PASSENGER AND IMMIGRATION LISTS BIBLIOGRAPHY 1538-1900

FIRST EDITION

PASSENGER AND IMMIGRATION LISTS BIBLIOGRAPHY 1538-1900

Being a Guide to Published Lists of Arrivals in the United States and Canada

FIRST SUPPLEMENT

(With Combined Index to Basic Volume and Supplement)

Edited by P. William Filby

GALE RESEARCH COMPANY * BOOK TOWER * DETROIT, MICHIGAN 48226

Editor: P. William Filby
Copy Editor and Indexer: Geraldine McIntosh
Assistant Editor: Kathryn Fischer

Production Supervisor-Internal: Laura Bryant
Production Supervisor-External: Carol Blanchard
Senior Production Assistant-Internal: Louise Gagné

Art Director: Art Chartow

Publisher: Frederick G. Ruffner
Executive Vice President/Editorial: James M. Ethridge
Editorial Director: Dedria Bryfonski
Director, Directories Division: John Schmittroth, Jr.
Senior Editor, Special Editorial Projects: Robert C. Thomas

Library of Congress Cataloging in Publication Data

Filby, P. William, 1911-
Passenger and immigration lists bibliography, 1538-1900.

Includes index.
1. Ships--Passenger lists--Bibliography. 2. Registers of births, etc.--United States--Bibliography. 3. United States--Genealogy--Bibliography. 4. United States--Emigration and immigration--Bibliography. 5. United States--History--Sources--Bibliography. I. Filby, P. William, 1911- . Passenger and immigration lists bibliography, 1538-1900. II. Title.
Z5313.U5F54 1981 Suppl. [CS47] 016.929'373 84-13702
ISBN 0-8103-1644-7

Printed in the United States of America

To

Dorothy M. Lower
Formerly Head, Genealogy Department
Allen County Public Library, Fort Wayne, Indiana
And
Mary Keysor Meyer
Formerly Genealogy Librarian
Maryland Historical Society, Baltimore, Maryland

****

For Many Years the Friends of Genealogists

Contents

Preface

This first supplement to the *Passenger and Immigration Lists Bibliography* contains over 600 new sources which have appeared from 1981 to 1984 or which had not been found during previous searches in earlier works. Together, the basic volume and this supplement represent over 1,900 sources, thus replacing the last edition of Harold Lancour's classic *Bibliography of Ship Passenger Lists,* revised by Richard J. Wolfe in 1963, which contained 262 sources.

Lancour first attempted such a list in 1937, and in 1963, Wolfe made a complete revision, restricting his dates to 1538-1825, coinciding with the end of unofficial immigration, when the U.S. Government began to control the influx. In the late 1970s, Mr. Frederick G. Ruffner, President of the Gale Research Company, encouraged me to compile a consolidation of the names of new arrivals to these shores under the title *Passenger and Immigration Lists Index (PILI);* it appeared in 1981 in three volumes containing 500,000 personal names taken from lists referred to in my *Bibliography.* When the 1983 supplement to *PILI* was published, a total of 900,000 names became available. These names, however, were taken from only 900 sources, so names in the remaining 1,000 sources have yet to appear in the *Index.* The 1,000 sources contain well over one million names—the 600 sources in this one supplement to the *Bibliography* alone contain 900,000 names. The *Bibliography* volumes will be invaluable to those whose search fails to find a certain name or names in *PILI,* since a check of the volumes may suggest a source in print with the missing name. For example, if an ancestor came from Yorkshire, England, and the *Bibliography* index under "Yorkshire" shows that entry number 1245 is a source that has a list of 120 passengers from there to Georgia in 1775, it is possible that the source may have the name required. This then is one of the chief values of the *Bibliography:* the basic volume and the supplement enable researchers to make a further search for sources having names not listed in *PILI.*

The supplement has the same criterion for source inclusion as the original work, where, in the words of Wolfe, "The standard for including a list is *proof of overseas origin* [of the immigrants named] . . . *usefulness* being the deciding factor in borderline cases. . . ." In addition to passenger and port lists, I have included, both in the basic volume and the supplement, sources of naturalization lists and declarations of intention to acquire citizenship in which often the actual date of immigration is given. I have also included several compilations of the "Great Registers" of Arizona, California, and Oregon, containing names of thousands of voters, some of whom indicated overseas birth. Another type of material, new in the supplement, is entitled "Queries," a section often found in genealogical magazines and used by searchers in their quests for information on ancestors: e.g., "I am searching for data on Johann Stein, who arrived in New York in 1872 on the *Peacock* from Bremen. . . ."

As before, my chief resources have been Mr. Gunther E. Pohl, Mrs. Mary K. Meyer, and Miss Dorothy M. Lower. Mr. James H. Nelson of Allen County Public Library, Fort Wayne, has filled the void left by Dorothy Lower upon her retirement, and it is through him that this volume is so complete and current. As a final check, I visited Allen County Public Library in Fort Wayne, the Genealogical Society at Salt Lake City, the New York Public Library, and frequently the Library of Congress and the Maryland Historical Society. Everywhere I received tremendous help from the staff. Canada was well served by Terrence M Punch, and in England I obtained much help from Anthony J. Camp, Director of the Society of Genealogists, and Francis Leeson, Editor of the *Genealogists' Magazine,* London. It is useful to note here that Mr. Leeson of Sea Lane, Ferring, Sussex, maintains a very fine Surname Index in which he has listed thousands of emigrants' names which are still in manuscript and unlikely to be seen in *PILI,* since it encompasses only published lists.

At the Library of Congress, even with their busy schedules, Judith F. Austin, Samuel M. Andrusko, Judith P. Reid, and Virginia S. Wood always found time to help me. Similar treatment came from Kip Sperry and David F. Putnam at the Genealogical Society in Salt Lake City. Michael Cassady transcribed almost fifty German lists and made them available to me. Gail Breitbard sent me copies of her new periodical, *The Lost Palatine,* filled with useful lists.

I would also like to acknowledge help in various ways from the following: Cleadie B. Barnett, Robert M. Bartram, Carl R. Bogardus, M.D., Dr. Dorothy Boyd-Rush, Jackie Marie Clegg, Peter Wilson Coldham, Jane E. Darlington, George Hancocks, Willard Heiss, Edgar Heyl, Thomas L. Hollowak, Dr. Arta F. Johnson, Robert J. Koenig, Jo Ann Kuhr, Andrew B. M. MacEwan, Gene Mosley, Sylvia Lee Nimmo, Nils W. Olsson, Robert E. Owen, J. Carlyle Parker, Ann Reinert, A. Hester Rich, Clifford Neal Smith, Margie Sobotka, Loretto D. Szucs, Dr. Michael H. Tepper, Nick Vine Hall, and Ella-Kate Wilson. Without the cooperation of directors of institutions, assistance from their staffs could not have been given, and I thank Dr. Rick J. Ashton (Allen County Public Library), William B. Keller (Chief Librarian, Maryland Historical Society), and Lyn Hart (George Peabody Library of The Johns Hopkins University).

Susan Sullivan (French and Spanish) and Gary E. Myer-Bruggey (German) did much for me with annotations on the works included in this bibliography. A special accolade must be awarded to Mr. Myer-Bruggey, professional genealogist, who controlled the German input, both identifying and obtaining materials in Germany. The comprehensiveness of the German content is his doing.

At all times I have received unstinting help from Gale Research Company. Frederick G. Ruffner, President, suggested the book and encouraged me throughout; Robert C. Thomas, Dennis LaBeau, Miranda C. Herbert, and Barbara McNeil followed the compilation closely and gave advice when necessary. Last but not least, I thank Geraldine McIntosh, who served as copy editor of the bibliography and polished every entry, checked cross references, picked up errors, and prepared the index. Without her skill the work would have been the poorer.

Such is the enthusiasm of librarians and genealogists, I am receiving new lists weekly, so it is intended to further update this work at intervals. I therefore request any finders to furnish me with references that may be added: 8944 Madison St., Savage, Md., 20763.

P. William Filby, F.S.G.
formerly Director, Maryland Historical Society,
Baltimore, Maryland

How to Use This Bibliography

The arrangement of this bibliography is alphabetical by author name or, if there is none or it is unknown, by title of the article, journal, pamphlet, or book. Full publication information is given, including reprint information, followed by an annotation describing the contents of the work and frequently naming the original location of the passenger or ship list, immigration register, church record, naturalization data, or possibly census, military mustering-out roll, or archival source in the "old country." Foreign titles are usually translated in the first line of the annotation.

Item Number

Every entry is preceded by an item number, which is used in the index to refer to the entry. The numbers are not consecutive, but they do follow one another in ascending order. Gaps were left in the numbering so that late arriving, recently researched, newly prepared items could be inserted in the correct alphabetical sequence right up to press time. Item numbers in the supplement are assigned so that the entries will correctly interfile with those in the basic volume. The item number is useful with reference to the three-volume *Passenger and Immigration Lists Index,* and its supplements, where, next to the personal name of an immigrant, along with age, place and year of arrival at a North American port or date of naturalization, is cited the number of the individual item in this bibliography which supplies the source information needed for further research. To sum up: the source number given in *PILI* is the same as the item number in this bibliography. It is the reason these are companion works.

Subject Index

Following the bibliographical entries is a general index. *In this supplement, the indexing of the basic volume and the supplement is combined, with supplement item numbers appearing in boldface.* The index is planned to provide access through the names of the places of emigration or immigration, ports of departure or arrival, and places of settlement, wherever any or some of these are mentioned in a title or annotation. It includes ship names with the dates of particular voyages, if those are cited. Since the information given is not always the same from one item to another, it may be fruitful for a searcher to look not only under the place-names, but also under the collective name of the people(s). The usual specific term relating to the nationality, province, or faith group has been used wherever possible; therefore, in a given quest, look, for example, under Danes or Germans, Moravians, Mennonites, or Quakers (as well as under the place names).

Genealogists and other experienced researchers know how helpful it is to be flexible and expansive in the use of an index, especially one covering this period before as well as after the rise of national states in Europe and before as well as after the colonial era on this side of the Atlantic. Acadia included Maine as well as Nova Scotia; what is now Alabama was "West Florida" at the time of arrival of some immigrants; and one writer, concerned with the New England destination of 1,700 German emigrants, defined the New England states as "the original American colonies from Massachusetts to Georgia." Therefore, specific place-names cited in titles or annotations are entered, unlocated, wherever they fall in the alphabet, and only some of them were able to be consolidated under a larger, obvious political jurisdiction or language group.

Readers are reminded that the index refers to the item number, not the page number, and that numbers in boldface refer to items in this supplement.

Passenger and Immigration Lists Bibliography 1538-1900 First Supplement

0056.1 — 0056.5
ADAMSON, RAYMOND J. "I Pledge Allegiance." In *Ancestoring* [Augusta Genealogical Society, Georgia].
0056.1
---No. 3 (1981), pp. 3-13 (1793-1822).
0056.2
---No. 4 (1981), pp. 28-34 (1822-1838).
0056.3
---No. 5 (1982), pp. 29-40 (1838-1857).
0056.4
---No. 6 (1983), pp. 57-64 (1857-1858).
0056.5
---No. 7 (1983), pp. 53-58 (1858-1868). In progress.

Concerns late 18th and largely 19th-century immigrants to Georgia from Europe, chiefly from the United Kingdom. Information extracted from minutes books of the Superior Court of Richmond County, Georgia, for the years 1793-1868. Immigrant's name, place of birth or country to which allegiance was owed, type of document, names of persons signing the affidavit, date of court action. Often included are age and the date and port of arrival. Lists 1,200 names so far, through the year 1868. This work continues.

* * *

0090
ALBERS, ERV. "Birth and Death of a Town: Mannhaven in Mercer County, North Dakota, Was an Important River Town for Settlers and Grain Farmers." In *Heritage Review,* vol.13:2 (May 1983), pp. 31-35.

A 1918 list of 500 Mercer County landowners born in Russia, Rumania, Austria, Hungary, or Brazil. Only some specify country of birth. Information includes date of birth and name of wife.

* * *

0092
"ALDINGBOURNE EMIGRANTS TO AMERICA IN 1832." In *The Sussex Genealogist,* vol. 4:1 (July, 1979), pp. 10-11.

Tells of 38 persons, paupers, and of payments made in England on their behalf. Taken from appendix to Aldingbourne, West Sussex, overseers' accounts for the year 1832.

* * *

0097
ALLISON, ROBERT J. *Naturalization Records of Clearfield County [Pa.], 1822-1862*. Clearfield, Pa.: the compiler, 1981. n. pag. [57 pp.]

About 600 persons named. Nineteenth-century records, with date and place of arrival and place of origin. Many from Ireland.

* * *

0101
AMEN, DELBERT D., and SUSAN K. AMEN. "Declarations of Intent, Washita County, Oklahoma." In *Oklahoma Genealogical Society Quarterly,* vol. 26:1 (Mar. 1981), pp. 36-43.

About 200 persons named, with date of birth, date of entry, port of entry, name of vessel, date of application for citizenship, birthplace, and occupation. Many names differ in spelling from those in item no. 0104.

* * *

0104
AMEN, DELBERT D., and SUSAN K. AMEN. "U.S. Citizenship Declarations of Intent Filed by Germans from Russia in Washita County, Oklahoma, 1907-1935." In *Clues,* 1981, pt. 2, pp. 47-53.

Refers to over 150 persons, with names, dates and places of birth, dates and ports of entry, vessels, dates of application for first papers, and occupations. Many names differ in spelling from those in item no. 0101.

* * *

0110.1 — 0110.3
"ANCESTOR TABLES." In *Swedish American Genealogist.*
0110.1
---Vol. 1:4 (Dec. 1981), p. 162-166.
0110.2
---Vol. 2:1 (Mar. 1982), pp. 34-38; vol. 2:2 (June 1982), pp. 79-81; vol. 2:3 (Sept. 1982), pp. 130-136; vol. 2:4 (Dec. 1982), pp. 180-182.
0110.3
---Vol. 3:1 (Mar. 1983), pp. 31-37; vol. 3:2 (June 1983), pp. 82-89; vol. 3:3 (Sept. 1983), pp. 124-128. In progress.

Focuses on late 19th century. Family details are foremost in these entries. Several give the date of emigration to America. Continuing in future issues.

* * *

0123.1
ANUTA, MICHAEL. *East Prussians from Russia.* Menominee, Mich.: the author, 1979. 212p.

Reference is to the 1880s and 1890s and the arrival of 250 immigrants from East Prussia and Russia. Pages 172-211 list names, dates of birth and death, countries of origin, places and dates of entry to the U.S., and names of spouses. There is a supplement to this work; see item no. 0123.2.

* * *

0123.2
ANUTA, MICHAEL. *East Prussians from Russia: Supplement.* N.p., n.d. 32pp.

Contains an amended list of late 19th-century immigrants from East Prussia and Russia, corrected 6/1/1979. Affects over 200 entries. See pp. 20-32 for names, and item no. 0123.1 (above) for the original work.

* * *

0158
ASHBY, JOE H. "Alaska's Greatest Institution, the Pioneer's Home." In *Illinois State Genealogical Society Quarterly,* vol. 13:4 (Winter 1981), pp. 221-224.

Names of 65 pioneers at Sitka Home in the former capital of Alaska, October 1, 1920. Data includes places and dates of birth and dates of their arrival in Alaska, late 19th, early 20th centuries. Originally appeared in *The Pathfinder,* October 1920, p. 15.

* * *

0160
ASHTABULA COUNTY GENEALOGICAL SOCIETY. *Index of the Naturalization Records of Ashtabula County, Ohio, 1875-1906.* Jefferson, Ohio: the society, 1982. 110p.

Almost 4,000 names, with microfilm references.

* * *

0176.1 — 0176.12
AUGLAIZE COUNTY. "Naturalizations Taken from Index Cards in the Probate of the Auglaize County Courthouse." In *Fallen Timbers Ances-Tree* [Auglaize County, Ohio].
0176.1
---Vol. 2:7 (July-Aug. 1980), p. 3 (Nos. 1-50, A-BR).
0176.2
---Vol. 2:8 (Sept. 1980), p. 3 (Nos. 51-97, BU).
0176.3
---Vol. 2:9 (Oct. 1980), p. 2 (Nos. 98-140, BU-DI).
0176.4
---Vol. 2:9 (Oct. 1980), p. 3 (Nos. 141-166, DI-EI).
0176.5
---Vol. 2:10 (Nov. 1980), p. 3 (Nos. 167-220, EI-FR).
0176.6
---Vol. 3:1 (Jan.-Feb., 1981), pp. 3-4 (Nos. 221-335, GA-HE).
0176.7
---Vol. 3:2 (Mar.-Apr. 1981), pp. 2-3 (Nos. 336-442, HI-KO).
0176.8
---Vol. 3:4 (July-Aug. 1981), pp.3-4 (Nos. 443-520, LA-MI).
0176.9
---Vol. 3:5 (Sept.-Oct. 1981), p. 6 (Nos. 521-560, MI-OP).
0176.10
---Vol. 3:6 (Nov. 1981), pp. 2-3 (Nos. 561-640, PA-SC).
0176.11
---Vol. 4:1 (Jan.-Feb. 1982), pp. 5-6 (Nos. 641-748, SC-TO).
0176.12
---Vol. 4:2 (Mar.-Apr. 1982), pp. 6-7 (Nos. 749-836, TO-ZW).

Place of origin of almost all: Germany; date of naturalization: mostly last half of 19th century.

* * *

0190
AXTMANN, L. "Passenger Lists." In *Heritage Review,* vol. 11:3 (Sept. 1981), p. 45.

Names of 31 Germans from Russia bound for North and South Dakota in 1898. Includes ages and occupations.

* * *

0205
BACA, LEO. *Czech Immigration Passenger Lists.* Vol. 1. Richardson, Texas: Old Homestead Publishing Co., 1983. 158 p.

Names of 6,300 Czech immigrants: 3,600 through New Orleans before 1880, 2,000 through Galveston before 1872, and the remainder through New York and Baltimore, 1879. Country of origin, ports of departure and arrival, date of arrival, and age.

* * *

0232
BAKER, JOYCE. "List of Emigrants Intended for New England in the Good Shipp the *Confidence* of London of CC tonnes, John Jobson, Master . . . Southampton 24th Aprill, 1638." In *The Hampshire Family Historian* [Portsmouth, Eng.], vol. 1 (May 1978), pp. 27-28.

This list was derived from *The New England Historical and Genealogical Register,* vol.2 (Jan. 1848), p. 108. Reveals family groupings and ages, but spellings are archaic and sometimes incorrect. Tepper (item no. 9151 in the basic volume of this bibliography) is more accurate.

* * *

0251
BALFOUR, GWYNETH S. "Washington County, Oregon, Records — Index to Naturalizations." In *Genealogical Forum of Portland, Oregon: Quarterly Bulletin,* vol. 33:2 (Dec. 1983), pp. 77-86.

Covers surnames beginning A through G in the years 1853-1926, with dates of naturalization and reference to location of the information in the county records.

* * *

0253
BALTIMORE PORT. *Passenger Arrivals at the Port of Baltimore 1820-1834, from Customs Passenger Lists.* General ed. Michael H. Tepper. Transcribed by Elizabeth P. Bentley. Baltimore: Genealogical Publishing Co., 1982. 786 pages.

Lists 50,000 immigrants: 75% were Germans and most of the others British or Irish. Alphabetical arrangement: name, age, sex, occupation, country of origin, country or place intended, name of ship, date of arrival. Includes an excellent commentary on passenger lists by Michael H. Tepper. Data taken from National Archives micropublications: Quarterly abstracts of vessels arriving at Baltimore (M 596); Passenger lists of vessels arriving at Baltimore (M 255); and State Department transcripts of passenger lists.

* * *

0254
BANGERTER, LAWRENCE B. *The Compass: A Concise and Factual Compilation of All Vessels and Sources Listed, with References Made of All of Their Voyages and Some Dates of Registration.* Vol. 1. Logan, Utah: Everton Publishers, 1983. 171p.

Information extracted from "U.S. Customs Passenger Lists, Port of Baltimore, 1820-1891," on microfilm in the U.S. National Archives; from *A Bibliography of Ship Passenger Lists,* compiled by Harold Lancour, 3rd ed., 1963; and from records in the Genealogical Society of Utah. Almost 6,000 ships' crossings listed, with origin or place of embarkation, destination or place of debarkation, and registration date. Almost all in the 18th and 19th centuries.

* * *

0340
BARNES, ROBERT. "Passenger List of Convicts." In *The Notebook: Baltimore County Genealogical Society,* no. 20 (Sept. 1983), pp. 1-2.

A dozen convicts and statement of reasons for conviction, transported on the *Reformation* from the city of Exon, England, in 1722. Taken from Baltimore County land records, liber IS #G, p. 34.

* * *

0358.2
BARNETT, CLEADIE B. "Account of Money Paid by John Campbell to 25 Families of Scotch Emigrants Who Arrived at St. Andrews and Settled in Charlotte County. Nov. 1804." In *We Lived: A Genealogical Newsletter of New Brunswick Sources,* no. 15 (Oct. 1982), p. 190.

Scottish arrivals and the amounts they were paid as newly arrived settlers in New Brunswick. Involves 27 persons.

* * *

0358.6
BARNETT, CLEADIE B. "English Emigrants Who Ask for Land on the New St. Andrews Road, 1837." In *We Lived: A Genealogical Newsletter of New Brunswick Sources,* no. 15 (Oct. 1982), p. 191.

Names 31 persons and involved, all told, with families and members of households, 145 new arrivals in Canada.

* * *

0358.13
BARNETT, CLEADIE B. "List of Passengers Embarked in the *Thetis* of Troon, Robt. Smith, Master, and Who Have Contracted to be Landed at Bathurst, Bay Chalure." In *We Lived: A Genealogical Newsletter of New Brunswick Sources,* no. 13 (Feb. 1982), pp. 149-150.

Refers to arrival of 79 laborers at Chaleur Bay in northeast New Brunswick in 1837. The ship was registered from a Scottish port.

* * *

0358.15
BARNETT, CLEADIE B. "List of Passengers not Paying Debts — Ship *Rosina* from Fordnock or Greenock to St. John, New Brunswick, 1803." In *We Lived: A Genealogical Newsletter of New Brunswick Sources,* no. 7 (July 1980), p. 80.

Records on 15 passengers, with names of accompanying family members. Scottish port of departure.

* * *

0358.17
BARNETT, CLEADIE B. "List of Passengers Shipwrecked in Gulf of St. Lawrence and Rescued from the Ship *Helen Thomson,* Forwarded [from?] St. John, N. B., Portland, and Montreal." In *We Lived: A Genealogical Newsletter of New Brunswick Sources,* no. 15 (Oct. 1982), pp. 183-184.

Lists 93 passengers and their ages. Nineteenth century; no dates given.

* * *

0358.19
BARNETT, CLEADIE B. [List of Persons from Scotland Brought in Through the Port of St. John. . . .] In *We Lived: A Genealogical Newsletter of New Brunswick Sources,* no. 14 (June 1982), pp. 175-176, 164.

Names 127 ship passengers and their locations in 1816. The information includes ages and occupations.

* * *

0358.21
BARNETT, CLEADIE B. "A List of the Crew and Such Persons as have Contracted to take their Passage on Board the Ship *Prudence* of Londonderry, Berthen & Registe'd 281 Tons, Robert Phillips, Master for Saint John, N.B." In *We Lived: A Genealogical Newsletter of New Brunswick Sources,* no. 15 (Oct. 1982), pp. 180-182.

Names 180 persons, with ages, places of origin, and occupations. Reference is to an 1838 crossing from Ulster to New Brunswick.

* * *

0358.26
BARNETT, CLEADIE B. "List of the Passengers Embarked in the Barque *Robert Watt of Saint Andrew,* Ralph Salliman, Master, and Who Have Contracted to be Landed at Saint Andrews, New Brunswick . . . 1837." In *We Lived: A Genealogical Newsletter of New Brunswick Sources,* no. 14 (June 1982), pp. 173-174.

Concerns 291 Canadian arrivals, almost all laborers. Names and ages only.

* * *

0358.31
BARNETT, CLEADIE B. "Passenger List: Ship *Favourite,* 1815." In *We Lived: A Genealogical Newsletter of New Brunswick Sources,* no. 7 (July 1980), pp. 78-80.

For 133 passengers from Glasgow to St. John, New Brunswick, this gives name, age, sex, occupation, and location of former residence, including specific place name, county, and parish.

* * *

0358.36
BARNETT, CLEADIE B. "The Province of New Brunswick, to the Parish of Saint Andrews: For Support of Emigrant Poor from 11 January 1841 to 10 January 1842, inclusive." In *We Lived: A Genealogical Newsletter of New Brunswick Sources,* no. 15 (Oct. 1982), pp. 187-190.

Spans the years 1841 to 1843. Names 48 immigrants who were supplied in the first year and 92 in the second. Exact dates and places of origin given.

* * *

0358.41
BARNETT, CLEADIE B. "Return of Loyalist[s] Embarked on Board the Transport for St. John River in the Bay of Fundy." In *We Lived: A Genealogical Newsletter of New Brunswick Sources,* no. 15 (Oct. 1982), pp. 184-186.

Lists 145 passengers, with occupation and former place of residence for each. No dates or names of ships.

* * *

0358.46
BARNETT, CLEADIE B. "Sick Emigrants from the Brig *William Henry,* to the Parish of St. Andrews Drs., 1827." In *We Lived: A Genealogical Newsletter of New Brunswick Sources,* no. 15 (Oct. 1982), p. 187.

These were 40 impoverished immigrants supported temporarily by a local church in New Brunswick.

* * *

0440
BAUER, ARMAND, and ELAINE BAUER. "Passenger Lists." In *Heritage Review,* vol. 11:4 (Dec. 1981), p. 40.

The S. S. *Hammonia* brought 96 Germans from Russia to New York via Hamburg in 1876. Ages given.

* * *

0444
BAUER, ELAINE, and ARMAND BAUER. "Family Register of the Odessa Reformed Church [near Sutley, South Dakota]." In *Heritage Review,* vol. 13:4 (Dec. 1983), pp. 41-45.

Germans from Russia who came in the latter half of the 19th century. Years of arrival not given. Supplies names and dates of birth of 63 immigrants.

* * *

0446
BAUER, MARGARET. "Norddeutscher Lloyd, Passagier-Liste des Post-Dampfschiffes *Oder* von Bremen nach New York am 17 November 1875." In *Peoria Genealogical Society Newsletter,* vol. 10:4 (Apr. 1982), pp. 2-3.

Passenger list from a vessel of the North German Lloyd line, the steamship *Oder,* Bremen to New York, November 17, 1875. Includes 120 names, with places of origin. Some listed were American travelers, not newly arriving immigrants.

* * *

0464
BECKER, MARSHALL JOSEPH. "Pre-Penn Settlements of the Delaware Valley." In *The Pennsylvania Genealogical Magazine,* vol. 32:3 (1982), pp. 227-234.

Dutch and Swedes in the Delaware valley in the seventeenth century. Several names, with dates and places of settlement. This location was named Lenape, "site of Hopokehocking, on the peninsula where Wilmington now stands."

* * *

0470.1 — 0470.2
"BEDFORD COUNTY [Pennsylvania] NATURALIZATION RECORDS, vol. 1." In *St. Clair's, Bedford.*
0470.1
---Vol. 1:1 (June 1981), pp. 9-10.
0470.2
---Vol. 1:2 (Sept. 1981), pp. 11-12.

Refers to 17 persons, with much genealogical data on each, including dates of immigration and dates of admission to citizenship.

* * *

0472
BEHR, HILDEGARD. "Auswandererschicksale aus Langenholtensen." In *Zeitschrift fuer Niederdeutsche Familienkunde,* Jahrgang 53:2 (Mar. 1978), pp. 37-39.

Fate of emigrants from Langenholtensen, Germany. Concerns 10 departures for America in second half of 19th century. Much biographical data.

* * *

0491
BELL, RAYMOND MARTIN. "Pennsylvania German Pioneers Ship List #28." *Western Pennsylvania Genealogical Society Quarterly,* vol. 8:2 (Nov. 1981), pp. 75-76.

List #28 from vol. 1, Strassburger & Hinke, *Pennsylvania German Pioneers* (item no. 9041 in basic volume of this bibliography). Bell has made a list of families and attempted to get the correct spelling of names. Covers 1727-1775.

* * *

0515 — 0518
"BERKS COUNTY [Pennsylvania] NATURALIZATION RECORDS." In *Berks of Old.*
0515
---Vol. 1:1 (May 1983), pp. 23-24.
0516
---Vol 1:2 (Aug. 1983), p. 24.
0517
---Vol. 1:3 (Nov. 1983), p. 25.
0518
---Vol. 1:4 (Feb. 1984), p. 25. In progress.

First half of 19th century. Includes names of more than a hundred persons, so far, mostly Irish and German. This continues.

* * *

0540
BEVERLY, TREVIA WOOSTER. "Washington County, Texas, Naturalization Papers, 1872-1880: Book B." In *Stirpes,* vol. 21:4 (Dec. 1981), pp. 223-228.

Refers to 225 persons, with dates of arrival in U.S., ages, countries of origin, and dates of naturalization.

* * *

0611
BOBELENYI, ROSE M. "1882 to 1982: Hungarians Celebrate 100 Years in South Bend, Indiana." In *South Bend Area Genealogical Society Quarterly,* vol. 8:1 (Sept. 1983), pp. 17-18.

Identifies several Hungarians arriving in Boston in 1882, bound for South Bend.

* * *

0614
BOCKSTRUCK, LLOYD DEWITT. "Passenger Lists of the Ship *Charming Molly* to Essex County, Virginia." In *The Virginia Genealogist,* vol. 26:3 (July-Sept. 1982), pp. 219-220.

Names of 110 persons who arrived in 1764 and 1765. The original list was compiled in 1779 so that headrights could be claimed.

* * *

0620
BOCKSTRUCK, LLOYD DEWITT. "Some Immigrants to Middlesex County in the Colony of Virginia, 1674-1702." In *The Virginia Genealogist,* vol. 25:1 (Jan.-Mar. 1981), pp. 15-22; vol. 25:2 (Apr.-June 1981), pp. 92-97.

Over 200 persons, all indentured servants, with names of persons to whom bonded, dates of arrival, and names of ships.

* * *

0624
BODDIE, WILLIAM WILLIS. [Witherspoon Colony.] In *History of Williamsburg.* Columbia [S.C.]:State Company, 1923, pp. 9-17.

Details of arrivals of 11 members of the Witherspoon family in 1734 and later years, including dates of arrival in South Carolina and elsewhere. Written by Robert Witherspoon, 1780.

* * *

0626
BOEHM, WILHELM. "Memories of Years Ago." In *Clues,* 1980, pt. 2, pp. 46-48.

Details concerning some of the 94 persons who arrived in New York from Katharinental, Russia, on the S.S. *Spaarndam,* 1891. About 25 names and families. Recorded in the *North Dakota Herold,* Feb. 2 and 9, 1917.

* * *

0633
BOGARDUS, CARL R., SR., and WILLIAM R. GREEAR. *Persons of Foreign Birth in Nineteenth Century Scott County, Indiana, 1817-1894.* Scottsburg, Ind.: Muscatatuck Press, 1969. 29p.

Lists 615 immigrants to Scott County, Indiana, with dates and countries of birth, and often dates of arrival.

* * *

0635
BOHNERT, BRUNO. "Amerika-Auswanderer aus der Pfarrei Prinzbach im 19. Jahrhundert." In *Ortenau,* vol. 57 (1977), pp. 292-295.

Emigrants to America from the parish of Prinzbach in the 19th century. About 40 persons, most with birth dates and additional family data, 1839 to about 1860.

* * *

0678.1 — 0678.3
BORGSTEDT, CLARICE. "Harris County, Texas. Naturalization Intent Records." In *The Roadrunner.*
0678.1
---Vol. 1:3 (May 1975), pp. 38-39.
0678.2
---Vol. 2:3 (May 1976), pp. 34-35.
0678.3
---Vol. 3:2 (Feb. 1977), pp. 35-36.

About 250 immigrants with ages, native countries, and dates of declarations. Covers the years 1886-1892.

* * *

0683
BOSS, FRIEDER. "Auswanderer nach Nordamerika und Russisch-Polen aus Hoechst, Lichtenberg und Umstadt." In *Hessische Familienkunde,* vol. 13:2 (June 1976), cols. 105-110.

Emigrants to North America and Russian Poland from Hoechst, Lichtenberg, and Umstadt. Over 200 individuals or heads of families from 48 communities in the former Archduchy of Hesse-Darmstadt, Germany, 1834-1838. From notices in the newspaper, *Wochenblatt fuer den Kreis Dieburg*, 1834-1838. Item no. 0685 in the basic volume of this bibliography is an English-language translation of this article.

* * *

0692
BOVE, SUSAN BARBER. *The Early Italian Immigrants to Seneca Falls, New York (1884-1930).* Canandaigua, N.Y.: the author, 1983. 74pp.

Mentions names throughout the text and lists 50 Italians who served the U.S. in World War I (p.61) and over 800 immigrants, pp. 69-74: "List of Italian immigrants from census records." Most date from 1905-1925.

* * *

0770
BRADLEY, BARBARA. "Naturalization Records." In *The Johnson County [Kansas] Genealogist*, vol. 11:2 (June 1983), pp. 64-68; vol. 11:3 (Sept. 1983), pp. 91-92; vol. 11:4 (Dec. 1983), pp. 131-132.

Records for the years 1870-1890 found in the vault of the Clerk of the District Court, Johnson County, Kansas, "Book A," Declaration of Intention only. Name, age, country of birth, and date of declared intention to acquire citizenship of 330 persons.

* * *

0773
BRANDOW, JAMES C. *Genealogies of Barbados Families.* Baltimore: Genealogical Publishing Co., 1983. 753p.

Contains every article pertaining to family history published in *Caribbeana*, 1909-1919, and *The Journal of the Barbados Museum and Historical Society*, 1933 to date. Lists 15,000 names, including some of Barbados Quakers. Throughout the 17th and 18th centuries, there was a continuous flow of settlers from Barbados to virtually every port on the Atlantic seaboard.

* * *

0776
BRANDOW, JAMES C. *Omitted Chapters from Hotten's Original Lists of Persons of Quality . . . and Others Who Went from Great Britain to the American Plantations, 1600-1700: Census Returns, Parish Registers, and Militia Rolls from the Barbados Census of 1679/80.* Baltimore: Genealogical Publishing Co., 1982. 245p.

Hotten included only a portion of the lists available to him. Nearly two-thirds of the important Barbados census of 1679/80 was not used, and many similar lists were wholly or partially omitted. About 6,500 names left out of Hotten (item no. 3283 in the basic volume of this bibliography) are listed for the first time anywhere in the work cited above.

* * *

0856
BRAUN, FRITZ. "The Eighteenth-Century Emigration from the Palatinate: New Documentation." Translated and edited by Don Yoder. In *Pennsylvania Folklife*, vol. 15:3 (Spring 1966), pp. 40-48.

List of 18th-century German emigrants, abstracted from Braun, *Auswanderer aus Kaiserslauten* . . . (item no.0845 in the main volume of this bibliography). Much genealogical data on each emigrant. Also in item no. 9968, Yoder, *Rhineland Emigrants*, pp. 33-40.

* * *

0923
BRECHT, SAMUEL KRIEBEL. "The Migrations of the Schwenkfelders." In *Genealogical Record of the Schwenkfelder Families: Seekers of Religious Liberty Who Fled from Silesia to Saxony and Thence to Pennsylvania in the Years 1731 to 1737.* New York: Rand McNally (for the Schwenkfelder Church, Pennsburg, Pa.), 1923, pp. 34-44.

The Schwenkfelders came to Pennsylvania in six "waves" in the years 1731 to 1737. Over 300 names are listed, with places of origin, ships, dates, and ports of arrival. Details of the emigrations are contained in the text. Members of the first four movements are also listed in Strassburger's *Pennsylvania German Pioneers. . .* , nos. 9041-42 in the basic volume of this bibliography. The fifth and sixth migrations appear for the first time.

* * *

0924
BREHAUT, MRS. W. M. "The Scotchfort Settlers." In *Historic Highlights of Prince Edward Island.* Charlottetown: Prince Edward Island Historical Society, 1955, pp. 80-85.

Lists several Scots who arrived at Prince Edward Island in 1772 on the *Alexander.*

* * *

0926.4
BREITBARD, GAIL. "Comparing Some Immigration & Naturalization Records." In *The Lost Palatine*, no. 16 (1984), p.2

Compares data on 18th-century immigrants' names in three separate sources: Giuseppi, *Naturalizations of Foreign Protestants in the American and West Indian Colonies*, item no. 2564 in the main vol. of this bibliography; Strassburger, *Pennsylvania German Pioneers*, item nos. 9041-9042 in main vol.; and the 1790 Pennsylvania census.

* * *

0926.8
BREITBARD, GAIL. "Heads of Households of the 1709/10 Palatines Who Went from Germany thru the Port of Rotterdam to London." In *The Lost Palatine*, no. 10 (1983), pp. 7-10.

Lists hundreds of immigrants who indicated Mohawk Valley, New York, as destination. Many names taken from Knittle's *Early Eighteenth Century Palatine Emigration* (item nos. 3983, 3990, 3997, 4003, 4010 in the main volume of this bibliography).

* * *

0926.10
BREITBARD, GAIL. "Immigrants not Found in S. & H." In *The Lost Palatine*, no. 4 (1982), pp. 4-5.

About 30 names not listed in the classic work of Strassburger & Hinke, *Pennsylvania German Pioneers . . . 1727 to 1808* (item nos. 9041-9042 in the basic volume of this bibliography). Includes dates of birth, arrival, and naturalization, 18th, 19th centuries.

* * *

0926.12

BREITBARD, GAIL. "Juniata Co., Pa., Naturalizations (from *The National Genealogical Quarterly,* 1967)." In *The Lost Palatine*, no. 18 (1984), p. 11.

German names taken from Marian S. Sowers: "Juniata County, Pennsylvania, Naturalization Records," (item no. 5593 in the basic vol. of this bibliography), with notes by Gail Breitbard. Covers the years 1789-1848.

* * *

0926.16

BREITBARD, GAIL. "Naturalizations Excerpted from *Naturalizations of Foreign Protestants in the American Colonies.*" In *The Lost Palatine,* no. 10 (1983), p. 13.

Refers to the years 1740-1765. Information on 50 persons named in work by Giuseppi (item no. 2564 in main vol. of this bibliography). Date and place of naturalization given for each.

* * *

0926.18

BREITBARD, GAIL. "Naturalizations of Lancaster County German/Swiss in 1729." In *The Lost Palatine,* no. 6 (1982), pp. 6-7.

Names only, of about 100 persons in colonial Pennsylvania.

* * *

0926.21

BREITBARD, GAIL. "Palatines & Servants Imported on *The King of Prussia,* 10-3-1764." In *The Lost Palatine,* no. 16 (1984), pp. 5-6.

Names and other data taken from the work of the same title cited in item no. 6441 in the main volume of this bibliography. Breitbard comments on the information extracted. This was immigration to Philadelphia. The servants were English.

* * *

0926.26

BREITBARD, GAIL. "1709 Germantown, Pa., Naturalizations." In *The Lost Palatine,* no. 6 (1982), pp. 3-4.

About 50 immigrants, some of them Quakers and Mennonites who refused to take the naturalization oath by swearing.

* * *

0926.36

BREITBARD, GAIL. "Some Early Georgia Palatine Immigrants." In *The Lost Palatine.*" No. 7 (1982), pp. 5-7; no. 8 (1983), pp. 7-8; no. 9 (1983), pp. 2-3.

About 500 immigrants whose names have been excerpted from *A List of the Early Settlers of Georgia* by Coulter and Saye (item no. 1322 in the basic volume of this bibliography). Most were from Salzburg, Austria. Ages and dates of arrival often given, 1730s-1740s. All names taken from among immigrants classified as "Persons Who Went from Europe to Georgia at the Trustees' Charge," meaning those whose passage was paid for them.

* * *

0926.38

BREITBARD, GAIL. "Some Early Lancaster County, Penna., Naturalizations." In *The Lost Palatine,* no. 11 (1983), p. 3.

Focuses on the 18th century and has about 100 names taken from H. Frank Eshleman, *Historic Background and Annals of the Swiss and German Pioneer Settlers* . . . (1917). Mostly names only, with few dates.

* * *

0926.40

BREITBARD, GAIL. "Some Early New York State Naturalizations." In *The Lost Palatine,* no. 11 (1983), pp. 10-11.

Names of about 200 New York Mohawk Valley Palatines from the year 1710, taken from "Persons Naturalized by Act of Assembly 1714-1772," in Chambers: *The Early Germans of New Jersey* (no.1138).

* * *

0926.42

BREITBARD, GAIL. "Some Early South Carolina Immigrants." In *The Lost Palatine,* no. 11 (1983), pp. 4-5.

Names and ages of persons applying for financial assistance for passage from Germany to South Carolina in 1765.

* * *

0926.44

BREITBARD, GAIL. "Some Early Virginia Immigrants." In *The Lost Palatine,* no. 5 (1982), pp. 4-5.

Names of about 100 immigrants from the first half of the 18th century. Dates of arrival given and sometimes name of ship.

* * *

0926.46

BREITBARD, GAIL. "Some Early West Virginia Landowners." In *The Lost Palatine,* no. 15 (1983), p. 8.

German names extracted from Edgar B. Sims, *Index to Land Grants in West Virginia* (1952). Many have name of ship and an 18th-century date of arrival.

* * *

0926.49

BREITBARD, GAIL. "Some 1816 Residents of Mississippi." In *The Lost Palatine,* no. 15 (1983), pp. 1-2.

German names extracted from the 1816 Mississippi census. Many entries include date of immigration.

* * *

0926.51

BREITBARD, GAIL. "Some Maryland Naturalizations." In *The Lost Palatine,* no. 14 (1983), p. 5.

About 100 German immigrants cited, with dates of naturalization and sometimes dates of arrival and names of ships. 18th century.

* * *

0926.52
BREITBARD, GAIL. "Some Names from *Naturalizations of Foreign Protestants in the American Colonies.*" In *The Lost Palatine,* no. 18 (1984), p. 10.

German names from Giuseppi's *Naturalizations. . .* (item no. 2564 in the basic vol. of this bibliography), with notes by Gail Breitbard. See also item no. 0926.63 in this supplement.

* * *

0926.53
BREITBARD, GAIL. "Some Naturalizations from *The Hoosier Journal of Ancestry.*" In *The Lost Palatine,* no. 11 (1983), pp. 9-10.

Late 19th and early 20th centuries naturalizations in various Indiana counties. Names of 50 new citizens.

* * *

0926.55
BREITBARD, GAIL. "Some Palatines Lost in the Naturalization Records." In *The Lost Palatine,* no. 8 (1983), pp. 6-7.

About 50 names, with place of residence and date of naturalization for each. 18th century. Occasionally the name of an immigrant's ship is given.

* * *

0926.57
BREITBARD, GAIL. "Some Shenandoah Valley Naturalizations." In *The Lost Palatine,* no. 8 (1983), pp. 3-4.

Excerpted from Augusta County, Virginia, court records for the 18th century. Names and dates of naturalization of 30 persons.

* * *

0926.59
BREITBARD, GAIL. "Some South Carolina Immigrants." In *The Lost Palatine,* no. 13 (1983), p. 6-7.

About 200 immigrants from the ship *Frankland,* 1766. All Germans. Names and ages given.

* * *

0926.63
BREITBARD, GAIL. "Tidying Up Naturalizations." In *The Lost Palatine,* no. 17 (1984), p. 3.

Corrections to many names listed in *Naturalizations of Foreign Protestants in the American and West Indian Colonies,* by M.S. Giuseppi, item no. 2564 in the basic volume of this bibliography.

* * *

0929
BRENDLE, A.S. "List of Immigrants." In *A Brief History of Schaefferstown.* York, Pa.: Dispatch Publishing Co., 1901, pp. 193-195.

About 150 immigrants named, chiefly from the Palatinate and Switzerland between 1727 and 1787. Includes most of the early settlers of a Pennsylvania community called Schaefferstown and its vicinity. Originally appeared in *Pennsylvania Archives,* 2nd ser., vol. 17, 1892.

* * *

0971
BROSZ, ALLYN R. "U.S. Citizen Declarations of Intent Filed by Germans from Russia in Hutchinson County, South Dakota, 1877-1878." In *Clues,* 1980, pt. 2, pp. 22-23.

Applications for first papers by 65 immigrants, most of whom arrived on the S.S. *Mosel* in 1877 or 1878. Names, year of birth, date and port of entry to the U.S., and date of the declaration of intention to acquire citizenship.

* * *

0977
BROWN, R. D. "Devonians and New England Settlement Before 1650." In *The Devonian Association for the Advancement of Science, Literature and Art: Report and Transactions,* vol. 95 (1963), pp. 219-243.

A list of people from Devonshire who came to New England, showing their places of origin and destinations and other biographical information, with references to the source of the information. Derived mostly from Banks, *Topographical Dictionary of 2,885 English Emigrants to New England, 1620-1650* (item no. 0275 in the basic volume of this bibliography). Brown's findings alter and augment some of Banks's statistics.

* * *

1001
BUCHANAN, A.W. PATRICK. *The Buchanan Book: the Life of Alexander Buchanan, Q.C., of Montreal. . . .* Montreal [Canada]: n.p., 1911.

Pages 211-212 list members of the family and others related to a James Buchanan, who emigrated from Ireland to America, early 19th century.

* * *

1005
BUECKNER, FLOSSIE. "Naturalization Records Book 'A': Galveston County, Texas." In *The Roadrunner,* vol. 6:2 (Feb. 1980), pp. 15-26.

About 200 names, dates of birth and of immigration, countries of origin, and date of each one's intention to acquire citizenship.

* * *

1006.1 — 1006.5
BUECKNER, FLOSSIE. "Naturalization Records from Harris County, Texas." In *The Roadrunner.*
1006.1
--- Vol. 5:4 (Aug. 1979), pp. 19-24.
1006.2
--- Vol. 6:3 (May 1980), pp. 6-8.
1006.3
--- Vol. 7:4 (Aug. 1981), p. 7.
1006.4
--- Vol. 8:2 (Feb. 1982), pp. 21-22, 31.
1006.5
--- Vol. 9:3 (May 1983), pp. 112-114.

Acquisition of citizenship in the years 1891-1894. Name, date of naturalization, country of origin, age, and page reference in the court files for about 240 persons. Title varies.
There is some doubt about continuation of this research, as it concludes: "I will not go down there again soon, as my car was towed away from its place in the parking lot and it cost me a fortune."

* * *

1012
BUESING, WOLFGANG. "Zur Amerika Auswanderung der Familie Rumsfeld." In *Norddeutsche Familienkunde*, part 1 (1978), pp. 146-147.

Concerning emigration to America of members of the Rumsfeld family. Tells of eight who came to America, 1866-1877. Much biographical data. See also Meyerholz, item no. 5633.

* * *

1014
BUMSTED, J. M. *The People's Clearance: Highland Emigration to British North America.* Edinburgh: Edinburgh University Press; Winnipeg: University of Manitoba Press, 1982. pp.224-287.

Scots to British North America: 1,500 passengers on 19 passenger lists. Arrival on various ships mentioned in other publications: the *Hector*, 1773; the *Lovely Nelly*, ca. 1774; the *Friendship* and the *Lovely Nelly*, 1775; the *Jane*, the *Lucy*, and the *British Queen*, 1790; the *Dove of Aberdeen*, the *Sarah of Liverpool*, 1801; the *Commerce*, 1803; the *Oughton*, 1804; the *Humphreys*, the *Spencer*, the *Isle of Skye*, the *Elizabeth & Ann*, 1806; the *Clarendon*, 1808; and the *Prince of Wales*, 1813 and 1815. Red River settlers in 1811 are also listed.

* * *

1031.5
BURGERT, ANNETTE K. *Early Pennsylvania Pioneers from Mutterstadt in the Palatinate.* (Immigrant Origins Monograph Ser., 4.) Worthington, Ohio: AKB Publications, 1983. 29p.

Considers 32 immigrants and gives family details about each. Emigration occurred in the first half of the 18th century.

* * *

1031.8
BURGERT, ANNETTE K. *Eighteenth Century Emigrants from German-Speaking Lands to North America.* Vol. 1: *The Northern Kraichgau.* (Publications of The Pennsylvania German Society, 16.) Breinigsville, Pa.: The Pennsylvania German Society, 1983. 461 p.

Names of hundreds of German-language immigrants, mostly 18th century. Much extra genealogical information.

* * *

1031.12
BURGERT, ANNETTE K. *Eighteenth Century Pennsylvania Emigrants from Hassloch and Boehl in the Palatinate.* (Immigrant Origins Monograph Ser., 2.) Worthington, Ohio: AKB Publications, 1983. 32p.

Concerns 41 immigrants and gives family details about each. Emigration occurred in the first half of the 18th century.

* * *

1033.4
BURGERT, ANNETTE K. *The Hochstadt Origins of Some of the Early Settlers at Host Church, Berks County, Pa.* (Immigrant Origins Monograph Ser., 3.) Worthington, Ohio: AKB Publications, 1983. 40p.

Considers 34 immigrants and gives family details about each. Emigration occurred in first half of 18th century. See also nos. 0889 and 1032 in the main volume of this bibliography for more on Host Church, Berks County.

* * *

1033.11
BURGERT, ANNETTE K. *Pennsylvania Pioneers from Wolfersweiler Parish, Saarland, Germany.* (Immigrant Origins Monograph Ser., 1.) Worthington, Ohio: AKB Publications, 1983. 44p.

List of emigrants from the Wolfersweiler area to Pennsylvania, beginning in 1709. Much additional information on these settlers given throughout book.

* * *

1035.14
BURKHARDT, JUDITH. "England to Virginia in 1635." In *The Second Boat*, vol. 2:1 (May 1981), pp. 4-5.

Two lists, published in *The New England Historical and Genealogical Register*, vol. 3:3 (July 1849), pp. 388-390, and cited in Somerby, item no. 8862 in the basic volume of this bibliography. Variations in spelling of names. Includes 200 names and ages.

* * *

1035.25
BURKHOLDER, JOSEPH C. "Benedict Brechbuhl, Hans Burkholder and the Swiss Mennonite Migration to Lancaster, Penna. The Swiss Emigration." *Papers Read Before the Lancaster County Historical Society*, May 6, 1927, vol. 21:5, pp. 57-62.

Concerns the many 18th-century Swiss Mennonite arrivals.

* * *

1050.1 — 1050.7
"BUTTE COUNTY, CALIFORNIA, GREAT REGISTER." In *Genealogical Goldmine* [Paradise Genealogical Society].
1050.1
---Vol. 15:1 (June 1982), pp. 9-14 (A).
1050.2
---Vol. 15:2 (Sept. 1982), pp. 15-20 (A-B).
1050.3
---Vol. 15:3 (Dec. 1982), pp. 9-14 (B).
1050.4
---Vol. 15:4 (Mar. 1983), pp. 9-14 (B).
1050.5
---Vol. 16:1 (June 1983), pp. 9-14 (B).
1050.6
---Vol. 16:2 (Sept. 1983), pp. 9-14 (B).
1050.7
---Vol. 16:3 (Dec. 1983), pp. 9-14 (B-C). In progress.

Covers the years 1878-1879. Supplies information on name, age, place of origin, occupation, residence, date of registration, and sometimes date of naturalization. Great Registers were voter registration lists. This has 900 entries just in names beginning A through C, and the transcription continues.

* * *

1068.1 — 1068.3
"CALIFORNIA SPECIAL CENSUS 1852, Calaveras County." In *Orange County California Genealogical Society Quarterly.*
1068.1
--- Vol. 18:4 (Dec. 1981), p. 107.
1068.2
--- Vol. 19:2 (June 1982), pp. 54-56; vol. 19:3 (Sept. 1982), pp. 95-99.
1068.3
--- Vol. 20:1 (Mar. 1983), pp. 12-13. In progress.

Since this was a census, not every person named was an immigrant, but many do indicate countries of birth other than the U.S.A. Data supplies age, sex, and occupation. These issues are the beginning of a work that continues.

* * *

1076.1 — 1076.4
"CAMBRIA COUNTY [Pennsylvania] NATURALIZATION RECORDS." In *Conemaugh Country,*
1076.1
--- Vol. 1:1 (June 1981), pp. 10-11.
1076.2
--- Vol. 1:2 (Sept. 1981), p. 9.
1076.3
--- Vol. 1:3 (Dec. 1981), pp. 9-12.
1076.4
--- Vol. 1:4 (Mar. 1982), pp. 9-10.

About 80 persons, mostly from Great Britain and Ireland, with dates of admission and sometimes dates of arrival. Citizenships granted in 1835 and 1836.

* * *

1133.4
CASSADY, MICHAEL. "1863 Passengers Minnesota Bound." In *The Minnesota Genealogist,* vol. 13:4 (Dec. 1982), pp. 166-170.

Information on 200 passengers from the *Germania,* Antwerp to New York, 1863, with ages and places of origin. Most were going to St. Paul.

* * *

1133.6
CASSADY, MICHAEL. "From Europe to Iowa: Iowa-Bound Passengers on Four Ships." In *Hawkeye Heritage,* vol. 17:3 (Summer-Fall 1982), pp. 119-122.

About 150 passengers from Hamburg and Bremen to New York, 1854-1862, with data on age, sex, occupation, and country of origin.

* * *

1133.8
CASSADY, MICHAEL. "From Germany to Iowa: A List of Iowa-Bound Passengers on the Bark, *Kopler.*" In *Hawkeye Heritage,* vol. 16:4 (Fall-Winter 1981), pp. 188-189.

Covers 70 passengers, with data on age, sex, occupation, and place of origin. Arrival in New York was in 1853.

* * *

1133.10
CASSADY, MICHAEL. "Immigrants to Indiana from Customs Ship Passenger Lists at New York." In *The Hoosier Genealogist,* vol. 23:3 (Sept. 1983), pp. 55-61.

More than 300 European passengers between the years 1850 and 1864. Age, sex, occupation, place of origin (England and the Continent, mostly Germany, with some specific locations given). At New York port of arrival, all signified their intention of going to Indiana. Taken from National Archives microfilm, with reel reference numbers to facilitate research.

* * *

1133.12
CASSADY, MICHAEL. "Iowa-Bound Arrivals at Port of New York." In *Hawkeye Heritage,* vol. 18:3 (Fall 1983), pp. 128-135.

Passengers from Hamburg and Bremen to New York in the years 1848, 1862, 1864, and 1865. About 300 named Iowa as destination. Data includes ages, sex, occupations, and places of origin.

* * *

1133.14
CASSADY, MICHAEL. "*Mount Stewart Elphinstone* Passenger List." In *Nebraska Ancestree,* vol. 5:2 (Fall 1982), pp. 59-61.

In an 1849 sailing from Glasgow to New York, 126 passengers. Data for each includes age, sex, occupation, country of origin, and destination.

* * *

1133.16
CASSADY, MICHAEL. "Ohio-Bound Passengers." In *The Report: The Ohio Genealogical Society,* vol. 22:2 (Summer 1982), pp. 85-88.

Refers to immigrants on three crossings from LeHavre to New York: the *St. Nicholas* and the *Oneida* in 1849 and the *Langen* in 1853. More than 300 passengers, most from France and Germany, some from Switzerland. Names, ages, and places of origin.

* * *

1133.18
CASSADY, MICHAEL. "Ohio-Bound Passengers." In *The Report: The Ohio Genealogical Society,* vol. 22:4 (Winter 1982), pp. 203-206.

Mid-19th-century sailings from the Continent, with most of the 450 passengers headed for western New York state (Buffalo), Ohio, and Michigan. The *Havre* and the *Oneida* embarked from LeHavre in 1845; the *Belgique* from Antwerp in 1857; and the *John Bertram* from Hamburg in 1864. All to the port of New York. Names, ages, sex, countries of origin, and destinations.

* * *

1133.20
CASSADY, MICHAEL. "Ohio-Bound Passengers." In *The Report: The Ohio Genealogical Society,* vol. 23:1 (Spring 1983), pp. 7-10.

Almost 400 passengers on three vessels to New York: the *Emerald* from LeHavre in 1845; the *New Hampshire* from Antwerp with German passengers, 1847; and the S.S. *Union* from Bremen in 1868. Data includes names, ages, sex, and occupations.

* * *

1133.22

CASSADY, MICHAEL. "Ohio-Bound Passengers." In *The Report: The Ohio Genealogical Society,* vol. 23:2 (Summer 1983), pp. 96-99.

Departures from Antwerp, Bremen, and Liverpool to New York, 1838-1868 on 11 ships. Age, sex, place of origin. Passengers boarding at Antwerp and Bremen were German for the most part; mostly Irish boarded at Liverpool: 525 passengers in all.

* * *

1133.23

CASSADY, MICHAEL. "Ohio-Bound Passengers." In *The Report: The Ohio Genealogical Society,* vol. 23:4 (Winter 1983), pp. 211-213.

Covers German port departures for New York, 1838-1868. Over 400 passengers. Name, with occupation, sex, and age. Passengers on the *Alexander,* the *Elizabeth,* the *Charlotte Louise,* the *Charles Crooker,* the *Georgiana,* the *Hannibal,* the *Arestedes and* the *Tuisko.*

* * *

1133.24

CASSADY, MICHAEL. "Passenger List for Brig *Russia.*" In *Nebraska Ancestree,* vol. 5:1 (Summer 1982), pp. 17-18.

Names 81 Irish passengers on the brig *Russia,* from Dublin to New York, 1849. Data includes age, sex, occupation, place of origin, and destination. Taken from microfilm of the National Archives, Washington, D.C.

* * *

1133.26

CASSADY, MICHAEL. "Passenger List for Ship *Cultivator.*" In *Nebraska Ancestree,* vol. 5:1 (Summer 1982), pp. 16-17.

An 1867 crossing of the *Cultivator* from Liverpool to New York with 56 passengers. Names, ages, occupations, countries and counties of origin, and destinations. Transcribed from microfilm of the National Archives, Washington, D.C.

* * *

1133.28

CASSADY, MICHAEL. "Passenger List of the Ship *Albert.*" In *M.C.G.S. Reporter* [Milwaukee County Genealogical Society], vol. 13:2 (Spring 1982), pp. 61-67.

Lists 300 passengers on ship's crossings from Bremen to New York in 1858. Names, ages, sex, occupations, countries of origin, and places of destination.

* * *

1133.30

CASSADY, MICHAEL. "Passenger List, the Bark *Franklin,* 30 April 1849." In *The New York Genealogical and Biographical Record,* vol. 113:3 (July 1982), pp. 131-132.

From Hamburg, 55 passengers: names, ages, sex, occupations, countries of origin, and destinations.

* * *

1133.32

CASSADY, MICHAEL. "Passenger List, the Brig *Gil Blas,* 1 May 1849." In *The New York Genealogical and Biographical Record,* vol. 114:2, (Apr. 1983), pp. 99-101.

Covers 98 passengers from Bremen to New York. Name, age, sex, occupation, place of origin, and destination.

* * *

1133.34

CASSADY, MICHAEL. "Passenger Lists Excerpts." In *Wisconsin State Genealogical Society Newsletter,* vol. 28:3 (Jan. 1982), p. 139.

Passengers on board the bark, *Langen,* Le Havre to New York, 1853. Prussian and Swiss immigrants, mostly farmers. The Swiss were bound for Ohio; the Prussians for Wisconsin.

* * *

1133.36

CASSADY, MICHAEL. "Passengers in the Brig *Dettmar,* 1849." In *New York Genealogical and Biographical Record,* vol. 114:1 (Jan. 1983), pp. 6-8.

On a Bremen to New York crossing, 155 passengers. Names, ages, sex, occupations, destinations.

* * *

1133.38

CASSADY, MICHAEL. "Ship Passenger Lists." In *Illinois State Genealogical Society Quarterly.*
---Vol. 15:1 (Spring 1983), pp. 2-8.

Five ships from the Continent in the 1850s and 1860s carried 344 passengers whose destination was given as Illinois. Most were from Germany. Sailings were from Antwerp, the *Belgique* in 1857; from Bremen, the *Olympia* in 1857 and the *Coriolan* and the *Ferdinand* in 1864; from Hamburg, the *John Bertram* in 1864. All sailings to New York. Lists provide name, age, sex, occupation, and country of origin.

* * *

1133.40

CASSADY, MICHAEL. "Ship Passenger Lists." In *Illinois State Genealogical Society Quarterly,* vol. 15:4 (Winter 1983), pp. 269-274.

About 270 arrivals on seven ships to New York, 1850-1883, with passengers' final destination, Illinois. Age, sex, occupation, place of origin (mostly Germany).

* * *

1133.42

CASSADY, MICHAEL. "Ship Passengers Minnesota Bound, 1859, 1868, 1883." In *Minnesota Genealogist,* vol. 14:4 (Dec. 1983), pp. 185-190.

Lists 160 passengers on four ships: the *Arestedes,* the *Smidt,* the *Tuisko,* and the *Parthia.* Names, ages, sex, occupations, and countries of origin: Germany, Sweden, and Norway.

* * *

1133.44
CASSADY, MICHAEL. "Ship Passengers Minnesota Bound, 1868, 1888." In *Minnesota Genealogist*, vol. 14:1 (Mar. 1983), pp. 36-47.

About 300 passengers on these four crossings: the *Republic* and the *Goethe* from Bremen, 1868; the *City of Richmond* and the *Aurania* from Liverpool and Queenstown, 1888. Names, ages, sex, occupations, places of last recent residence, and destinations.

* * *

1133.46
CASSADY, MICHAEL. "Ship Passengers Minnesota Bound, 1892." In *Minnesota Genealogist*, vol. 14:2 (June 1983), pp. 89-93; vol. 14:3 (Sept. 1983), pp. 141-149.

About 320 passengers, mostly from Sweden and Norway to New York. Names, ages, sex, occupations, and places of last prior residence. Mostly Minnesota destinations specified. Some of the ships involved were the *Etruria*, the *Anchoria*, and the *Wyoming*.

* * *

1133.48
CASSADY, MICHAEL. "Wisconsin-Bound Passengers on Bark *Kopler*." *Wisconsin State Genealogical Society Newsletter*, vol. 29:1 (June 1982), p. 10; vol. 29:2 (Sept. 1982), p. 81.

In the year 1853, these 70 passengers from Hamburg arrived in New York. Data includes ages, sex, occupations, and countries of origin.

* * *

1133.52
CASSADY, MICHAEL. "Wisconsin-Bound Passengers on Board the Bark *Jupiter*, Arrived New York from Bremen, 28 May 1864." In *Wisconsin State Genealogical Society Newsletter*, vol. 29:4 (Apr. 1983), pp. 223-224.

Lists 56 passengers, with data on age, sex, occupation, and place of origin.

* * *

1133.54
CASSADY, MICHAEL. "Wisconsin-Bound Passengers on Board *The John Bertram*, Arrived New York from Hamburg, 18 June 1864." In *Wisconsin State Genealogical Society Newsletter*, vol. 30:1 (June 1983), pp. 15-16.

About 60 emigrants from Germany, with data for each giving age, sex, occupation, and place of origin. Over half indicated they were bound for Milwaukee.

* * *

1133.56
CASSADY, MICHAEL. "Wisconsin-Bound Passengers on Board the *Orpheus*, Arrived New York from Bremen, 12 July 1861 (and on the *Thusneleta*, New York from Bremen, 10 August 1861)." In *Wisconsin State Genealogical Society Newsletter,* vol. 30:2 (Sept. 1983), pp. 83-84.

About 90 passengers, all Germans, with information on ages, sex, occupations, and, occasionally, places of origin and destination (Milwaukee).

* * *

1133.58
CASSADY, MICHAEL. "Wisconsin-Bound Passengers on Ship, *Charlotte*." In *Wisconsin State Genealogical Society Newsletter*, vol. 29:2 (Sept. 1982), p. 82; vol. 29:3 (Jan. 1983), pp. 29-30.

Refers to 80 passengers from Bremerhaven, destination Milwaukee, 1867. Name, age, sex, occupation, origin.

* * *

1133.60
CASSADY, MICHAEL. "Wisconsin-Bound Passengers on Ship *Marmion*." In *Wisconsin State Genealogical Society Newsletter*, vol. 29:1 (June 1982), p. 9.

Concerns a sailing from Liverpool to New York in 1849. Listing specifies name, age, sex, and occupation of each of 50 passengers who had declared Wisconsin as destination.

* * *

1133.62
CASSADY, MICHAEL. "Wisconsin-Bound Passengers on the *Sir Robert Peel*, Arrived New York from Hamburg, 24 June 1862." In *Wisconsin State Genealogical Society Newsletter*, vol. 30:3 (Jan. 1984), p. 158.

Names of 62 arrivals from Germany in 1862. The information provides names, ages, sex, occupations, and places of origin. These listings will continue in a future issue of the Newsletter.

* * *

1138
CHAMBERS, THEODORE FRELINGSHUYSEN. "Palatines in New York in 1710." In *The Early Germans of New Jersey. . . .* (1895). Repr. Baltimore: Genealogical Publishing Co., 1969, pp. 632-637.

Appendix VII includes not only Palatines in New York in 1710, but other names as well: persons naturalized in New York by Act of Assembly, 1714-1772.

* * *

1139.1
CHANDLER, M.J. "Emigrants from Britain to the Colonies of America and the West Indies." In *The Journal of the Barbados Museum and Historical Society*, vol. 36:1 (1979), pp. 28-43.

Indentured servants in the 17th century: names, ages, places of origin or occupation, and destinations. The original list was compiled by Thomas Tanner, clerk of the Worshipful Company of Fishmongers. Although a few of the 410 names also appear in Ghirelli (item no. 2524 in the main volume of this bibliography) and cover nearly the same dates, 1682-1686, the two lists are different.

* * *

1139.6
CHANDLER, R.E. "End of An Odyssey: Acadians Arrive in St. Gabriel, Louisiana." In *Louisiana History,* vol. 14:1 (Winter 1973), pp. 69-87.

Lists of more than 200 Acadians who arrived in New Orleans in 1767 and later settled at St. Gabriel, Iberville Parish, Louisiana. Place of origin variously believed to be Nova Scotia, Maryland, or Saint Domingue (Santo Domingo, now the Dominican Republic). Lists of names with distribution of lands; names of immigrants, their ages and families, pp. 80-87.

* * *

1163
CHOLOCHWOST, TOMASZ L. "Baltimore's Polish Pioneers." In *Maryland Magazine of Genealogy*, vol. 5:1, (Spring 1982), pp. 3-7.

Ship lists of Polish citizens, giving country of birth, place of last prior residence, age, sex, occupation.

* * *

1186
"CLARK COUNTY, INDIANA: INDEX TO NATURALIZATIONS, Books 2, 3, and 4, 1888-1927." In *Southern Indiana Genealogical Society Quarterly*, vol. 3:1 (Jan. 1982), pp. 8, 11.

Names of 200 persons, with age of each at time of naturalization.

* * *

1188
CLARKE, JAMES. "The Emigration." In *Memorials of the Clarke Family. . . .* Indianapolis: Indianapolis Printing and Publishing House, 1875, pp. 23-25.

Records the emigration of James Clarke with 38 other Britishers from Liverpool in 1816.

* * *

1194
CLARKE, R.S.J. "References to Emigrants on Co. Down Gravestones." In *Ulster Genealogical and Historical Guild Newsletter*, vol. 1:8 (1982), pp. 258-264; vol. 1:9 (1983), pp. 290-293.

Death records that indicate emigration took place (Irish to America) and when and where death occurred. Taken from Clarke's *Gravestone Inscriptions: Co[unty] Down [Ireland]*, vols. 1-19. Nineteenth and twentieth-century dates.

* * *

1211
CLAY, ROBERT Y. "Powhatan County, Virginia, Oaths of Allegiance, 1777." In *The Virginia Genealogist*, vol. 27:3 (July-Sept., 1983), pp. 190-196.

Eighteenth-century records included with loose papers of Powhatan County, now preserved at the Virginia State Library, Richmond. Over 300 names, mostly British.

* * *

1213.1 — 1213.3
"COCHISE COUNTY, TERRITORY OF ARIZONA, GREAT REGISTER, 1890." In *Copper State Bulletin*.
1213.1
---Vol. 15:3 (Fall 1980), pp. 106-110 (Letters A, B); vol. 15:4 (Winter 1980/1981), pp. 146-52 (B, C).
1213.2
---Vol. 16:1 (Spring 1981), pp. 15-21 (C,D); vol. 16:2 (Summer 1981), pp. 50-58 (D-G); vol. 16:3 (Fall 1981), pp. 67-82 (G-M); vol. 16:4 (Winter 1981), pp. 97-108 (M-Q).
1213.3
---Vol. 17:1 (Spring 1982), pp. 26-28 (Q,R); vol. 17:2 (Summer 1982), pp. 52-58 (R,S); vol. 17:3 (Fall 1982), pp. 71-74 (S-V); vol. 17:4 (Winter 1982), pp. 105-110 (W-Z and suppl.).

Voter registration and poll lists used to be called the Great Register. Over 2,000 names, each with age, country of birth, occupation, local residence, naturalization date, and name and location of the court.

* * *

1217.1 — 1217.9
COLDHAM, PETER WILSON. *Bonded Passengers to America*. 9 vols. in 3. Baltimore: Genealogical Publishing Co., 1983.
1217.1
--- Vol. 1. History of Transportation, 1615-1775. 193p.
1217.2
--- Vol. 2. Middlesex, 1617-1775. 334p.
1217.3
--- Vol. 3. London, 1656-1775. 179p.
1217.4
--- Vol. 4. Home Counties, 1655-1775: Surrey, Hertfordshire, Kent, Essex, and Sussex. 231p.
1217.5
--- Vol. 5. Western Circuit, 1664-1775: Cornwall, Devon, Dorset, Hampshire, Somerset, and Wiltshire, With a List of the Rebels of 1685. 95p.
1217.6
--- Vol. 6. Oxford Circuit, 1663-1775: Berkshire, Gloucestershire, Herefordshire, Monmouthshire, Oxfordshire, Shropshire, Staffordshire, and Worcestershire. 95p.
1217.7
--- Vol. 7. Norfolk Circuit, 1663-1775: Bedfordshire, Buckinghamshire, Cambridgeshire, Huntingdonshire, Norfolk, and Suffolk. 95p.
1217.8
--- Vol. 8. Northern Circuit, 1665-1775: Cheshire, Cumberland, Durham, Lancashire, Northumberland, Westmorland, Yorkshire, and Flint. 54p.
1217.9
--- Vol. 9. Midland Circuit, 1671-1775: Derbyshire, Leicestershire, Lincolnshire, Northamptonshire, Nottinghamshire, Rutland, Warwickshire, and Strays [misc.]. 60p.

Includes about 50,000 names relative to British emigration, with dates of embarkation and other details. Note: *Middlesex* and *London*, vols. 2 and 3, were published earlier as *English Convicts in Colonial America* (Polyanthos, 1975, 1976) and cited in the basic volume of this bibliography as items 1222 and 1223. Of the nine vols. listed above, tome 1 contains vols. 1 and 2; tome 2 has vols. 3 and 4; and tome 3 the remainder.

* * *

1235
COLDHAM, PETER WILSON. *Lord Mayor's Court of London: Depositions Relating to Americans, 1641-1736.* (National Genealogical Society Publications, 44) Washington, DC: National Genealogical Society, 1980. 119pp.

Refers to American debtors and money they owed in England in the 17th and 18th centuries. Facts indicate emigration and sometimes help determine time. Pages 80 and 81 list prisoners transported to Barbados in 1648 and British royalist exiles to Barbados in 1656.

* * *

1239
COLDHAM, PETER WILSON. "Passengers and Ships to America, 1618-1668." (Genealogical Gleanings in England.) In *National Genealogical Society Quarterly*, vol. 71:3 (Sept. 1983), pp. 163-192; vol. 71:4 (Dec. 1983), pp. 284-296.

Data taken from English Port Books in the Public Records Office, London. Names of ship, master, and port; destinations (Canada and elsewhere in America); date and name of shipper or passenger. Quite often the shipper (merchant) was the passenger (immigrant). No actual passenger lists given. In progress.

* * *

1245
COLDHAM, PETER WILSON. "Some Emigrants to Georgia, 1774-1775." (Genealogical Gleanings in England.) In *National Genealogical Society Quarterly*, vol. 66:2 (June 1978), pp. 117-118.

About 120 servants from Whitby, Yorkshire, and Orkney, Scotland, sailed on the *Marlborough*, bound for work on Thomas Brown's plantations. Names only.

* * *

1255
COLDHAM, PETER WILSON. "Some Scottish Emigrants, 1771-1774." In *National Genealogical Society Quarterly*, vol. 61:4 (Dec. 1973), pp. 262-263.

A description of the contents of a box of Treasury Papers (PRO: T1/500) concerning emigration from Scotland. Cites 10 names.

* * *

1257
COLDHAM, PETER WILSON. "The 'Spiriting' of London Children to Virginia, 1648-1685." In *The Virginia Magazine of History and Biography*, vol. 83:3 (July 1975), pp. 280-287.

A description of some 17th-century kidnappings, with a list of about 30 children who were taken to Virginia.

* * *

1260
COLDHAM, PETER WILSON. "The Voyage of the *Neptune* to Virginia, 1618-1619, and the Disposition of Its Cargo." In *The Virginia Magazine of History and Biography*, vol. 87:1 (Jan. 1979), pp. 30-67.

Although this concerns mainly a law case about illegal happenings on board the *Neptune*, chartered by the Virginia Company, names of several persons who stayed in Virginia are given.

* * *

1284
[COMPTON FAMILY ARRIVALS at the Port of Quebec, Canada, 1865-1869.] In *The Midland Ancestor*, vol. 4:2 (Aug. 1975), p. 48.

Sixteen Comptons, giving ages, names of vessels, and dates of arrival, on a list contained in a letter from C. MacKinnon, Canadian Archivist, to a correspondent, Mrs. Simmons, who had inquired about one William Compton who arrived in Canada in the 1860s.

* * *

1286
CONNER, CARA MILLER. "Christian Mueller: a Mennonite Pioneer." In *Journal of the American Historical Society of Germans from Russia*, vol. 6:4 (Winter 1983), pp. 17-23.

Several Mennonites from Russia to the U.S. in the 1870s mentioned in the text. Much about the Mennonite connection between Russia and the U.S.

* * *

1290
CONRAD, GLENN R. *The First Families of Louisiana.* Baton Rouge [La.]: Claitor's Publishing Division, [1970]. Vol. 1, pp. 1-140.

Many hundreds of immigrants from Europe, mainly French and German, arriving in Louisiana, 1717-1731. A two-volume set.

* * *

1307
CORNELL, NANCY J. "Naturalization Papers, Irwin County [Georgia] Superior Court Minutes." In *The Southern States Armchair Researcher*, vol. 1:3 (Fall 1983), pp. 142-144.

Records for the years 1841 and 1842 list 60 persons from Ireland, with dates of arrival in the U.S. and in Georgia, ages, and dates of naturalization or of declaration of intention to acquire citizenship.

* * *

1357.1 — 1357.2
COX, RICHARD J. "Maryland Runaway Convict Servants, 1745-1780." In *National Genealogical Society Quarterly*.
1357.1
---Vol. 68:2 (June 1980), pp. 105-114; vol. 68:3 (Sept. 1980), pp. 232-233; vol. 68:4 (Dec. 1980), pp. 299-304.
1357.2
---Vol. 69:1 (Mar. 1981), pp. 51-58; vol. 69:2 (June 1981), pp. 125-132; vol. 69:3 (Sept. 1981), pp. 205-214; vol. 69:4 (Dec. 1981), pp. 293-300.

A dissertation on the plight of servants, with a list of more than 700 of them. Information includes age, name of person to whom contracted, location before fleeing, occupation, and sometimes the place of origin in Great Britain or Ireland.

* * *

1385
"CRAWFORD COUNTY [Indiana] DECLARATIONS OF INTENTION to Become Citizens, Crawford County Civil Order Book A." In *The Hoosier Journal of Ancestry*, vol. 7:2 (Apr. 1980), p. 18.

About 50 persons, all from United Kingdom, with ages, places and dates of birth, places and dates of departure from Britain and of arrival in America. Most declarations filed 1817-1824.

* * *

1398.1 — 1401
CRIGLER, ARTHUR D., GRACE R. SCOTT, *et al.*,contributors. "Naturalization Entries 1833-1871: Court Minute Books, Mobile County, Alabama." In *Deep South Genealogical Quarterly*.
1398.1
---Vol. 17.1 (Feb. 1980), pp. 29-35; vol. 17:2 (May 1980), pp. 68-69; vol. 17:3 (Aug. 1980), pp. 99-100.
1399
---Vol. 18:2 (May 1981), pp. 76-79; vol. 18:4 (Nov. 1981), pp. 150-154.
1400
---Vol. 19:1 (Feb. 1982), pp. 43-47; vol. 19:2 (May 1982), pp. 97-101; vol. 19:4 (Nov. 1982), pp. 201-205.
1401
---Vol. 20:2 (May 1983), pp. 96-98; vol. 20:3 (Aug. 1983), pp. 127-130.

Continuation of abstracts listed in item nos. 1386-1398 in the basic volume of this bibliography. Crigler moved to another state and Grace Scott has died. Lucille S. Mallon has continued the series although her name is not carried on the work.

* * *

1418
CUNNINGHAM, JOHN. "The Emigrant Children of the Vaughan Charitable Charter School, Kesh Co., Fermanagh." In *Ulster Genealogical and Historical Guild Newsletter*, vol. 1:8 (1982), pp. 252-257.

A list of about 60 Irish children, with each one's place of origin, destination, date of emigration, and age. Tells of 38 who were sent to the U.S. or Canada between 1846 and 1929.

* * *

1420
CUNZ, DIETER. "German Settlers in Early Colonial Maryland." In *Maryland Historical Magazine*, vol. 42:2 (June 1947), pp. 101-108.

Seventeenth-century arrivals, with data on the immigration and naturalization of about 30 of them.

* * *

1433
CUSHING, J. ELIZABETH, TERESA CASEY, and MONICA ROBERTSON. *A Chronicle of Irish Emigration to Saint John, New Brunswick, 1847*. St. John: The New Brunswick Museum, 1979. 77 p.

A record of over 900 immigrants, with considerable information about each.

* * *

1436
D., S.E. "The Voyage of the *Valiant*, 1817." In the Charlottetown [Prince Edward Island] *Patriot*, 24 Nov. 1932, p. 4.

The story of the *Valiant* mentions about 50 passengers and cites the Rev. Matthew Smith's 1898 account of the crossing. Smith's "Voyage of the *Valiant*," is entry no. 8753 in the basic volume of this bibliography.

* * *

1439
DAICY, BRENDA. "Notes on Knight Immigrants to America." In *The Second Boat*, vol. 4:2 (Aug. 1983), pp. 45-47.

Much information on immigrants with the surname Knight.

* * *

1443
DALBY, BARBARA, MARGARET KERN, and LORETTO D. SZUCS. "Naturalization Records of the District Court of Eastern Michigan, 1810-1893." In *The Detroit Society for Genealogical Research Magazine*, vol. 46:1 (Fall 1982), pp. 9-12, A-D; vol. 46:2 (Winter 1982), pp. 75-78, D-K; vol. 46:3 (Spring 1983), pp. 103-106, K-P; vol. 46:4 (Summer 1983), pp. 173-177, P-Z.

Completed coverage of the years indicated, with -- for each of about 1,300 entries -- filing date of intention to become a citizen, date of final oath, country of origin, and reference to original document file number. Abstracted and indexed at the Federal Archives and Records Center in Chicago. Published also in book form, with limited distribution.

* * *

1446.1 — 1446.3
DALE, JANET. "P.E.I. Passenger Lists: A Genealogical Myth Struck Down." In *The Island Magazine*.
1446.1
---No. 1 (Fall-Winter 1976), pp. 34-39. "List of Emigrants Shipped on Board the *Lovely Nelly* of Whavon for St. Johns Island, North America. Carsthorn, 1st May 1775. Passengers on Board the *Lucy* and *Jane*."
1446.2
---No. 2 (Spring-Summer 1977), pp. 39-42. "List of Passengers on Board the *Lovely Nelly* Bound for St. Johns Island; Brig *Rambler* from Tobermory, N. Britain, 14th July 1806."
1446.3
---No. 3 (Fall-Winter 1977), pp. 21-27. "*Clarendon* Passenger List, Oban to Charlottetown, 1808; *Elizabeth and Ann* of Newcastle, 1806; *Spencer* of Newcastle, 1806; Barque *Lulan* from Glasgow, 1848; Brig *Isle of Skye* of Aberdeen, 1806; and *Lively* from Britain, 1775."

For years it was believed that many passenger lists of ships crossing to Canada were available, but a thorough search has revealed that only a few are still extant. They are, however, available. In these to Prince Edward Island, about 850 immigrants are named, with ages, occupations, places of residence, counties of origin, and stated reasons for emigrating. St. John Isle was an early name for Prince Edward Island, hence the references to "St. Johns" in the 18th and 19th century records. All from English and Scottish ports.

* * *

1447.1 — 1447.4
"DALLAS COUNTY, TEXAS, INDEX TO NATURALIZATION RECORDS." In *Dallas Genealogical Society Quarterly.*
1447.1
---Vol. 26:4 (Dec.1980), pp. 186-192 (A-Ba).
1447.2
---Vol. 27:1 (Mar. 1981), pp. 300-306 (Ba-Bo); vol. 27:2 (June 1981), pp. 335-341 (Bo-Ch); vol. 27:3 (Sept. 1981), pp. 411-417 (Ca-Cz; vol. 27:4 (Dec. 1981), 461-475 (Da-Fr).
1447.3
---Vol. 28:1 (Mar. 1982), pp. 8-26 (Fr-He); vol. 28:2 (June 1982), pp. 75-98 (He-Ku); vol. 28:4 (Dec. 1982), pp. 236-246 (La- Lu).
1447.4
---Vol. 29:1 (Mar. 1983), pp. 1-27 (M-Q); vol. 29:2 (June 1983), pp. 86-98 (R-S); vol. 29:3 (Sept. 1983), pp. 134-150 (S); vol. 29:4 (Dec. 1983), pp. 188-205 (S-Z).

Over 3,000 new citizens from Great Britain, Ireland, and the continent of Europe in the latter half of the 19th century. Country of birth or allegiance and name of the district court.

* * *

1450.1
DARLINGTON, JANE E. "Marion County [Indiana] Naturalizations, 1843-1853." In *The Hoosier Genealogist*, vol. 21:1 (Mar. 1981), pp. 12-21; vol. 21:2 (June 1981), pp. 39-46.

In two parts: A-L, M-Z. Names of 300 persons, with each date of birth, dates and ports of embarkation and debarkation, country of origin, date of filing for citizenship papers or date of admission to citizenship. For the years 1832-1842, see item 1450 in the main volume.

* * *

1451.6
DAUGHTERS OF THE AMERICAN REVOLUTION, Old Ridge Road Chapter, abstractors. *Naturalization Records, Allen County, Indiana; Court House - Fort Wayne Indiana, Old Records Office, Circuit Court Order Books A, B, C, D, E.* n.p., 1978. 79 pp.

About 1,000 names, with places of origin, ages, dates and places of arrival, and dates of naturalization.

* * *

1451.15 — 1451.16
DAVIS, HARRIET. "Marion County [Oregon] Records: Foreign Born and Physically Disabled Electors of 1900." In *Beaver Briefs.*
1451.15
---Vol. 15:3 (Summer 1983), pp. 59-66 (Aumsville-Engelwood precincts); vol. 15:4 (Fall 1983), pp. 79-80, 91-96 (Fairfield-Marion precincts).
1451.16
---Vol. 16:1 (Winter 1984), pp. 15-17 (Marion-Mt. Angel precincts).

Abstracts naming persons identified as foreign-born or disabled in the year 1900 in the official register of electors for precincts in Marion County, Oregon. Name, age, occupation, place of birth, and date of first papers or naturalization. This work continues in later issues of the publication. More than 350 names so far.

* * *

1451.45
DAVIS, ROBERT S., JR. "Georgia Returns of Qualified Voters, 1867: Naturalized Citizens of Augusta and Richmond County." In *National Genealogical Society Quarterly*, vol. 70:1 (Mar. 1982), pp. 19-26.

About 450 names, with places of origin and dates and places of naturalization.

* * *

1451.49
DAVIS, ROBERT SCOTT, JR. "Scottish and English Immigrants to the Georgia Frontier, 1774-1775." In *National Genealogical Society Quarterly*, vol. 70:3 (Sept. 1982), pp. 190-194.

About 230 persons, indentured servants from Kirkwall, Orkney Islands, in 1774-1775, sent from Scotland on the *Georgia Packet*. Name, place of origin, age, occupation, and stated reason for coming to America.

* * *

1457.1 — 1457.3
"DEARBORN COUNTY [Indiana] NATURALIZATION Book 1, 1838-1845." In *The Hoosier Journal of Ancestry.*
1457.1
---Vol. 5:3 (July 1978), p. 16 (Lists entries 1-11).
1457.2
---Vol. 8:1 (Jan. 1981), p. 18 (entries 12-18).
1457.3
---Vol. 8:2 (Apr. 1981), pp. 103-104 (entries 19-29).
In progress.

Early new citizens in southeastern Indiana. Dates of birth, immigration, and naturalization; countries of origin, and places of arrival. Fewer than 30 are listed so far, but the work continues. See also next item: "Partial List of Others Who Applied. . . ."

* * *

1459
DEARBORN COUNTY [Indiana]: "Partial List of Others Who Applied for Naturalization in 1840." In *The Hoosier Journal of Ancestry*, vol. 8:2 (Apr. 1981), p. 104.

Names only, without additional information. This is intended to be a continuing feature. See also item above: "Dearborn County [Indiana] Naturalization Book 1. . . ."

* * *

1461
DEARING, BETTY. "The *Mayflower* Company." In *Ash Tree Echo*, vol. 11:1 (Jan. 1976), pp. 33-35.

Lists passengers on the first crossing of the *Mayflower*, with details of events in their lives to thirty years later, 1650.

* * *

1498
DE KALB COUNTY, ILLINOIS "Circuit Court Book A, 1838-1845, Naturalization." In *Cornsilk: Quarterly of the Genealogical Society of DeKalb County, Illinois*, vol. 2:2 (Summer 1983), pp. 44-45.

Lists of new citizens, 1838-1845, from Illinois court records for DeKalb County. For reference to naturalizations in the years 1853-1908, see item no. 2421.

* * *

1500
DELICAET, PAUL. "Passengers Aboard the *Thetis*, Cork to Bathurst, New Brunswick, in April 1837." In *The Irish Ancestor*, nos. 1 and 2 (1980), pp. 65-66.

Names and ages of 71 passengers, most from County Cork, Ireland. The *Thetis* was registered at Troon, Scotland, sailing to Chaleur Bay.

* * *

1505
DeMARCE, VIRGINIA EASLEY. *Mercenary Troops from Anhalt-Zerbst, Germany, Who Served with the British Forces During the American Revolution*. (German-American Genealogical Research Monograph, No. 19.) McNeal, Arizona: Westland Publications, 1984. 2 vols.

Vol. 1, surnames A through Kr; vol. 2, Ku through Z. Name, age, origin, notes on person, and source of the reference.

* * *

1525
DES MOINES COUNTY GENEALOGICAL SOCIETY, copier. *Naturalization Index, 1849-1857, Des Moines County, Iowa*. Burlington, Iowa.: the society, n.d. 21p.

Indexes 1,000 names, with references to locations in the official records.

* * *

1536
DEVILLE, WINSTON. "The Guillorys Arrive from Santo Domingo." In *Louisiana Genealogical Register*, vol. 28:1 (Mar. 1981), pp. 23, 24, 31.

Extracted from passenger lists taken from manifests of the Customs Service, Port of New Orleans, book 7, 1868-1870, W.P.A. of Louisiana (1940). Lists 89 passengers, many with the name Guillory, on the schooner *Jeannette* from St. Marc, Haiti, to New Orleans, 1870.

* * *

1634
DILLER, CORINNE HANNA. "Immigrant Ancestors of Miami Valley, Ohio, Quaker Families." In *Miami Valley Genealogical Society: Genealogical Aids Bulletin*, vol. 13:3 (Winter 1984), pp. 64-67.

All 18th century arrivals: 32 names, with places of birth, places and times of settlement, and names of spouses.

* * *

1638
DOAN, JAN. "Richland County Naturalizations." In *Illinois State Genealogical Society Quarterly*, vol. 14:2 (Summer 1982), pp. 102-104.

Lists 350 naturalized citizens in the state of Illinois. Names only.

* * *

1639
DOBSON, DAVID. *Directory of Scots Banished to the American Plantations, 1650-1775*. Baltimore: Genealogical Publishing Co., 1983, 239p.

Lists 3,000 Scots, with each occupation, place of residence in Scotland, place of capture and captivity, parents' names, date and cause of banishment, name of ship, and date and place of arrival in colonies. Much extra information on families. Most of these prisoners had been taken at uprisings in Scotland in 1715 and 1745.

* * *

1640.1 — 1640.2
DOBSON, DAVID. *A Directory of Scottish Settlers in North America*. Baltimore: Genealogical Publishing Co., 1984.
1640.1
---Vol. 1. 267p.

Uncovers the names of 5,000 Scottish immigrants before 1825 and 1,000 from the years 1625-1685.

1640.2
---Vol. 2. 216p.

Lists 4,000 Scottish immigrants before 1825.

* * *

1641
DOLLINGER, MARION DEUTER. "The Seventh Day Adventist Church of Bowdle, South Dakota." In *Clues*, 1980, pt. 2, pp. 41-43.

About 30 immigrant Germans from Russia in 1889, who organized the Church of Bowdle.

* * *

1654.1 — 1654.2
"DOUGLAS COUNTY (WA) NATURALIZATION INDEX, 1888-1973." In *The Appleland Bulletin* [Genealogical Society of North Central Washington].
1654.1
---Vol. 11:2 (Winter 1983), pp. 40-43 (A-H); vol. 11:3 (Spring 1983), pp. 70-72 (H-L); vol. 11:4 (Summer 1983), pp. 96-97 (L-M).
1654.2
---Vol. 12:1 (Fall 1983), pp. 9-13 (P-Z).

About 700 names taken from books in the Douglas County Courthouse, Waterville, Washington. Data includes reference to citation in county records, country of birth, and date of naturalization. Names beginning with N and O were apparently omitted or missing.

* * *

1659
DRAKE, CHARLES E. "Virginia Headrights: Genealogical Content and Usage." In *The Quarterly of The Virginia Genealogical Society*, vol. 20:2 (Apr.-June 1982), pp. 50-52.

Headrights (titles to land) do not necessarily give clues to the date of arrival in America, but with these in Virginia, granted to 35 indentured servants and transported Britishers, it is probable that the dates of arrival were only a few years before the granting of headrights in the years 1677-1679.

* * *

1677
DREILING, B.M. *Golden Jubilee of the German-Russian Settlement of Ellis and Rush Counties, Kansas.* Hays, Kansas: Ellis County News, 1926, 128p.

Names of many Germans from Russia, with details of the great emigration from Russia following the drafting of Germans in 1874. Indicates places of domicile in Russia and destination and settlement in America (Ellis and Rush counties, Kansas). Lists are on pp. 13-18, 34-35, 41-42, 47, 60-61, and 65. Further, pp. 122-128 provide a consolidated list of German-Russian immigrants in Ellis and Rush counties for the years 1876-1878: names and areas of origin, with dates of arrival.

* * *

1728.4 — 1728.5
DURBIN, LINDA L. "Pierce County [Washington] Voter Registration Surfaces at Swap Meet." In *Bulletin of the Seattle Genealogical Society.*
1728.4
---Vol. 30:4 (Summer 1981), pp. 251-256.
1728.5
---Vol. 31:1 (Fall 1981), pp. 10-17.

Covers the years 1916-1920. Some 300 names, with registration date, residence, age, occupation, and birthplace. About 100 foreign-born give place and date of naturalization and name of court.

* * *

1750
"EARLY ARRIVALS." In *The International Genealogical Exchange* [Kountze, Texas], (May 1981), p. 5.

Scottish prisoners of war were sent by Cromwell to New England, 1651-1652. This names 37 of them at the iron works in Lynn, Massachusetts. From Suffolk Court files, Massachusetts archives.

* * *

1820.1 — 1820.3
"1892 GREAT REGISTER OF SISKIYOU COUNTY, California." In *Genealogical Society of Siskiyou County.*
1820.1
---Vol. 11:4 (Summer 1983), pp. 21-23 (A, B).
1820.2
---Vol. 12:1 (Fall 1983), p. 24 (B).
1820.3
---Vol. 12:2 (Winter 1983), pp. 3-5 (B). In progress.

Voter registration lists (the "Great Registers") provided name, age, occupation, place of birth, and the address at the time. This is to continue in future issues. For Siskiyou County names in the years 1866-1878, see item no. 8484.

* * *

1828
ELNIFF, PAULINE S. "Certificates of Naturalization, 1907-1921 [Lawrence, Kansas]." In *The Pioneer*, vol. 7:2 (Fall 1983), pp. 59-62.

Family information provided here for fifty persons listed, with ages and dates of declaration or naturalization. Copied from certificate stubs numbered 50701-50750 in vol. 3815 at the office of the Clerk of the District Court, Lawrence, Kansas.

* * *

1831
"EMIGRANT FILES [IRISH] ON FILE AT THE AUGUSTAN LIBRARY." In *Irish-American Genealogist*, no. 8 (1977), pp. 17-18.

About 200 Irish immigrants of the 18th and 19th centuries, with places of origin. Full information is available from the Augustan Library, Torrance, California.

* * *

1832
EMIGRANTS AT WORSHIP: *125 Years of Chisago Lake Methodism: A History of the Congregation, 1858-1983. First United Methodist Church, Lindstrom, Minnesota.* Lindstrom, Minn.: First United Methodist Church [1983]. 85 p.

Mentions several immigrants, with family data. See also item no. 6406 in the basic volume of this bibliography concerning a work by Karl Olin on the Chisago Lake meeting of the Congregational Church, 1855-1867.

* * *

1860
ENGLAND, LOUISE C. "Canadian Passenger Lists." In *Clues*, 1983, pt. 2 pp. 31-36.

About 700 Germans from Russia arrived at the port of Halifax, 1897-1899. Age, occupation, name of ship, and often destination. Many to U.S.A.

* * *

1862
"ENGLISH & WELSH EMIGRANT INDEX." In *The English Genealogist*, vol. 4:2, (1981), pp. 368-372.

About 500 names, dates of birth, and places of arrival in North America (U.S. and Canada). Dates of arrival seldom given; covers 17th to 19th centuries. From files maintained by the Augustan Society Library in Torrance, California, where full information is available.

* * *

1865
ENS, ADOLF, and RITA PENNER. "Quebec Passenger Lists of the Russian Mennonite Immigration, 1874-1880." In *The Mennonite Quarterly Review*, vol. 48:4 (Oct. 1974), pp. 527-531.

This article discusses the existence of the Quebec Lists in the Public Archives of Canada at Ottawa, nos. 9-11, microfilm nos. C-4528-4530. In Table I, "Steamships carrying Mennonite Immigrants, Liverpool/Glasgow to Quebec, 1874-1880," are listed 30 ships, with dates of arrival in Quebec and the number of Mennonites on board, their places of origin and names of the leaders of groups on the ships. Forty names in all.

* * *

1867 — 1868.1
ERICSON, TIMOTHY L. "Index to Pierce Series 26, Immigration & Naturalization Papers." In *Wisconsin State Genealogical Society Newsletter.*
1867
As in basic volume of this bibliography: vol. 26, A through Tim.
1868.1
---Vol. 27:1 (June 1980), p. 49. Tin through Z.

This completes the series and replaces item no. 1868 in the main volume of this bibliography. The number of names totals about 100. The series provides a list of alien residents signed up in that region for all phases of the procedure for becoming a citizen in the years 1907-1925. Prepared in the Area Research Center, University of Wisconsin, River Falls.

* * *

1869
ERIE SOCIETY FOR GENEALOGICAL RESEARCH, compiler. *Erie County, Pennsylvania, Naturalizations, 1825-1906*. Erie, Pa.: the society, 1983, 179 pp.

Involves over 12,000 persons, with names, ages, dates of immigration, dates of declaration of intention to become a citizen and of naturalization, etc. Some indicate place of residence at time of declaration or naturalization.

* * *

1870
ERNST, LORENZ. "Auswanderer aus Woerrstadt (Rheinhessen)." In *Hessische Familienkunde*, vol. 6:5 (Jan. 1963), cols. 279-280.

Emigrants from Woerrstadt (in Rhenish Hessia or Hesse). Lists 20 Germans, most to Pennsylvania, 1743-1754. See also item no. 2192 (basic vol.) for a similar emigration in the same years.

* * *

1873
ESHLEMAN, H. FRANK. *Historic Background and Annals of the Swiss and German Pioneer Settlers of South-Eastern Pennsylvania . . . to the Time of the Revolutionary War*. Lancaster, Pa., 1917. Repr. Baltimore: Genealogical Publishing Co., 1969. 386pp.

Spine has short title: *Annals of the Swiss and German Pioneers of Pennsylvania*. History of religious intolerance during several centuries, culminating in a large emigration to the Susquehanna and Schuylkill valleys in Pennsylvania during colonial times. Many of the 2,000 persons came to Pennsylvania and the text has much information about them.

* * *

1918
FAIRFIELD COUNTY, OHIO: *Index to Naturalizations*. [Lancaster, Ohio]: Ohio Genealogical Soc., Fairfield County Chapter, 1983. 48pp.

Mainly 1840-1870. Places of emigration given; many from Germany. About 1,700 names, with dates of naturalization.

* * *

1921.1 — 1921.4
THE FAMINE IMMIGRANTS: *Lists of Irish Immigrants Arriving at the Port of New York, 1846-1851*. Ira A. Glazier, Editor, and Michael Tepper, Associate Editor. Baltimore: Genealogical Publishing Co.
1921.1
---Vol. 1 (January 1846-June 1847). 1983, 841p.
1921.2
---Vol. 2 (July 1847-June 1848). 1983, 722p.
1921.3
---Vol. 3 (July 1848-March 1849). 1984, 695p.
1921.4
---Vol. 4 (April 1849-Dec. 1850). 1984, 750p.

Customs lists, offering an enumeration of Irish passengers arriving in New York as a result of failure of the potato crop during the winter of 1845-1846. Names, ages, sex, family relationships, occupations, ships' names, and ports of embarkation. The first volume has 85,000 entries; the second and fourth 75,000 each; the third, 70,000.

* * *

1924
FANDRICH, ESTHER (DIEGEL). "Passenger Lists." In *Heritage Review*, vol. 14:1 (Feb. 1984), p. 14.

Passengers on the ship *Columbia* from Glasgow to New York in 1905. All 19 were Germans from Russia destined for North Dakota and Nebraska. Ages given.

* * *

1966.1 — 1966.8
"FAYETTE COUNTY [Pennsylvania] NATURALIZATION RECORDS." In *La Fayette*: History and Genealogy of Fayette County, Pennsylvania.
1966.1
---Vol. 1:1 (Apr. 1981), pp. 13-14 (yr. 1802).
1966.2
---Vol. 1:2 (July 1981), pp. 13-14 (yr. 1802).
1966.3
---Vol. 1:3 (Oct. 1981), pp. 13-14 (yrs. 1802-1805).
1966.4
---Vol. 1:4 (Jan. 1982), pp. 12-13 (yrs. 1805-1808).
1966.5
---Vol. 2:1 (Apr. 1982), p. 12 (yr. 1808).
1966.6
---Vol. 2:2 (July 1982), pp. 12-13 (yrs. 1808-ca.1809).
1966.7
---Vol. 2:3 (Oct. 1982), pp. 12-13 (yrs. 1808-ca.1809).
1966.8
---Vol. 2:4 (Jan. 1983), p. 12 (yrs. 1809-1815). In progress.

Almost all Irish, listed with occupations, dates of admission, and names of sponsors. Includes more than 170 so far, and the work continues.

* * *

1970
FEIL, JERRY. "Passenger Lists." In *Heritage Review*, vol. 13:1 (Feb., 1983), p. 38.

Vessels *Kaiser Wilhelm der Grosse* and *Polynesia*, crossing from Bremen and Hamburg to New York in the years 1888, 1901, and 1903, carried 65 passengers traveling from Russia to the Dakota Territory. Lists give names, ages, and family relationships.

* * *

1981
FERGUSON, MARY. "1900 - Great Register of Santa Clara County [Calif.]. In *Santa Clara County Historical and Genealogical Society Quarterly*, vol. 18:4 (Spring 1982), pp. 85-87.

Provides 115 names, ages, and addresses. Taken from a section of the Great Register called the Burnett Division.

* * *

2004.5
FESER, PHYLLIS HERTZ. "Passenger Lists." In *Heritage Review*, vol. 11:3 (Sept. 1981), p. 48.

The 1893 arrival of Germans from Russia. Names of a hundred immigrants and their ages.

* * *

2004.11
FESER, PHYLLIS HERTZ. "Passenger Lists." In *Heritage Review*, vol. 12:3 (Sept. 1982), p. 44.

Germans from Russia, 1901, 1908. Thirty arrivals: names and ages.

* * *

2004.13
FESER, PHYLLIS HERTZ. "Passenger Lists." In *Heritage Review*, vol. 12:4 (Dec. 1982), pp. 49-51.

Germans from Russia arriving in New York, 1886. Cites 600 names and ages.

* * *

2005
FESER, PHYLLIS HERTZ, and ELAINE BAUER. "Passenger Lists." In *Heritage Review*, vol. 11:3 (Sept. 1981), pp. 46-47.

Among Germans from Russia arriving in 1903, this lists about 150, with age of each.

* * *

2043
FILBY, P. WILLIAM. "Sailing List of Sussex Emigrants to Canada Circa 1836." In *Canadian Genealogist*, vol. 4:1 (1982), pp. 9-12.

Names taken from *Egremont Papers*, West Sussex Record Office. Age, occupation, and interesting comments on each.

* * *

2048.1
FILBY, P. WILLIAM, with MARY KEYSOR MEYER, editor. *Passenger and Immigration Lists Index: 1982 Supplement*. Detroit: Gale Research Co., 1983. 950p.

Identifies an additional 200,000 passengers (500,000 names are in the main volume) who arrived between the years 1600 and 1900, with data on when and where they landed and who came with them. Entries refer to the books, magazines, and documents to consult for further details.

* * *

2048.2
FILBY, P. WILLIAM, with MARY KEYSOR MEYER, editor. *Passenger and Immigration Lists Index: 1983 Supplement*. Detroit, Gale Research Co., 1984. ca. 950p.

Identifies an additional 200,000 passengers (700,000 having been listed in the earlier works) who arrived between the years 1600 and 1900. Includes date and place of each immigrant's arrival, age, and names of persons accompanying. Entries refer to the books, magazines, or documents to consult for further details.

* * *

2090
FLOM, GEORGE T. "The First Swedes in Burlington. Other Early Settlements in the State down to 1855: Swede Point, Bergholm, Swede Bend, Mineral Ridge. The Founders of These Settlements. Two Early Settlements in Northeastern Iowa." In *The Iowa Journal of History and Politics*, vol. 3:4 (Oct. 1905), pp. 607-615.

Names many immigrants to Iowa from 1846 on.

* * *

2095
FORSTER, WALTER O. *Zion on the Mississippi: the Settlement of the Saxon Lutherans in Missouri, 1839-1841*. St. Louis: Concordia Publishing House, 1953. 606p.

"Lists and tables," pp. 535-558, names about 800 passengers from Bremerhaven in November 1838, arriving in New Orleans in January 1839, on the ships *Copernicus*, *Johan Georg*, *Republik*, and *Olbers*. There are also other groups: passengers on the *Amalia* (which sank), and members of what were called the New York Group and Gruber's Group. Ages, occupations, former places of residence, and ships' names.

* * *

2130.1 — 2130.4
FOTHERGILL, GERALD. "Licences to Pass from England Beyond the Seas." In *The Genealogist* [London]. New series
2130.1
---Vol. 23:[1] (1907), pp. 32-38; vol. 23:2 (1907), pp. 115-119; vol. 23:3 (1907), pp. 167-170; vol. 23:4 (1907), pp. 235-239.
2130.2
---Vol. 24:1 (1908), pp. 56-59; vol. 24:2 (1908), pp. 124-127; vol. 24:4 (1908), pp. 274-275.
2130.3
---Vol. 25:1 (1909), pp. 52-54; vol. 25:2 (1909), pp. 99-103; vol. 25:3 (1909), pp. 172-175; vol. 25:4 (1909), pp. 257-263.
2130.4
---Vol. 26:1 (1910), pp. 44-48; vol. 26:2 (1910), pp. 155-159; vol. 26:4 (1910), pp. 240-243.

Covers the years 1624-1638. Names many persons who went to Holland, where licenses were more easily given, and thence to New England. Hotten, in his *Original Lists of Persons of Quality* . . . (item no. 3283 in the basic volume of this bibliog.), printed the licenses of all those bound straight for America; thus, this list will contain names left out by Hotten as being settlers in Europe. The last list in 1910 states this was to be continued, but no further installments were published.

* * *

2158
FOX, MRS. JOE NEALE. "Naturalization Records from Todd County, Kentucky, Circuit Court Records." In *Kentucky Ancestors*, vol. 18:4 (Apr. 1983), p. 201.

Refers to the years 1828-1867, providing names of 13 persons, ages, countries of origin, and dates of the declarations of intention to become a citizen.

* * *

2180
"FRANKLIN COUNTY [Indiana] CITIZENSHIP RECORD I (Naturalizations)." In *The Hoosier Journal of Ancestry*, vol. 7:2 (Apr. 1980), pp. 26-27.

Mostly 1830s. Involves 30 persons.

* * *

2307
FURIN, L. "Passenger Lists." In *Heritage Review*, vol. 12:3 (Sept. 1982), p. 44.

About 40 persons from Rumania on the S.S. *Mainz*, Bremen to New York, 1900. Names, ages, occupations.

* * *

2320
GALE, JOHN. "Passenger Lists." In *Heritage Review*, vol. 14:1 (Feb. 1984), pp. 14-16.

About 350 Germans from Russia who arrived at New York on German ships in 1894. Ages and occupations given along with names. The information was submitted by Alice Essig.

* * *

2338
GARTNER, AL, and LAURA GARTNER. "Passenger Lists." In *Heritage Review*, vol. 11:3 (Sept. 1981), p. 45.

Emigration of 20 persons from Speier, Russia, to Mandan, North Dakota, in 1900. Passage of these Germans from Russia was via Bremen-New York. Ages given.

* * *

2341.1 — 2341.2
GASH, DONNA. "Naturalization Records, from Index at Vermilion County, Illinois, Courthouse." In *Illiana Genealogist*.
2341.1
---Vol. 16:1 (Winter 1980), pp. 12-15 (Letters A-B).
---Vol. 16:2 (Spring 1980), pp. 39-42 (Letters C-E).
---Vol. 16:3 (Summer 1980), pp. 73-74 (Letters F-G).
---Vol. 16:4 (Fall 1980), pp. 107-109 (Letters H-J).
2341.2
---Vol. 17:1 (Winter 1981), pp. 17-20 (Letters K-L).
---Vol. 17:2 (Spring 1981), pp. 60-63 (Letters M-O).
---Vol. 17:3 (Summer 1981), pp. 77-79 (Letters P-R).
---Vol. 17:4 (Fall 1981), pp. 114-120 (Letters S-Z).

Latter half of 19th century, mostly 1880-1900. About 1,400 names, with each date of naturalization or of application for citizenship, and indication of country of birth.

* * *

2398
GAUTREY, A.J. "Discovering Those Country Cousins [in U.S.A.]." In *Sussex Family Historian*, vol. 2:3 (Dec. 1975), pp. 77-79.

Story of author's visit in 1975 to relatives in America, with information on the Gautrey family and relatives who emigrated from Sussex in 1868.

* * *

2419.1 — 2419.3
"GENEALOGICAL QUERIES." In *Swedish American Genealogist*.
2419.1
---Vol. 1:1 (Mar. 1981), pp. 38-39; vol. 1:2 (June 1981), pp. 84-90; vol. 1:3 (Sept. 1981), pp. 137-139.
2419.2
---Vol. 2:1 (Mar. 1982), 39-46; vol. 2:2 (June 1982), pp. 82-93; vol. 2:3 (Sept. 1982), pp. 137-141; vol. 2:4 (Dec. 1982), pp. 183-186.
2419.3
---Vol. 3:1 (Mar. 1983), pp. 38-46; vol. 3:2 (June 1983), pp. 90-94; vol. 3:3 (Sept. 1983), pp. 129-135. In progress.

Involves Swedish arrivals in the last half of the 19th century. All queries give copious information on the families being researched, and most give date of emigration, with city of origin and the destination in America. This is work in progress, intended to continue in later issues.

* * *

2421
GENEALOGICAL SOCIETY OF DEKALB COUNTY, ILLINOIS, compiler. *Naturalization Records of DeKalb County, Illinois*. Sycamore, Ill.: the society, 1981. 131p.

Covers the years 1853-1908, and provides full name, age, date of arrival, country of origin, date of U.S. naturalization, and name of witness for each of 2,600 persons. See item no. 1498 for reference to naturalizations in DeKalb County between 1838 and 1845.

* * *

2423
GENERAL LIST OF CITIZENS OF THE UNITED STATES RESIDENT IN THE COUNTY OF CONTRA COSTA [California] ***and Registered in the Great Register. . . .*** n.p., 1898. 88p. Folio.

About 4,000 persons named, with occupations, ages, countries of birth, places of local residence, dates of naturalization, dates of voter registration. Late 19th, early 20th centuries. The Great Register document is an official list.

* * *

2428
GEORGE, BERNICE A. "Petitions for Naturalization--Laurens County, S.C." In *The Georgia Genealogical Magazine*, no. 42 (Fall 1971), pp. 463-466 or pp. 55-58.

Among 50 names, many Irish. Years of naturalization: 1800-1825. Data includes countries and often counties of origin, often dates and places of arrival, dates of petition for citizenship and names of witnesses. Taken from original applications on file with the Clerk of Court at Laurens, South Carolina, Label 2, rolls 51-98.

* * *

2518
GEUE, ETHEL HANDER. "Ship *Canapus*, Departed Bremen; Arrived Galveston, December 19, 1848." In *The Roadrunner*, vol. 7:4 (Aug. 1981), p. 6.

Names 30 persons, with ages and places of origin and destination. Extracted from Geue, *New Homes in a New Land . . . 1847-1861* (item no. 2504 in main volume of this bibliography) and previously taken from microfilm in state archives, Austin, Texas.

* * *

2525.15
GIBBS, ANN. "Earliest Ripley County [Indiana] Naturalizations, 1818-1843." In *The Hoosier Genealogist*, vol. 22:3 (Sept. 1982), pp. 63-67.

About 100 persons, each name with age, place of origin, date of immigration, and date of naturalization or of first papers.

* * *

2525.40
GIBBS, ANN. "Switzerland County [Indiana] Naturalizations, Oct. 1825- Apr. 1829." In *The Hoosier Genealogist*, vol. 22:2 (June 1982), pp. 42-44.

About 80 persons, mostly from Switzerland and the British Isles. Indicates date of intention to become a citizen; identifies name of court and country of origin.

* * *

2526.10
GIBSON, J.S.W. "Sponsored Emigration of Paupers from Banbury Union, 1834-1860." In *The Oxfordshire Family Historian*, vol. 2:7 (Spring 1982), pp. 211-215.

Many to Australia and Canada, 1830s-1850s. Ages, destinations, sometimes occupations and name of ship.

* * *

2526.40
GIBSON, J.S.W., and others. "Pauper Emigration." In *The Oxfordshire Family Historian*, vol. 2:8 (Summer 1982), pp. 259-265.

About 200 persons, most of whom went to Australia. A few to Canada in the 1840s.

* * *

2528
GIESINGER, ADAM. "Immigration of Refugees from Russia to Canada in the 1920s." In *Journal of American Historical Society of Germans from Russia*, vol. 6:2 (Summer 1983), pp. 19-26.

A list of about 50 immigrants from Hamburg on the *S.S. Montrose* in 1924, destined for St. John, New Brunswick, and sponsored by the Association of German Canadian Catholics (Volksverein Deutsch Canadischer Katholiken, VDCK).

* * *

2763.10
[GRAY FAMILY] "Index to Passenger Lists of Vessels Arriving at Port of Philadelphia, 1800-1906." In *The Long Gray Line*. vol. 1:2 (1982), pp. 17-26.

Refers to 19th-century arrivals of a family named Gray, with some variations in the spelling of the name. Each entry specifies age, sex, occupation, nationality, ship, date of arrival. About 550 names.

* * *

2763.20
GREAT REGISTER *Containing the Names and Registration of the Domiciled Inhabitants of the County of Santa Clara . . . 1884.* San Jose, Calif., 1884. Folio.

Lists 8,496 names with information on age, birthplace, occupation, local residence, date and place of naturalization, and date of registration.

* * *

2763.25 — 2763.33
"THE GREAT REGISTER OF FRESNO COUNTY [California]." In *Ash Tree Echo*.
2763.25
---Vol. 11:4 (Oct. 1974), pp. 223-226 (Auberry and Belmont precincts).
2763.26
---Vol. 12:2 (Apr. 1977), pp. 69-72; vol. 12:3 (July 1977), pp. 134-135. (Belmont precinct).
2763.27
---Vol. 13:1 (Jan. 1978), pp. 1-4 (Belmont, Big Sandy, Butler precincts); vol. 13:3 (July 1978), pp. 140-146 (Black Mountain, Bryant, Cantua, and Crescent precincts); vol. 13:4 (Oct. 1978), pp. 163-169 (Central Colony, Clark's Valley, and Centerville precincts).
2763.28
---Vol. 14:1 (Jan. 1979), pp. 32-35, 39 (Chicago, Colles, and Bry Creek precincts); vol. 14:2 (Apr. 1979), pp. 65-69, 54 (East Fresno); vol. 14:3 (July 1979), pp. 101-103 (Easterby); vol. 14:4 (Oct. 1979), pp. 146-149, 157 (Firebaugh, Fancher precincts).
2763.29
---Vol. 15:1 (Jan. 1980), pp. 3-7 (Fresno Colony); vol. 15:2 (Apr. 1980), pp. 58-62 (Fowler), vol. 15:3 (July 1980), pp. 94-99 (Fowler).
2763.30
---Vol. 16:1 (Jan. 1981) pp. 44-47 (Fresno nos. 2 and 3); vol. 16:2 (Apr. 1981), pp. 93-96 (Fresno nos. 2 and 3); vol. 16:3 (July 1981), pp. 121-122 (Fresno no. 3); vol. 16:4 (Oct. 1981), pp. 182-183 (Fresno no. 3).
2763.31
---Vol. 17:1 (Jan. 1982), pp. 12-13 (Fresno no. 3, cont'd); vol. 17:2 (Apr. 1982), pp. 58-59 (Fresno no. 4); vol. 17:3 (July 1982), pp. 93-96 (Fresno nos. 4-6); vol. 17:4 (Oct. 1981), pp. 201-204 (Fresno no. 6).
2763.32
---Vol. 18:1 (Jan. 1983), pp. 12-15 (Fresno no. 6 cont'd); vol. 18:2 (Apr. 1983), pp. 89-92 (Fresno nos. 6-7); vol. 18:3 (July 1983), pp. 126-130 (Fresno no. 7); vol. 18:4 (Oct. 1983), pp. 199-203 (Fresno no. 8).
2763.33
---Vol. 19:1 (Jan. 1984), pp. 229-236 (Fresno no. 9).

Covers voter registrations in Fresno in the years 1896-1898 and lists 900 so far. Names, ages, and occupations given. Not all were immigrants, but 800 from various other countries are listed, with naturalization dates. Continues.

* * *

2763.54 — 2763.56
"THE GREAT REGISTER OF KERN COUNTY, California, Vol. 1: 1866-1877." In *Kern-Gen* [Kern County Genealogical Society].
2763.54
---Vol. 18:1 (Mar. 1981), pp. 16-21 (A); vol. 18:3 (Sept. 1981), pp. 70-72 (B); vol. 18:4 (Dec. 1981), pp. 102-104 (B).
2763.55
---Vol. 19:1 (Mar. 1982), pp. 19-22 (B); vol. 19:2 (June 1982), pp. 36-40 (B,C); vol. 19:3 (Sept. 1982), pp. 73-78 (C); vol. 19:4 (Dec. 1982), pp. 96-101 (C).
2763.56
---Vol. 20:1 (Mar. 1983), pp. 13-17 (C,D); vol. 20:2 (June 1983), pp. 48-53 (D,E); vol. 20:3 (Sept. 1983), pp. 74-79 (E,F); vol. 20:4 (Dec. 1983), pp. 108-109 (F,G). In progress.

A continuing work on the latter half of the 19th century. Age, residence, occupation, place of birth and voter registration date for about 350 names in the first part of the alphabet, A-G. Some copied by Shirley C. Ford and Evelyn D. Lynn. Foreign-born listed with naturalization dates.

* * *

2769.1 — 2769.10
"THE GREAT REGISTER, TULARE COUNTY, CALIFORNIA, 1872." In *Sequoia Genealogical Society Newsletter.*
2769.1
---Vol. 9:3 (Nov. 1982), pp. 3-6 (A-B).
2769.2
---Vol. 9:4 (Jan. 1983), pp. 3-6 (B-C).
2769.3
---Vol. 9:5 (Feb. 1983), pp. 3-6 (C-E).
2769.4
---Vol. 9:6 (Mar. 1983), pp. 3-6 (F-H).
2769.5
---Vol. 9:7 (Apr. 1983), pp. 3-6 (H-K).
2769.6
---Vol. 9:8 (May 1983), pp. 3-6 (K-M).
2769.7
---Vol. 10:1 (Sept. 1983), pp. 3-6 (M-R).
2769.8
---Vol. 10:2 (Oct. 1983), pp. 3-6 (R-S).
2769.9
---Vol. 10:3 (Nov. 1983), pp. 3-6 (S-Y).
2769.10
---Vol. 10:4 (Dec. 1983), pp. 3-6 (Y-Z and suppl.).

About 2,000 names, with ages, places of birth and local residence, dates of voter registration, and occupations. Most of those listed were born in the U.S. and were not immigrants. For Great Register listings in Tulare County in the year 1888, see item nos. 2765-2768 in the main volume of this bibliography. For an explanation of the Great Registers, see item no. 1890 in the main volume.

* * *

2770
"GREENE COUNTY [Iowa] NATURALIZATION RECORDS INDEX." In *Hawkeye Heritage*, vol. 15:4 (Fall 1980), pp. 208-221.

Over 500 names, with countries of birth and dates of naturalization.

* * *

2771
GREENLEE, JANET. *Naturalization Index of Scott County, Iowa, 1842-1930.* Des Moines: Iowa Genealogical Society, 1981. 228p.

A work of 10,000 names, with countries of origin and year of naturalization. Includes reference to location of each name in the county records. Sponsored by Scott County Genealogical Society, Davenport.

* * *

2824
GRUNDY, MARTHA JONET PAXSON. "The Paxson Brothers of Colonial Pennsylvania: the First Three Generations." In *National Genealogical Society Quarterly*, vol. 71:3 (Sept. 1983), pp. 193-216.

A discussion of the seventeenth and eighteenth-century immigration of various members of the Paxson family who settled in Pennsylvania. Often supplies dates of emigration from England (Buckinghamshire).

* * *

2829.1 — 2829.3
GUENTHER, KURT. "Hessian Emigrants to America." In *Germanic Genealogist.*
2829.1
---No. 19 (1979), pp. 69-76, Parts 4, 5: 1835-1836. This replaces and adds to item 2829 in the basic volume of this bibliography.
2829.2
---No. 20 (1980), pp. 142-144, Part 6: 1837.
2829.3
---No. 22 (1981), pp. 219-222, Parts 7,8: 1838-1839.

All from counties of the province Nether-Hesse, northeastern part of the former territory of Hesse-Cassel. About 750 names, with each person's place of settlement, sex, and number of family members in the years 1835-1839. Reprinted in pamphlet form by the Augustan Society in Torrance, Calif., 1983, 24p. The years 1832-1835 were covered in item no. 2828 in the basic volume of *PILB*.

* * *

2852
HAAR, MARTIN. *Moessinger Heimatbuch.* Moessingen [Germany]: Gemeinde Moessingen, 1973.

Local history of Moessingen. Beginning on p. 25, there is a discussion of emigration from that community in Baden-Wuerttemberg, Germany. Pp. 33-45 list about 400 names and family groups emigrating to America, 1829-1900. Many entries include year of birth, emigration date, occupation, and names of parents.

* * *

2854
HACKER, WERNER. "American Emigrants from the Territories of the Bishopric of Speyer." Translated and edited by Don Yoder. In *Pennsylvania Folklife*, vol. 21:4 (Summer 1972), pp. 43-45.

Much information on the 80 emigrants. An 18th century migration from Germany. Data abstracted from Hacker, *Auswanderungen aus dem frueheren Hochstift Speyer nach Suedost Europa . . .* (item no. 2856 in main volume of this bibliography). Also in item no. 9968 in this supplement: Yoder, *Rhineland Emigrants*, pp. 69-71.

* * *

2855
HACKER, WERNER. "Auswanderer aus dem Territorium der Reichsstadt Ulm, vor allem im ausgehenden 17. und im 18. Jahrhundert." In *Ulm und Oberschwaben: Zeitschrift fuer Geschichte und Kunst*, vols. 42/43 (1978), pp. 161-257.

Emigrants from the territory of the imperial city of Ulm, primarily at the end of the 17th century and in the 18th. Lists 813 Germans, of whom over 100 gave their destination as America (primarily Georgia, South Carolina, and Pennsylvania). The data includes name of community of origin and date of document mentioning the emigration.

* * *

2855.5
HACKER, WERNER. *Auswanderungen aus Baden und dem Breisgau: Obere und mittlere rechtsseitige Oberrheinlande im 18. Jahrhundert archivalisch documentiert.* Stuttgart: Konrad Theiss, 1980.

Emigration from Baden and the Breisgau region, upper and middle lands east of the upper Rhine River, documented from 18th century archival sources in Germany. Lists 11,666 persons, of whom over 1,000 came to America, name of each one's community of origin, date of record mentioning emigration, and planned country of destination.

* * *

2857
HACKER, WERNER. *Kurpfaelzische Auswanderer vom Unteren Neckar: Rechtsrheinische Gebiete der Kurpfalz.* (Sonderveroeffentlichung des Stadtarchivs Mannheim, 4) Stuttgart [Germany]: Konrad Theiss, 1983. 208pp.

Electoral Palatine emigrants from the Lower Neckar region, electoral Palatine territories "to the right of the Rhine" (i.e. east of the Rhine). Lists 2,300 persons who left this area, of whom over 500 came to America in the 18th century. The information includes community of origin, date of record mentioning the emigration, and country of destination.

* * *

2865
HAIMAN, MIECISLAUS. *Polish Pioneers of Pennsylvania.* (Annals of the Polish Rom. Cath. Union Archives and Museum, vol. 6) Chicago, Ill.: Polish R.C. Union of America, 1941. 72p.

Names of many pioneers who came to Pennsylvania, mainly 18th century.

* * *

2884.1 — 2884.5
HALL, CHARLES M. "Surname Index." In *The Palatine Immigrant.*
2884.1
---Vol. 1:1 (Summer 1975), pp. 7-24;
2884.2
---Vol. 1:2 (Fall 1975), pp. 15-35;
2884.3
---Vol. 1:3 (Winter 1976), pp. 13-24;
2884.4
---Vol. 1:4 (Spring 1976), pp. 9-28;
2884.5
---Vol. 2:2 (Fall 1976), pp. 11-22.

About 1,500 German emigrants, chiefly 18th century, with, for each, place of origin, year of departure from Europe or arrival in America, religion, and place of settlement (usually city, county, and state).

* * *

2885
HALL, CHARLES M., and HERITAGE INTERNATIONAL. *The Antwerp Emigration Index.* Salt Lake City [Utah]: Heritage International, [1979]. n. pag. [91p.]

About 5,000 individuals or groups migrating out of Europe in 1855 from Germany, France, Switzerland, Italy, the Netherlands, Belgium, and other countries. Not all came to North America. Name, age, place of origin, ship, and passport.

* * *

2906
HARRIS, CARRIE. "Door County [Wisconsin] Naturalization Book 4." In *Wisconsin State Genealogical Society Newsletter*, vol. 30:1 (June 1983), p. 84.

Covers the years from 1904 to 1906. Names of 28 newly naturalized, with countries of origin (mostly Scandinavian), dates and places of filing, and names of witnesses.

* * *

2907.1 — 2907.2
HARRIS, CARRIE. "Record of Final Citizenship, Door County [Wisconsin] Circuit Court. Vol. 2." In *Wisconsin State Genealogical Society Newsletter.*
2907.1
---Vol. 27:2 (Sept. 1980), p. 82; vol. 27:3 (Jan. 1981), pp. 141- 142; vol. 27:4 (Apr. 1981), pp. 199-200.
2907.2
---Vol. 28:1 (June 1981), p. 23.

Spans the years 1870-1890. About 150 names, with places and years of birth, ports and dates of arrival, names of witnesses, dates and places of oath of intent, and dates of swearing in. Almost all Europeans, with a large number from Scandinavia.

* * *

2910
"HARRIS COUNTY, TEXAS: OATHS OF ALLEGIANCE, vol. 3." In *The Roadrunner*, vol. 8:2 (1982), p. 20.

Cites 15 names, with country of origin, date and port of arrival, age, and date of the swearing of allegiance. Covers the years 1903-1906.

* * *

2915
HART, L.H. "Some Importations from Lunenburg [Virginia] Order Books." In *The Southside Virginian*, vol. 1:1 (Oct. 1982), p. 25.

Nine persons who claimed lands in Lunenburg County, 1746-1750, stating place of origin in Great Britain and number of years since immigration.

* * *

2919
HARVEY, D.C. *Holland's Description of Cape Breton Island, and Other Documents.* (Public Archives of Nova Scotia, pub. 2). Halifax: Public Archives of Nova Scotia, 1935, pp. 147-168.

A census of Cape Breton Island in 1818 (see Appendix B) lists inhabitants of various areas, with specific locality, age, time on the Island, country of origin, country of parents, trade, marital status, children. Identifies 1,022 households for which it is possible to determine year of arrival.

* * *

2965
HAYNES, EMMA SCHWABENLAND. "List of Volga German Refugees Who Arrived at Frankfurt on the Oder from Minsk on December 9, 1922." In *Journal of the American Historical Society of Germans from Russia*, vol. 5:1 (Spring 1982), pp. 21-29; vol. 5:2 (Summer 1982), pp. 55-66.

Almost 900 Volga Germans: name, date of birth, father's name, names of relatives in America. All from Russia following the drought of 1921. Many came to America, although there is no evidence to determine which came.

* * *

2973.2
HAYNES, EMMA SCHWABENLAND. "Passenger Lists." In *Clues*, 1980, pt. 2, pp. 52-60.

Germans from Russia destined for Kansas and the Dakotas in the years 1876-1899, 1908, 1922. Names of 1,000 persons, with their ages and occupations. All came by way of New York.

* * *

2974.1
HAYNES, EMMA SCHWABENLAND. "Passenger Lists." In *Clues*, 1981, pt. 1, pp. 79-88.

Mostly Germans from Russia destined for New York, with some to Baltimore or Halifax, Nova Scotia. Spans the years 1849-1910. About 1,000 names, with ages and occupations.

* * *

2974.2
HAYNES, EMMA SCHWABENLAND. "Passenger Lists." In *Clues*, 1981, pt. 2, pp. 27-38.

About 1,000 passengers, mostly Germans from Russia, 1876-1913. Age, occupation, and sometimes destination (mostly to New York).

* * *

2974.3
HAYNES, EMMA SCHWABENLAND. "Passenger Lists." In *Clues*, 1982, pt. 1, pp. 79-88.

About 1,000 names, mostly of Germans from Russia arriving in New York in 1873 or between 1888 and 1913. Ages and occupations given. Some cite places of origin and destinations.

* * *

2974.4
HAYNES, EMMA SCHWABENLAND. "Passenger Lists." In *Clues*, 1982, pt. 2, pp. 23-28.

About 700 passengers, mostly Germans from Russia, 1886-1911. Data includes age, occupation, and often destination (usually New York).

* * *

2974.5
HAYNES, EMMA SCHWABENLAND. "Passenger Lists." In *Clues*, 1983, pt. 1, pp. 90-100.

About 1,500 passengers named, all Germans from Russia, most giving destinations in U.S.A. Arrival at various U.S. ports: 1879, 1892, 1899, 1906, 1912-1913, 1923.

* * *

2974.6
HAYNES, EMMA SCHWABENLAND. "Passenger Lists." In *Clues*, 1983, pt. 2, pp. 37-44.

Sailings from Hamburg to New York, 1905-1907, brought these 800 Germans from Russia. Names, ages, occupations, origins, and destinations given.

* * *

2978
HAYNES, EMMA SCHWABENLAND. "Ships Bringing the Largest Number of Russian Germans to North America." In *Journal of American Historical Society of Germans from Russia*, vol. 6:2 (Summer 1983), pp. 15-18.

No immigrants are named, but this is the most comprehensive listing of ships concerned with the immigration of Russian Germans.

* * *

2984
HAZUKA, JEAN. "Tripp County [South Dakota] Naturalization Records." In *South Dakota Genealogical Society*, vol. 2:1 (July 1983), pp. 21-26.

County record Book 1 has 42 names, with dates of birth between 1856 and 1888 and dates of naturalization falling in the years 1910-1914. Books 2-4 have 250 names but no other information.

* * *

2995
HEFFNER, DONNA. "Passenger Lists." In *Heritage Review*, vol. 12:1 (Feb. 1982), p. 38.

Names 25 Germans from Russia who sailed on the *Kaiser Wilhelm der Grosse* from Bremen to New York in 1899. Ages and occupations given. Place of settlement was indicated as Bowdle, South Dakota.

* * *

3015.5
HELMS, KATE, and GENE LUNDERGAN. "Index to the Naturalization Papers of Brown County [Wisconsin], Located at the Area Research Center, The University of Wisconsin, Green Bay." In *Wisconsin State Genealogical Society Newsletter,* vol. 25:3 (Jan. 1979), pp. 131-132 (Brown County, pp. 37-38); vol. 25:4 (Apr. 1979), pp.

185-186 (Brown County, pp. 39-40); vol. 26:2 (Sept. 1979), pp. 75-76 (Brown County, pp. 41-42); vol. 26:3 (Jan. 1980), pp. 133-134 (Brown County, pp. 43-44); vol. 26:4 (Apr. 1980), pp. 189-190 (Brown County, pp. 45-46); vol. 27:2 (Sept. 1980), pp. 77-78 (Brown County, pp. 47-48); vol. 27:3 (Jan. 1981), pp. 135-136 (Brown County, pp. 49-50); vol. 27:4 (Apr. 1981), pp. 195-196 (Brown County, pp. 51-52); vol. 28:1 (June 1981), pp. 17-18 (Brown County, pp. 53-54); vol. 28:2 (Sept. 1981), pp.79-80 (Brown County, pp. 55-56); vol. 28:3 (Jan. 1982), pp. 145-146 (Brown County, pp. 57-58); vol. 28:4 (Apr. 1982), pp. 207-208 (Brown County, pp. 59-60); vol. 29:1 (June 1982), pp. 19-20 (Brown County, pp. 61-62).

Spans the years 1841-1978. Names almost 4,000 newly naturalized citizens, with dates of naturalization and citation of references in the county records. This data replaces, adds to, and completes the information in item no. 3015 in the basic volume of this bibiliography.

* * *

3018
HELPINGSTINE, JEANNE, indexer. *Declarations of Intent 1852-1951, and Naturalization Books 1855-1945, Knox County, Indiana.* [Vincennes, Ind.: Northwest Territory Genealogical Society] 1981. 66, 20, 5pp.

Declarations of Intent [to acquire citizenship], Books A-J; Naturalization Books AA-KK; and additional names not in those books. Includes about 3,600 names, with book and page reference for each.

* * *

3028
HENDERSON, F. J. R. "Cuba: English and Irish Immigrants." In *The Scottish Genealogist*, vol. 17:2 (June 1970), pp. 62-63.

One hundred persons who wished to reside in Cuba in the years 1818-1819 and 1853-1858. Name, age, marital status, date and place of petition (mostly Havana).

* * *

3068
HETRICK, AL, and CLEON HETRICK. "Declaration of Intention Records for Sandusky County, Ohio." In *Sandusky County Heritage,* vol. 3:1 (Winter 1983), pp. 8-12; vol. 3:2 (Spring 1983), pp. 44-49; vol. 3:3 (Summer 1983), pp. 80-86; vol. 3:4 (Fall 1983), pp. 113-116. Title varies.

Covers the 1860s to 1880s, with names of aliens applying for citizenship, the date, their countries of origin, and names of sponsors. Issues cited above cover volumes 2-6 of the court records. Item no. 3069 is part of this series and lists minors. This series continues.

* * *

3069
HETRICK, CLEON, and AL HETRICK. "Declaration of Intention Records of Aliens Who Arrived in the United States Under Eighteen Years." In *Sandusky Country Heritage,* vol. 2:5 (1982), pp. 103-105.

Names, ages, dates of arrival (1840s - 1850s), counties of origin, dates of declaration (1859-1860), sponsors. File in Probate Court in and for the County of Sandusky and the State of Ohio. Taken from vol. 1 (1859-1860). Lists 109 persons.

* * *

3077
HEWLETT, BERNARD. "The *Mayflower* and the Pilgrim Fathers." In *The Midland Ancestor* (U.K.), vol. 6:4 (Mar. 1982), pp. 128-129.

Provides names and genealogies of each of 30 passengers.

* * *

3197
HINMAN, ROYAL R. *A Catalogue of the Names of the First Puritan Settlers of the Colony of Connecticut from 1635, with Time of the Arrival in the Colony . . . .* Hartford, Conn.: Case, Tiffany & Co., 1852. 801p.

Originally intended to cover the whole alphabet but concluded in the D's with Danielson (part 5); in 1856, a part 6 was published under title, *A Family Record of the Descendants of Sergt. Edward Hinman*, with pp. 803-884 devoted entirely to the Hinman family. No further parts were published. Mentions names of hundreds of first settlers and often gives dates of arrival from England and names of ships.

* * *

3208
HIPPENSTIEL, HAROLD FRANKLIN. *The Hippenstiel Families in America.* Bethlehem, Pa.: the compiler, 1925. 20pp. folio.

Gives names of late 18th-century Hippenstiel family members who arrived in Philadelphia in 1819 on the S.S. *Osgood.* Much family history.

* * *

3246
HOFMANN, ROBERTA. "Cass County [Ind.] Naturalization Applications??" In *The Hoosier Genealogist*, vol. 23:2 (June 1983), p. 54.

List of names of 42 alien residents applying for first papers, taken from *Logansport [Ind.] Daily Journal*, Oct. 10 and Nov. 7, 1876. Information includes port of origin, 1840s to 1870s. The names do not appear in *An Index to Indiana Naturalization Records* (item no. 3434). Some doubt that those listed were all from Cass County, hence the question marks in the title.

* * *

3251
HOLDER, JEAN, assisted by GRACE HUBLEY. *Nova Scotia Vital Statistics from Newspapers, 1829-1834.* (Genealogical Association of the Royal Nova Scotia Historical Society, Publication 6.) Halifax: the society, 1982. 164p.

Some of the 3,485 entries give data on immigration. Contains a list of ships.

* * *

3260
HOLLOWAK, THOMAS L. "Zwischendecks-Passagiere, Dampfers *Hohenzollern.*" In *Maryland Genealogical Society Bulletin*, vol. 24:2 (Spring 1983), pp. 120-126.

Reference is to steerage passengers on the steamship *Hohenzollern* in a crossing from Bremen to Baltimore, arriving May 1886. Provides only names and nationalities of the 903 passengers.

* * *

3275
HOLMES, MAURICE. "Decatur County [Indiana] Naturalizations, 1867-1874." In *The Hoosier Genealogist*, vol. 21:4 (Dec. 1981), pp. 87-90.

Names 120 persons, with ages, countries of origin, dates of arrival, and dates of declaration of intention to acquire citizenship.

* * *

3277
HOPFAUF, DIANNE. "Passenger Lists." In *Heritage Review*, vol. 11:3 (Sept. 1981), pp. 48-49.

Germans from Russia migrating to the Dakotas in 1903: 62 listed.

* * *

3279
HOTTEN, JOHN CAMDEN. "List of Passengers on the Ship *Fortune*." In *The Second Boat*, vol. 3:1 (May 1982), p. 7.

Early British arrivals in the American plantations: 30 persons in 1621. The list was submitted by Robert Martin but originally appeared in Hotten, *The Original Lists of Persons of Quality*, p. 28. See main volume of this bibliography, item no. 3283, for *Original Lists*. . . .

* * *

3295
HOWE, HENRY. "First German and Swiss Settlements." In *Historical Collections of Ohio*, vol. 2, pp. 266-267.

Ten German-Swiss families who came to Amboy, New Jersey, on the *Eugenius*, 1819, under the leadership of Fr. Jacob Tisher. The families finally settled in Monroe County, Ohio.

* * *

3300
HUEBSCH, HELLA, and RUTH RECTOR. "Auswanderer nach Arkansas (USA) 1833: Auf der Suche nach Namen und Herkunftsorten einer deutschen Reisegesellschaft." In *Hessische Familienkunde*, vol. 16:2 (June 1982), cols. 117-122.

Emigrants to Arkansas, 1833: the search of a group of German travelers for familiar names and fellow countrymen from their own home communities. About 150 emigrants, in the ship *Olbers*, Bremen, 5 March 1833, to New Orleans, arrived 30 April 1833. Some indicate place of origin and have descendants still to be found in the U.S.

* * *

3330.1 — 3330.4
"HUNTINGDON COUNTY [Pennsylvania] NATURALIZATION RECORDS, 1798-1802." In *A Standing Stone*.
3330.1
---Vol. 1:1 (June 1981), p. 12.
3330.2
---Vol. 1:2 (Sept. 1981), p. 12.
3330.3
---Vol. 1:3 (Dec. 1981), p. 12.
3330.4
---Vol. 1:4 (Mar. 1982), pp. 12-14.

About 100 persons, mostly from Great Britain and Ireland, with each date of admission to citizenship. The first two issues cited above cover 1798; the third, 1799; and the fourth, 1802.

* * *

3365
HUTCHINSON, CECIL ALAN. *Frontier Settlement in Mexican California: The Hijar-Padres Colony, and its Origins, 1769-1835*. (Yale Western Americana Ser., 21.) New Haven, Conn.: Yale University Press, 1969.

Refers to what is now the state of California in the year 1833. Arrivals were about 125 members of a community called the Farias Colony (Mexican) and others who accompanied them. In Appendix D, pp. 419-422, there is a list providing names, ages, and, often, the marital status.

* * *

3370
HUTCHISON, PAUL PHELPS. "The Early Scots in Montreal." In *The Scottish Genealogist*, vol. 29:2 (June 1982), pp. 33-40.

Concerns arrivals in the 18th century and later. Lists several names, with dates of entry into Canada and family and business information.

* * *

3371
HUXFORD, FOLKS. "Declarations of Citizenship, Abstracted from Minutes of Irwin Co. Superior Court, 1820-1847." In *Georgia Historical Magazine*, no. 41 (Summer 1971), pp. 301-304.

Irish immigrants in Georgia. About 60 names, with each person's country of origin, date of arrival in U.S., port of entry, and date of filing the declaration.

* * *

3375
"IMMIGRANT ANCESTORS." In *The Palatine Immigrant*, vol. 8:4 (Spring 1983), pp. 183-187.

All 1710 arrivals from German-speaking locales. Names were furnished by descendants, along with other genealogical details. These immigrants were called "the 1709ers." Same issue carries an article on "Publications on the 1709ers," pp. 180ff. Hank Jones has indicated the origins of some of these immigrants.

* * *

3394
"IMMIGRANTS FROM KRATZKA, RUSSIA, Who Settled in Russell County, Kansas." In *The Russell Record*, March 1, 1948. In *Clues*, 1977, pt. 1, pp. 49-51.

Names about 70 persons who arrived in the 1870s from a village not far from Saratov. (Spelled Katzka in one source.)

* * *

3430
"INDENTURED SERVANTS, 1774-5." In *The Georgia Genealogical Society Quarterly*, vol. 7:2 (Summer 1971), pp. 118-119.

Two muster rolls of 118 servants bonded to Lt. Col. Thomas Brown of Georgia, originally from Great Britain. Taken from records in the Public Record Office, London. Names only.

* * *

3434
AN INDEX TO INDIANA NATURALIZATION RECORDS *Found in Various Order Books of the Ninety-Two Local Courts Prior to 1907*. Indianapolis: Family History Section, Indiana Historical Society, 1981. 172pp.

Provides access to naturalization records in the various Indiana courthouses, not in the state archives and not usually found in the county clerks' record books in the separate counties. From material compiled by the Work Projects Administration. Transcription is poor; use with caution. Over 40,000 names.

* * *

3436
"INDEX TO NATURALIZATIONS, THURSTON COUNTY [WASHINGTON], 1853-1883." In *Olympia Genealogical Society Quarterly*, vol. 9:1 (Jan. 1983), pp. 20-23; vol. 9:2 (Apr. 1983), pp. 40-45; vol. 9:3 (July 1983), pp. 73-75.

Includes 700 names, with page references to the Thurston County courthouse records in the state of Washington. This is an untranscribed, facsimile list. The first issue cited above covers names beginning A-G; the second, H-Q; the third, R-Z.

* * *

3438.1 — 3438.6
IRELAND, GORDON. "Servants to Foreign Plantations from Bristol, England, to Barbados, 1654-1686." In *The Journal of the Barbados Museum and Historical Society*.
3438.1
---Vol. 14:2 (Nov. 1946-Feb. 1947), pp. 48-69 (nos. 1-472, A-C); vol. 14:3 (May 1947), pp. 143-158 (nos. 473-851, C-G); vol. 14:4 (Aug. 1947), pp. 196-212 (nos. 852-1185, G-J).
3438.2
---Vol. 15:4 (Aug. 1948), pp. 216-226 (nos. 1186-1400, J-L).
3438.3
---Vol. 16:1/2 (Nov. 1948-Feb. 1949), pp. 95-100 (nos. 1401-1512, L-M); vol. 16:3 (May 1949), pp. 152-156 (nos. 1513-1602, M).
3438.4
---Vol. 17:2/3 (Feb.-May 1950), pp. 143-158 (nos. 1603-1916, M-R).
3438.5
---Vol. 18:1/2 (Nov. 1950-Feb. 1951), pp. 86-100 (nos. 1917-2208, R-S); vol. 18:3/4 (May-Aug. 1951), pp. 180-200 (nos. 2209-2617, S-W).
3438.6
---Vol. 19:1 (Nov. 1951), pp. 47-48 (nos. 2618-2656, W- Y).

Name, description, place of origin, bondmaster, date of arrival in Barbados, reference. Compare item nos. 3438 and 3440 in the basic volume of this bibliography. This series of articles lists 2,656 persons.

3453
"IRISH AND ENGLISH IMMIGRANTS ARRIVING AT THE PORT OF NEW ORLEANS, October 20, 1849, British Passenger Ship *Euphemia*." In *The Southwestern Genealogist*, vol. 11:3 (May-June 1972), p. 44.

Lists about 100 immigrants who boarded ship at Liverpool or Cardiff. Names only. See also item no. 2742 in the main volume for this same subject.

* * *

3455.1 — 3455.5
"IROQUOIS [Illinois] NATURALIZATION RECORDS — Declaration of Intention." In *The Iroquois Stalker*.
3455.1
---Vol. 4:1 (Winter 1974), pp. 9-14; vol. 4:2 (Spring 1974), pp. 40-55.
3455.2
---Vol. 5:2 (Spring 1975), pp. 43-53; vol. 5:3 (Summer 1975), pp. 71-80; vol. 5:4 (Fall 1975), pp. 94-106.
3455.3
---Vol. 6:1 (Winter 1976), pp. 16-26; vol. 6:2 (Spring 1976), pp. 45-55; vol. 6:3 (Summer 1976), pp. 78-86; vol. 6:4 (Fall 1976), pp. 104-115.
3455.4
---Vol. 7:1 (Winter 1977), pp. 24-29; vol. 7:2 (Spring 1977), pp. 50-56; vol. 7:3 (Summer 1976), pp. 78-83; vol. 7:4 (Fall 1977), pp. 92-94.
3455.5
---Vol. 11 (Winter 1981), p. 7.

Declarations of intention to acquire citizenship in Iroquois County, Illinois, between the years 1891 and 1929. Title varies.

* * *

3457.1
IRVIN, MRS. JOHN M. "Calumet County [Wisconsin] Naturalizations." In *Wisconsin State Genealogical Society Newsletter*."
3457.1
---Vol. 30:2 (Sept. 1983), pp. 89-90 (A-B); vol. 30:3 (Jan. 1984), pp. 163-164 (B-D). In progress.

Focuses on latter half of 19th century. Information includes names, countries of origin (a preponderance from Germany), and dates of the declarations of intention to acquire citizenship. These listings are still being compiled and will continue to be published.

* * *

3495
JANSEN, NORBERT. *Nach Amerika: Geschichte der liechtensteinischen Auswanderung nach den Vereinigten Staaten von Amerika*. Vaduz: Verlag des Historischen Vereins fuer das Fuerstentum Liechtenstein, 1976. 216p.

To America: history of emigration from Liechtenstein to the U.S.A. Pp. 169-213 contain a list of about 700 individuals or families emigrating to the U.S. in the 19th and 20th centuries. Year of birth and community of origin specified. Some include names of parents, their own place of settlement in the U.S., and occupation.

* * *

3509
"JENNINGS COUNTY [Indiana] NATURALIZATION." In *The Hoosier Journal of Ancestry*, vol. 7:4 (1980), p. 36.

Twenty persons named, with countries of origin, length of residence in the U.S., and dates of naturalization: 1865-1900.

* * *

3545
JODER, KARL. "Swiss Emigrants from 1694-1754 Who Settled in the Palatinate, Alsace-Lorraine, Baden-Wuerttemberg, and Pennsylvania." In *Mennonite Family History*, vol. 2:4 (Oct. 1983), pp. 132-136.

About 50 of these were bound for Pennsylvania, and the dates of arrival are stated. List includes 600 names, all told, with places of origin and places of settlement. Taken from the *Rodel weggezogener Mannrechten* (Vol. B XIII 443) at the cantonal Staatsarchiv in Bern, Switzerland.

* * *

3570.1 — 3570.5
JOHNSON, ARTA F., editor. "Immigrant Ancestors." In *The Palatine Immigrant*.
3570.1
---Vol.5:1 (Summer 1979), pp. 44-46; vol. 5:2 (Autumn 1979), pp. 87-91; vol. 5:3 (Winter 1980), pp. 138-143; vol. 5:4 (Spring 1980), pp. 183-187. (This replaces and adds to item 3570 in the basic volume of this bibliography.)
3570.2
---Vol. 6:1 (Summer 1980), pp. 44-47; vol. 6:2 (Fall 1980), pp. 87-93; vol. 6:3 (Winter 1981), pp. 138-143; vol. 6:4 (Spring 1981), pp. 189-191.
3570.3.
---Vol. 7:1 (Summer 1981), pp. 46-47; vol. 7:3 (Winter 1982), pp. 112-114.
3570.4.
---Vol. 8:1 (Summer 1982), pp. 20-25; vol. 8:2 (Autumn 1982), pp. 80-87; vol. 8:3 (Winter 1983), pp. 139-144; vol. 8:4 (Spring 1983), pp. 186-191.
3570.5.
---Vol. 9:1 (Summer 1983), pp. 28-33; vol. 9:2 (Autumn 1983), pp. 90-95; vol. 9:3 (Winter 1984), pp. 137-142. In progress.

Continuing listings of mostly Mennonite German immigrants who settled in Pennsylvania between 1710 and 1815. The majority were from Baden-Durlach in the Palatinate. Dates of arrival and present locations of descendants are included in the listings.

* * *

3577
JOHNSON, ARTA F. *Kinfolk in Germany — Kinfolk in Maryland*. Columbus, Ohio: the author, 1983, 42p.

The Rhine-valley, Klein-Schifferstadt origins and relationships of people who settled in Maryland in the early 1700s. Involves the Brunner, Goetzendanner, Sturm, and Thomas families. Emigration data throughout the text.

* * *

3605
JONES, GEORGE FENWICK. "German-Speaking Settlers in Georgia, 1733-1741 [Based on the Earl of Egmont's List]." In *The Report: a Journal of German-American History*, 38 (1982), pp. 35-51.

Provides 750 names taken from lists of one of the founders of the Georgia Colony. Facts on each immigrant include date of birth, date of arrival, occupation, nationality, and miscellaneous other information.

* * *

3609
JONES, GEORGE F., and DON SAVELL. "The Fourth Transport of Georgia Salzburgers." In *Concordia Historical Institute Quarterly*, vol. 56:1 (Spring 1983), pp. 6-26; vol. 56:2 (Summer 1983), pp. 52-63.

Extracts from diaries kept by travelers on the *Loyal Judith*, from London to Ebenezer, Georgia, arriving December 1741. Passengers mentioned throughout text, and a complete list of 61, with ages and occupations, on pp. 62-63.

* * *

3615
JONES, HENRY Z., JR. "Emigrants from Laudenheim, Germany, to New York in 1709/10." In *National Genealogical Society Quarterly*, vol. 70:2 (June 1982), pp. 97-102.

A hundred Palatines, with much information on their lives.

* * *

3624
JONES, HENRY Z., JR. "A Partial Listing of the Palatine Families of New York." In *Germanic Genealogist*, vol. 6:1 (no. 25), (1981) pp. 185-187.

This involves about 500 German immigrants from the years 1709 and 1715-1750, whose names have been traced to their German home villages and communities.

* * *

3627
JONES, HENRY Z., JR., and ANNETTE K. BURGERT. "A New Emigrant List: Bonfeld 1710-1738." In *Der Reggeboge: Quarterly of the Pennsylvania German Society*, vol. 14:4 (Oct. 1980), pp. 3-20.

Bonfeld is located in the Neckar Valley area of southern Germany. Article lists 250 names with considerable information on families.

* * *

3688
JUSTUS, NORMA MIZE. *A Compilation of Persons Drawing Pensions . . . With Some Naturalization and Pardon Records from Lawrence County, AR*. Powhatan, Arkansas: the compiler [1983]. 8p.

"Loose" naturalization records (i.e. unbound), containing 13 names, with countries of origin and dates of naturalization, 1855-1887.

* * *

3690.1
KAMINKOW, JACK, and MARION KAMINKOW, transcribers. *A List of Emigrants from England to America, 1718-1759*. New, enl. edition. Baltimore: Magna Carta Book Co., 1981. 292p.

Adds 48 recently discovered records to the more than 3,000 listed in the earlier (1964) edition (item 3690 in main volume of this bibliography). New material involves 18th-century servants' indentures found at the Guildhall, London.

* * *

3702
KAMPHOEFNER, WALTER D. *Westfalen in der Neuen Welt: eine Sozialgeschichte der Auswanderung im 19. Jahrhundert*. (Beitraege zur Volkskultur im Nordwestdeutschland, pt. 26.) Muenster: Coppenrath, 1982. 211p.

Westphalia in the New World: a social history of emigration in the 19th century, part of a series on N.W. Germany. Appendix B, pp. 184-190 has about 130 Germans from Westphalia keyed to their places of appearance in the 1850 U.S. censuses of St. Charles and Warren counties, Missouri. The immigrants were probably from Tecklenburg.

* * *

3704
KANELY, EDNA A. "Passenger Lists — Ships *James Eduard, Jason, Providence, Rebecca Francis, Ulysses* Arrived in Baltimore in September 1833." In *Maryland Genealogical Society Bulletin*, vol. 22:1 (Winter 1981), pp. 10-17.

About 340 passengers arrived on five ships in 1833. The *James Eduard* listed 55 from Germany destined for Ohio. The *Providence*, sailing from Amsterdam to Baltimore, carried 140 passengers from Germany and supplies data on age, sex, place of origin, and occupation of each. The *Jason* brought 132 persons. Children were not named on the lists.

* * *

3707.1 — 3707.19
KANKAS, EDNA, compiler. "Great Register for General Election, Sept. 30, 1879 [Siskiyou County, California]." In *Genealogical Society of Siskiyou County*.
3707.1
---Vol. 2:3 (Spring 1974), pp. 6-8. (A-B).
3707.2
---Vol. 2:4 (Summer 1974), pp. 6-9. (B-C).
3707.3
---Vol. 3:1 (Fall 1974), pp. 6-9. (C-D).
3707.4
---Vol. 3:2 (Winter 1974), pp. 6-9. (D-G).
3707.5
---Vol. 3:3 (Spring 1975), pp. 7-11. (G-J).
3707.6
---Vol. 3:4 (Summer 1975), pp. 21-22. (J-K).
3707.7
---Vol. 4:1 (Fall 1975), pp. 11-14. (K-M).
3707.8
---Vol. 4:2 (Winter 1975), pp. 17-19. (M-N).
3707.9
---Vol. 6:3 (Spring 1978), pp. 27-28. (N-P).
3707.10
---Vol. 6:4 (Summer 1978), pp. 23-24. (P).
3707.11
---Vol. 7:1 (Fall 1978), pp. 6-7. (P-R).
3707.12
---Vol. 7:2 (Winter 1978), p. 18. (R).
3707.13
---Vol. 7:3 (Spring 1979), pp. 17-18. (S).
3707.14
---Vol. 7:4 (Summer 1979), pp. 10-11. (S).
3707.15
---Vol. 8:1 (Fall 1979), pp. 19-20. (S).
3707.16
---Vol. 8:2 (Winter 1979), pp. 18-19. (S-T).
3707.17
---Vol. 8:3 (Spring 1980), pp. 9-10. (T-V).
3707.18
---Vol. 8:4 (Summer 1980), pp. 23-24. (V-W).
3707.19
---Vol. 9:1 (Fall 1980), pp. 22-24. (W-Z).

About 2,000 names fill this voter registration list for the year 1879. The data includes age, birthplace, occupation, and local residence for each entry.

* * *

3709
KAPP, RONALD O. "Immigrant Members of St. John's Ev[angelical] Lutheran Church, Northfield Township, Washtenaw County, Michigan." In *Family History Capers*, vol. 7:1 (July 1983), pp. 10-14.

Nineteenth-century immigrants, 170 in number, of whom 97 were born in Wuerttemberg, Germany.

* * *

3745
KAULBACK, RUTH E. "Miscellany." In *Historic Saga of LeHeve (LaHave)* [N.S.]. Halifax: the author, 1971. 105p.

Lists of persons coming to Nova Scotia, taken from the Public Archives of Nova Scotia, published as Chapter 5, pp. 66-89. Some lists made by John Dick acquired the title, "Dick Foreign Protestants." Includes more than 1,000 passengers from Germany, France, and Switzerland, 1750-1752. Name, origin, trade. Many names transcribed erroneously.

* * *

3755
KEARNY COUNTY HISTORICAL SOCIETY, KANSAS. "1880 Federal Census of Kearny County and Citizens Naturalized in Kearny County." In *History of Kearny County, Kansas*. Dodge City, Kansas: the society, 1964. Vol. 1, pp. 433-435.

Historical source names 160 residents of Kearny County, Kansas, in the year 1880, with ages, occupations, and places of birth. About half were born outside the U.S. Newly naturalized citizens numbered 40 between 1909 and 1937. Data on naturalization includes countries of origin; many from Russia.

* * *

3771
KEITH, ARTHUR LESLIE. "The German Colony of 1717." In *The William and Mary Quarterly*, ser. 1, vol. 26:2 (Oct. 1917), pp. 79-95; vol. 26:3 (Jan. 1918), pp. 178-195; vol. 26:4 (Apr. 1918), pp. 234-249.

Mentions names of "High Germans" who arrived in 1717 and established a colony at Germanna, Virginia. Much information on subsequent movements and descendants.

* * *

3806
KERNAN, JOHN DEVEREUX. "Notices from The Shamrock Newspaper of New York 1810-1812." In *The Irish Genealogist*, vol. 6:3, (Nov. 1982), pp. 370-377.

These "notices" are reprints of the passenger lists of 15 ships that sailed from Ireland between 1810 and 1812 with 500 passengers. Information given includes places of origin and relationships of family members aboard. Taken from an incomplete set of newspapers in the Sterling Library of Yale University.

* * *

3810
KERWIN, MARION BINGENHEIMER. "Manifest of Passengers on Board the Bark *Irad Ferry*. In *Wisconsin State Genealogical Society Newsletter*, vol. 30:3 (Jan. 1984), pp. 157.

Most of these 125 arrivals were from Switzerland, destined for western states. Arrival in New York was in 1843. Name, age, sex, and, occasionally, occupation.

* * *

3813
KEY CITY GENEALOGICAL SOCIETY, copier. *Book 1 of Naturalization Declarations, 1832-1856, Dubuque County, Iowa*. Des Moines Iowa Genealogical Society, 1982. 61p.

Copied from the original records located in Dubuque County Court House. Almost 3,000 entries, with ages, countries of origin, and dates of declarations of intention to acquire citizenship.

* * *

3820
KINGSBURY, SUSAN MYRA, editor. "A List of Men Nowe Sent for Plantacon (*sic*) in Virginia, September 3, 1620." In *The Records of the Virginia Company of London*. Washington, D.C.: U.S. Government Printing Office, 1933. Vol. 3, pp. 396-397.

Very early arrivals from England in the Virginia Colony: 50 names. Taken from a document in the New York Public Library, List of Records no. 205: the Smyth of Nibley Papers, pp. 138-139.

* * *

3836
KIRKWOOD, PATRICIA. "Passenger List *Medora*: 1836, District of New York — Port of New York." In *The English Genealogist*, vol. 5:1 (1983), pp. 473-474.

List from the ship manifest naming 30 passengers from London taken on board the ship *Medora* of Newburyport in 1836. Names, ages, sex, occupations, and countries of origin. Most were from England.

3840.1 — 3840.3
"KLAMATH COUNTY [Oregon] GREAT REGISTER — 1869." In *Redwood Researcher*.
3840.1
---Vol. 15:4 (May 1983), pp. 14-19.
3840.2
---Vol. 16:1 (Aug. 1983), pp. 14-19.
3840.3
---Vol. 16:2 (Nov. 1983), pp. 8-13. In progress.

Register of the domiciled inhabitants, copied from the Great Register. With each name is the age, place of origin, occupation, place of local residence, and date and place of registration, 1866-1869. To be continued.

* * *

3844
KLEIN, TONY A. "Passenger Lists." In *Heritage Review*, vol. 11:3 (Sept. 1981), pp. 45-46.

Germans from Russia who sailed on the *Friesland* out of Antwerp for New York in 1893 are listed here, thirty in number. Settlement was in North Dakota in towns named Zeeland and Hague.

* * *

4030
KNUTSON, FLORENCE. "The Family Tree and Norwegian Homeplace of the Hefte Folks." In *Seattle Genealogical Society Bulletin*, vol. 33:1 (Fall 1983), pp. 3-4.

Names of 12 persons, including seven Hefte family members, who left Golreppen, Hallingdal, Norway, in 1853 for America.

* * *

4049
KOEDEL, BARBARA. "Ship Passenger List, 1787." In *The Genealogical Magazine of New Jersey*, vol. 55:2 (May 1980), pp. 54-56.

An 18th-century ship named *Mayflower* under Capt. John Stilwell anchored at Billingsport, New Jersey, 1787, after crossing from Cork, Ireland, with 73 passengers, including 56 redemptioners. Some indicate specific destinations.

* * *

4058
KOENIG, ROBERT J. *Except the Corn Die*. Giddings, Texas: the author, 1975. 474p.

An account of 800 German Christians who left Germany in the 1830s as a protest against State interference in their religious liberty. Includes names of those who actually made the journey; they are not fictional characters, although this is a historical novel.

* * *

4061
KONRAD, ALLEN. "Passenger List." In *Heritage Review*, vol. 12:2 (May 1982), p. 88.

Forty Germans from Russia who settled in Kulm, North Dakota, passengers from the S.S. *Kaiser Wilhelm der Grosse*, in a sailing from Bremen to New York in 1902. Information supplied: names, ages, occupations, and places of origin.

* * *

4255
KREBS, FRIEDRICH. "18th-Century Emigrants from the Palatinate, Lower Alsace, and Rheinhessen." Translated and edited by Don Yoder. In *Pennsylvania Folklife*, vol. 21:3 (Spring 1972), pp. 46-48.

Abstracted from two works listed in the basic volume of this bibliography: item no. 4133, "Amerika-Auswanderer des 18. Jahrhunderts aus dem Gebiet der Pfaelz . . . ," and no. 4308, "Einige Amerika-Auswanderer des 18. Jahrhunderts aus Rheinhessen." Also in no. 9968 of this supplement: Yoder, *Rhineland Emigrants*, pp. 66-68. About 60 names.

* * *

4268
KREBS, FRIEDRICH. "Eighteenth-Century Emigration from the Duchy of Zweibruecken." Translated and edited by Don Yoder. In *Pennsylvania Folklife*, vol. 17:1 (Autumn 1967), pp. 42-48.

About 75 German arrivals and much genealogical data. Names also listed in item no. 9968, Yoder, *Rhineland Emigrants*, pp. 45-51.

* * *

4319
KREBS, FRIEDRICH. "An Emigrant to America in 1749 from Rhodt [Palatinate]." In *Pennsylvania Genealogical Magazine*, vol. 29:1 (1975), p. 61.

Christian Carl Brand and his family of eight arrived in Philadelphia in October 1749. Twelve passengers listed.

* * *

4349
KREBS, FRIEDRICH. "Emigrants to America from the Duchy of Zweibruecken." Translated and edited by Don Yoder. In *Pennsylvania Folklife*, vol. 21:4 (Summer 1972), pp. 46-48.

About 50 eighteenth-century arrivals from Germany. Abstracted from item no. 4141 in the basic volume of this bibliography: Krebs, "Amerika-Auswanderer des 18. Jahrhunderts aus dem Gebiet des Herzogtums Zweibruecken." Also in no. 9968 in this supplement: Yoder, *Rhineland Emigrants*, pp. 72-74.

* * *

4374
KREBS, FRIEDRICH. "New Materials on 18th-Century Emigration from Wuerttemberg." Translated and edited by Don Yoder. In *Pennsylvania Folklife*, vol. 16:2 (Winter 1966-1967), pp. 22-23.

Abstracted from a work cited in the main volume of this bibliography: item no. 4245, Krebs, "Beitraege zur Amerikaauswanderung des 18. Jahrhunderts aus Altwuerttemberg." Also in item no. 9968 in this supplement: Yoder, *Rhineland Emigrants*, pp. 43-44. About 40 names cited.

* * *

4376
KREBS, FRIEDRICH. "New Materials on the 18th-Century Emigration; from the Speyer State Archives." Translated and edited by Don Yoder. In *Pennsylvania Folklife*, vol. 16:1 (Autumn 1966), pp. 40-41.

Abstracted from Krebs, "Amerikaauswanderer des 18. Jahrhunderts . . . ," a work cited in the basic volume of this bibliography: item no. 4122. Also in this supplement in no. 9968: Yoder, *Rhineland Emigrants*, pp. 41-42. Names of about 50 Germans in America.

* * *

4480
KUHNS, OSCAR. "A Genealogical Trip to Switzerland." In *The Pennsylvania-German*, vol. 7:6 (Oct. 1906), pp. 311-312.

Traveling in Switzerland in 1900, Kuhns recorded the names of about 25 persons who had emigrated to the U.S. in 1709-1710.

* * *

4483
KUHNS, OSCAR. "Lancaster County, Pennsylvania, Families from the Canton of Zurich, Switzerland," (and) "Some Lancaster County Families from the Canton of Berne, Switzerland." In *National Genealogical Society Quarterly*, vol. 8:3 (Oct. 1919), pp. 36-41.

Twenty Swiss settled in Pennsylvania in the 17th century, immigrants of the Brethren who were Mennonites.

* * *

4485.1
KUHR, JO ANN. "Galveston Passenger Ship Lists." In *Clues*, 1982, pt. 1, pp. 89-92.

Germans from Russia, 1897-1908. Names 350 passengers, with ages, places of origin, and often destinations.

* * *

4485.2
KUHR, JO ANN. "Galveston Passenger Lists." In *Clues*, 1982, pt. 2, pp. 29-31.

Mostly Germans from Russia, 1898-1910. About 450 passengers, with ages, occupations, places of origin, and often destinations.

* * *

4490
LACHER, CONNIE. "Passenger Lists." In *Heritage Review*, vol. 13:3 (Sept. 1983), p. 47.

Germans from Russia, sailing from Hamburg to New York in 1899. The 17 gave their destinations as South Dakota (the cities of Eureka and Menno) and Montreal in the province of Quebec.

* * *

4504.1 — 4504.3
"LANCASTER COUNTY [Pennsylvania] NATURALIZATION RECORDS." In *Lancaster Legacy*.
4504.1
---Vol. 1:1 (June 1983), pp. 29-30.
4504.2
---Vol. 1:2 (Sept. 1983), pp. 23-24.
4504.3
---Vol. 1:3 (Dec. 1983), p. 23. In progress.

Early 19th-century lists that include many Irish names. Sponsors also listed. This is a continuing series that covers the years 1800-1802 so far.

4514
LANDERS, JO. "Emigrant List." In *Landers' Landings,* vol. 3:3 (Dec. 1983-Jan. 1984), pp. 3-4.

A list of 70 persons, most from Germany, with the name Landers or variations of this spelling. The data includes places of origin and arrival, dates of arrival, names of ships, and the source of the information. Spans 17th to 19th centuries.

* * *

4532
LAPP, JANET M. "Passenger Lists." In *Heritage Review,* vol. 11:3 (Sept. 1981), p. 45.

Germans from Russia in the years 1898 and 1909 traveling to Eureka, South Dakota. For the Atlantic crossing, this lists 24 passengers, with ages and occupations.

* * *

4537
"LAWRENCE COUNTY [Indiana] NATURALIZATIONS." In *The Hoosier Journal of Ancestry,* vol. 6:3 (July 1979), pp. 29-30.

Abstracted from 1852 naturalizations records. These are record book entries 1-37. Country of origin, age, and places of departure and arrival are listed. Many Irish in this first installment of what was intended as a continuing feature.

* * *

4594
LEHMAN, DANIEL R. "Bishop Hans Lehman, Immigrant of 1727." In *Pennsylvania Mennonite Heritage,* vol. 3:4 (Oct. 1980), pp. 16-23.

Page 16 mentions several emigrants on the *James Goodwill,* which left Rotterdam and arrived at Philadelphia in 1727. All from Zweibruecken, Germany. A few also mentioned on subsequent pages.

* * *

4598
LEISTNER, DORIS. "Crawford County, Indiana, Naturalizations." In *The Hoosier Genealogist,* vol. 22:1 (Mar. 1982), pp. 20-29.

Concerns a hundred new citizens between 1822 and 1896: name of each, with date and place of birth, date and port of embarkation, date and port of entry to U.S.A., and county of residence.

* * *

4599
LEISTNER, DORIS. "Orange County [Indiana] Naturalizations, 1840-1905." In *The Hoosier Genealogist,* vol. 22:4 (Dec. 1982), pp. 88-92.

Spans the years 1840-1878 and 1905, listing the names of 80 new citizens. The information includes places and dates of birth, ports and dates of embarkation, ports and dates of entry to the U.S., and places of residence at the time of naturalization.

* * *

4606
LERSKI, JERZY JAN. "List of the Polish Exiles in the United States of North America." In *A Polish Chapter in Jacksonian America: the United States and the Polish Exiles of 1831.* Madison: University of Wisconsin Press, 1958, pp. 172-180.

In the appendix are the following lists of Polish exiles: 234 who came from Trieste to New York on the frigates *Guerriera* and *Hebe* in 1831; 16 to New York on the corvette *Lipsia,* July 1834; 11 to Boston on American merchant vessel *Cherokee,* July 1834; and 39 to New York on the corvette *Adria* in May 1835.

* * *

4609
LESLIE, KIM C. *Roots of America: an Anthology of Documents Relating to American History in the West Sussex Record Office, Chichester, England.* Chichester: West Sussex County Council, 1976. 114p.

Pages 33-36, 38-40, and 42 give details concerning several emigrants from Sussex to America, chiefly in the 1830s. About 80 names.

* * *

4646
"LIST OF EMIGRANTS ARRIVED AT THE PORT OF CHARLOTTETOWN [Prince Edward Island] During the Year Ended 31st December, 1855." In *Prince Edward Island Journal of the House of Assembly,* 1856. Appendix B, pp. 48-49.

Probably British arrivals on the schooner *Dragonet.* Data includes names of 57 persons, their ages, and the amounts they paid for passage.

* * *

4649
"LIST OF EMIGRANTS ON SCHOONER DOLPHIN, from Scotland to Georgetown, P.E.I., 1848." In *Prince Edward Island Journal of House of Assembly, 1849. Appendix I, pp. 37-38.*

Names 55 arrivals at Prince Edward Island and gives their ages.

* * *

4676
"LIST OF GERMANS AND ACADIAN FAMILIES Who Went by an English Vessel to New Orleans to Settle . . . 1769." In *New Orleans Genesis,* vol. 22 (July 1983), pp. 370-373.

Names 57 Germans and 32 Acadians with families who, though their first vessel was lost in the Gulf of Mexico as it put in at Espiritu Santo Bay, arrived in New Orleans, October 24, 1769. Ages given.

* * *

4727
"LIST OF REBEL PRISONERS IMPORTED by Capt. Edwd Trafford in the *Elizabeth & Anne* From Liverpole [*sic.*], 1716." In *Calendar of Virginia State Papers,* Vol. 1: 1652 to 1781. Richmond, Virginia: the state, 1875, pp. 185-186.

Arriving at Yorktown, 112 indentured and unindentured servants.

4747
LIST OF THE NAMES AND REGISTRATION of the Domiciled Inhabitants of the County of Humboldt Copied from the Great Register of Humboldt County [Calif.], 1884. n.p., 1884. 68p. Folio.

Carries 5,092 names, with age, birthplace, occupation, local residence, date and place of naturalization, and date of registration.

* * *

4810
LOETE, JOAN. "Passenger List of Ship *Kroonland*, Sailing from Antwerp on March 3, 1906, Landing in New York, March 13, 1906." In *Smoke Signals*, vol. 9:1 (Spring 1982), pp. 30-31.

Names 30 persons, many from Belgium, with ages, places of origin, and destinations.

* * *

4814
LOGAN, ROBERT ARCHIBALD. "Highlanders of Skye in North Carolina and Nova Scotia, 1771-1818." In *The Scottish Genealogist*, vol. 12:4 (Feb. 1966), p. 92.

Names of Scottish Highlanders who settled in North Carolina and Nova Scotia late in the 18th century or early in the 19th.

* * *

4891
LUCHSINGER, JOHN. "The Planting of the Swiss Colony at New Glarus, Wis." In *Collections of the State Historical Society of Wisconsin*, vol. 12 (1892), pp. 335-382.

A discussion of the colony, with a list on p. 367 of 26 men, 23 women, and 73 children, original settlers of New Glarus in 1845 from the Canton of Glarus, Switzerland.

* * *

4900
LUNDBERG, GERTRUDE W. "Passenger List from Havre de Grace, France, to America on the Ship *Rhone*." In *Chicago Genealogist*, vol. 15:1 (Fall 1982), pp. 20-23.

Arrival of 200 passengers from France and Germany in New York in 1841. Data indicates ages and sex. Some specify occupations.

* * *

4902
LUNDBERG, GERTRUDE W. "Ship's Passenger List." In *Chicago Genealogist*, vol. 15:4 (Summer 1983), pp. 191-193.

A hundred passengers on the *Alwina* from Bremen to New York, 1841.

* * *

4903
LUNDBERG, GERTRUDE W. "Ship's Passenger List, Great Britain to the United States." In *Chicago Genealogist*, vol. 15:3 (Spring 1983), pp. 153-157.

Names of about 220 immigrants who arrived on the *Eutaw* from Liverpool in July 1841. Includes age, sex, and occupation.

* * *

4905
LUNDBERG, GERTRUDE W. "Ship's Passenger Lists." In *Chicago Genealogist*, vol. 15:2 (Winter 1982-1983), pp. 88-98.

About 450 passengers, mostly from England, some from Germany, arriving in New York, 1840-1841, giving ages, occupations, and places of origin.

* * *

4906
LUNDBERG, GERTRUDE W. "Ship's Passengers — Regulations for Captains." In *Illinois State Genealogical Society Quarterly*, vol. 15:2 (Summer 1983), pp. 79-84.

Passenger lists indicate 18 on the schooner *Cornelia*, arriving New York, 1841; 43 on the *Sheffield*, Liverpool to U.S. and Canada, 1841; 240 on the *Isaac Allerton*, Liverpool to New York, 1841. Almost all the newly arrived were English or Irish. Data includes name, age, sex, occupation, and country of origin. The regulations referred to in the title are merely incidental to the lists of 300 passengers.

* * *

4908.1 — 4908.3
LYNGSVAER, ROALD. "Norwegian Emigrants to America; ed. by Gene C. Moen." In *Hawkeye Heritage*.
4908.1
---Vol. 16:2 (Spring 1981), pp. 83-91. Vinje Subdivision.
4908.2
---Vol. 16:3 (Summer 1981), pp. 153-158. Myrkdalen Subdivision.
4908.3
---Vol. 16:4 (Fall-Winter 1981), pp. 190-200. Oppheim Subdivision.

About 1,200 names, with for each, date of birth, sometimes name of spouse, often date of emigration (mostly latter half of 19th century), and occasionally, destination in America. Taken from Lyngsvaer's *Aettebok for Vossestrand*, Voss, 1971.

* * *

4912
McBRIDE, RANSOM. "A Change of Destination for Some 100 'Emigrants' from Virginia & Maryland to South Carolina, 1718." In *The North Carolina Genealogical Society Journal*, vol. 9:3 (Aug. 1983), pp. 165-167.

Describes the transportation of 100 persons sentenced in London for felonies, who were en route to Maryland and Virginia when their ship, the *Eagle*, was attacked by pirates. Later, the *Eagle* was rescued by ships from Charleston, and the convicts landed there. The hundred are listed on p. 167.

* * *

4913
McBRIDE, RANSOM. "List of Scottish Rebel Prisoners Transported to America in the Aftermath of Culloden — 1746." In *The North Carolina Genealogical Society Journal*, vol. 6:2 (May 1980), pp. 78-94.

Names 800 prisoners transported to America after the Jacobite Rebellion of 1745-1746. Much information on the ships and the places of debarkation, with ages, occupations, counties of origin, and physical descriptions of the immigrants.

* * *

4915
McCANN, ALISON. *Emigrants and Transportees from West Sussex, 1778–ca.1874.* (Lists and Index, 9) Chichester, Sussex: West Sussex Record Office, 1980. n. pag. [18p.]

Name; place of origin (all England); destinations: Australia, Canada and America. Convicts transported, 1778-1853, with nature and date of offense specified. Involves 800 persons.

* * *

4968
McDIARMID, GARNET. "The Original Emigrants to McNab Township, Upper Canada, 1825." In *The Scottish Genealogist*, vol. 28:3 (Sept. 1981), pp. 109-121; and in *Families*, vol. 21:1 (1982), pp. 13-21.

A study of more than 150 emigrants from Scotland in 1825 to what is now the province of Ontario.

* * *

5012.17
MacMILLAN, SOMERLED. *The Emigration of Lochaber MacMillans to Canada in 1802*. Paisley, Scotland: the author, 1958. 14p.

A study of the MacMillan family, with lists and mention of the names of those who accompanied Archibald MacMillan in 1802 from Lochaber in south Inverness County, Scotland.

* * *

5012.18
MacMILLAN, SOMERLED. "Passenger List of the Emigrants to Canada in 1802." In *The Clan MacMillan Magazine*, vol. 1:4 (1964), pp. 23-26.

About 300 Scottish immigrants, with wives and children unnamed here, and places of origin cited.

* * *

5012.37
McNABB, MICHELE. "Naturalization Records — Minors, Champaign County [Illinois]." In *Champaign County Genealogical Society Quarterly,* vol. 5:3 (1983), pp. 59-62.

Names of 140 minors naturalized between 1886 and 1896 and of 14 in the years 1903-1906. Many from Germany. Name, age, and the names of two sponsors given for each.

* * *

5012.40
McNABB, MICHELE. "Soldiers' Naturalization Records, volume 'B' (1866-1892), [Champaign County, Illinois.]" In *Champaign County Genealogical Society Quarterly,* vol. 5:4 [Mar. 1984], p. 97.

Provides 11 names, with dates of application, names of witnesses, and countries of origin.

5033
MAGEE, PEGGY. "Passenger Lists." In *Gaelic Gleanings*, vol. 1:1 (Nov. 1981), pp. 19-22.

The Brig *Emeline*, departed Newry, Ireland, for Philadelphia, 1825, with 200 passengers. Data names the parishes and counties of origin and gives ages and occupations.

* * *

5034
MAGEE, PEGGY. "Passenger Lists." In *Gaelic Gleanings*, vol. 1:2 (Feb. 1982), pp. 59-60.

Totals 68 passengers from these ships: the *Ajax*, Liverpool to New Orleans, 1820; the *Herald*, Liverpool to Baltimore, 1834; the *Fairy Queen*, St. John, New Brunswick, to Portland and Falmouth, Maine, 1849; the *Catharine*, Havana to New Orleans, 1820.

* * *

5038
MAGNUSON, MARY LOU. "To Minnesota from Sweden." In *Bulletin of the Seattle Genealogical Society*, 31:1 (Fall 1981), pp. 31-34; 31:2 (Winter 1981), pp. 98-101.

Concerns 360 persons emigrating from Sweden between 1880 and 1904 and later settling in Minnesota. Date of arrival, age, and place of settlement in Minnesota given for each.

* * *

5120
MAHRENHOLTZ, HANS. "Norddeutsche in aller Welt: Auswanderungen aus den Aemtern Catlenburg/Lindau, Duderstadt und Gieboldehausen, 1831-1863 bezw. 1839-1866." In *Suedhannoverscher Heimatkalender,* (1965), pp. 63-65.

North Germans the world over: emigration from the jurisdictions of Catlenburg-Lindau, and Duderstadt and Gieboldehausen, 1831-1863 and 1839-1866, respectively. About 50 emigrants to America, with places of origin, dates of birth, family data, occupations, and dates of emigration. Not as complete as the item described in no. 5119 in the basic volume of this bibliography.

* * *

5228
MANNY, MRS. ARNOLD (MARGARET). "Citizenship [Iowa]." In *Cedar Tree*, vol. 14 (1983), p. 13.

About 80 persons who were naturalized 1868, County Court, Dubuque; Iowa Circuit Court. Mostly from Ireland and Luxembourg.

* * *

5231
MANTLE, HALLIE. "Passenger List of the Sailboat *Oregon*." In *Pioneer Times*, vol. 2:2 (Apr. 1978), pp. 95-101.

Mostly French, many of whom settled in Osage County, Missouri. Arrival in 1843 at the port of New Orleans, 300 persons. Information includes names, ages, sex, occupations, and countries of origin.

* * *

5233
MARES, CLAIRE. "SS *Texas*, Port of Embarkation: Liverpool; Arrival Date: 30 Jan. 1882 to the Port of Baltimore, Maryland." In *Roots and Leaves*, vol. 6:2 (Summer 1983), p. 39.

These 15 arrivals were mostly stowaways from England. Names and ages given.

* * *

5235
MARES, CLAIRE. "Ship Passenger Listings, 1874 (Partial)." In *Roots and Leaves*, vol. 6:3 (Fall 1983), pp. 41-47.

Nine ships to Baltimore, Maryland, 1874, brought 270 passengers from Liverpool, England; Bremen or Bremerhaven, Germany; and Glasgow, Scotland. Age, sex, occupation, country of origin, and, often, destination given for each newly arriving immigrant.

* * *

5237
MARES, CLAIRE. *Ship Passenger Lists, Port of Baltimore [Maryland], 4 May through 30 December 1874.* [Fremont, Nebraska:] Eastern Nebraska Genealogical Society, 1984. 111p.

Some 7,500 passengers from several countries in Europe, including Russia, but nearly all from Germany and Bohemia. Age, sex, occupation, country of origin, destination, name of ship, port of embarkation, date of arrival. Of the 113 vessels involved, most sailed from Bremen.

* * *

5277
MARTIN, D.L. "A List of Names of Persons from New Brunswick Going Through to Upper Canada, 1801." (Upper Canada Sundries, R.G.S. A1 vol., pp. 675-680.) In *We Lived: A Genealogical Newsletter of New Brunswick Sources*, no. 15 (Oct. 1982), p. 186.

Names of 20 persons cited in a letter to Thos. Barclay and received in Quebec, Dec. 25, 1801.

* * *

5323
MARWOOD, ALICE. "Ship's Lists." In *The British Columbia Genealogist*, vol. 11:2 (Summer 1982), pp. 37, 40.

Arrivals in British Columbia on various ships: 40 passengers on the *Oregon*, 1861; 46 on the *Brother Jonathan* from San Francisco via Portland, 1860; 17 on the *Princess Royal* from London, 1861. All lists taken from the *Daily British Colonist*, Victoria, B.C.

* * *

5390
"MAYFLOWER PASSENGERS." In *The Boulder Genealogical Society Quarterly*, vol. 2:3 (Nov. 1970), pp. 10-15.

Names 120 persons and their places of origin, with details of happenings to those settlers after the landing in America in 1620.

* * *

5394.1 — 5394.7
MERCER, GERALD A., copier. "Naturalization Records of Riverside County, California." In *Lifeliner*.
5394.1
---Vol. 11:1 (Sept. 1975), p. 38 (1903-1904); vol. 11:2 (Dec. 1975), pp. 39-44 (1904-1907); vol. 11:3 (Mar. 1976), pp. 113-116 (1908-1910); vol. 11:4 (June 1976), pp. 193-194 (1910-1911).
5394.2
---Vol. 13:4 (June 1978), pp. 145-150 (1911-1914).
5394.3
---Vol. 14:1 (Sept. 1978), pp. 39-42 (1914-1916); vol. 14:2 (Dec. 1978), pp. 77-82 (1916-1917).
5394.4
---Vol. 15:4 (June 1980), pp. 175-181 (1918).
5394.5
---Vol. 16:3 (1980-1981), pp. 134-137 (1919-1920).
5394.6
---Vol. 17:1 (1981-1982), pp. 32-35 (1920-1921); vol. 17:2 (1981-1982), pp. 65-68, 80 (1921-1922); vol. 17:3 (1981-1982), p. 141 (1922); vol. 17:4 (1981-1982), pp. 176, 180 (1922).
5394.7
---Vol. 18:1 (1982-1982), pp. 40-43 (1923-1924); vol. 18:4 (June 1983), pp. 172-175 (1924-1925).

About 600 naturalizations, 1903-1925. Origins of the new citizens: Canada, Great Britain, and elsewhere in Europe. Most entries include dates of arrival in the United States and witnesses' names. These items replace, with additions, entry no. 5394 in the basic volume of this bibliography.

* * *

5400
MERCER, JULIA E. *Bermuda Settlers of the 17th Century: Genealogical Notes from Bermuda.* Baltimore: Genealogical Publishing Co., 1982. 276 p.

Originally published in *Tyler's Quarterly*, vols. 23-29, 1942-1947. The collected notes, retitled by the publisher, consist of abstracts of the earliest known records of Bermuda settlers and form a supplement to Hotten's *Original Lists of Persons of Quality. . .* (item no. 3283 in the basic volume of this bibliography). Many of the early settlers in Bermuda — or their descendants — removed to the mainland and were among the earliest settlers of the Carolinas, Georgia, and Virginia.

* * *

5608
MEYER, MARY KEYSOR. "List of Passengers Taken on Board the Ship, *Ornen*, of Shein, from Antwerp." In *Wisconsin State Genealogical Society Newsletter*, vol. 28:3 (Jan. 1982), pp. 139-140; vol. 28:4 (Apr. 1982), p. 201.

A hundred arrivals from Belgium and Germany to Wisconsin, 1843. Specifies ages, occupations, and countries of origin.

* * *

5630
MEYER, MARY KEYSOR. "Some Cumberland County, Pennsylvania, Naturalizations." In *National Genealogical Society Quarterly*, vol. 70:3 (Sept. 1982), p. 196.

From Ireland, 25 new citizens, with occupations given and dates of arrival in the U.S. Covers the years 1783-1801.

5633
MEYERHOLZ, HEINRICH. "Die Rumsfelds kamen aus Niedersachsen." In *Norddeutsche Familienkunde*, (1977), pt. 1, pp. 13-17.

The Rumsfelds came from Lower Saxony. The article concerns about 15 members of the Rumsfeld/Rumsfield family who came to America in the 1860s. *See also* Buesing, no. 1012.

* * *

5650
MILLER, MARCUS L. "Germantown Residents Naturalized in 1691." In *Mennonite Family History*, vol. 2:3 (July 1983), pp. 102-104.

Names of 62 new citizens in colonial Pennsylvania, many with dates of arrival in the U.S. and the names of the ships that brought them.

* * *

5723
MOCHA, FRANK, editor. *Poles in America: Bicentennial Essays*. Stevens Point, Wisconsin: Worzalla Publishing Co., 1978. 203p.

Information on many Polish immigrants. Names, ages, and ships mentioned throughout the book.

* * *

5726.1
MOELLER, KURT DETLEV. "Namen russlanddeutscher Auswanderer nach Suedamerika in den hamburgischen Auswandererlisten der Jahre 1876-1878. In *Jahrbuch 1940, Deutscher Volksbund fuer Argentinien, Buenos Aires*, pp. 141-152.

Names of Russian-German emigrants to South America in the Hamburg emigration lists for 1876-1878. Place of origin, age, destination, name of ship and date of departure. Continued in item no. 5726.2.

* * *

5726.2
MOELLER, KURT DETLEFF. "Namensliste der ersten russlanddeutschen Einwanderer, in den Jahren 1876/1878." In *Anuario, suplemento de la Revista Mensual "La Union," 1944. Jahrbuch . . . "Der Bund."* Buenos Aires: Deutscher Volksbund fuer Argentinien, pp. 132-138.

List of names of the first Russian-German immigrants, 1876-1878. Concerns arrivals in South America. A continuation of item no. 5726.1.

* * *

5745
MOLTMANN, GUNTER. *Aufbruch nach Amerika: Friedrich List und die Auswanderung aus Baden und Wuerttemberg, 1816-1817....* Tuebingen: Rainer Wunderlich, 1979. 408p.

Departure for America: Friedrich List and the emigration from Baden and Wuerttemberg, 1816-1817. . . . Includes copies and transcriptions of many newspaper notices, ships' lists, emigration permits with names, and other data, that indicate places of origin of emigrants from the duchies of Baden and Wuerttemberg in southwestern Germany who left for America during the second decade of the 19th century. Ages, destinations, and occupations also given. Covers 200-300 persons.

5747
"MONATLICHE VERSAMMLUNG DES DEUTSCHEN PIONIER-VEREINS." In *Der Deutsche Pionier*, vol. 9:3 (June 1877), pp. 126-128.

Monthly meeting of the German Pioneer Society, founded in Cincinnati in the 19th century. Pp. 126-127 contain a list of 50 newly-accepted members of the Deutscher Pionier Verein, announced at their regular monthly meeting in May 1877. Date of birth, place of origin, and year of emigration from Germany. On the same subject, see also item no. 1578 in the basic volume of this bibliography and, in this supplement, nos. 9999.3 and .6.

* * *

5755
"MONROE COUNTY [INDIANA] NATURALIZATIONS." In *The Hoosier Journal of Ancestry*.

---Vol. 7:3 (July 1980), p. 31.
---Vol. 9:2/3 (July 1982), p. 110.
---Vol. 10:1 (Mar. 1983), pp. 41-42.

Complete transcription of naturalizations dated 1854-1859 in the county records. Names, places of birth, dates and places of departure and arrival in America. Involves 53 persons in all. Contents include a list from the years 1860-1862 of names without further information.

* * *

5776
MOODY, ROSEMARY COSSMAN. "The Emigrants of Kreis Adenau." In *Illinois State Genealogical Society Quarterly*, vol. 14:1 (Spring 1982), pp. 13-18.

Refers to people from the Rhineland Palatinate in Germany. Records found by Joseph Scheben span the years 1831-1911, although the majority cover 1850-1880. Surnames only are given, but more than 700 of them, with an offer of more information from the source.

* * *

5817
MORGAN, MARY M. "Wells County [Indiana] Naturalization Final Oaths." In *The Hoosier Genealogist*, vol. 23:4 (Dec. 1983), pp. 93-95.

Names of 213 persons naturalized in Wells County. Taken from the Circuit Court Final Oath Books in 1942. Names only.

* * *

5819
MORGAN COUNTY GENEALOGICAL SOCIETY, OHIO, compiler. *Genealogical Extracts from Naturalization Records, Morgan County, Ohio.* McConnelsville, Ohio: the society, 1982. 50p.

Provides 800 names with each nationality, date of declaration of intent and date of naturalization. Other information given for some.

* * *

5820
[MORIARTY, GEORGE ANDREWS] *The English Ancestry and Connections of Early Emigrants to New England: A List of Articles Appearing in The New England Historical and Genealogical Register, 1909-1928.* Boston: Boston Evening Transcript, 1929.

During the years 1909 to 1928, *The New England Historical and Genealogical Register*, Boston, published pedigrees and clues to the English ancestry of a list of 600 early immigrants. These were reprinted in the *Boston Evening Transcript*, March 13 and March 25, 1929, compiled by G.A. Moriarty.

* * *

5825
MORRIS, JEAN S. "Western Pennsylvania Naturalizations." In *Western Pennsylvania Genealogical Society Quarterly Magazine*, vol. 8:1 (Aug. 1981), pp. 6-10.

Covers the years 1798-1799 and names 150 immigrants, with places of residence, birth dates, and dates of naturalization.

* * *

5829
MORTON ALLAN DIRECTORY *of European Passenger Steamship Arrivals for the Years 1890-1930 at the Port of New York, and for the Years 1904-1926 at the Ports of New York, Philadelphia, Boston, and Baltimore*. 1931. Reprinted, Baltimore: Genealogical Publishing Co., 1980. 268p.

A complete list taken from official sources of the dates of passenger steamship arrivals. Of course, not all were bearing immigrants, and hardly any would be entirely immigrant ships. The passenger list published on board usually showed, as first class, Americans returning to the U.S.; "zwischen," or between decks, a mixture of travelers and immigrants; and lower, or steerage, almost all immigrants. See also item no. 0254 for a consolidated ship list covering the 18th and 19th centuries.

* * *

5860
MUELLER, FRIEDRICH. "Westfaelische Auswanderer im 19. Jahrhundert — Auswanderung aus dem Regierungsbezirk Minden, Part 1: 1816-1900 (Erlaubte Auswanderung)." In *Beitraege zur westfaelischen Familienforschung*, vols. 38/39 (1980-1981), pp. 3-711.

Westphalian emigrants in the 19th century: emigration from the governmental district of Minden, part I, 1816-1900 (cases of permitted emigration). Similar in format to Mueller's earlier work, on Muenster, cited in item no. 5861 of the basic volume of this bibliography. Covers 9,632 persons, of whom 5,000 emigrated to America. Places of origin, dates of birth, countries or continents of destination. Alphabetical lists of surnames, communities of origin, and destinations.

* * *

5867.1 — 5867.2
MUIRHEAD, BEVRA J. "Alien Declarations of Intent to Become Citizens: From Book 3 in the Erie County Clerk's Office at Buffalo, 1838-1842." In *Tree Talks*.
5867.1
---Vol. 20:2 (June 1980), pp. 85-86 (Immigration and Naturalization, pp. 61-62); vol. 20:3 (Sept. 1980), pp. 145-146 (Immigration and Naturalization, pp. 63-64).
5867.2
---Vol. 21:1 (Mar. 1981), p. 21 (Immigration and Naturalization, p. 65).

A hundred names, with countries of origin and dates of declarations.

* * *

5901
MURPHY, RONALD C. "Preliminary Research in the U.S.A.: Naturalization Records." In *Ulster Genealogical and Historical Guild Newsletter*, vol. 1:8 (1982), pp. 240-251.

Records of the Franklin County Court, St. Albans, Vermont, 19th century. Names of almost 500 Irish residents with dates of declarations concerning citizenship, ages at declaration, places of origin, and places of residence in Vermont.

* * *

5911
MYER-BRUGGEY, GARY E., and MARY K. MEYER. "Passengers on Board the Ship, *Lucilla*, from Bremen to Baltimore, 3 August 1840." In *Maryland Magazine of Genealogy*, vol. 5:2 (Fall 1982), pp. 89-95.

Names 150 passengers, with ages, places of birth, places of residence in America, and occupations.

* * *

5935
MYERS, MRS. LESTER F. "Abstracts from Aliens' Declarations of Intention to Become Citizens and Other Naturalization Proceedings . . . Saratoga County [N.Y.]: Supplement." In *Tree Talks*, vol. 21:3 (Sept. 1981), p. 145 (Immigration-Naturalization, p. 67).

Adds nine names to those of the early 19th-century British and Irish immigrants listed in the December 1966 issue of *Tree Talks*. See item no. 5934 in the basic volume of this bibliography for reference to three earlier installments of this research.

* * *

5970
MYERS, ELEANOR (Mrs. Lester F.). "Naturalization Papers, 1820-1839, from Steuben County [New York]." In *Tree Talks*, vol. 21:1 (Mar. 1981), pp. 21-22 (Immigration and Naturalization, pp. 65-66); vol. 21:3 (Sept. 1981), pp. 145-148 (Immigration and Naturalization, pp. 67-70); vol. 22:2 (June 1982), p. 83 (Immigration and Naturalization, p. 71).

Lists 39 persons receiving citizenship papers. Names, places of birth, ports of embarkation, dates of arrival in the U.S., places of residence in this country, and dates of acquisition of citizenship. "Immigration and Naturalization," cited above, is a subsection of *Tree Talks*, with its own pagination.

* * *

5982
NAESETH, GERHARD B. "Another Early Passenger List Submitted." In *Budstikken*, Dec. 1981, p. 32.

One hundred passengers on the *Olav Kyre*, Bergen to Quebec, 1848. Gives age and place of origin for each.

* * *

5985
NAESETH, GERHARD B. "The 1842 Immigrants from Norway." In *Norwegian-American Studies*, vol. 25 (1972), pp. 225-257.

Contains the names of over 500 immigrants, specific places of origin, if known, some ages, and details of their life after arrival. These immigrants travelled on the *Washington*, the *Ellida*, the *Clarissa*, the *Triton*, the *Hector*, the *Tuslina*, the *Samos*, and the *Emilie*, all into New York.

*   *   *

5996
"NAMES OF THE PEOPLE LATELY ARRIVED from Ireland in the Ship *Brittania*, Jas. Clindinnon, Master." In *The Georgia Genealogical Society Quarterly*, vol. 5:2 (June 1969), pp. 100-101.

Excerpt from the March 1772 entry in "Proceedings and Minutes of the Governor and Council, August 6, 1771, to February 13, 1782," *Colonial Records of the State of Georgia*, vol. 12. Names 217 immigrants, all heads of household. Other passengers and family members not named.

*   *   *

5997
"THE NAMES OF THE PERSONS WHO CAME OUT OF ENGLAND and Arrived in Maryland on June 29, 1650, at the Charge and Cost of Robert Brooke, Esquire." In *The Family Tree* [Howard County, Maryland, Genealogical Society] no. 18 (Dec. 10, 1980), p. 2.

Lists 36 immigrants of the Brooke family with maid servants and man servants included.

*   *   *

6002
"NATURALIZATION APPLICATIONS, BEAVER COUNTY, PENNSYLVANIA." In *Gleanings: Journal of the Beaver County Genealogical Society*, vol. 8:2 (Dec. 1983), pp. 5-10.

Covers the years 1849-1854. About 300 names, each with country of origin and date of naturalization.

*   *   *

6013.7
NATURALIZATION PAPERS OF FULTON AND BEDFORD COUNTIES, PENNSYLVANIA. (Publications, vol. 5.) McConnellsburg, Pa.: Fulton County Historical Society, 1983. 72p.

A list equally divided between British and German immigrants of the nineteenth century. Involves 1,157 families. Dates of birth, places of origin, dates and places of arrival, and sometimes places settled. Names of many witnesses to declarations of intent are included.

*   *   *

6013.19
"NATURALIZATION PAPERS ON MICROFILM at San Bruno, CA, Archives." In *Santa Clara County Historical and Genealogical Society Quarterly*, vol. 19:2 (Fall 1982), pp. 29-30 (letters A-H); vol. 19:3 (Winter 1982), pp. 73-74 (H-R); vol. 19:4 (Spring 1983), pp. 88-90 (R-Z; n.s.? A-G). In progress.

A running alphabetical transcription of some California naturalization and first-papers information from the years 1846-1850. The records are housed in archives at San Bruno, California. Include dates of birth and countries of origin. A continuing feature.

6013.40
"NATURALIZATION PROCEDURES: MONTGOMERY COUNTY Records at Independence, KS." In *The Descender*, vol. 16:4 (Nov. 1983), pp. 15-17.

Provides names of 40 new citizens, most from Germany, between 1907 and 1919. Dates of naturalization given.

*   *   *

6013.55
"NATURALIZATION PROCEEDINGS — HARRIS COUNTY, TEXAS." In *The Living Tree News*, vol. 7:3 (Spring 1981), pp. 77-79.

Records from the years 1899-1903. Includes country of origin and names of witnesses. Thus far, 32 new citizens' names transcribed. This was intended to continue in later issues.

*   *   *

6099
NELSON, WILLIAM. "The Shipp Called the *Griffin* Arrived in Dellaware River. . . 1689." In *Patents and Deeds and Other Early Records of New Jersey, 1664-1703*. Paterson, N.J.: Press Printing and Publishing Co., 1899. Repr. by Genealogical Publishing Co., Baltimore, 1976, pp. 590-591.

Refers to 20 passengers, with ages and family relationships indicated. Originally titled *Documents Relating to the Colonial History of the State of New Jersey*, vol. 21, 1899, pp. 590-591; also *New Jersey Archives*, 1st ser., vol. 21. The *Patents and Deeds. . .* title was a change made by the publisher.

*   *   *

6104
NEU, HEINRICH. "Beitraege zur Geschichte der rheinischen Amerika-Auswanderung im 18. Jahrhundert." In *Rheinische Vierteljahrsblaetter*, pt. 2 (1936), pp. 176-185.

Contributions to the history of Rhenish emigration to America in the 18th century. Tells of 30 individuals or families from Germany's Rhineland who emigrated to America in the years 1752-1764 and settled in Maine.

*   *   *

6111.1 — 6111.13
"NEW ENGLAND SHIP AND PASSENGER LISTS." In *Boulder Genealogical Society Quarterly*.
6111.1
---Vol. 2:3 (Nov. 1970), pp. 10-15 (Yr. 1620, the *Mayflower*).
6111.2
---Vol. 3:1-2 (Feb./May 1971), pp. 22-26 (1622-1624).
6111.3
---Vol. 3:3 (Aug. 1971), pp. 21-24 (1625-1629).
6111.4
---Vol. 3:4 (Nov. 1971), pp. 22-25 (1630).
6111.5
---Vol. 4:1 (Feb. 1972), pp. 28-32 (1630).
6111.6
---Vol. 4:2 (May 1972), pp. 27-30 (1630).
6111.7
---Vol. 4:3 (Aug. 1972), pp. 26-30 (1630-1632).

6111.8
---Vol. 4:4 (Nov. 1972), pp. 36-39 (1633-1634).
6111.9
---Vol. 5:1 (Feb. 1973), pp. 25-29 (1634).
6111.10
---Vol. 5:2 (May 1973), pp. 23-27 (1634).
6111.11
---Vol. 5:3 (Aug. 1973), pp. 35-40 (1635).
6111.12
---Vol. 5:4 (Nov. 1973), pp. 30-34 (1635-1637).
6111.13
---Vol. 6:1 (1974-1975), pp. 28-32 (1638-1640).

Place of origin, with genealogical data and account of events after arrival in America.

* * *

6121
"NEW ORLEANS CUSTOM HOUSE Passenger Lists, Book 1, 1813-1837, Jan.-Dec. 1821." In *Irish Genealogy Digest,* Fall 1982, p. 26.

Two sailings out of Belfast in the year 1821 produce names of 24 new arrivals. The *Edw. Downes* and the brig *Edward* brought Irish and possibly others to New Orleans.

* * *

6131
"NEW U.S. CITIZENS NATURALIZED, JUNE 2, 1936, Judge Warren Steel, Presiding, Yuba County Court, Marysville, California 95901." In *Diggers Digest, Sutter-Yuba Genealogical Society,* vol. 8:2 (1981), p. 41.

Records on eleven new citizens from various countries of origin.

* * *

6154
NEWBAUER, ELLA C. "The Swiss Settlements of Madison County, Illinois." In *Transactions of the Illinois State Historical Society,* Publication 12 (1906), pp. 232-237.

Names of several 19th-century immigrants in Madison County, Ill.

* * *

6185
NICHOLSON, MARY ANN. "Stolen Children." In *The Scottish Genealogist,* vol. 29:1 (Mar. 1982), pp. 11-15.

About 100 children forcibly taken from Scotland to Philadelphia, 1697-1698. Ages, 10-16, and terms of service stipulated.

* * *

6194
NICKCHEN, JUERGEN. "Auswanderer aus dem Kirchspiel Ransweiler im 19. Jahrhundert." In *Mitteilungen zur Wanderungsgeschichte der Pfaelzer,* 1981/3; *Pfaelzisch-Rheinische Familienkunde,* Jahrgang 30, vol. 9:12, pp. 673-677.

Emigrants from the parish of Ransweiler in the 19th century. Data taken originally from churchbooks for the years 1823-1842 supply the names of 150 German emigrants. In a publication on Palatines and Rhinelanders.

6200
NIMMO, SYLVIA, editor. *New York Passenger Arrivals, 1849-1868. Passenger Lists Transcribed by Michael Cassady.* Papillion, Neb.: the editor, 1983. 118p.

Compilation of 33 passenger lists, transcribed from microfilm at the National Archives, Washington, D.C. Over 11,000 passengers, of whom 5,500 were British and 4,000 were German. Stated destination of 2,000 of them was Utah. Names, ages, occupations, countries of origin, and sex. Names of ships and ports and the dates of departure and arrival are included.

* * *

6211
"NOTES ON THE PIONEERS." In *Quarterly of the Pennsylvania German Society,* vol. 11:2 (Summer 1977), pp. 19-21.

Germans to Pennsylvania, 18th century. Names of ships and dates of arrival included, with genealogical details.

* * *

6225
NUGENT, NELL MARION. *Cavaliers and Pioneers: Abstracts of Virginia Land Patents and Grants. Supplement: Northern Neck Grants No. 1, 1690-1692.* Indexed by Susan B. Sheppard. (Virginia State Library Publications, 47.) Richmond: Virginia State Library, 1980. 18p.

Supplement to three volumes previously published (item nos. 6219-6223 in basic vol. of this bibliog.). About 160 names, with much information.

* * *

6251
"THE OATH OF ALLEGIANCE." In *The Bulletin of the Northumberland County Historical Society,* vol. 3:1 (July 1966), pp. 19-20.

About 110 persons who took oaths of allegiance in Northumberland, Virginia, in April 1652. The pledge in that year of the colonial era was of allegiance to the Commonwealth of England.

* * *

6254
"OATHS OF ALLEGIANCE, HARRIS COUNTY, TEXAS, Vol. 2, Oct. 1896." In *The Roadrunner,* vol. 8:3 (1975), pp. 3-6.

About 80 persons from various countries, with ages and dates of the swearing of allegiance.

* * *

6346
"OCHLING FAMILY as Listed on Ship Passenger List." In *Tuscarawas Pioneer Footprints,* vol. 11:3 (Aug. 1983), p. 36.

About 75 members of the Ochling family, who came to New York from Germany on the *Neptune,* February 1837.

* * *

6372.1 — 6372.2
"OHIO COUNTY [Indiana] NATURALIZATION Book 1." In *The Hoosier Journal of Ancestry.*
6372.1
---Vol. 8:3 (July 1981), pp. 219-220.
6372.2
---Vol. 9:2/3 (July 1982), p. 111.

Spans the years 1848-1852. New citizens mostly of Irish and German stock. Age, place of birth, dates and places of departure and of arrival. Intended as a continuing series.

* * *

6406.6
OLSON, LOLA. "Passenger Lists." In *Heritage Review,* vol. 13:3 (Sept. 1983), p. 47.

Names 17 Germans from Rumania crossing from Hamburg to New York in 1899. Destination was Cathay, North Dakota. Ages and occupations given.

* * *

6410.5
OLSSON, NILS WILLIAM. "Declarations of Intention and Naturalization in New Sweden, ME, 1873-1900." In *Swedish American Genealogist,* vol. 1:3 (Sept. 1981), pp. 93-118.

Good background material for study of Swedish immigration. Covers naturalizations and declarations of intention in the U.S. Superior Court of Aroostook County, Houlton, Maine. Names, years of arrival, birth dates, and much family information.

* * *

6410.10
OLSSON, NILS WILLIAM. "Declarations of Intention by Swedes in Rockford [Illinois], 1859-1870." In *Swedish American Genealogist,* vol. 1:1 (Mar. 1981), pp. 7-14.

Provides names of Swedish residents of Rockford, Illinois, in the 1860's who declared their intention to acquire citizenship. Dates of declarations included.

* * *

6410.15
OLSSON, NILS WILLIAM. "Emigrants from Gotland [Sweden] to America, 1819-1890." In *Swedish American Genealogist,* vol. 2:3 (Sept. 1982), pp. 102-109.

Provides 120 names, with much information on each. Derived from Swedish sources.

* * *

6410.20
OLSSON, NILS WILLIAM. "Naturalizations of Scandinavians in Los Angeles County [California], 1856-1887." In *Swedish American Genealogist,* vol. 3:3 (Sept. 1983), pp. 104-107.

About 50 names, with countries of allegiance, dates of declarations and naturalization, and names of witnesses.

* * *

6410.25
OLSSON, NILS WILLIAM. "Naturalizations of Swedes in Rock Island County [Illinois], 1855-1864." In *Smoke Signals, Blackhawk Genealogical Society,* vol. 10:1 (Spring 1983), pp. 8-20: and in *Swedish American Genealogist,* vol. 2:1 (Mar. 1982), pp. 18-27.

Names, dates of declarations of intention and dates of naturalization. The article also contains "Declarations of Intention of Swedes in Rock Island, Il (1855-1859)," and "Naturalizations of Swedes (Minors) in the Circuit Court of Rock Island County, Il (1858-1862)." The article on minors gives date of arrival in the U.S. and names of witnesses at the naturalization for each. About 200 persons naturalized in one decade.

* * *

6410.30
OLSSON, NILS WILLIAM. "Naturalized Scandinavian Seamen in Boston, 1815-1840." In *Swedish American Genealogist,* vol. 1:3 (Sept. 1981), pp. 125-133.

Many seamen became naturalized so they could be employed on U.S. ships. Here, over 100 are listed, 65 of them Danish. Date of each naturalization (1815-1840), age, height, complexion, and birthplace.

* * *

6410.35
OLSSON, NILS WILLIAM. "The Swedish Brothers of Minneapolis: an Early Mutual Aid Society." In *Swedish American Genealogist,* vol. 1:2 (June 1981), pp. 45-67.

List of members of the Society, 1876-1888, with, for each, the Minneapolis address, place of birth, and dates of birth, arrival in U.S., and admission to the Society. Names 284 persons.

* * *

6410.40
OLSSON, NILS WILLIAM. "A Swedish Directory for Boston, 1881." In *Swedish American Genealogist,* vol. 2:3 (Sept. 1982), pp. 97-99.

Svensk Kalender i Boston, utgifven af Eric Wretlind, Boston, 1881, has a list of Swedish Americans, with dates of birth and of arrival in America, places of origin, and Boston addresses. Olsson has published a sample sheet with names of 29 persons, ten of whom had come as immigrants.

* * *

6412.40
OLSSON, NILS WILLIAM. "Swedish Seamen Who Deserted in U.S. Ports, 1841-1858." In *Swedish American Genealogist,* vol. 3:4 (Dec. 1983), pp. 141-157.

Lists 437 Swedish seamen who left their ships in American ports. Rank, age, places of birth and residence, port where sailor jumped ship, and date.

* * *

6412.50
OLSSON, NILS WILLIAM. "Who Was Daniel Larson of Haurida?" In *Swedish American Genealogist,* vol. 2:3 (Sept. 1982), pp. 110-117.

Article includes a list of 45 passengers who arrived in Boston on board the *Montreal* on Nov. 19, 1851. Ages and occupations are given. Larson (or Larsson) led the emigrants from Sweden to North America.

* * *

6413.20
O'MAHONY, S.C. "Emigration from the Limerick Workhouse, 1848-1860." In *The Irish Ancestor,* no. 2 (1982), pp. 83-94.

Lists many Irish emigrants to the U.S.A. and some to Canada and Australia.

* * *

6413.30
O'MAHONY, S.C. "Emigration from the Workhouse at Ennistymon, Co. Clare." In *The Irish Ancestor,* 1981, no. 2, pp. 79-82.

About 50 impoverished Irish to the United States and Canada between 1850 and 1860.

* * *

6425
OVERTON, JULIE. "Naturalization Records - Clark County, Ohio." In *Ohio Records & Pioneer Families,* vol. 23:3 (July-Sept. 1982), pp. 122-123.

About 40 persons, with mention of places of origin, dates of immigration (1890-1902), places of residence in Ohio, ages, and occupations. Includes data on families.

* * *

6428.1 — 6428.16
OWEN, ROBERT E. "Lists of Luxembourgers." In *Luxembourg Society of Wisconsin Newsletter.*
6428.1
---Vol. 4:6 (June 1982), pp. 5-6.

Arrival of 55 persons from Luxembourg on seven ships, Le Havre to New York, in the years 1853-1855.

6428.2
---Vol. 4:7-8 (July-Aug. 1982), pp. 5-6.

Lists 29 Luxembourgers and 68 Dutch from two ships out of Antwerp and Le Havre to New York in the year 1856.

6428.3
---Vol. 4:9 (Sept. 1982), pp. 5-6.

Names 57 Luxembourgers and 34 Dutch on five ships sailing from Antwerp and Le Havre to New York in the years 1854-1856.

6428.4
---Vol. 4:11 (Nov. 1982), pp. 5-6.

33 Luxembourgers and 39 Dutch on eight ships, 1855-1856, Antwerp and Le Havre to New York.

6428.5
---Vol. 4:12 (Dec. 1982), pp. 5-6.

39 Luxembourgers and 35 Prussians, Dutch, and Belgians on six ships, 1855-1857 and 1882, Antwerp, Le Havre, and Liverpool to New York.

6428.6
---Vol. 5:2 (Feb. 1983), p. 8.

45 Luxembourgers on three ships, 1851-1854, Antwerp and Le Havre to New York.

6428.7
---Vol. 5:3 (Mar. 1983), pp. 3-4.

86 Luxembourgers on four ships, 1852-1855, Antwerp and Le Havre to New York.

6428.8
---Vol. 5:2 [i.e. 4] (Apr. 1983), pp. 3-4.

86 Luxembourgers on four ships, 1852-1855, Antwerp and Le Havre to New York.

6428.9
---Vol. 5:5 (May 1983), pp. 5-6.

91 Luxembourgers on two ships, 1855, Le Havre to New York.

6428.10
---Vol. 5:6 (June 1983), pp. 5-6.

108 Luxembourgers on one ship, 1857, Antwerp to New York.

6428.11
---Vol. 5:7 (July 1983), pp. 5-6.

85 Luxembourgers on five ships, 1857, Antwerp and Le Havre to New York.

6428.12
---Vol. 5:8 (Aug. 1983), pp. 5-6.

49 Luxembourgers and 13 Dutch on nine ships, 1855-1857, Antwerp and Le Havre to New York.

6428.13
---Vol. 5:8 [i.e. 9] (Sept. 1983), pp. 5-6.

106 Germans on one ship, 1856, Antwerp to New York.

6428.14
---Vol. 5:10 (Oct. 1983), pp. 5-6.

25 Luxembourgers, 30 Germans, and 5 Dutch on six ships, 1848-1864, Antwerp and Le Havre to New York.

6428.15
---Vol. 5:11 (Nov. 1983), pp. 5-6.

86 Luxembourgers on two ships, 1855, Le Havre to New York.

6428.16
---Vol. 5:12 (Dec. 1983), pp. 5-6.

78 Luxembourgers and 11 Germans on two ships, 1852-1855, Antwerp and Le Havre to New York.
All names taken from records in the U.S. National Archives, with ages, sex, occupations, places of origin, and places of arrival. Luxembourgers, while having a distinct cultural and legal identity, were often listed on ship passenger manifests under the nationality which the originator of the list apparently assumed they had. German, Prussian, Dutch, Belgian, and French are seen in the records. Names of individuals listed under these nationalities have been included in the collection of the Luxembourg Society of Wisconsin on the basis of collateral knowledge of Society members or circumstantial logic.

* * *

6508.3
"PASSENGER LISTS." In *Gaelic Gleanings*, vol. 1:3 (May 1982), pp. 100-101.

Irish passengers on the brig *Leander*, sailing from Londonderry to Wilmington in 1831. On 100 passengers, the data includes names, ages, occupations, countries of origin, and destinations.

* * *

6508.5
"PASSENGER LISTS." In *Gaelic Gleanings*, vol. 2:1 (Nov. 1982), pp. 19-20.

Irish on the brig *Paragon* out of Bangor, Wales, with a call at Cork. One hundred arrived at Newport, Rhode Island, in 1851. Names and ages listed.

* * *

6508.6
"PASSENGER LISTS." In *Gaelic Gleanings*, vol. 2:3 (May 1983), p. 115.

Scottish and Irish arrivals: the *Stephen Baldwin*, Liverpool to Philadelphia, 1845; and the brig *Sophia*, Demerara to Baltimore, 1871. Names, sex, ages, and occupations. All Irish on the *Stephen Baldwin;* Scottish on the *Sophia*. Twenty passengers in all.

* * *

6508.7
"PASSENGER LISTS." In *Gaelic Gleanings*, vol. 2:4 (Aug. 1983), pp. 160-161.

About 100 passengers on board the brig *Pleiades*, Liverpool to Wilmington, Delaware, 1831. Age, place of origin, occupation.

* * *

6508.8
"PASSENGER LISTS." In *Gaelic Gleanings*, vol. 3:1 (Nov. 1983), pp. 25-26.

All from Ireland on the *Eliza Warwick* and *Isabella G. Briggs*, Liverpool to Baltimore, in the years 1841-1842. Names and ages of the 80 passengers.

* * *

6515
"PASSENGER LISTS." In *M. C. G. S. Reporter* [Milwaukee County Genealogical Society] vol. 14:1, (Winter 1983), pp. 26-27.

Departures from Sweden and France in 1848: the bark *Charles Lottie* from Gothenburg to New York and the *Tremont* from Le Havre to New York. Names and ages of about 150 passengers in all. Data taken from National Archives microfilm M257, reel 73.

* * *

6535
"PASSENGERS ABOARD THE BUCHANNON, Newry to New York, August 1765." In *The Irish Ancestor*, vol. 12:2 (1980), p. 52.

From an article in the *Belfast Newsletter*. Names, only, of sixty passengers from the British Isles.

* * *

6572
"PASSENGERS FROM GERMANIA to the U.S., 1821-1823." In *Germanic Genealogist*, no. 14 (1978), pp. 335-345; no. 22 (1981), pp. 244-245.

About 700 passengers, various ports; age, sex, occupation. Origins: mostly German, but all from regions east of the Rhine and north of the Danube. Names of ships mentioned occasionally.

* * *

6604
"PASSENGERS ON THE MAYFLOWER." In *The Mayflower Quarterly*, vol. 46:4 (Nov. 1980), pp. 177-182.

Membership roster of the Connecticut Society of *Mayflower* Descendants, containing a list of *Mayflower* passengers with more than the usual information about them and their families.

* * *

6608
"PASSENGERS ON THE SHIP ERIN WHICH LEFT DUBLIN, Ireland, and Arrived in New York in 1811." In *The International Genealogical Exchange*, Feb. 1981, [p. 9].

Complete list of 64 arrivals, originally published in *The Shamrock*, an early New York periodical.

* * *

6656
PAULK, MICKEY McVEY. "Hancock County, Mississippi, Naturalization Records, vol. 1 (1856-1905), Books 1-2" In *The Southern Genealogist's Exchange Quarterly*, vol. 23:4 (Winter 1982), pp. 194-198.

Name, date, place of birth of about 200 persons who acquired citizenship between 1856 and (despite title date) 1923.

* * *

6659
PEARSON, MARY SPRINGER. "Naturalization Proceedings, Abstracted from vols. 1-6, 1897-1903 . . . , Court of Harris County, Texas." In *The Living Tree News*, vol. 7:2 (Winter 1980), pp. 38-40; vol. 7:3 (Spring 1981), pp. 77-79.

Names, dates, countries of origin, witnesses. Involves about 80 new citizens.

* * *

6660
PEARSON, MARY SPRINGER. "Petitions for Naturalization, District Court of Jackson County, Texas." In *The Living Tree News*, vol. 9:2 (Winter 1982), pp. 42-48.

From twenty applications for citizenship in Texas between 1890 and 1910 or 1920. Detailed information on each.

* * *

6686

PENROSE, MARYLY B. "New York Naturalizations, 1789." In *New York Genealogical and Biographical Record*, vol. 112:1 (Jan. 1981), pp. 16-17.

About 180 names, with no other information. Taken from a work entitled *Laws of the State of New York, 1792*, vol. 2, pp. 279-280.

*   *   *

6717

PETERSON, WILLIAM R., and NILS WILLIAM OLSSON. "Declarations of Intention by Swedes in Cadillac, MI, 1875-1882." In *Swedish American Genealogist*, vol. 3:1 (Mar. 1983), pp. 19-27.

Refers to declarations of intention to become citizens by more than 100 Swedish residents of Wexford County, Michigan, between 1875 and 1882. Name, age, township, place of origin, port of entry, year of arrival, and date of filing. Much family information given in the commentary.

*   *   *

6750

PHEIL, SHARON. "Passenger Lists." In *Heritage Review*, vol. 10:4 (Dec. 1980), p. 46.

Germans from Russia on the S.S. *Friesland*, Antwerp to New York, June 1900. Forty passengers destined, mostly, for the Dakotas.

*   *   *

6758

PHILLIPS, ESTYLLE, and CATHERINE SUMMERS. "Citizenships, 1852, Harrison County, Indiana; Naturalizations, 1841-1844, Harrison County, Indiana." In *Ancestral Lines*, vol. 7:1 (Winter 1981), p. 24.

Names 57 persons, with countries of origin and dates of naturalization.

*   *   *

6778

PIONEER SONS AND DAUGHTERS, compilers. *Declarations of Intent, May 1848 - Oct. 1889, Polk Co., Ia.* Des Moines: the compilers, 1983. 45p.

A list of 1,630 names, each with country of origin and filing date of the application for first papers in Polk County, Iowa.

*   *   *

6912

PRITCHETT, MORGAN H., and KLAUS WUST. "German Immigrants to Baltimore: The Passenger Lists of 1854. Part 1." In *The Report: A Journal of German-American History,* vol. 38 (1982), pp. 52-109.

Names and places of origin of 5,400 passengers, most of whom departed from Bremen. Taken from 18 passenger lists. An additional 21 lists remain to be copied.

*   *   *

6987

PUNCH, TERRENCE M. "Ansbach Troopers in Nova Scotia in the 1780s." In *The Nova Scotia Genealogist*, vol. 1:2 (1983), pp. 64-65.

Ansbach troopers were Germans who fought in the American Revolution. Twenty of them who did not return to Germany are named in a discussion of their lives in North America after the war.

*   *   *

7005

PUNCH, TERRENCE M. "Carmarthen to Halifax." In *Gaelic Gleanings*, vol. 2:3 (May 1983), pp. 96-98.

Welsh emigrants on board the schooner, *Two Brothers*, bound for Shelburne, Nova Scotia, in 1818. Almost 100 named, with their occupations.

*   *   *

7012

PUNCH, TERRENCE M. "'Foreign Protestant' Settlement in Nova Scotia from Queen Ann to the *Ann*." In *Genealogical Journal*, vol. 11:3 (Fall 1982), pp. 91-97.

The "foreign Protestants" were 100 Germans and Swiss who arrived in Canada in 1750. Queen Anne was on the British throne when Nova Scotia was ceded to the English in 1713; she died in 1715, but it was not until 35 years later that the British interested settlers from other countries to come to Nova Scotia. This 1750 crossing of the *Ann* was from Rotterdam to Halifax.

*   *   *

7016

PUNCH, TERRENCE M. "Foreign Protestants in Nova Scotia, 1750-1752." In *The Palatine Immigrant*, vol. 7:1 (Summer 1981), pp. 2-10.

Mostly German arrivals at Halifax on the *Gale* in 1752. The data provides names, ages, occupations, and places of origin of about 100 passengers.

*   *   *

7073

PUNCH, TERRENCE M. "Loyalists Whom Gilroy Missed: Ship Harbour." In *Newsletter of the Genealogical Association of Nova Scotia*, vol. 4:2 (Autumn 1982), p. 73.

Marion Gilroy, *Loyalists and Land Settlement in Nova Scotia* (1937), has an incomplete list of Loyalists, and Punch has added to it. He has also ascertained that 30 soldiers and their families were from Ireland about 1770.

*   *   *

7075

PUNCH, TERRENCE M. "Offer Made, Offer Taken: Passengers on the *Ann* to Nova Scotia, 1750." In *The Palatine Immigrant*, vol. 7:4 (Spring 1982), pp. 184-191.

A European agent named John Dick organized emigration and made attractive offers for passengers. This lists 100 of the Nova Scotia arrivals, most designating place of origin. There are variations in transcription.

7076
PUNCH, TERRENCE M. "Passenger Lists of 'Foreign Protestants' to Nova Scotia, 1751." In *Canadian Genealogist*, vol. 4:2 (1982), pp. 85-100.

German passengers on the *Speedwell* to Halifax and on the *Gale* from Rotterdam to Halifax; Swiss on the *Gale* from Rotterdam to "Nouvelle Ecosse" (Nova Scotia); Germans on the *Murdoch* and on the *Pearl*, both to *Halifax*. About 400 passengers in all.

* * *

7078
PUNCH, TERRENCE M. "Passengers on the *Aide-de-Camp.*" In *Genealogical Research in Nova Scotia*, 1978, p. 80.

Nine passengers who inserted a notice of thanks concerning their crossing in a local newspaper. All from Ireland to Halifax, Nova Scotia. 19th century.

* * *

7079
PUNCH, TERRENCE M. "Passengers on the *Pearl*, 1752." In *The Palatine Immigrant*, vol. 8:2 (Autumn 1982), pp. 63-69; and in *Northwest Trail Tracer*, vol. 4:3 (Sept. 1983), pp. 20-23.

Mostly Germans sailing out of Rotterdam for Halifax. Names, ages, occupations, places of origin for 250 persons.

* * *

7105
PUNCH, TERRENCE M. "Wann Sie in Harrietsfeld Deutsch Sprachen." In *The Nova Scotia Genealogist*, vol. 1:1 (1983), pp. 22-25.

"When in Harrietsfield speak German." A list of 35 "Hessians" (meaning German-speaking auxiliary troops in British service during the American Revolutionary War), who were granted land in Harrietsfield, near Halifax, Nova Scotia, in 1784. Much information on each settler.

* * *

7119
QUATTLEBAUM, PAUL. "German Protestants in South Carolina in 1788." In *The South Carolina Historical and Genealogical Magazine*, vol. 47:4 (Oct. 1946), pp. 195-204.

A petition of German Protestant congregations for the incorporation of their churches. From other sources, it has been determined that many were recent arrivals from Germany. This supplements Bernheim: *History of the German Settlements and of the Lutheran Church in North and South Carolina*, 1872, pp. 288-311.

* * *

7121
QUATTLEBAUM, PAUL. "Some German Protestants in South Carolina in 1794." In *The South Carolina Historical and Genealogical Magazine*, vol. 51:2 (Apr. 1950), pp. 75-77.

Petition for the incorporation of St. John's Lutheran Church and of St. Peter's (Piney Woods) Lutheran Church, listing 73 names, probably recent arrivals from Germany.

* * *

7124.1 — 7124.8
"QUERIES: A 'Can You Help' Genealogy Service." In *Clues*.
7124.1
---1979, pt. 2, pp. 15-17;
7124.2
---1980, pt. 1, pp. 73-75;
7124.3
---1981, pt. 1, pp. 70-72;
7124.4
---1981, pt. 2, pp. 19-20;
7124.5
---1982, pt. 1, pp. 66-71;
7124.6
---1982, pt. 2, pp. 47-48;
7124.7
---1983, pt. 1, pp. 66-73;
7124.8
---1983, pt. 2, pp. 28-30. In progress.

About Germans from Russia in the 1880s. Includes 300 individual names so far. Many of the queries reveal emigration data. Continuing.

* * *

7127.2 — 7127.15
"QUERIES." In *Palatine Patter*.

Item	*Issue*	*Pub. date*	*Page nos.*
7127.2	no.18	Oct. 1980	pp. 3-4
7127.4	no.20	May 1981	pp. 2-5
7127.5	no.21	Aug. 1981	pp. 5-6
7127.6	no.22	Nov. 1981	p. 4
7127.7	no.23	Feb. 1982	p. 5
7127.8	Special	May 1982	pp. 1-9
7127.9	no.25	Aug. 1982	pp. 6-8
7127.10	no.26	Nov. 1982	pp. 4-5
7127.11	no.27	Feb. 1983	pp. 5-10
7127.12	no.28	May 1983	pp. 6-11
7127.13	no.29	Aug. 1983	pp. 4-11
7127.14	no.30	Nov. 1983	pp. 6-10
7127.15	no.31	Feb. 1984	pp. 3-9 In progress.

Many of the queries from readers contain date and place of arrival or other useful information. Nos. 1-17 had few queries and no emigration data. All Germans to North America, 500 so far. 18th, 19th centuries.

* * *

7129
RACINE, JUANITA. "Caddo Parish Courthouse, Shreveport, Louisiana, Index Files, 1867-1882." In *The Genie*, vol. 15:1 (Jan. 1981), pp. 44-46.

Taken from the "Index to Judicial Records, Naturalizations," for the 1870s: 110 names.

* * *

7130
RACINE, JUANITA. "Direct Index to Civil Suits 1880-1925: Naturalizations." In *The Genie*, vol. 15:1 (Jan. 1981), p. 46; vol. 15:2 (April 1981), pp. 96-98.

Concerns Caddo Parish, Shreveport, Louisiana. Supplies 160 names.

* * *

7137
RAPP, ALICE R. "Persons from Austria, Hungary, Prussia & Russia, from the 1900 Census, Carroll Township, Cambria County, Pennsylvania." In *Eastern & Central European Genealogist*, no. 4 (1980), pp. 168-171.

Lists name, date and place of birth, and year of immigration.

* * *

7138
RAPP, ALICE R. "Research Report: Courthouse, Cambria County, Ebensburg, Pennsylvania." In *Eastern & Central European Genealogist*, no. 3 (1979), pp. 111-117.

Over 300 names, with special treatment for Kowalski-Kowal-Kowalczik variations and Lipinski-Lupinski-Lapinski variations. Dates and places of birth, places of Pennsylvania residence, sometimes dates of arrival, and of declarations of intention concerning citizenship.

* * *

7140
RASIMUS, HANS. *Auswanderer aus Jockgrim im 19. Jahrhundert.* (Schriften zur Wanderungsgeschichte der Pfaelzer, 29. Beitraege zur Heimatgeschichte, Schriftenreihe des Landkreises Germersheim, vol. 1) Kaiserslautern: n.p., 1980. 416p.

Emigrants from Jockgrim[m] in the 19th century, a West-German village in the Rhenish Palatinate. Tells of 451 departures, with half emigrating to America. Birth and marriage data, dates of emigration, and first places of settlement in America. Includes some information on their ownership of land and other possessions in Jockgrimm.

* * *

7199
RAWLINGS, GWEN. *The Pioneers of Inverness Township, Quebec: An Historical and Genealogical Story, 1800-1978.* Ed. by Elizabeth Harwood. Cheltenham, Ont.: Boston Mills Press, 1979, pp. 18-23.

First settlers, 1819; Ulster Scots arrive, 1827-1830; Arran Scots arrive, 1829-1832. Much on Megantic County, Quebec.

* * *

7200
RAY, MAGDALA T. "Wisconsin-Bound Passengers on Board the Ship *Marianne*, Arrived Baltimore, 18 July 1855, from Bremen." In *Wisconsin State Genealogical Society Newsletter*, vol. 30:2 (Sept. 1983), p. 83.

German passengers on the *Marianne* and the *Admiral* in 1855 and on the *Columbia* in 1856 landed at Baltimore en route to Wisconsin. Names 28 persons, with indication of ages, sex, and occupations.

* * *

7202
REAMAN, GEORGE ELMORE. *The Trail of the Black Walnut.* [Toronto] McClelland & Stewart, 1957.

Appendix A, pp. 204-208, gives locations and dates of first settlements in Upper Canada, with first recorded settlers and dates; Appendix B, pp. 209-220, tells of persons or families migrating from the American colonies to Upper Canada: name, place migrated from, date (1776-1834), place migrated to, with other information, mainly family and religion. Appendix C, p. 221, includes a list of names from a survey of the River Thames, Ontario, 1793; Appendix D, p. 222, contains assessment statistics from Somerset County, Pennsylvania, in 1802, with names of some who went to Canada and settled in Vaughan Township, York County, Ontario; Appendix E, pp. 223-225, gives a comparison of family names of the earliest settlers in Ontario's Waterloo Township with names in the Kaiserslautern-Pfalz area in Germany, as prepared by Felix Braun. This work is available in more recent editions or as reprint.

* * *

7204
REAMAN, G. ELMORE. *The Trail of the Huguenots in Europe, the United States, South Africa and Canada.* London: Frederick Muller Ltd., 1963; repr. Baltimore: Genealogical Publishing Co., 1966, 1972.

Part 4, "The Trail Crosses the Atlantic," records Huguenots in American colonies: South and North Carolina; New England (Rhode Island, Boston); New York, Pennsylvania, Virginia; and in Canada (Maritimes, Ontario, Niagara, Bay of Quinte, Essex, and Kent). There are many references to family names of Huguenots, and on pp. 280-298 are listed full names with dates of arrival. Late 17th century and much of 18th century.

* * *

7228
"A RECORD OF THE PERSONS WHO HAVE DECLARED THEIR INTENTION TO BECOME CITIZENS of the United States of America Before the Clerk of the District Court of the U.S., Within and for the Third Judicial District in the Territory of Oregon, 1850-1853." In *Olympia* [Washington] *Genealogical Society Quarterly*, Oct. 1982, pp. 103-109.

Untranscribed facsimile records of first papers for about 200 persons. Countries of origin and dates of declarations included.

* * *

7242
REEB, PAUL. "They Were 'Russians' Viewed with Favor." In *Heritage Review*, vol. 13:4 (Dec. 1983), pp. 29-33.

Discusses 12 families who left Russia in 1889 and traveled to Scotland, South Dakota, with the intention of settling ultimately in Colorado.

* * *

7323
"RETURN, IN REFERENCE TO THE EXPENSES OF TRANSPORT of Emigrants over the Red River Route During the Summer of 1871." In *Dominion Sessional Papers*, 1872 (no. 7), SP 64, Ottawa, pp. 1-7.

Also has title, "Return Shewing Number of Emigrants Passed Over the Route from Fort William to Fort Garry for year ended Dec. 1871." Refers to about 125 immigrants: names, ages, countries of origin, trades or occupations, religious denominations, and last previous places of residence. Most were from the United Kingdom.

* * *

7370
RICHARDS, MATTHIAS HENRY. *The German Emigration from the New York Province into Pennsylvania.* (The Pennsylvania-German Society Proceedings and Addresses . . . 1898. Vol. 9, 1899.) Lancaster, Pa.: the society, 1899, pp. 395-397.

A list of about 150 first settlers from New York to the area of Tulpehocken, Pennsylvania, in the early 1700s. Many taken from Rupp (item no. 7820 in the basic volume of this bibliography). Names only. See annotation for item 0889 in the basic volume for information on the overseas origins of these settlers.

* * *

7470
"RILEY COUNTY, KANSAS, NATURALIZATION RECORDS, 1866-1892." In *Kansas Kin*, vol. 19:3 (Aug. 1981), pp. 48-49, 55.

Names of over 500 new citizens, with page references to the original entries in the district court records of Manhattan, Kansas. Additional information not copied.

* * *

7480
RILING, MILDRED. "Governor Spotswood's Germans." In *The Palatine Immigrant*, vol. 7:3 (Winter 1982), pp. 109-111.

Lutherans and other German Protestants brought to Virginia between 1714 and 1717 by Governor Alexander Spotswood (1676-1740). Cites 40 names. Taken from W.W. Scott, *A History of Orange County, Virginia* (1970, repr. 1974) and the *Virginia Magazine of History* vol. 12, pp. 367-370, with corrections and additions by the author.

* * *

7510.1 — 7510.2
RINGUETTE, ADRIEN L. "From the Province of Perche to New France, and from the Province of Quebec to New England." In *French Canadian and Acadian Genealogical Review.*
7510.1
---Vol. 8:1-2 (1980), pp. 37-109.
7510.2
---Vol. 9:1-4 (1981), pp. 194-229.

Lists many French to America and some from Canada to New England, with dates of emigration between 1613 and 1640. Mostly concerns the Ringuette and Lauthier families moving from Perche to Canada and some then from Quebec to New England.

* * *

7515.1 — 7515.2
"RIPLEY COUNTY [Indiana] NATURALIZATIONS." In *The Hoosier Journal of Ancestry.*
7515.1
---Vol. 1:2 (Apr. 1969), p. 4.
7515.2
---Vol. 5:1 (Jan. 1978), p. 23.

Beginning of transcription of records from the 1850s. Age, dates of immigration and naturalization, ports of departure and arrival. Many German names. Planned for continuation.

* * *

7521
RITTER, ERNST. "Auswanderung aus Lippe-Detmold nach Amerika, 1851, 1861, 1863-1866." In *Norddeutsche Familienkunde*, Jahrgang 30, pt. 2 (Apr.-June 1981), pp. 170-178.

Emigration from Lippe-Detmold to America, 1851, 1861, 1863-1866. Detmold was the capital of this former state of Lippe in N.W. Germany. Compiled from notices appearing in the newspaper, *Fuerstlich Lippisches Regierungs- und Anzeigeblatt* of Detmold, giving names of about 200 citizens who emigrated to America. Place of origin and date of newspaper item given for each.

* * *

7607
ROBERTS, CHARLES R. "The First Swiss Settlements in America." In *Lehigh County* [Pennsylvania] *Historical Society, Annual Publication*, vol. 3, (1923), pp. 9-13.

Names of several 18th-century immigrants from Switzerland.

* * *

7621
ROBERTSON, LOIS, contributor. "Ship List of North German Bark *Goeshe*, 3 July 1868." In *Illinois State Genealogical Society Quarterly*, vol. 9:2 (Summer 1977), pp. 129-130.

Identical with the article in *Midwest Genealogical Register* (item no. 7620 in the basic volume of this bibliography). Reprinted in the *I.S.G.S.Q.* because a great number of these immigrants stated that their destination was Illinois.

* * *

7640
ROCKETT, CHARLES WHITLOCK. *Some Shipboard Passengers of Captain John Rockett from Europe to New York City (1828-1841).* Mission Viejo, Calif.: the compiler, 1983. 46 p.

Lists 1,500 passengers aboard packet ships sailing from Le Havre to New York and commanded by Capt. John Rockett between 1828 and 1842. Passengers were largely from France, Germany, and Switzerland. Names, ages, sex, occupations, and countries of origin are given.

7664
ROGERS, CHARLOTTE SCHMIDT. "Naturalizations & Declarations of Belgian Glassworkers of Jeannette, Westmoreland County [Pennsylvania]." In *Western Pennsylvania Genealogical Society Quarterly*, vol. 9:1 (Aug. 1982), pp. 18-26.

Spans the years 1889-1904 and involves 300 persons. Names, ages, places of residence, dates of declaration of intention to acquire citizenship and of naturalization, and names of witnesses or sponsors.

* * *

7667
ROGERS, ELWIN E. "Almost Scandinavian: Scandinavian Immigrant Experience in Grant County [South Dakota], 1877-1920." In *South Dakota Historical Collections*, vol. 41 (1982), pp. 439-452.

Appendix A lists about 425 Scandinavian landowners in Grant County by township through 1901: name, township, plat, date (1881-1901). Appendix B, Scandinavian-born residents in Grant County, 1880, by township. About 200, with ages, places of birth (mostly Sweden and Norway), and occupations.

* * *

7755
"ROWAN COUNTY, N.C., NATURALIZATION RECORDS, from the District of Salisbury." In *The Palatine Immigrant*, vol. 6:1 (Summer 1980), pp. 5-9.

Names of about 100 persons naturalized in North Carolina between 1763 and 1767 and of a few German immigrants who had settled west of the Catawba River, 1760s-1780s.

* * *

7765
ROYER, DONALD M. "The French Huguenot, Palatine, Lancaster Co. Connection: A Treatise on the French Huguenot Roots of the Royer Family of Lancaster County [Pennsylvania]." In *The Palatine Immigrant*, vol. 9:2 (Autumn 1983), pp. 72-81.

A good discussion of the Huguenots and their exodus from Germany. Pages 79-81 list some French Huguenot settlers in Lancaster County in the early 18th century. Extracted from Stapleton, *Memorials of the Huguenots in America* . . . , 1901 (item no. 8935 in the basic volume of this bibliography).

* * *

7840.1 — 7840.51
"SACRAMENTO COUNTY, CALIFORNIA: Extracts from 'The Great Register,' 1860-1871." In *Genealogical Research News* [Carmichael, California].
7840.1
---Vol. 5:9 (Sept. 1967), pp. 3-6 (Letter A).
7840.2
---Vol. 5:10 (Oct. 1967), pp. 7-10 (A).
7840.3
---Vol. 5:11 (Nov. 1967), pp. 11-14 (A).
7840.4
---Vol. 5:12 (Dec. 1967), pp. 1-6 (A, B).
7840.5
---Vol. 6:1 (Jan. 1968), pp. 7-10 (B).
7840.6
---Vol. 6:2 (Feb. 1968), pp. 15-20 (B).
7840.7
---Vol. 6:3 (Mar. 1968), pp. 9-16 (B).
7840.8
---Vol. 6:4 (Apr. 1968), pp. 9-16 (B).
7840.9
---Vol. 6:5 (May 1968), pp. 13-20 (B).
7840.10
---Vol. 6:6 (June 1968), pp. 13-20 (B).
7840.11
---Vol. 6:7 (July 1968), pp. 7-14 (B).
7840.12
---Vol. 6:8 (Aug. 1968), pp. 13-20 (B).
7840.13
---Vol. 6:9 (Sept. 1968), pp. 1-8 (B).
7840.14
---Vol. 6:10 (Oct. 1968), pp. 3-13 (B, C).
7840.15
---Vol. 6:11 (Nov. 1968), pp. 11-18 (C).
7840.16
---Vol. 6:12 (Dec. 1968), pp. 13-20 (C).
7840.17
---Vol. 7:1 (Jan. 1969), pp. 11-18 (C).
7840.18
---Vol. 7:2 (Feb. 1969), pp. 9-16 (C, D).
7840.19
---Vol. 7:3 (Mar. 1969), pp. 11-18 (D).
7840.20
---Vol. 7:4 (Apr. 1969), pp. 3-10 (D).
7840.21
---Vol. 7:5 (May 1969), pp. 1-8 (D-F).
7840.22
---Vol. 7:6 (June 1969), pp. 11-18 (F).
7840.23
---Vol. 7:7 (July 1969), pp. 3-8 (G).
7840.24
---Vol. 7:8 (Aug. 1969), pp. 11-16 (G, H).
7840.25
---Vol. 7:9 (Sept. 1969), pp. 11-18 (F-H).
7840.26
---Vol. 7:10-11 (Oct.-Nov. 1969), pp. 13-24 (H).
7840.27
---Vol. 7:12 (Dec. 1969), pp. 1-8 (H-J).
7840.28
---Vol. 8:1 (Jan. 1970), pp. 5-12 (J, K).
7840.29
---Vol. 8:2 (Feb. 1970), pp. 41-42 (K).
7840.30
---Vol. 8:3 (Mar. 1970), pp. 83-86 (K).
7840.31
---Vol. 8:4 (Apr. 1970), pp. 97-104 (K, L).
7840.32
---Vol. 8:5 (May 1970), pp. 145-150 (L).
7840.33
---Vol. 8:6 (June 1970), pp. 168-175 (L, M).
7840.34
---Vol. 8:7 (July 1970), pp. 182-193 (M).
7840.35
---Vol. 8:8 (Aug. 1970), pp. 225-236 (M).
7840.36
---Vol. 8:9 (Sept. 1970), pp. 257-262 (M).

7840.37
---Vol. 9:1 (Feb. 1971), pp. 11-18 (M).
7840.38
---Vol. 9:2 (Mar. 1971), pp. 39-40 (N).
7840.39
---Vol. 9:3 (Apr. 1971), pp. 77-82 (N).
7840.40
---Vol. 9:4 (May 1971), pp. 119-120 (N, O).
7840.41
---Vol. 9:5 (June 1971), pp. 150-157 (O).
7840.42
---Vol. 9:6 (July 1971), pp. 171-178 (O).
7840.43
---Vol. 10:1 (Jan./Feb. 1972), pp. 3-10 (O, P).
7840.44
---Vol. 10:2 (Mar./Apr. 1972), pp. 45-52 (P).
7840.45
---Vol. 10:3 (May/June 1972), pp. 81- 88 (P).
7840.46
---Vol. 10:4 (July/Aug. 1972), pp. 213-220 (P).
7840.47
---Vol. 10:5 (Sept./Oct. 1972), pp. 238-246 (P).
7840.48
---Vol. 10:6 (Nov./Dec. 1972), pp. 259-266 (P-R).
7840.49
---Vol. 11:1 (Jan.-Mar. 1973), pp. 21-26 (R).
7840.50
---Vol. 11:2 (Apr.-June 1973), pp. 45-52 (R).
7840.51
---Vol. 11:3 (July-Sept. 1973), pp. 69-76 (R . . .).
No others published.

Title varies. Compiled originally by Lucile B. Rowe, later by W.K. Holbrook, Pauline Boden, and possibly others. About 4,000 names in all, with ages, places of birth, occupations, places of residence, dates and places of naturalization, names of courts, dates of registration, dates sworn. The Great Registers were early voter registration records. See item no. 1890 in our basic volume for more on the Great Registers in California counties.

* * *

7846
SADOWSKY, LORRAINE. "Passenger Lists." In *Heritage Review*, vol. 12:1 (Feb. 1982), pp. 39-40.

Germans from Russia, Bremen to New York, 1889 and 1898. Names, ages, occupations, places of last residence, and the destinations: Eureka and Bowdle, South Dakota, for 150 arrivals.

* * *

7852
SAINSBURY, W. NOEL, editor. "A List of His Majesty's Subjects and Slaves Transported . . . to Jamaica, 1675." In *Calendar of State Papers. Colonial Ser., 1675-1676.* London: Her Majesty's Stationery Office, 1893. Vol. 9, pp. 285-287.

Names 250 persons traveling to Jamaica on the *Hercules*, the *America*, and the *Henry and Sarah* in 1675. Some 950 slaves were also transported on these crossings, but their names are not listed.

* * *

7855
SALINGER, SHARON V. "Send No More Women: Female Servants in Eighteenth-Century Philadelphia." In *The Pennsylvania Magazine*, vol. 107:1 (Jan. 1983), pp. 29-48.

Lists a few women who came to Philadelphia, mostly from Great Britain.

* * *

7896
SAUER, PHILIP VON ROHR. "Heinrich von Rohr and the Great Emigration of 1839." In *Concordia Historical Institute Quarterly,* vol. 56:2 (Summer 1983), pp. 64-70.

Tells of the emigration of 1,239 Old Lutherans from Hamburg, Germany, to New York via Liverpool. The final destination: Buffalo, N.Y., in 1839. Names several of the emigrants and describes the part Heinrich von Rohr played in organizing the emigration.

* * *

7899
SAUNDERS, DOROTHY CHAPMAN. "Huguenot & Dutch Settlers of New Amsterdam & New Jersey." In *The Second Boat*, vol. 4:3 (Nov. 1983), pp. 89-94.

About 60 "additional founders of American families," who came to New York between 1630 and 1667. Includes some not in Colket's *Founders of Early American Families* (item no. 1262 in the basic volume of this bibliography). Date and place of birth, date of arrival in the U.S., sometimes name of ship. Many of these settlers were from Holland. Some details of their lives in America are given.

* * *

7912
SCARLOTT, JEAN. *Court Appointed and Chosen Guardians, Carroll County, Ohio, from Will Book A, 1833-1843.* Carrollton, Ohio: Carroll County Genealogical Society, 1981, pp. 14-16.

Alien and naturalization records, Common Pleas Journal A, 1833-1839. Provides 150 names, with page reference.

* * *

7945
SCHALL, NED. "Passenger Lists." In *Heritage Review*, vol. 10:4 (Dec. 1980), pp. 46-47.

Mention of the Russian colonies of origin in this list of 200 Germans from Russia in 1893. Names, ages, and occupations are given. Crossing was from Bremen to New York on the S.S. *Lahn* and the *H.H. Meier*.

* * *

7948
SCHALL, NED. "Passenger Lists." In *Heritage Review*, vol. 12:3 (Sept. 1982), pp. 43-44.

Germans from Russia, Bremen to New York, 1889 and 1893. Names, ages, and occupations of 170 immigrants destined to settle in the Dakotas.

* * *

7951.3 — 7951.5
SCHALL, NED. "Passenger Lists." In *Heritage Review.*
7951.3
---Vol. 13:1 (Feb. 1983), p. 37.
7951.5
---Vol. 13:3 (Sept. 1983), p. 47.

Germans from Russia in the years 1888 and 1889, all destined for the Dakota Territory. Crossing was from Bremen to New York. Names, ages, and occupations given for about 175 new arrivals.

* * *

8010
SCHARF, J. THOMAS, and THOMPSON WESTCOTT. "The Swedish Settlements on the Delaware." In *History of Philadelphia, 1609-1884*. Philadelphia: L.H. Everts, 1884. Vol. 1, pp. 61-71.

Lists several persons who came in the 17th century.

* * *

8042
SCHELBERT, LEO, and SANDRA LUEBKING. "Swiss Mennonite Family Names: An Annotated Checklist." In *Pennsylvania Folklife*, vol. 26:5 (Summer 1977), pp. 2-24.

A study of the migration of Swiss Brethren in the 17th century and, later, their departure for America, chiefly to Pennsylvania in the 18th century. Lists 182 families (with variations in the spelling of names), details of emigration, and mention of final destinations. Also in item no. 9968, Yoder, *Rhineland Emigrants*, pp. 122-144.

* * *

8197
SCOTT, KENNETH. *Early New York Naturalizations: Abstracts of Naturalizations Records from Federal, State, and Local Courts, 1792-1840*. Baltimore: Genealogical Publishing Co., 1981. 452p.

Refers to records on 10,000 persons and their declarations of intention to acquire citizenship and their naturalization. Many include family information. Name, age, place of residence, place of birth, port and approximate date of arrival in America, sometimes the occupation or trade.

* * *

8209
SCOTT, KENNETH. "New Jersey Naturalization Records, 1838-1844." In *National Genealogical Society Quarterly*, vol. 69:1 (Mar. 1981), pp. 27-33.

Involves 190 persons, specifying country of origin, often date of arrival, with port and miscellaneous other information.

* * *

8250
SCOTT, KENNETH. "Some New Haven County, Connecticut, Naturalizations, 1803-1844." In *National Genealogical Society Quarterly*, vol. 71:3 (Sept. 1983), pp. 217-219.

A sampling of 73 names taken from a large collection available in the Connecticut State Library in Hartford. Date and place of birth, and sometimes date and place of arrival, with date of naturalization and name of the court.

8278
SEABURY, JOHN ALDEN. "A Record of the Names of the Passengers on the Good Ship *Mayflower* in December 1620, from Whom Descent May Now be Proved. . . ." In *The Mayflower and Alden Kindred Historiographer*, vol. 2:4 (Nov. 1923), pp. 26-35.

Traces descendants of *Mayflower* passengers to the fourth generation, listing 1,069 persons.

* * *

8361.1 — 8361.9
SEWELL, PATRICIA. "Great Register - San Diego County, 1866-1873." In *San Diego Leaves and Saplings.*
8361.1
---(A,B) vol. 1:1 (Winter 1973), pp. 25-28 (and pp. 1-4); (B) vol. 1:2 (Spring 1973), pp. 53-56; (B) vol. 1:3 (Summer 1973), pp. 93-96 (and pp. 5-8); (B,C) vol. 1:4 (Winter [i.e., Fall?] 1973), pp. 129-132 (and pp. 9-12).
8361.2
---(C) vol. 2:2 (Spring 1974), pp. 45-50 (and pp. 13-16); (C,D) vol. 2:3 (Summer 1974), pp. 81-84 (and pp. 17-20); (D,E) vol. 2:4 (Fall 1974), pp. 117-120 (and pp. 21-24).
8361.3
---(E,F) vol. 3:1 (Winter 1975), pp. 7-10 (and pp. 25-28); (F,G) vol. 3:2 (Spring 1975), pp. 43-46 (and pp. 29-32); (G,H) vol. 3:3 (Summer 1975), pp. 79-82 (and pp. 33-36); (H) vol. 3:4 (Fall 1975), pp. 115-118 (and pp. 37-40).
8361.4
---(H-K) vol. 4:1 (Winter 1976), pp. 7-10 (and pp. 41-44); (K,L) vol. 4:2 (Spring 1976), pp. 73-76 (and pp. 45-48); (L,M) vol. 4:3 (Summer 1976), pp. 103-108 (and pp. 49-54); (M) vol. 4:4 (Fall 1976), pp. 145-150 (and pp. 55-60).
8361.5
---(M,N) vol. 5:1 (Winter 1977), pp. 27-28 (and pp. 61-62); (N-P) vol. 5:4 (Fall 1977), pp. 128-131 (and pp. 63-66).
8361.6
---(P-R) vol. 6:3 (Summer 1978), pp. 103-106 (and pp. 67-70).
8361.7
---(R) vol. 7:2 (Spring 1979), pp. 63-66 (and pp. 71-74); (R) vol. 7:3 (Summer 1979), pp. 99-102 (and pp. 75-78); (R,S) vol. 7:4 (Fall 1979), pp. 133-138 (and pp. 79-84).
8361.8
---(S) vol. 8:1 (Winter 1980), pp. 15-18 (and pp. 85-88); (S) vol. 8:2 (Spring 1980), pp. 68-71 (and pp. 89-92); (S) vol. 8:3 (Summer 1980), pp. 100-105 (and pp. 93-98); (S,T) vol. 8:4 (Fall 1980), pp. 138-143 (and pp. 99-104).
8361.9
---(T-W) vol. 9:1 (Winter 1981), pp. 31-40 (and pp. 105-114); (W-Z) vol. 9:2 (Spring 1981), pp. 19-36 (and pp. 115-132); (Omissions) vol. 9:3 (Summer 1981), pp. 99-101 (and pp. 133-135).

Transcription of names A through Z, with emendations at the end, from records on about 460 eligible voters. About 25 percent of them were immigrants, who gave dates of naturalization. For every entry: name, address, age, and occupation.

* * *

8361.30 — 8361.32
SEWELL, PATRICIA. "Great Register - San Diego County, 1880-1887." In *San Diego Leaves and Saplings.*
8361.30
---(A-B) Vol. 9:2 (Spring 1981), pp. 19-36 (and pp. 115-132); (A-B) vol. 9:3 (Summer 1981), pp. 102-110 (and pp. 136-144); (B) vol. 9:4 (Fall 1981), pp. 111-128 (and pp. 145-162).
8361.31
---(B-C) Vol. 10:1 (Jan-Mar. 1982), pp. 13-24 (and pp. 163-174); (C) vol. 10:2 (Apr.-June 1982), pp. 37-44 (and pp. 175-182); (C) vol. 10:3 (July-Sept. 1982), pp. 77-87 (and pp. 183-192); (C-D) vol. 10:4 (Oct.-Dec. 1982), pp. 121-130 (and pp. 193-202).
8361.32
---(D) Vol. 11:1 (Jan.-Mar. 1983), pp. 1-8 (and pp. 203-210); (D-E) vol. 11:2 (Apr.-June 1983), pp. 41-48 (and pp. 211-218); (E-F) vol. 11:3 (July-Sept. 1983), pp. 79-88 (pp. 219-228); (F) vol. 11:4 (Oct.-Dec. 1983), pp. 119-124 (and pp. 229-234). In progress.

Focuses on California in the 1870s, with about 1,000 names and addresses taken from voter registration lists of the time (which is what Great Registers were). Foreign-born entries include date of naturalization. Covers names A-F. Continuing in later issues.

* * *

8363
SEYFERT, HON. A.G. "Migration of Lancaster County [Pennsylvania] Mennonites to Waterloo County, Ontario, Canada, from 1800 to 1825." *Papers Read Before the Lancaster County Historical Society, March 5, 1926,* vol. 30:3, pp. 33-41.

Many names, Most from Holland, Germany, and Switzerland.

* * *

8365.6 — 8365.11
SHELBY COUNTY GENEALOGICAL SOCIETY [Ohio]. "Certificate of Citizenship Granted, from Minute Books, Shelby County, Clerk of Courts." In *Shelbyana.*
8365.6
---No. 7 (Apr. 1981), pp. 11-12. Book 4 (1841-1843).
8365.7
---No. 9 (Oct. 1981), pp. 11-12. Book 5 (1843-1844).
8365.8
---No. 10 (Jan. 1982), pp. 11-12. Book 6 (1844-1848).
8365.9
---No. 11 (Apr. 1982), pp. 11-12. Book 7 (1848-1852).
8365.10
---No. 13 (Oct. 1982), p. 17. Book 8 (1853-1854).
8365.11
---No. 19 (Apr. 1984), pp. 9-11. Book 8 (1854-1858).

Names of 300 persons, with countries of origin and sometimes ages. For earlier instalments of this research, covering the years 1820-1841, see item nos. 8365.52-8365.57.

* * *

8365.25 — 8365.27
SHELBY COUNTY GENEALOGICAL SOCIETY [Ohio]. "Declarations of Intent, from Minute Books, Shelby County, Clerk of Courts Office." In *Shelbyana.*
8365.25
---No. 7 (Jan. 1981), p. 12. Book 4 (1841-1843).
8365.26
---No. 9 (Oct. 1981), p. 12. Book 5 (1843).
8365.27
---No. 10 (Jan. 1982), p. 12. Book 6 (1844-1848).

Alien residents obtaining first papers for citizenship between 1841 and 1848 in Ohio's Shelby County numbered 56. Various countries of origin.

* * *

8365.40 — 8365.45
SHELBY COUNTY GENEALOGICAL SOCIETY [Ohio]. "Naturalization Records." In *Shelbyana.*
8365.40
---No. 14 (Jan. 1983), pp. 11-12 (A-He).
8365.41
---No. 15 (Apr. 1983), pp. 9-10 (He-Schn).
8365.42
---No. 16 (July 1983), pp. 9-10 (Scho-Z; n.s.? A-Br).
8365.43
---No. 17 (Oct. 1983), pp. 9-10 (Bu-La).
8365.44
---No. 18 (Jan. 1984), pp. 9-10 (La-St).
8365.45
---No. 19 (Apr. 1984), p. 9 (St-Z).

Transcription of new-citizen records for the years 1814-1856. The first issues above include 220 names; the later issues (the new series?) provide about 200. Many entries provide information on countries of origin and the name of the place the document (for citizenship papers) was executed. For others naturalized in Shelby County in some of these same years, see items above and below.

* * *

8365.52 — 8365.57
SHELBY COUNTY GENEALOGICAL SOCIETY [Ohio]. "Naturalizations, Taken from the Minute Books in the Clerk of Courts Office, Shelby Co., Ohio." In *Shelbyana.*
8365.52
---No. 2 (Jan. 1980), pp. 11-13. Books 1-3 (1820-1837).
8365.53
---No. 8 (July 1981), p. 11. Book 1-A (1824-1833).
8365.54
---No. 3 (Apr. 1980), pp. 11-12. Book 3 (1837-1838).
8365.55
---No. 4 (July 1980), pp. 11-12. Book 3 (1838-1839).
8365.56
---No. 5 (Oct. 1980), pp. 11-12. Book 3 (1839-1840).
8365.57
---No. 6 (Jan. 1981), pp. 11-12. Book 4 (1840-1841).

Provides full names, ages, and countries of origin of nearly 200 new citizens. In 1981 the title changed to "Certificate of Citizenship Granted, from Minute Books, Shelby Co., Clerk of Courts" (item nos. 8365.6-8365.11). Compiled by Barbara Adams and, later, by members of the Shelby County Genealogical Society. Replaces and adds to the data in item nos. 0050-0052 in the basic volume of this bibliography.

* * *

8368
SHELLEY, JANE, and ELSIE M. WASSER. *Naturalization and Intentions of Madison County, Illinois: An Index 1816-1900*. Edwardsville, Ill.: the compilers, 1983. 163p.

Almost 10,000 new citizens listed in this Illinois county during the 19th century. Names, dates of declarations of intention to acquire citizenship, dates of naturalization, and citations of source in the original records.

* * *

8395
SHERMAN, JOHN H. "'Second Boat' Ancestors." In *The Second Boat*, vol. 4:2 (Aug. 1983), pp. 49-55.

John Sherman's 346 ancestors listed. Many entries name the ships and indicate dates of arrival.

* * *

8404
SHIELTZ, RUTH, and RITA TIMMERMAN. "Naturalization Records, Mercer County, Ohio." In *Miami Valley Genealogical Society, Genealogical Aids Bulletin*, vol. 12:2 (Fall 1982), p. 53.

German immigrants, primarily, new citizens between 1852 and 1884 in Ohio. Involves 26 persons: Names, countries of origin, ages, dates of first papers, and dates of acquisition of citizenship.

* * *

8408
SHILSTONE, E.M. "A List of Persons Who Left Barbados in the Year 1679." In *The Journal of the Barbados Museum and Historical Society*, vol. 1:3 (May 1934), pp. 155-180.

Records taken from the Public Record Office, London, concerning about 500 persons who left Barbados for Virginia, New York, Jamaica, and elsewhere. Dates, ships, and destinations. Article submitted to the *Journal* by the Honorary Secretary of the Barbados Museum.

* * *

8426.1 — 8426.6
"SHIP PASSENGER LISTS." In *The Family Tree*.
8426.1
---Vol. 1:1 (July 1969), pp. 18-30.
8426.2
---Vol. 1:2 (?Aug. 1969), pp. 14-32, 56.
8426.3
---Vol. 1:3 (Nov.-Dec. 1969), pp. 3-19, 41.
8426.4
---Vol. 1:4 (Jan.-Feb. 1970), pp. 6-17, 67.
8426.5
---Vol. 1:5 (Mar.-Apr. 1970), pp. 24-32, 42-52.
8426.6
---Vol. 1:6 (May-June 1970), pp. 6-26.

Refers to emigration from the British Isles in the years 1634-1635, the 1680s, and 1811-1816. It reprints lists published in four other sources: Drake, Hotten, Nicholson, and Hacket & Early (item nos. 1672, 3283, 6179, and 2859, respectively, in the main volume of this bibliography). The series concludes in the first issue of *Family Tree's* vol. 2 (July-Aug. 1970): item no. 8425 in the basic volume of this bibliography. Altogether there are about 4,000 names, with dates of arrival.

8435
SHORROCKS, D. M. M. "Transportation of Felons from Sandwich [Kent, England] to Virginia, 1721-1773." In *The Virginia Magazine of History and Biography*, vol. 68:3 (July 1960), pp. 295-299.

Names of a few prisoners and the dates of their transportation to the colonies. The article describes prison methods at Sandwich.

* * *

8484.1 — 8484.38
SIMPSON, WILOGENE, compiler. "Great Register, Siskiyou County, 1866-1878: Registered Voters in Siskiyou County, California." In *Genealogical Society of Siskiyou County*.
8484.1
---Vol. 1:1 (Fall 1972), pp. 15-17 (Letter A).
8484.2
---Vol. 1:2 (Winter 1972), pp. 13-15 (A, B).
8484.3
---Vol. 1:3 (Spring 1972), pp. 31-33.(B).
8484.4
---Vol. 1:4 (Summer 1973), pp. 2-4 (B).
8484.5
---Vol. 2:1 (Fall 1973), pp. 4-6 (B, C).
8484.6
---Vol. 2:2 (Winter 1973), pp. 4-6 (C).
8484.7
---Vol. 2:3 (Spring 1974), pp. 3-5 (C, D).
8484.8
---Vol. 2:4 (Summer 1974), pp. 3-5 (D).
8484.9
---Vol. 3:1 (Fall 1974), pp. 3-5 (D, E).
8484.10
---Vol. 3:2 (Winter 1974), pp. 3-5 (E).
8484.11
---Vol. 3:3 (Spring 1975), pp. 4-5 (F).
8484.12
---Vol. 3:4 (Summer 1975), pp. 16-17 (F).
8484.13
---Vol. 4:1 (Fall 1975), pp. 20-21 (F, G).
8484.14
---Vol. 5:4 (Summer 1977), pp. 12-14 (G).
8484.15
---Vol. 6:1 (Fall 1977), pp. 27-29 (G, H).
8484.16
---Vol. 6:2 (Winter 1977), pp. 7-8 (H).
8484.17
---Vol. 6:3 (Spring 1978), pp. 24-25 (H).
8484.18
---Vol. 6:4 (Summer 1978), pp. 17-18 (H).
8484.19
---Vol. 7:1 (Fall 1978), pp. 3-6 (H-J).
8484.20
---Vol. 7:2 (Winter 1978), p. 19 (J).
8484.21
---Vol. 7:3 (Spring 1979), p. 19 (J).
8484.22
---Vol. 7:4 (Summer 1979), pp. 14-15 (J, K).
8484.23
---Vol. 8:1 (Fall 1979), pp. 7-8 (K).
8484.24
---Vol. 8:2 (Winter 1979), pp. 12-13 (K, L).

8484.25
---Vol. 8:3 (Spring 1980), pp. 23-24 (L).
8484.26
---Vol. 8:4 (Summer 1980), pp. 19-20 (L, M).
8484.27
---Vol. 9:1 (Fall 1980), pp. 28-29 (M).
8484.28
---Vol. 9:2 (Winter 1980), pp. 24-25 (M).
8484.29
---Vol. 9:3 (Spring 1981), pp. 20-21 (M).
8484.30
---Vol. 10:1 (Fall 1981), pp. 15-17 (M).
8484.31
---Vol. 10:2 (Winter 1981), pp. 30-32 (M).
8484.32
---Vol. 10:3 (Spring 1982), pp. 7-9 (N, O).
8484.33
---Vol. 10:4 (Summer 1982), pp. 5-7 (M-P).
8484.34
---Vol. 11:1 (Fall 1982), pp. 10-12 (P).
8484.35
---Vol. 11:2 (Winter 1982), p. 30 (Q).
8484.36
---Vol. 11:3 (Spring 1983), pp. 21-23 (R).
8484.37
---Vol. 11:4 (Summer 1983), pp. 3-5 (R).
8484.38
---Vol. 12:1 (Fall 1983), pp. 21-23 (S). In progress.

Transcription of 19th-century records involving (so far) names beginning A through S. Other data: age, country of origin, occupation, local residence. For foreign-born citizens, the original records include date and place of naturalization and name of court. Not all named are immigrants, since this was a list of the eligible voters. For Siskiyou County's 1892 list, see item nos. 1820.1 and .2. This transcription is a continuing project.

* * *

8499
SKINNER, JEAN C. "Excerpts from Passenger Lists." In *Wisconsin State Genealogical Society Newsletter*, vol. 28:2 (Sept. 1981), p. 66.

German passengers on three ships that arrived in New York in 1852: the *Probus*, the *Emperor*, and the *Hermine*. Destination indicated was Milwaukee or elsewhere in Wisconsin. Names and ages given. Forty persons involved.

* * *

8505
SKINNER, JEAN C. "Excerpts from Ship Passenger Lists." In *Wisconsin State Genealogical Society Newsletter*, vol. 28:4 (Apr. 1982), pp. 201-202.

Irish and Germans destined to settle in Wisconsin, 100 in number. Names, ages, occupations, countries of origin. Arrival at New York in 1852.

* * *

8506
SKINNER, JEAN C. "Mid-West-Bound Passengers on the Bark *Hansa*, Bremen to New York, arrived Dec. 9, 1852." In *Wisconsin State Genealogical Society Newsletter*, vol. 29:4 (Apr. 1983), p. 224.

These 37 immigrants are each named with age, occupation, and places of origin and destination.

* * *

8507
SKINNER, JEAN C. "Passenger Lists." In *Wisconsin State Genealogical Society Newsletter*, vol. 29:2 (Sept. 1982), p. 81; vol 29:3 (Jan. 1983), p. 154.

Arrivals in Wisconsin in 1852. Information concerning name, age, occupation, and place of origin of each of 47 persons.

* * *

8508
SKINNER, JEAN C. "Ship Passenger Lists." In *Wisconsin State Genealogical Society Newsletter*, vol. 27:4 (Apr. 1981), pp. 191-192.

Wisconsin arrivals: 150 persons who came from Bremen by way of New York in 1852 on the *Kunigrude* and the *Beta*. Data provides name, age, sex, occupation, and place of origin. Many named Milwaukee as destination.

* * *

8509.1
SKINNER, JEAN C. "Wisconsin-Bound Passengers." In *Wisconsin State Genealogical Society Newsletter*, vol. 30:1 (June 1983), p. 16.

German immigrants who arrived in New York in 1852 as passengers on the *Middlesex*, the *Patricia*, the *Elize*, and the *Andrew*. Thirty indicated Wisconsin as destination, also providing name, age, occupation, place of birth, and place of residence.

* * *

8509.2
SKINNER, JEAN C. "Wisconsin-Bound Passengers on Bark *Peter*." In *Wisconsin State Genealogical Society Newsletter*, vol. 29:1 (June 1982), p. 9.

German arrivals in the year 1852. Names of 16 persons, with ages, places of birth, prior places of residence, occupations, and destinations.

* * *

8514
SLEZAK, EVA. "A Cache of Czechs." In *Maryland Genealogical Society Bulletin*, vol. 23:2 (Spring 1982), pp. 166-167.

Forty arrivals from Bohemia, selected from a complement of 239 passengers crossing from Bremen to Baltimore on the S.S. *Baltimore* in 1868. Names, ages, and occupations given.

* * *

8515
SLEZAK, EVA. "Passenger List - the Barque *Virginia* Arrived in Baltimore, June 1841." In *Maryland Genealogical Society Bulletin*, vol. 22:4 (Fall 1981), pp. 296-307.

Mostly Germans were among 150 passengers on the *Virginia*, Bremen to Baltimore, 1841. Names, ages, sex, occupations, places of origin, and destinations given.

8525
SMALLMAN, MARY BIONDI. "Index to Aliens from Naturalization Book I, County Clerk's Office, Canton [St. Lawrence County, New York]." In *Tree Talks*, vol. 22:2 (June 1982), pp. 83-84 (Immigration and Naturalization, pp. 71-72).

About 160 new citizens listed, with ages, and sometimes names of towns in New York's St. Lawrence County. No dates given.

* * *

8528
SMELTZER, MARJORIE R. "An Irish-Palatine Family in Kansas." In *The Kansas City Genealogist*, vol. 24:1 (Summer 1983/1984), pp. 5-7.

Names of members of the Smeltzer, Smelzer, Smelser families who came to America in the 18th-century from Germany via England and Ireland.

* * *

8543
SMITH, CLIFFORD NEAL. *British Deportees to America, Part 3: 1766-1767*. (British-American Genealogical Research Monograph, 3). McNeal, Ariz.: Westland Publications, 1981. 73p.

Criminals, convicts, and "refugees from injustice" named in British Home Office Papers in the Public Record Office, London. For material on earlier years and more ample comment, see item nos. 8530 and 8541 in the main volume of this bibliography.

* * *

8570.7
SMITH, CLIFFORD NEAL. "Deserters, Dischargees, and Prisoners of War from the British Seventh Regiment of Foot (Fusiliers) During the American Revolution." In *National Genealogical Society Quarterly*, vol. 67:4, (Dec. 1979), pp. 255-263.

Former British military who remained in North America, 500 of whom are named here, most having left service between the years 1775 and 1783. Many settled in the Carolinas or Georgia.

* * *

8570.10
SMITH, CLIFFORD NEAL. "Deserters, Dischargees, and Prisoners of War from the British Tenth Regiment of Foot (North Lincolnshire) During the American Revolution." In *National Genealogical Society Quarterly*, vol. 71:2 (June 1983), pp. 114-120.

List of 230 British soldiers who may have remained in the U.S. after the American Revolution. The list includes names of a few Germans who were recruited into the British Army.

* * *

8570.15
SMITH, CLIFFORD NEAL. "Deserters, Dischargees, and Prisoners of War from the British Fifteenth Regiment of Foot (The Yorkshire East Riding) During the American Revolution." In *National Genealogical Society Quarterly*, vol. 70:1 (Mar. 1982), pp. 15-17.

Fifty names, with dates of desertion or discharge between 1777 and 1780. All probably remained in the U.S.

* * *

8584
SMITH, CLIFFORD NEAL. *Eighteenth-Century Emigrants from Kreis Simmern (Hunsrueck), Rheinland-Pfalz, Germany, to Central Europe, Pfalzdorf am Niederrhein, and North America*. (German-American Genealogical Research Monograph, 15 [i.e. 16]) McNeal, Ariz.: Westland Publications, 1982. 23p.

Improves on lists referred to in item no. 8652 from the compilation of Walter Diener and E. Siegel. Identifies earlier emigrants from Simmern not included in their work. Provides about 200 names, with the numbers of persons accompanying, places of origin, and destination. Covers the years 1750 to 1803. This publication was erroneously printed as no. 15, but it is actually 16.

* * *

8595
SMITH, CLIFFORD NEAL. *Emigrants from the Former Amt Damme, Oldenburg [Now Niedersachsen], Germany, Mainly to the United States, 1830-1849*. (German-American Genealogical Research Monograph, 12) McNeal, Ariz.: Westland Publications, 1981. 84p.

About 1,500 names, with each date of arrival, and sometimes destination and place of German origin.

* * *

8596
SMITH, CLIFFORD NEAL. *Emigrants from the Island of Foehr to Australia, Canada, Chile, the United States, and the West Indies, 1850-1875*. (German-American Genealogical Research Monograph, 17) McNeal, Ariz.: Westland Publications, 1983. 33p.

About 700 emigrants from this former Danish possession, now a part of West Germany. Names, ages, occupations, places of origin, destinations, and date of departure.

* * *

8606
SMITH, CLIFFORD NEAL. *Emigrants from the West-German Fuerstenberg Territories (Baden and the Palatinate) to America and Central Europe 1712, 1737, 1787*. (German-American Genealogical Research Monograph, 9.) McNeal, Ariz.: Westland Publications, 1981. 46p.

Eighteenth century German emigration: 1,200 names and important details, including dates and places of arrival.

* * *

8636
SMITH, CLIFFORD NEAL. *Immigrants to America (Mainly Wisconsin) from the Former Recklinghausen District [Nordrhein-Westfalen, Germany] Around the Middle of the Nineteenth Century*. (German-American Genealogical Research Monograph, 15) McNeal, Ariz.: Westland Publications, 1983. 28p.

The Recklinghausen district was formerly a dependency of the Muenster administrative region, and is today a city in the Ruhr. About 300 names, with each individual's date and place of birth, occupation, and date of emigration: mostly 1840s and 1850s. Taken from a monograph by A. Doridor entitled *Auswanderung nach Nordamerika aus dem ehemaligen Kreise Recklinghausen um die Mitte des 19. Jahrhunderts*.

* * *

8646
SMITH, CLIFFORD NEAL. *Missing Young Men of Wuerttemberg, Germany, 1807: Some Possible Immigrants to America*. (German-American Genealogical Research Monograph, 18) McNeal, Ariz.: Westland Publications, 1983. 43p.

A list of about 1,000 young men declared missing in 1807. Taken from the *Koeniglich-Wuerrtembergische Staats- und Regierungs-Blatt* (Royal Wuerttemberg State and Government Sheet, Stuttgart, 1807), pp. 69-72, 144, 433-440. Most are believed to have made their way to America by clandestine means (as stowaways or by jumping ship, etc.). With the names, are the occupations and places of origin.

* * *

8653
SMITH, CLIFFORD NEAL. *Nineteenth-Century Emigration from the Siegkreis, Nordrhein-Westfalen, Germany, Mainly to the United States*. (German-American Genealogical Research Monograph, 10) McNeal, Ariz.: Westland Publications, 1980. 55p.

Covers the years 1857-1883, with much information on the 800 emigrants. The index includes over 2,000 names.

* * *

8655.20
SMITH, CLIFFORD NEAL. "Pfalzdorf am Niederrhein as a Possible Staging Area for Eighteenth-Century German Emigration to America." In *Genealogical Journal*, vol. 11:4 (Winter 1982-1983), pp. 143-147.

A Lower-Rhine Palatine village in Germany provided 66 emigrants in the 1700s. Surnames and dates of departure are provided.

* * *

8657 — 8659
SMITH, CLIFFORD NEAL. *Reconstructed Passenger Lists for 1850: Hamburg to Australia, Brazil, Canada, Chile, and the United States. Part 2: Passenger Lists 26 through 42*. (German and Central European Emigration Monograph, 1, pt. 2) McNeal, Ariz.: Westland Publications, 1980. 86p.

Provides 2,200 names, with occupation and birthplace of each emigrant. All except two of the sailings were to New York in 1850. For lists 1-25, see item no. 8656 in the main volume of this bibliography.

8658
---*Part 3: Passenger Lists 43 through 60*. (German and Central European Emigration Monograph, 1, pt. 3) McNeal, Ariz.: Westland Publications, 1981. 63p.

Lists 1,250 passengers to Chile, Canada, and the United States. All ships to U.S. arrived in New York; two went to Australia and two to Chile.

8659
---*Part 4: Supplemental Notes on Emigrants' Places of Origin*. (German and Central European Emigration Monograph, 1, pt. 4) McNeal, Ariz.: Westland Publications, 1981. 58p.

This part contains no names, but is essential for use with parts 1-3, (described above and in item no. 8656 in the basic volume of this bibliography). Almost 6,000 names are listed in parts 1- 3.

* * *

8667
SMITH, CLIFFORD NEAL. "Some Eighteenth-Century Emigrants to America from Durlach, Wuerttemberg-Baden, Germany." In *The Palatine Immigrant*, vol. 8:3 (Winter 1983), pp. 98-104.

Approximately 100 emigrants named, with considerable detail about them and their families.

* * *

8695
SMITH, CLIFFORD NEAL. "Unrecognized Refugees from Injustice." In *Genealogical Journal*, vol. 8:3 (Sept. 1979), pp. 125-134.

A comparison of names listed in Smith, *British Deportees to America: Part 1: 1760-1763* (item no. 8534 in the basic volume of this bibliography) and the first volume of Coldham, *Convicts in Colonial America*, (item no. 1222, basic vol. of this bibliography). Includes names of over 500 convicts sent to America between 1760 and 1765. Information differs in the two sources.

* * *

8773
SNEDDEN, HOWARD E. "Naturalizations Recorded in Order Book A, Supreme Court, Territory and State of Iowa, 1838-1853." In *Hawkeye Heritage*, vol. 16:2 (Apr.-June 1981), pp. 62-63.

New citizens in 19th-century Iowa, mostly from Great Britain, naturalized between 1840 and 1851. Twenty are named.

* * *

8774
SOBOTKA, MARGIE. *Czech Immigrant Passenger List (for Nebraska) 1879*. Omaha, Neb.: the compiler, 1982. 10p.

Czechoslovakian departures were mostly from Hamburg or Bremen. Arrival in 1879 was at the port of New York for the 700 named here, from several listings in the Czech newspaper, *Pokrok Zapadu*, that same year. Names only, without additional information.

* * *

8805
"SOME MARYLAND PLANTERS, 1704." In *National Genealogical Society Quarterly*, vol. 71:2 (June 1983), p. 130.

The *Thirsby*, alias the *Wye River Merchant*, sailed in 1703 from Plymouth, Devon, to the Patuxent River, Maryland, with 40 passengers. Arrival was in February of 1704.

8864.1 — 8864.8
"SOMERSET COUNTY [Pennsylvania] NATURALIZATION RECORDS, 1855-1856." In *Somerset Past*.
8864.1
---Vol. 1:1 (Apr. 1981), p. 14.
8864.2
---Vol. 1:2 (July 1981), p. 14.
8864.3
---Vol. 1:3 (Oct. 1981), pp. 14-15.
8864.4
---Vol. 1:4 (Jan. 1982), p. 14.
8864.5
---Vol. 2:1 (Apr. 1982), p. 14.
8864.6
---Vol. 2:2 (July 1982), p. 14.
8864.7
---Vol. 2:3 (Oct. 1982), pp. 14-15.
8864.8
---Vol. 2:4 (Jan. 1983), p. 14.

Provides 125 names, with dates of application filed or admission as a citizen in the years 1855 and 1856. Almost all from Germany. For coverage of an earlier period, same place, see Iscrupe, *Naturalization Records, 1802-1854* . . . (item no. 3458 in the basic volume of this bibliography).

* * *

8865
"SONOMA [California] NATURALIZATIONS - 30/31 August 1875, Sonoma County Court. Abstract from *The Sonoma Democrat*, September 4, 1875." In *The Sonoma Searcher*, vol. 10:3 (Mar. 1983), p. 30.

New citizens in 1875: 35 are named. No other information given.

* * *

8867
"SOURCES FOR THE IDENTIFICATION OF EMIGRANTS FROM IRELAND to North America in the 19th Century." In *Ulster Genealogical and Historical Guild Newsletter*, vol. 1 (1978), pp. 7-18.

Article names about 200 Irish who sailed for Quebec or the United States in the 1830s (mostly). Provides data on name, place of residence in the homeland, religion, and destination.

* * *

8877
SPEAR, BURTON W. "Passengers Aboard the *Mary & John*." In *The Second Boat*, vol. 1:2 (Aug. 1980), pp. 4-8.

Lists *Mary and John* passengers, taken from Banks, *Winthrop Fleet of 1630* . . . (item no. 0281 in the basic volume of this bibliography). On p. 8 Spear proffers a list of 59 persons who may have been passengers on the same crossing: the conjectural list is not given in Banks.

* * *

8893
SPERRY, KIP. "Some North Americans in the Old Parochial Registers of Scotland." In *National Genealogical Society Quarterly*, vol. 69:4 (Dec. 1981), pp. 261-267.

Extracts from the Old Parochial Registers of the Church of Scotland, which recorded social events, including whereabouts of immigrants, and family affairs, mostly first half of nineteenth century. About 200 names cited.

* * *

8900
SPIELMAN, J.R. "Passenger Lists." In *Heritage Review*, vol. 12:1 (Feb. 1982), p. 38.

About 100 Germans from Russia who crossed from Bremen to New York in 1884-1885. Names, ages, and occupations.

* * *

9027
STIENS, ROBERT E. "Passenger List, 1893." In *Germanic Genealogist*, vol. 6:2 or no. 22 (1981), pp. 225-226.

Refers to the steamship *Russia*, sailing in 1893 from Hamburg and Le Havre to New York, with 133 passengers aboard. Native countries of the passengers: mainly Austria, Prussia, and Russia. Names, ages, sex, and places of last previous residence given.

* * *

9028
STIENS, ROBERT E. "Passenger List of the *Sorrento*, 1892." In *Germanic Genealogist*, no. 20 (1980), pp. 134-137.

In December of 1892, the *Sorrento* left Hamburg with 271 persons, arriving in New York in January of 1893. List includes information on age, sex, country of origin — mostly Austria and Prussia — and place of last previous residence.

* * *

9033
STIENS, ROBERT E. "Passengers from Russia." In *Eastern & Central European Genealogist*, no. 4 (1981), pp. 164-167.

Hamburg lists for the years 1892-1893, from sources at the Genealogical Society in Salt Lake City. Names 350 passengers from Russia, with ships, dates, ages, sex, and ports of arrival.

* * *

9035
STIENS, ROBERT E., contributor. "Three Passenger Lists." In *Germanic Genealogist*, vol. 6:3/4 or nos. 23/24 (1982), pp. 285-299.

Supplies names of arrivals at the ports of Baltimore and New York in January 1893 on the *Amalfi*, the *Italia*, and the *Weimar*. Over 1,700 persons from Eastern and Central European places are named, with ages, sex, and countries of origin. Data taken from U.S. National Archives microfilm, M 237, roll 602. A reprint of the article from *Eastern and Central European Genealogist* described in item no. 9034 in the basic volume of this bibliography.

* * *

9037.1 — 9037.2
STILES, MRS. PHILIP (CASSANDRA), and MRS. RICHARD (WAVA) WHITE. *"Charlotte* and *Sully* Arrived in New York on July 22, 1833." In *Tuscarawas Pioneer Footprints*.

9037.1
---Vol. 11:1 (Feb. 1983), pp. 3-4; vol. 11:2 (May 1983), pp. 21,23; vol. 11:3 (Aug. 1983), pp. 29-30; vol. 11:4 (Nov. 1983), pp. 43-44.
9037.2
---Vol. 12:1 (Feb. 1984), pp. 5-6.

About 200 passengers who sailed from Le Havre, with ages, occupations, and countries of origin. Most from Germany and Switzerland. Several settled in Tuscarawas County, Ohio.

* * *

9039
STITH, WILLIAM. *The History of the First Discovery and Settlement of Virginia*. Williamsburg, Va.: William Parks, 1747. 415p.

Names of many adventurers and immigrants from early 17th century are mentioned throughout the text. Several reprints of this source exist.

* * *

9072
STUHL, BERNHARD. "Auerbacher Amerika-Auswanderer im 19. Jahrhundert." In *Bergstraesser Heimatblaetter: Beitraege zur Heimatkunde von Bensheim und Umgebung*, no. 6 (26 July 1980), and no. 7 (2 Aug. 1980), n.pag.

Emigrants to America from Auerbach (now part of Bensheim, south of Darmstadt in West Germany) in the 19th century. About 50 individuals or family groups who left that Upper Palatine village between 1830 and the end of the 19th century for America. Date of birth, names of parents, places of settlement in America, and some other biographical details.

* * *

9074
SUELFLOW, ROY A., editor. *The Chronicle of Pastor L.F.E. Krause, First Lutheran Pastor to Work in Wisconsin*. Translated by Roy A. Suelflow. [Mequon, Wisc., Trinity Lutheran Church of Freistadt, 1970?]. n. pag. [50pp.]

Germans settled in Milwaukee in about the 1840s are named in this small book. Pages are unnumbered, but see 1, 7, 11, 14, 22, and 28, where about 50 names are to be found.

* * *

9076
SULLIVAN, LARRY E. "The Records of the Ethnic Political Association as a Genealogical Source: The Associated Friends of Ireland in the City of Baltimore." In *Maryland Magazine of Genealogy*, vol. 5:1 (Spring 1982), pp. 23-33.

Names of about 300 members of the Association, 1831-1834, who were born in Ireland. All arrived in Baltimore prior to 1831.

* * *

9078
"SURNAME INTEREST LISTINGS." In *The English Genealogist*, no. 11 (1979), p. 257 (ref. nos. 1-5); no. 12 (1979), pp. 306-309 (refs. 6-40); no. 13 (1980), pp. 354-356 (refs. 41-63); no. 14 (1981), pp. 387-389 (refs. 64-90); nos. 15/16 (1982), pp. 439-440 (refs. 91-110); no. 17 (1983), pp. 500-503 (refs. 111-140).

Beginning of a series intended to assist researchers with a wealth of information on English emigration: individual places of origin, dates of departure, destinations, and vital statistics. In progress.

* * *

9079
"SURNAME INTEREST LISTINGS." In *Germanic Genealogist*, no. 16 (1979), pp. 463-468 (ref. nos. 1-42); no. 18A (1979), pp. 24-35 (refs. 43-139); no. 18B (1979), pp. 54-60 (refs. 149-190); no. 19 (1980), pp. 101-106 (refs. 191-233); no. 20 (1980), pp. 175-178 (refs. 234-260); no. 21 (1981), pp. 207-212 (refs. 261-359); vol. 6:2, i.e., no. 22 (1981), pp. 239-243 (refs. 360-439); vol. 6:3/4, i.e., nos. 23/24 (1982), pp. 306-310 (refs 440-517); vol. 7:1, i.e., no. 25 (1983), pp. 341-355, 358 (refs. 518-622). In progress.

This series, intended to assist researchers, provides a wealth of information on German emigration, places of origin, dates of departure or arrival, destinations, and vital statistics spanning the centuries. A continuing feature.

* * *

9081
SWIERENGA, ROBERT P. *Dutch Emigrants to the United States, South Africa, South America, and Southeast Asia, 1835-1880: An Alphabetical Listing of Household Heads and Independent Persons*. Wilmington, Del.: Scholarly Resources, 1983. 346p.

Names 21,800 persons from 19th-century Dutch government records, with many more details than are normally given in such lists. It is coded in such a way that many unusual details become available. This volume, and the two-volume work, item no. 9082 (below), supply the most complete information available on Dutch emigrants of that period.

* * *

9082
SWIERENGA, ROBERT P. *Dutch Immigrants in U.S. Ship Passenger Manifests 1820-1880: An Alphabetical Listing by Household Heads and Independent Persons*. Wilmington, Del.: Scholarly Resources, 1983. 2 vols. 1,223p.

Vol. 1, Aab-Meller; vol. 2, Mellink-Z and Addendum. From a culling of 100,000 separate 19th-century ship manifests. By a special method of coding, provides more information than is given anywhere else. The most comprehensive listing of Dutch immigrants in the U.S. See related item by Swierenga above.

* * *

9090
SWITZER, LAURA. "List of 148 Passengers on Board the Ship, *Ocean*, Captn. Higgins, from Bremen to Baltimore." In *Maryland Magazine of Genealogy*, vol. 4:2 (Fall 1981), pp. 83-86.

Refers to Germans who arrived in Baltimore in 1841. Name, age, place of origin, and occupation.

* * *

9094

SWYGARD, NELLIE, and VERDA J. BAIRD, transcribers. *Jefferson County Iowa Naturalizations*. Des Moines, Ia.: Jefferson County Genealogical Society, 1982. 28p.

Records those who obtained citizenship between 1846 and 1904 and those who applied for first papers between 1870 and 1905. Includes 1,300 names, with countries of origin and date of the records for each.

* * *

9097

SZUCS, LORETTO DENNIS. *Naturalizations, Declarations of Intent, and Final Oaths, Circuit Court, Eastern District of Michigan, Detroit*. [Midlothian, Ill., the author, 1978] 31p.

Covers the 19th century from the 1830s on, listing name, age, date of petition, date of final oath, and country of origin for each of about 1,500 persons.

* * *

9117

TENBARGE, ELEANOR. "Naturalization Records—Vanderburgh County, Indiana." In *The Tri-State Packet*, vol. 4:2 (Dec. 1980), pp. 14-20.

New citizens in the years of the 1820s through the 1840s. This is a continuation of material published in earlier issues of the same publication. See items 9115-9116 in the basic volume of this bibliography for references to naturalization records covering the years 1850-1854.

* * *

9155

THARAN, BONNIE. "Clarion County [Pennsylvania] Naturalizations." In *Western Pennsylvania Genealogical Society Quarterly*, vol. 10:2 (Nov. 1983), pp. 126-135.

About 400 persons, with countries of birth (mostly Germany and Ireland), and dates of declaration of intention to acquire citizenship and of naturalization, 1830s to 1900s, mostly 1840s-1880s. Lists surnames beginning A through H in this issue.

* * *

9161

THORSELL, ELISABETH, transcriber. *Forteckning Over Emigranter Fran Ostergotland, 1851-1860*. Linkoping, Sweden: the transcriber, 1981. 20p.

List of emigrants from Ostergotland, Sweden, in the 1850s. Heads of households and single persons, 800 in all, who applied for passports. Names, occupations, places of origin, and dates of issuance of passports.

* * *

9207

TRAPP, GLENDA KAY. "Passenger Lists." In *The Tri-State Packet of the Tri-State Genealogical Society*, vol. 5:4 (June 1982), pp. 5- 10.

In voyages out of Bremen in 1895, the *Stuttgart* brought 350 passengers in steerage. Ports of arrival were New York and Baltimore. German and Polish names.

9225

TSCHAEKOFSKE, RON, and PHYLLIS HERTZ FESER. "Passenger Lists." In *Heritage Review*, vol. 11:3 (Sept. 1981), pp. 47-48.

Germans from Russia who crossed from Bremen to New York on the *Fulda* in 1886. About 100 are named.

* * *

9251

ULLE, ROBERT F. "Germantown: Gateway to the New World." In *Pennsylvania Heritage*, vol. 9:4 (Fall 1983), pp. 19-22.

Facts on some of the immigrants from Krefeld (or Crefeld), Germany, to Germantown, Pennsylvania, on the *Concord* in 1683. More information on this same subject is available in the article described in item no. 9252.

* * *

9252

ULLE, ROBERT F. "The Original Germantown Families." In *Mennonite Family History*, vol. 2:2 (Apr. 1983), pp. 48-51.

Details concerning several Germans from Krefeld (or Crefeld) who arrived on the *Concord* in 1683 and settled in Germantown, Pennsylvania.

* * *

9254

ULSTER GENEALOGICAL & HISTORICAL GUILD. *Subscribers' Interest*. Belfast: the society, 1983. 81p.

A list of approximately 2,400 entries recording the interests of members, in which many give date of someone's emigration to Canada or the U.S. Other data on families are given.

* * *

9256

UNGER, CLAUDE W., translator. "The Old Goschenhoppen Burial Register, 1752-1772." In *Pennsylvania Folklife*, vol. 17:2 (Winter 1967-1968), pp. 32-34.

From *The Perkiomen Region*, 1921-1925. Some mention of dates of emigration. Also in item no. 9968, Yoder, *Rhineland Emigrants*, pp. 109-111.

* * *

9317

UNITED STATES, WORKS PROJECTS ADMINISTRATION, State of Kansas. *A Guide to Hillsboro, Kansas*. Hillsboro, Kansas: Mennonite Brethren Publishing House, 1940. 91p.

About 100 names listed from early records, mostly 1873 and 1874. Largely Germans.

* * *

9332
URLSPERGER, SAMUEL. *Detailed Reports on the Salzburger Emigrants Who Settled in America.* (Wormsloe Foundation Publications) Athens, Ga.: Univ. of Georgia Press.

---[Reports on the Emigrants at Ebenezer, Georgia, 1738.] In vol. 5: 1738. (Wormsloe, 14), 1980, pp. 316-323.
---Signers of the letter of gratitude sent on 26 October 1739 to the Salzburgers' benefactors in Germany, with wives' names. In vol. 6: 1739. 1981, pp. 323-334, appendices 2-4.

Daily registers of pastors J.M. Boltzius and I.C. Gronau, who shepherded the exiles from Salzburg, Austria, and other settlers in Georgia, in the 1730s.

* * *

9362
VAN KOEVERING, ADRIAN. *Legends of the Dutch: the Story of a Mass Movement of Nineteenth Century Pilgrims.* Zeeland, Mich.: Zeeland Record Co., 1960. 618p.

Dutch emigrants who sailed from Rotterdam and Antwerp to New York, 1846-1847, are listed in appendices A-E on pp. 599-618. Names of about 650 persons are given, with data on age, sex, and occupation.

* * *

9417
VERDENHALVEN, FRITZ. *Die Auswanderer aus dem Fuerstentum Lippe (bis 1877).* (Sonderveroeffentlichungen des Naturwissenschaftlichen und Historischen Vereins fuer das Land Lippe, vol. 30) Detmold, Germany: Naturwissenschaftlicher und Historischer Verein fuer das Land Lippe, 1980. 535p.

Emigrants from the Principality of Lippe up to 1877. Coverage begins in the mid-1600s. This former jurisdiction was centered around the city of Detmold in the present-day Federal Republic of Germany. Heaviest movement was in the early 1800s. Most of the 10,000 emigrants came to America. Information includes name of village of origin, year of emigration, occupation, destination, and other facts. From a wide number of sources, including newspapers and city records.

* * *

9473
VOGT, DON J. "Whitman County, Washington, Germans from Russia, 1889 Whitman County Census." In *Clues*, 1981, pt. 1, pp. 56-61.

About 200 persons: names, ages, sex, and places of birth (Russia). Some came on the S.S. *Mosel* and arrived at New York in 1876.

* * *

9490
VOLZ, JACOB. "My Immigration to America." Ed. by Emma S. Haynes. In *Clues*, 1980, pt. 2, pp. 49-51.

Mentions about 30 Germans from Russia, many having the surname Bauer. Late 19th century.

* * *

9530
WALDENMAIER, NELLIE PROTSMAN. *Some of the Earlier Oaths of Allegiance to the United States of America.* n.p.: the author, 1944. 93pp.

Includes 1,572 names, with places where the oaths were administered and dates (mostly 1778). Actual texts of the oaths were extracted from records in the National Archives, the War Department, and the Library of Congress.

* * *

9554
WALKER, WAYNE. "Disbanded Soldiers in Dalhousie, Annapolis County [Nova Scotia], 1820." In *The Nova Scotia Genealogist*, vol. 1:3 (Nov. 1983), pp. 101-103.

Most of these soldiers came from the 99th or Prince of Wales Tipperary Regiment of Foot, almost all from Ireland. Data provides 48 names, with date of enlistment, place of birth, years served, date and place of discharge for each. Taken from London's Public Record Office document WO 25, vol. 548.

* * *

9556
WALL, O. J. "The Passengers on the ship *Strassburg* . . . May 28, 1878." In *Becker Family* . . . . Compiled by O.J. Wall. Freeman, S.D.: Pine Hill Press [1982], pp. 83-87.

Four destinations were named by these 650 German immigrants: Mountain Lake, Minnesota; Sutton, Nebraska; and communities identified as Newton and Burton, Kansas. Involves 100 families.

* * *

9576
WARD, CYRIL G. "Intending Emigrants from the Irish Constabulary." In *Genealogists' Magazine*, vol. 21:1 (Mar. 1983), pp. 23-24; vol. 21:3 (Sept. 1983), pp. 97-99.

Concerns resigning members of the Royal Irish Constabulary who, between 1834 and 1845, indicated their intention to emigrate. Surname, forename, county of birth, age at joining, year of joining and of resigning, and country of immigration. Most were destined for Australia or America. About 300 names.

* * *

9593
WARKE, TIMOTHY. "Gravestone Transcriptions of Irish Interest in Canada and the U.S.A." In *Ulster Genealogical & Historical Guild Newsletter*, vol. 1:9 (1983), pp. 297-308.

Reference is to gravestones in Acton, Ontario; the Pine Barrens of New Jersey; at the Bethsalem Presbyterian Church in Winston County, Mississippi; and in Lehigh County, Pennsylvania. Transcriptions often provide date of emigration and from that it is possible to approximate date of arrival.

* * *

9597
WARREN, JUDY. "Guests of the Present Seek Ghosts of the Past." In *Sussex Family Historian*, vol. 4:8 (June 1981), p. 244.

A list of English headed by the Rev. Henry Whitfield, Rector of Ockley, Surrey, who emigrated to found Guilford in Connecticut in the year 1639. Names of 24 persons are included.

9628
WEBER, ELDON D. "A List of Persons Emigrating from the Parish of Ashwell in the County of Hertfordshire, England, 1836, in *Hartley*. . . ." In *Newsleaf of Ontario Genealogical Society*, vol. 10:4 (Dec. 1980), n. pag.

Nine emigrants to Upper Canada, all agricultural laborers; ages given.

* * *

9638
WEFFER, HERBERT. *Auswanderer aus Stadt und Kreis Bonn von 1814 bis 1914*. (Veroeffentlichungen des Stadtarchivs Bonn, 19) Bonn: Ludwig Roehrscheid, 1977, pp. 119-396.

Emigrants from city and area of Bonn, 1814-1914. Concerns 1,000-1,500 Germans who departed for America. Names, with villages of origin, some dates of birth or ages, places of destination, and other supporting data.

* * *

9666
WELCH, GLORYA. "Excerpts from Ship Passenger Lists." In *Wisconsin State Genealogical Society Newsletter*, vol. 29:4 (Apr. 1983), p. 223.

Mostly Wisconsin-bound passengers among the 35 named who arrived at the port of New York in 1845. Data includes ages, occupations, and countries of origin.

* * *

9667
WELCH, GLORYA. "Ship *Probus*, Arrived in New York August 22, 1845, from Havre." In *Wisconsin State Genealogical Society Newsletter*, vol. 29:2 (Sept. 1982), p.81.

Norwegians to Milwaukee: names of 20 passengers given.

* * *

9668
WELCH, GLORYA. "Wisconsin-Bound Passengers on the Ship *John Hancock*, Arrived New York from Liverpool, 3 May 1853." In *Wisconsin State Genealogical Society Newsletter*, vol. 30:1 (June 1983), p. 15.

These passengers are believed to have been Swiss. Names and ages of 35 persons given.

* * *

9674
WENDLER, CARLOS J. "Founders of the Village Marienthal (Valle Maria), 21 July 1878, Near Parana in Entre Rios, Argentina." In *Clues*, 1980, pt. 1, pp. 50-51.

Germans to South America from Roman Catholic villages of the (Wiesenseite) Samara district of the Volga region, Russia. Names 63, with villages of origin.

* * *

9676
WENZLAFF, THEODORE C. "Passenger List." In *Heritage Review*, vol. 10:2 (Apr. 1980), p. 28.

Names of 19 Germans from Russia traveling to New York via Hamburg in 1874. Some went to Nebraska, others to the Dakota Territory.

* * *

9678.1 — 9678.3
WESTCOTT, LOIS. "Boulder County [Colorado] Naturalization Records (Papers)." In *Boulder Genealogical Society Quarterly*.
9678.1
---Vol. 13:4 (Nov. 1981), pp. 149-159 (Letters A-C).
9678.2
---Vol. 14:1 (Feb. 1982), pp. 15-25 (Letters D-I); vol. 14:2 (May 1982), pp. 58-62 (Letters J-K); vol. 14:3 (Aug. 1982), pp. 122-131 (Letters K-P); vol. 14:4 (Nov. 1982), pp. 163-168 (Letters P-S).
9678.3
---Vol. 15:1 (Feb. 1983), pp. 13-19 (Letters S-Z).

Names of about 750 persons, with countries of origin, dates naturalized, and names of witnesses. Title varies slightly in different issues of the publication.

* * *

9700 — 9702
WESTERN PENNSYLVANIA GENEALOGICAL SOCIETY, Pittsburgh, compilers. *A List of Immigrants Who Applied for Naturalization Papers in the District Courts of Allegheny County, Pennsylvania*. Pittsburgh: the society, 1981-1982.

9700
---Vol. 5: 1880-1887. (1981), 141 p.
9701
---Vol. 6: 1881-1891. (1981), 138p.
9702
---Vol. 7: 1892-1906. (1982), 220p.

Much information given, including date of intention to acquire citizenship, date of naturalization, place of residence, country of birth, and name of sponsor. Vols. 5 and 6 each present more than 8,000 names; vol. 7 more than 13,000.

* * *

9717.1 — 9717.4
"WESTMORELAND COUNTY [Pennsylvania] NATURALIZATION RECORDS, 1853." In *Old Westmoreland*.
9717.1
---Vol. 1:1 (Aug. 1980), pp. 21-23.
9717.2
---Vol. 1:2 (Nov. 1980), pp. 22-23.
9717.3
---Vol. 1:3 (Feb. 1981), pp. 21-24.
9717.4
---Vol. 1:4 (May 1981), pp. 19-20.

Provides 78 names, with dates of filing, dates of arrival in America, and places of residence in Pennsylvania in 1853. Naturalizations in prior years, 1802-1852, are covered in a work by Iscrupe, described in item no. 3460 in the basic volume of this bibliography.

* * *

9734
WHITE, WAVA R., and SANDRA STILES. "Manifests of Ships, *Charlotte* and *Sully*, Arrived New York, 1833." In *Ancestry*: Palm Beach County Genealogical Society, vol. 19:1 (Jan. 1984), pp. 23-31.

About 160 passengers on the *Sully* and about as many on the *Charlotte*, sailing from Le Havre to New York, arrived July 22, 1833. Ages, sex, occupations, countries of origin (mostly Germany, France, and Switzerland), and places of destination (mostly Ohio).

* * *

9754
"WHO'S YOUR ANCESTOR" Genealogical and Historical Society, compiler and publisher. *Naturalization Applications for Montgomery County, Indiana, 1850-1930*. Crawfordsville, Ind.: the society, (1982?). 67p.

Name, age, place of birth, year and place of emigration, date and place of arrival for about 1,000 alien residents of Montgomery County, Indiana. The information also includes the place of prior allegiance and the date an oath of allegiance was pronounced here, along with the name of the recording or county clerk at the time.

* * *

9777
WHYTE, DONALD. "Scottish Stone-Masons in Texas." In *The Scottish Genealogist*, vol. 13:2 (Oct. 1966), pp. 4-6.

A specialized list of 67 Scottish stonemasons who emigrated to Austin, Texas, in the 1880s.

* * *

9817
WILSON, EUNICE. "Passenger Lists at Kew [London]." In *Yorkshire Archaeological Society: Family History Section Newsletter,* vol. 9:4 (Aug. 1983), p. 107.

Illustrating the breadth of passenger lists at the Public Record Office, Kew, near London, there is mention of several emigrants, with their ships and dates of emigration.

* * *

9824
WILSON, REBA SHROPSHIRE, and BETTY S. GLOVER. *The Lees and Kings of Virginia and North Carolina, 1636-1976*. Ridgely, Tenn.: the authors, 1976, pp. 24-25.

Names of 20 persons brought to Virginia or North Carolina in the year 1694. Importation information taken from Virginia State Library, *Originals of Patents*, Book 8, p. 341.

* * *

9832
WISEMAN, WILLIAM A. "Emigrants from England to Settle in Maryland." In *Prince George's County Genealogical Society Bulletin*, vol. 14:5 (Jan. 1983), p. 73.

Refers to a crossing of the ship *Nancy* from London in 1774. Lists 18 passengers, with ages, occupations, and places of origin. Some were indentured servants. Data extracted from *The New England Historical and Genealogical Register*, vol. 62 (1908), p. 321. Also in Tepper, *Passengers to America*, p. 235 (item no. 9151).

9838
WODROW, ROBERT. [A List of Scots Transported to the New World in 1687.] In *The History of the Sufferings of the Church of Scotland, from the Restauration to the Revolution* . . . . Edinburgh: James Watson, 1722. Vol. 2, p. 612.

Refers to 21 men and women banished from Scotland in 1687.

* * *

9842
WODROW, ROBERT. [A Partial List of Scots Transported to Carolina in 1684.] In *The History of the Sufferings of the Church of Scotland, from the Restauration to the Revolution* . . . . Edinburgh: James Watson, 1722. Vol. 2, pp. 341-342.

Provides the names of 22 prisoners transported from Glasgow to Carolina in 1684.

* * *

9845
WODROW, ROBERT. [A Short List of Scots Transported to Jamaica in 1685.] In *The History of the Sufferings of the Church of Scotland, from the Restauration to the Revolution* . . . . Edinburgh: James Watson, 1722. Vol. 2, pp. 573-574.

Names nine prisoners transported in Dec. 1685 aboard the *Newhaven*.

* * *

9892
WOODBURN, CHARLES M. "Morgan County [Ohio] Naturalizations, 1819-1832." In *The Report, Ohio Genealogical Society*, vol. 22:2 (Summer 1982), pp. 89-90.

Names of 83 new citizens, most of them from the United Kingdom. Data includes age, place of origin, and date and place of arrival.

* * *

9897
WUST, KLAUS. "Direct German Immigration to Maryland in the 18th Century (A Preliminary Survey)." In *The Report: A Journal of German-American History*, no. 37 (1978), pp. 19-28.

An excellent study of the ships, commerce, and sea captains involved, along with a listing of a few immigrants and other information.

* * *

9949
YODER, DON. "Notes and Documents: Eighteenth-Century Letters from Germany." In *Pennsylvania Folklife*, vol. 19:3 (Spring 1970), pp. 30-33.

Some mention of emigrants and dates of arrival. Marginal. Also in item no. 9968, Yoder, *Rhineland Emigrants*, pp. 118-121.

* * *

9950
YODER, DON, editor. "Notes and Documents: I. A Letter to Germany (1806)." In *Pennsylvania Folklife*, vol. 16:1 (Autumn 1966), pp. 44-45.

The letter was from a family in Pennsylvania; contents concern chiefly the Bertolet family. Text in English and German. Also in item no. 9968, Yoder, *Rhineland Emigrants*, pp. 106-107.

* * *

9966
YODER, DON. "Personalia from the *Amerikanischer Correspondent*, 1826-1828." In *Pennsylvania Folklife*, vol. 17:2 (Winter 1967-1968), pp. 36-41.

Details concerning German immigrants, with a few dates of arrival. Also in item no. 9968, Yoder, *Rhineland Emigrants*, pp. 112-117.

* * *

9968
YODER, DON. *Rhineland Emigrants: Lists of German Settlers in Colonial America*. Baltimore: Genealogical Publishing Co., 1981. 170p.

Composed of 24 articles excerpted and reprinted from *Pennsylvania Folklife*, with new indexes. Lists about 4,000 names. Especially important because of the difficulty in finding early numbers of *Pennsylvania Folklife*.

* * *

9972.3 — 9972.4
"YORK COUNTY [Pennsylvania] NATURALIZATION RECORDS. . . ." In *Codorus Chronicles*.
9972.3
---Vol. 1:2 (Aug. 1983), p. 20.
9972.4
---Vol. 1:3 (Nov. 1983), pp. 20, 23, 27.

These issues cover the years 1798-1799 and list 13 new citizens, with names of some of the sponsors. For early listings after the turn of that century, see the item below.

* * *

9972.7 — 9972.8
"YORK COUNTY [Pennsylvania] NATURALIZATION RECORDS. . . ." In *Codorus Chronicles*.
9972.7
---Vol. 1:1 (May 1983), pp. 18, 33, 40-42.
9972.8
---Vol. 1:4 (Feb. 1984), n.pag. Title varies.

The May '83 issue covers the year 1802 and lists 46 new citizens originally from Scotland and Ireland. The other covers 1803-1804, with names of 13 persons. See item nos. 9972.3 and .4 for coverage of earlier years.

* * *

9981
ZIMMER, KLAUS. "Amerikaauswanderer aus der Reformierten Pfarrei Wolfersweiler vor 1750." In *Mitteilungen zur Wanderungsgeschichte der Pfaelzer*, 1982:1, pp. 39-45.

Emigrants to America from the Reformed parish of Wolfersweiler before 1750. Lists 50 German individuals or families who came to America between 1700 and 1750, with arrival dates and sometimes extensive additional genealogical data. Zimmer also examines Bell's article on emigrants from Wolfersweiler, item no. 0478 in the basic volume of this bibliography.

* * *

9982
ZIMMER, KLAUS. "Emigrants from the Ostertal." In *Journal of the Pennsylvania German Society*, vol. 16 (1982), pp. 24-27.

Translation into English of an article that appeared in vol. 9:9 (Dec. 1980) of *Mitteilungen zur Wanderungsgeschichte der Pfaelzer*. Refers to Germans from the Palatinate.

* * *

9984
ZSCHOKKE, E. "Caspar und Salomon Koepfli und die Gruendung der Schweizerkolonie 'Highland' in Illinois." In *Der Deutsche Pionier*, vol. 11:2 (May 1879), pp. 43-49; vol. 11:3 (June 1879), pp. 97-104.

Caspar and Salomon Koepfli and the founding of the Swiss colony, Highland, in Illinois. Contains names of 10 persons who settled in Highland in 1831 and their places of origin in the Canton of Lucerne in Switzerland.

* * *

9999.3
"ZWEIGVEREIN VON COVINGTON, KY." In *Der Deutsche Pionier*, vol. 9:4 (July 1877), pp. 170-173.

Branch [of German Pioneer] Society of Covington, Kentucky. Contains a list of founding members of the Covington, Kentucky, branch of the Deutscher Pionier Verein, whose headquarters were across the Ohio River in Cincinnati. Provides 125 names, usually with dates of birth, places of origin, and dates of emigration from Germany (ca. 1830-1856). See also item nos. 9999.6 and 5747.

* * *

9999.6
"ZWEIGVEREIN VON NEWPORT, KY." In *Der Deutsche Pionier*, vol. 9:4 (July 1877), pp. 173-176.

Branch Society of Newport, Kentucky. Contains a list of founding members of the Newport, Kentucky, branch of the Deutscher Pionier Verein (German Pioneer Society) of Cincinnati, Ohio. Includes 125 names, most with date of birth, place of origin, and date of emigration (ca. 1830-1856). See also item nos. 9999.3 and 5747.

* * *

Combined Index to Basic Volume and Supplement

An Explanation of the Index

Reference is to the entry number of the individual item, not to a page number. The boldface numbers indicate the new material in this supplement; the other references, in light face, indicate items in the basic volume of the bibliography. Cumulation of the two indexes was thought to give a complete picture of all that is contained in the two volumes and to provide one place to search both of them efficiently.

The alphabetical arrangement used is known as the word-by-word system (e.g., New Jersey and New York come before Newcastle). In foreign words, the diacritical marks have been omitted: thus, in German, an umlauted vowel appears without the umlaut, but with an e after the vowel, and the word is alphabetized accordingly.

Generally, this index includes place-names, nationalities, ships' names, naturalizations, occupations, religious groups, military units, and categories of arrivals entered as prisoners or indentured servants. Some surnames are to be found in the bibliography, but relatively few.

Entries that could be identified by date have an indication of that before the reference number.

Ships' names are given in italics throughout the book: *Virginia,* therefore, is a reference to a ship; Virginia to the place; *Oxford,* to a ship; Oxford to the place.

The following abbreviations were used in the index:

c.	= century	n.d.	= no date
ca.	= *circa*	n. pag.	= no pagination
ff.	= following	N.S.	= Nova Scotia

States have generally been indicated by the traditional standard abbreviations.

Perhaps it is worth pointing out that an expression like "Scottish departures" is a reference to Scots leaving their homeland for North America, not to the departure of Scots from this continent.

How to Use the Index for Rapid Reference

It is advisable to look first under the most specific place-names (of departure, arrival, or settlement) or the name of the people (the national name: French, Germans, etc.) from the country of emigration or the port of departure. Only if a nationality was not known from the material at hand was a given emigration assimilated to the nationality of the port of departure. Note that Silesia was divided between Poland and Czechoslovakia, but today some of it is in East Germany, and the source of the information and the port of departure may both be German. Whenever possible, therefore, multiple ways of access are provided in the index. The term *English* is used where the material refers explicitly to English places or people. If there is an indication that Scots, Welsh, or Irish were probably included aboard a sailing from an English port, the reference to that material may be found either under those groups, if they are identified, or under the more encompassing term *British.*

It is recognized that national states were not formed until after the dates of many of the migration movements mentioned, but use of the national names does apply to the language groups, does spotlight the conscious national heritage of many families, and is convenient for present-day researchers who may more readily be able to identify given place-names within current frontiers. Mixed lists of people from various countries are indexed merely as arrivals or departures under the place-names involved, instead of by nationality.

A reader in search of an author name or (possibly) a book or article title should look in the alphabetical sequence of the main part of the bibliography. Authors and titles are not in the index.

Passenger and Immigration Lists Bibliography
Index

This index covers material in both the basic volume of the Bibliography and this first supplement. Reference numbers in bold face are to the items that appear in the supplement at hand; those in regular type are to be found in the basic volume. The number refers to the individual item, not to a page.

A

Aachen, Germans from, n.d. 5436
Aargau, Swiss from, 1650-1800 4916
Aberdeen, Scots from
  to New York, 1834.................... 6450, 8520
  to Prince Edward Island, 1806 .... **1446.3**
Acadian settlement, St. Gabriel, La., 1767ff. **1139.6**
Acadians
  and French government pensions, 1767 2344
  and Hispaniola, 1764.......................2394
  and the *Saint-Jehan,* from France, 1636.. 2672, 2682
  during American Revolution, 1778 9880
  exiled,
    Beausejour to Miquelon and to France 2384
    fate of 3500
    France to Louisiana, 1785 7445
    Georgia to New York, 1756 6414
    Maryland to Louisiana, 1767 .... **1139.6**
    to Carolina(s), 1755-1768 7430
    to Cherbourg, 1767 2344
    to Connecticut, 1755-1768 7430
    to France, n.d. 3050-51
    to Georgia, 1755-1768 7430
    to islands, French-owned 2384
    to Maryland, 1755-1768 7430
    to Massachusetts,
      1750s 1658
      1755-1768 .... 2394, 7430
    to Miquelon, 1765-1767 .... 2354, 2384
    to New Orleans
      1767, 1769 .... **1139.6, 4676**
      1785 7445
    to New York, 1755-1768 .... 3503, 6414, 7430
    to Pennsylvania, 1755-1768 7430
    to Quebec, 1764 2394
    to St. Pierre, 1767 2354
    to South Carolina (Winyah), 1755-1756 5655
  incapacitated, South Carolina, 1756 5655
  petition to Governor of Mass., 1764 2394
  shipwrecked in Gulf of Mexico, 1769 ....**4676**
Acton, Ontario, gravestone transcriptions **9593**
Adams family, 1572-1640, 1675 .... 0048, 1292
Adelsverein, German society of nobles, 1845........8302
Adenau, Germans from, 1831-1911 .... **5776**, 8017
Admiral, with Wisconsin-bound Germans, 1855.....**7200**
Adria, Polish exiles aboard, 1835 ....**4606**
Aegir, Norwegians to New York on the,
 1836, 1837 1056
Africa, departure from Sierra Leone, 1870..........0289
Africa, West, arrivals from,
 New York, 1870 0289
Ahlfeld family, arrivals, 19th c. 3886
Aide-de-Camp, Ireland to Canada, 19th c...........**7078**
Aix-la-Chapelle, departures, n.d....................5436
Ajax. Liverpool to New Orleans, 1820 ....**5034**
Alabama
  arrivals, 1821-1822...........................5715
  French to, before 1764 9600
  Germans to, 1832-1852 5203-5204
  Irish to, 1832-1852 5203-5204
  naturalizations
    1764 (Mobile) colonial 9600
    1800s (Selma) 5218
    1833-1871 (Mobile) 1386-1397, **1398-1401**
    1880-1930 (Southern District) 4565
Alaska arrivals, late 19th, early 20th c. **0158**
Albany Township, Berks County, Pa., arrivals,
 1727-1757 3258
Albemarle, men aboard the, 1669-1676.............1153
Albert, Bremen to New York, 1858 .... **1133.28**

Albion,
Hull, England, to Fort Cumberland, N.S., 1774 5675
Irish to Canada on the, 1825 2832
New York to Texas, 1829 7740
Aldingbourne, West Sussex, paupers from, 1832 . . . . **0092**
Alexander,
Germany to New York, 1838-1868 . . . . **1133.23**
Scotland to Canada, 1772 . . . . **0924**
Alexandria County, Va., arrivals, 1801-1832 1768
Aliases, on prisoner lists 3700
Alien resident permits, New York 17th, 18th c. 8270
Allegheny County, Pa., naturalizations, 1880-1906 . . . . **9700-9702**
Allen, Captain, master of the *West Point,* 1849 3378
Allen, from Rotterdam to Pennsylvania, 1729 1732
Almshouses, Amsterdam, children from, to colonies, 1655 1988
Alsace-Lorraine,
French from, 1727-1775 2883
Germans from, to New York, 1820-1850 1874
Alsace, Lower, Germans from, 18th c. 4133
Alsatians to [?] Pennsylvania, 18th c. **4255**
Altenburg, Mo., Germans to, 1838-1839 4803
Alwina, Bremen to New York, 1841 . . . . **4902**
Alzey, Germans from, mid-18th c. 4308
Amalfi, with Central and Eastern Europeans
to Baltimore, 1893 . . . . 9034, **9035**
to New York, 1893 . . . . 9034, **9035**
Amalia, sinking of the, 1839, 1840(?) **2095**
Amboy, N.J., Germans and Swiss to, 1819 . . . . **3295**
Amelia County, Va., inhabitants, 1737-1745 0618
Amelia, of Belfast, to the Delaware River, runaways from, 1783 9158
America
to Jamaica, slaves aboard, 1675 . . . . **7852**
to Philadelphia, Mennonites, 1683 8490
American Merchant to Maryland, 1714 6077
American Revolution *see* Revolutionary War
Amish,
French, arrival of, 1831-1840 6431
German, arrival of, 1831-1840 6431
Amity, Irish to Canada on the, 1825 2832
Amsterdam, departures
Dutch from, to Delaware River area, 1661 1722
Elizabeth to Philadelphia, 1819 6500
Providence to Baltimore, 1833 . . . . **3704**
Amundson, Hans, and Swedish expedition, 1649 3760
Ancestry, clues to English **5820**
Anchoria, Norway and Sweden to New York, 1892 . . . . **1133.46**
Ancient and Honourable Artillery Company, members up to 1662 1936
Andover, Mass., Acadian French in exile 1658
Andrew, to New York, Germans aboard, 1852 . . . . **8509.1**
Anhalt, Germans from, 1850-1852 3886
Anhalt-Zerbst, Germans from, 18th c. **1505**
Anjou, French from, to Canada, 1636 5811
Ann
arrival of the, 1623 4692
England to Georgia, 1733 6494
England to Virginia, ca. 1623 5695
to Nova Scotia, 1750 . . . . **7012, 7075**
see also *Anne*
Annapolis, Md., documents in Hall of Records 9880
Annapolis, N.S., arrivals from Boston, 1760 9820
Annapolis Royal, Nova Scotia, the *Charming Molly* to, 1760 1072
Anne
British to Georgia on the, 1732 1312
to Carolina, 1723-1724 0608
to Plymouth [colony], 1623 . . . . 0255, 2713, 3408
to Virginia, 1723-1724 0608
see also *Ann*
Ansbach-Bayreuth,
Germans from, 18th c. 8640
troops from, in American war, 1777-1783 8905
Ansbach troopers to Nova Scotia, 1780s **6987**
Anstoss, Germans from, 1738 0212
Ant je Brons, Emden, Germany, to New York 1855, 1857 9664
Antigua,
English to, 1752-1756 2328
Scots to, 1774-1775 1088
Antoinette Marie, Bentheim and Rotterdam to New York, 1847 6895
Antwerp
Belgians from,
1843 . . . . **5608**
1906 . . . . **4810**
departures,
Belgique, 1857 . . . . **1133.18** and **.38**
Germania, 1863 . . . . **1133.4**
New Hampshire, 1838-68 . . . . **1133.20**
Ornen, 1843 . . . . **5608**
Dutch from, 1846-1847 . . . . **9362**
Germans from Russia via,
1893-1902 . . . . 2842, **3844, 6750**
Germans to N. America via,
1838-1868 (to N.Y.) . . . . **1133.20** and **.22**
1845 (to Galveston) 7405
Luxembourgers to New York via,
1848-1882 . . . . **6428.1** and **.16**
Antwerp Emigration Index for 1855 . . . . **2885**
Apatin, Yugoslavia, arrivals from, ca. 1900 6740
Appenhofen, Germans from, 18th c. 4259
Applewaite, Thomas, commander of the *Crown Milligo,* 1677 0356
Apprentices, bound,
Philadelphia,
1745-1746 . . . . 6054-56, 8357-58
1771-1773 . . . . 7207, 7222-23
search notices for 8242-8245
to Bermuda, from London, 1850 9995
Arabella, to New England,
1630, 1671 . . . . 6550, 7660
Arbella see *Arabella*
Arestedes
with passengers for Minn. 19th c. **1133.42**
with passengers for Ohio, 1838-1868 . . . . **1133.23**
Argentina, Germans from Russia to, 1878 . . . . **9674**
Argyleshire, Scots from, to North Carolina, 1767 5009
Argyll, Earl of, 1685 1110
Arizona, naturalizations, 19th c. **1213.1-.3**
Ark, to Maryland,
n.d. 1036, 6157

1634 .... 6070, 7141, 7976
Arkansas
Germans to, 1833 .... **3300**
naturalizations,
1809-1906 (statewide) 9280
1855-1887 (Lawrence County) **3688**
Aroostook County, Maine, naturalizations,
1873-1900 .... **6410.5**
Arran Island, Scots from, 1829-1832 .... **7199**
Arrivals
English and Welsh, 17th-19th c. **1862**
from Antwerp, indexed, 1855 .... **2885**
Germans from Russia, 1880s **7124.1-.8**
Scots, before 1700 .... **1640.1-.2, 1750, 6185**
Scottish exiles, 1687 .... **9838**
1600-1900, consolidation of lists **2048.1-.2**
1750 and earlier, consolidation of lists ... 9448, 9450
1700s, sources compared **0926.4**
1821-1823, State Dept. transcripts 9268
Ashley River region, S.C., French to, 1679 1916
Ashwell, Hertfordshire, English from, 1836 .... **9628**
Asperg, Germans from, 18th, 19th c. 0638
Associated Friends of Ireland, 1831-1834 .... **9076**
Atlantic, Aberdeen, to New York, 1834 ...... 6450, 8520
Atlantic seaboard,
Barbadians to, 17th, 18th c. **0773**
British to, 1654-1685 0943
naturalizations, 1817-1850 3530
settlers, 1607-1657 1262
Attakapas area, La., inhabitants, 1795-1823 9424
Auerbach, Germans from, 19th c. **9072**
Auglaize County, Ohio, nat'zations, 19th c. **0176.1-.12**
Augusta County, Va.,
arrivals, 1739-1740 .... 3816, 5831
Palatines naturalized, 18th c. **0926.57**
Augusta, Georgia
naturalized citizens, 1867 .... **1451.45**
Augustan Society Library, Torrance, Calif.,
Emigrant Files **1831, 1862**
Aurania, from Liverpool and Queenstown
to New York, 1888 .... **1133.44**
Austin, Texas, Scots to, 1880s **9777**
Australia
English to
1778-1853 .... **4915**
1830s-1850s **2526.10**
1840s **2526.40**
Foehr Islanders to, 1850-1875 .... **8596**
Germans to
1800s 1858
1825-1854 .... 3474, 5085
1847-1903 .... 3914, 4460, **8657**
Hamburg ships to Adelaide and Sydney, 1850 .. 8656
Irish to,
1834-1845 .... **9576**
1848-1860 .... **6413.20**
Poles (Old Lutherans) to, 1835-1854 3474
Wends to, 19th c. 1858
Austria, Salzburg departures,
to Georgia, 1734-1739 .... **0926.36,** 1134, 7820, 9055, 9330
Austrians
arrivals, 1850-1882 2172
from Guessing, 1884-1939 2762
from Imperial Circle of Vohenstrauss,
1843-1877 4596
in Pennsylvania, 1900 .... **7137**
to Georgia 1730s-1740s **0926.36,** 1134, **3609,** 7820, **9332**
to New York, 1893 .... **9027, 9028**
to North Dakota before 1918 .... **0090**
to Texas, 1858-1929 3830

B

Bacon, Anthony, captain of the *York,* 1740 9725
Baden,
Germans from,
1816-1817 .... **5745**
1830-1935 8120
Fuerstenberg territories, 1712, 1737, 1787 ... **8606**
Herbolzheim, n.d. 4033
Upper Rhine, 18th c. **2855.5**
Germans from, to Illinois, 1840s 1976
Baden-Durlach, Germans from
1710-1815 .... 3565-70, **3570.1-.5**
1738 4089
1749-1755 .. 4085, 4094, 4095, 4287, 4322, 4417, 4435
1700s **8667**
Baden-Wuerttemberg, Germans from
1727-1775 2883
18th, 19th c 0121, **8667**
1829-1900 .... **2852**
Baltimore
arrivals
from Bremen
1834 3080
1840, 1841 .... **5911, 8515**
1854, 1868 .... **6912, 8514**
1874 .... **5235, 5237**
1886 .... **3260**
from Glasgow, 1874 .... **5235**
from Liverpool,
1834 .... **5034**
1874 .... **5235**
1882 .... **5233**
from the Netherlands, 1784 9902
British to
1820-1834 .... **0253, 5034**
1874 .... **5235**
1882 .... **5233**
Central and Eastern Europeans to,
1893 .... 9034, **9035**
Czechoslovakians to,
1868 .... **8514**
1879 .... **0205**
Dutch to
1784 9902
1847 0675
Germans to,
1820-1834 .... **0253, 3704**
1841 .... **8515, 9090**
1854-56 .... 2414, **7200**

Baltimore, *cont'd*
1895 9207
from Hesse, 1854, 1855 2414
from Russia
1849-1910 .... **2974.1**
1873-1878 ...... 0438, 1882, 2969, 4019, 4497
Irish to
1811 .... 2859, 8796
1815-1816 1742
1820-1834 .... **0253, 5034**
by 1831 .... **9076**
1841-1842 .... **6508.8**
Poles to,
early on, n.d. **1163**
on the *Stuttgart,* 1895 .... **9207**
port passenger lists, 1874 .... **5237**
Scots to, 1871 .... **6508.6**
ships to,
Admiral, 1855 .... **7200**
Capellen tot den Pol, 1784 9902
Columbia, 1856 .... **7200**
Ferdinand, 1834 3080
Goethe, 1854 3705
Helena 1840 5623
Herald, 1834 .... **5034**
Hohenzollern, 1886 .... **3260**
Johannes, 1834 0285
Lucilla, 1840 .... **5911**
Marianne, 1855 .... **7200**
Neptune, 1840 5613
North America, 1784 9902
Ocean, 1841 .... **9090**
Stuttgart, 1895 .... **9207**
Texas, the, 1882 .... **5233**
various ships,
1833 .... **3704**
1874 .... **5235, 5237**
Virginia, the, 1841 .... **8515**
Baltimore County, Md.,
land records, 1722 .... **0340**
servants to, 1772-1774 1362
Banbury Union, Oxfordshire, emigration,
1830s-1850s **2526.10**
Baptismal records, French in "New France,"
1621-1700 6830
Baptist Herald, obituaries of Germans
from Russia, 1800s to 1950s 6381
Baptists in Delaware, Welsh, 1701-1713 1798
Barbados
British to,
1648, 1656 .... **1235**
1677 .... 1252, 9540
1600s **1139.1**
census of 1679-1680 .... **0776**
departures for, 1634-1635 8835
departures from,
to American colonies, 1678 3280
to Atlantic seabord, 17th, 18th c. **0773**
to Jamaica; Va.; N.Y.: 1679 .... **8408**
English to, 1654-1686 .... **3438.1-.6**
indentured servants to, 1683-1684 6179
prisoners to, ca. 1745 4920
Quakers in, n.d. **0773**
Scottish rebels to, 1716 8690
Barclay, Thomas, Quebec, 1801 .... **5277**
Barnet, Vt., Scots to, 1774 3670
Barriere, Michel Bernard, clergyman,
Louisiana, 19th c. 9424
Barron, Richard, and the *Oxford* prisoners,
1776 3110
"Basel Lists," 18th c., additions and
corrections to 8040
Basel, Swiss from
1650-1800 4916
1709-1795 1960
Basses Choyse, Va., inhabitants, 1625 5907
Bastrop, La., French to, 1797 6695
Bath County, N.C., arrivals, 1695-1702 2334
Bathurst, New Brunswick, arrivals, 1837 .... **0358.13**
Bauer family, Germans from Russia, 19th c. **9490**
Bavaria,
Austrians from Imperial Circle of
Vohenstrauss, 1843-1877 4596
Germans from,
18th c. 0558, **2854,** 4329, 8640, 8905
19th c. 0598, 3879, 3941
to American Revolution 8640, 8905
remaining after American Revolution 8640
see also Germans from Bavaria; Mercenary
troops, Ansbach-Bayreuth; Palatinate, Southern
Bavaria, Upper, Germans from, 1846-1852 0598
Bay Colony, English to, 1620-1640 0263
Bay of Fundy, N.B., Loyalists return, [18th c.] ... **0358.41**
Beaver County, Pa., nat'zations, 1849-1854 .... **6002**
Becker family arrivals, from Germany, 1878 .... **9556**
Bedford County, Pa., naturalizations,
19th c. **6013.7**
n.d. **0470.1-.2**
Bedfordshire, English from, 1663-1775 .... **1217.7**
Beihingen am Neckar, Germans from
1727-1934 8634
ca. 1895 7537
Beindersheim, Germans from, 19th c. 7967
Belfast
departures for Philadelphia
the *Ceres,* 1817 3075
the *Sarah Sheaffe,* 1836 1384
departures for Wilmington, the *Brothers*
1789-1790 .... 2044, 2046
Irish from, 1813-1837 .... 2080, **6121**
Belgians
in western Pennsylvania, 1889-1904 .... **7664**
to New York, 1906 .... **4810**
to Virginia, 1700 0953
to Wisconsin, 1843 .... **5608**
Belgique, Antwerp to N.Y., 1857 .... **1133.18** and **.38**
Belgium
arrivals from, 1848-1882 .... **6428.1-.16**
departures
for New Netherland, 1620-1664 8060
for Quebec, numerous ships, 1893 1697
from Antwerp *see* Antwerp
from Malmedy (formerly Prussian),
1843-1919 3740
Belleville, Tex., naturalization records,
1846-1847 6231-32
Bensheim, Germans from, 19th c. **9072**

Bergen, Teunis G., manuscripts 0508-09
Bergen, Norwegians from, 1848 . . . . **5982**
Bergholm, Ia., Swedes to, 1846-1855 . . . . **2090**
Bergzabern, Germans from, 1709-1766 4141
Berks County, Pa.,
  Germans at Host Church, 18th c. 1032, **1033.4**
  Germans to, 1732-1751 1032
  naturalizations, 19th c. **0515-0518**
Berkshire, English from, 1663-1775 . . . . **1217.6**
Bermuda
  British children to, 1850 9995
  earliest settlers, 17th c. **5400**
"Bern Lists," 18th c., additions and
 corrections to 8040
Bern, Swiss from
  1650-1800 4916
  1709-1795 1960
  to Pennsylvania, 17th c. **4483**
Bernkastel area, Germans from, n.d. 5408
Bernstadt Colony, Laurel County, Ky.,
 Swiss to, from 1881 8054
Bertolet family, Pennsylvania, 1806 . . . . **9950**
Berwick, Me. *see* Kittery; Lynn
Beta, Bremen to New York, 1852 . . . . **8508**
Bethlehem, Pa.,
  Moravian Archives 3171
  Moravian marriages, 18th c. 0454
  Moravians to, mid-18th c. 3660-61
Bethsalem Presbyterian Church, Winston County, Miss.,
 and gravestones of Irish **9593**
Bettina, German colony, New Braunfels, Texas,
 19th c. 9780
Beverly, Mass., arrivals, 1798-1800 3130
Bevis, Southampton, to New England, 1638 6606
Biencourt family, Canada, 17th, 18th c. 4846
Billigheim, Germans from, 18th c. 4329
Billingsport, N.J., Irish to, from Cork, 1787 . . . . **4049**
Birkenfeld, Germans from, 1697-1815 . . . . 5728, 9660
Birth dates of foreign-born,
  Tripp County, S.D., 1856-1888 . . . . **2984**
Birth records,
  Irish in America, ca. 18th c. 6276
  Maryland, 18th c. 0321, 0323, 0325, 0327
  see also Church records
Bischweiler, Zweibruecken, Germans from,
 1760-1764 8050
Bischwiller *see* Bischweiler
Bitburg, Germans from, 19th c. 5422
Board of Trade, London, lists of Palatines,
 1709 4772-4773
Boat hands *see* Seamen
Boehl, Palatines from,
  1726-1764 1034
  18th c. **1031.12**
Boeschen, Germans from, 1738 0212
Bohemians
  arrivals
    at Baltimore, 1874 . . . . **5237**
    via Crimea, 1874-1887 0008
    to Canada, n.d. 0008
    to Maryland, 1868 . . . . **8514**
    to North, South America, n.d. 0008
    to Saxony, 1772 6087
    to Wisconsin, 1907-1925 1867-68
Boltzius, J.M., pastor, leader of
  Salzburgers to Georgia, 1730s **9332**
Bonded immigrants
  Barbados, 1654-1686 . . . . **3438.1-.6**
  Massachusetts, 1847-1851 5328
  to various colonies before Revolution **1217.1-.9**
Bonded servants *see* Indentured servants
Bondmasters,
  Bristol, Eng., 1654-1686 3438
  British, 1654-1686 . . . . **3438.1-.6**
  New England, 1657-1686 3440
  Virginia, 1674-1702 . . . . **0620**
Bonfeld, Germans from, 1710-1738 . . . . **3627**
Bonn, Germans from, 1814-1914 . . . . **9638**
Bonny Bess, England to Virginia, ca. 1623 5695
Bosque County, Texas, Norwegians to,
 mid-19th c. 4026
Boston
  arrivals,
    1679 6560
    1715-1716 9750
    1762-1769 9750
  English to, 1620-1640 0263
  French Canadians to, 1763 2374
  French to, 1751 . . . . 3333, 3335
  Germans to
    1751 . . . . 3333, 3335, 4210
    1777 after Saratoga 0140
  Huguenots to, 17th, 18th c. **7204**
  Hungarians to, 1882 . . . . **0611**
  Irish to,
    from the North, 1804-1806 3450
    via Halifax, 18th, 19th c. 7095-7098
  Quakers to, on the *Speedwell,* 1656 1352
  Scandinavian seamen to, 1815-1840 . . . . **6410.30**
  Scots to, 1716-1766 9412
  Swedes to, 1881 and earlier **6410.40, 6412.50**
Boston Pilot, search notices for
 missing Irish, 19th c. 6417
Boulder County, Colo., nat'zations, n.d. **9678.1-.3**
Bounty Act of 1761 (South Carolina) 7343
Bounty grants, Georgia, 1756-1909 4890
Bounty payments to arrivals,
  New Brunswick, 1804 . . . . **0358.2**
  South Carolina, 1768 9598
Bowdle, S.D., Germans from Russia to,
  1889-1899 . . . . **1641, 2995, 7846**
Brac, Yugoslavia, departures for California,
 1891-1913 6785
Bradford, William,
  colonial governor 0695, 0756, 0768, 4692
Brand, Christian Carl, and family, to Philadelphia,
 1749 . . . . **4319**
Brandenburg, Germans from, 1835-1854 3474
Brandenburg, S.S., out of Bremen
  to New York, 1907 2424
  to Philadelphia, 1910 2424
Braunschweig *see* Brunswick
Brazil,
  British to, via Mobile, Alabama, 1866 5705
  departures for New York, 1870 0289

Brazil, *cont'd*
Germans to,
from Baden, n.d. 0119
from Duchy of Nassau, 1806-1866 9061
from Gemuenden (Hunsrueck), 1827-1897 ... 1612
from Malmedy, 1843-1919 3740
out of Hamburg, 1850 .... **8657**
Brazilian landowners, N.D., 1918 .... **0090**
Brechbuhl, Benedict, and Swiss Mennonites to Pa., 18th c. **1035.25**
Breisgau, Germans from, 18th c. **2855.5**
Bremen
emigration lists
1832-1849 9640
1849-1850 3967
German Lutherans from, 1838-1841 .... **2095**
Germans from Russia, 1874, 1875 .... 0438, 2966
to Baltimore,
many ships, 1874 .... 5235, 5237
the *Goethe*, 1854 3705
the *Herman*, 1889 7921
the *Hohenzollern*, 1886 .... **3260**
the *Johannes*, 1834 0285
the *Ocean*, 1841 .... **9090**
the *Stuttgart*, 1895 .... **9207**
the *Virginia*, 1841 .... **8515**
to Galveston, the *Canapus*, 1848 .... **2518**
to New Orleans
Balkan and Eastern Europeans, 1845 6127
the *Burgundy*, 1848 5153
the *Gen'l Washington*, 1845 0544
the *Wm. D. Sewall*, 1845 0544
to New York,
Czechs for Nebraska, 1879 .... **8774**
Germans from Lower Saxony, 1839 2242
Germans from Russia *see* Germans from Russia to N.Y. via Bremen
Iowa-bound, 1848-1865 .... **1133.6, 1133.12**
Ohio-bound, 1838-1868 .... **1133.22**
the *Albert*, 1858 .... **1133.28**
the *Alwina*, 1841 .... **4902**
the *Beta*, 1852 .... **8508**
the *Coriolan*, 1864 .... **1133.38**
the *Dettmar*, 1849 .... **1133.36**
the *Elisabeth*, 1832 0789
the *Ferdinand*, 1864 .... **1133.38**
the *Fulda*
1886 .... **9225**
1889 1765
the *Gil Blas*, 1849 .... **1133.32**
the *Goethe*, 1868 .... **1133.44**
the *H.H. Meier*, 1893 .... **7945**
the *Hansa*, 1852 .... **8506**
the *Helene*, 1849 0689
the *Jupiter*, 1864 .... **1133.52**
the *Kaiser Wilhelm der Grosse*
1899 .... **2995**
1902 .... **4061**
the *Kunigrude*, 1852 .... **8508**
the *Lahn*, 1893 .... **7945**
the *Mainz*, 1900 .... **2307**
the *Meier*, 1893 .... **7945**
the *Oder*, 1875 .... **0446**
the *Olympia*, 1857 .... **1133.38**
the *Orpheus*, 1861 .... **1133.56**
the *Republic*, 1868 .... **1133.44**
the *Salier*, 1882 6206
the *Stuttgart*, 1895 .... **9207**
the *Thusneleta*, 1861 .... **1133.56**
the *Union*, 1868 .... **1133.20**
various ships,
1852 .... 8500, 8503
1854-1862 .... **1133.6**
Wisconsin-bound passengers,
1847-1848 5821
to Texas,
Germans, 1845, 1851 .... 2474-76, 2514
Bremerhaven *see* Bremen
Brethren, Church of the,
early 18th c. 1732
Switzerland, 17th c. **4483**
Brethren, Mennonite, Swiss, 17th c. **8042**
Breton, Le Havre to Carolina, 1564 0228
Brideship, or *Tynemouth*, from England
to British Columbia, 1862 5321
Bridewell, English prisoners from, 18th c. 0608
Bristol, departures from, 1654-1686 .... 0943, 2899, 3438
to Pennsylvania, British, ca. 1682 2979
to Virginia, the *Joseph and Thomas*, 1707 0666
Britannia
founders off Newfoundland, 1842 9770
German passengers, 1773 4662
to Georgia, Irish aboard, 1772 .... **5996**
to Pennsylvania, 1773 1632
British,
arrivals,
1600s 3283
1620-1822 .... **3279,** 8790
1628-1640 .... 7237, **8426.1-.6**
1654-1680s 2890, **8426.1-.6,** 9590
1718-1759 .... 2324, 3690
1778-1874 .... **4915, 6508.7, 8426.1-.6**
on the *Bevis*, 1638 6606
on the *Eutaw*, 1841 .... **4903**
on the *Hercules*, 1635-1637 7111
on the *Laura*, out of Kent, 1748 1232
on the *Louisa*, Liverpool, 1834 0294
on the *Mary and John*, 1630 .... **8877**
on the *Mexico*, Liverpool, 1830 4860
colonies,
Germans to, 18th c. 4378
Scots to, 18th c. **1014**
foot regiments in North America
4th (King's Own) 8570
7th (Fusiliers) **8570.1**
10th (N. Lincolnshire) **8570.10**
15th (York, East Riding) **8570.15**
49th in Jamaica and N.Y., 1760-63 .... **8534**
99th (Prince of Wales), 1820 .... **9554**
forces in American Revolution
disbanded in Nova Scotia, 1820 .... **9554**
foot regiments that fought .... **8570, .1, .10, .15**
from Newcastle, 1685 0973
government, claim against, for Palatine debtors, 1710-1713 1811
in U.S., during War of 1812 8195

British, *cont'd*
in Virginia, 1777 ... **1211**
indentured servants,
1654-1692 ... 2524, 3438, 9580
1718-1759 ... 2554, 3510, 3690
1745-1780 ... **1357.1-.2**
infantry *see* foot regiments
military, siding with Americans, 1782-83 ... 8665
naturalized,
1802 ... 6047-48
1811-1816 ... 6031
"by particular acts," 1600s-1700s ... 3213-15
in Georgia, 1793-1868 ... **0056.1**
in Illinois (Morgan County), 1835-1894 ... 3368
in Indiana, 1817-1824 ... **1385**
in Iowa, 1838-1853 ... **8773**
in New Hampshire, 1792-1849 ... 8232
in New York
1782, 1785 (by legislative act) ... 5841
1782-1784 (statewide) ... 1906
1790-1828 (Southern District) ... 1140
1800-1840 (Saratoga County) ... 5934
1800-1855 (several counties) ... 0016
1807-1828 (Allegany County) ... 5972
1816-1870 (Cortland County) ... 1568
1830-1839 (Onondaga, Wayne Cos.) ... 5942
1830-1849 (Cayuga County) ... 5962
19th c. (Saratoga County) ... **5935**
in Ohio, 1819-1832 ... **9892**
in Pennsylvania
1795-1888 (Washington County) ... 8276-77
1798-1802 (Huntingdon County) ... **3330.1-.4**
1820-1840 (Western District) ... 2847
1835-1836 (Cambria County) ... **1076.1-.4**
19th c. (Fulton, Bedford Cos.) ... **6013.7**
in Texas
1880-1905 ... 8350
19th c. ... **1447.1-.4**
port departures *see* names of individual ports
prisoners, 1721-1780 ... **1357.1-.2, 8435,** 8530, 8534, 8541, **8543, 8695,** 9725
purchasers of land in Pennsylvania,
1681-1682 ... 0032
to American colonies, places unspecified,
17th c. ... **0776, 1139.1**
17th, 18th c. ... **1217.1-.9**
to Australia, 1778-1874 ... **4915**
to Baltimore, 1820-1834 ... **0253,** 0294
to Barbados,
1648, 1656 ... **1235**
1677 ... 9450
to Bermuda,
because of shipwreck, 1609-1610 ... 9227
children, 1850 ... 9995
to Boston,
1631 ... 9110
1712 ... 0154
to Brazil via Mobile, Ala., 1866 ... 5705
to British Columbia, ca. 1862
on the *Cyclone* ... 5304
on the *Mountain Wave* ... 5314
on the *Pacific* ... 5294
on the *Sierra Nevada* ... 5284
on the *Tynemouth* ... 5321

British, *cont'd*
via San Francisco, 1862 ... 5284, 5294, 5321
to Bucks County, Pa., 1687 and earlier... 0418, 0428
to Canada,
from London, 1862 ... 5304
from Sussex,
1778-1874 ... **4915**
1830s-1840s ... 9979
to Manitoba's Red River, 1871 ... **7323**
to Prince Edward Island,
18th, 19th c. ... **1446.1-.3, 4646**
to Delaware, 1831 ... **6508.7**
to Georgia,
1730s-1740s ... 1312, 3388
1774-1775 ... **1245, 3430**
1785-1790 ... 1078
1820-1868 ... 9890
to Jamaica, 1675 ... **7852**
to Maine, before 1630 ... 8880
to Maryland,
1650-1700s ... 0333, 0354, 0356, 2162, 9540
1703-1740 ... **4912, 8805,** 9725
1874, 1882 ... **5233, 5235**
to Massachusetts,
1630-1639 ... 0281, 1432, 3323, 4477
to Minnesota, 1888 ... **1133.44**
to New Brunswick,
1803 ... **0358.15**
1907 ... 7630
to New England,
1600s, 1700s ... 1046, 1672, 1674
1600-1649 ... 0124, **0232,** 0281, 0378, 1432, 3327, 4477, 5781, 6545, 6606, 7111, 8780
1654-1687 ... 0943, 4910, 6570, 9610, 9620
1700-1775 ... 0658
1843-1849 ... 7906-7907
see also specific place-names
to New Jersey,
1664 ... 1992
1674-1681 ... 3580, 8070
to New Netherland, 1639 ... 1984
to New Orleans, out of Wales, 1849 ... 2742
to New York,
1631-1637 ... 5781
1849-1868 ... **1133.26, 6200**
on the *Atlantic,* 1834 ... 6450
on the *Buchannon,* 1765 ... **6535**
on the *Lady Mary,* 1842 ... 9770
on the *Manhattan,* 1820 ... 6530
on the *Medora,* 1836 ... **3836**
on the *Orient,* 1842 ... 3796
on the *Scythia,* 1878 ... 8330
on the *West Point,* 1849 ... 3378
to Nova Scotia, from Yorkshire, 1774 ... 9975
to Philadelphia,
Gray family, 19th c. ... **2763.10**
Pennsylvania Packet, 1775 ... 4642
women servants, 18th c. ... **7855**
to Prince Edward Isl., 18th, 19th c. ... **1446.1-.3, 4646**
to South Carolina, 1718, 1728 ... 3510, **4912**
to Utah, 1849-1868 ... **6200**
to Virginia,
1631-1637 ... 3090, 5781
1677, 1686 ... 2162, 9540

British, *cont'd*
1700s 0225, 1782
1716, 1718 (ship diverted) **4727, 4912**
1721-1773 .... **2915, 8435**
18th c. 0225, 1782
to West Indies, places unspecified,
1631-1635 5781
1682-1686 .... **1139.1**
to West Jersey, 1664 1992
to Wisconsin,
1849 .... **1133.60**
1907-1925 1867-68
see also English; Irish; Scottish and Scots; Welsh
British Columbia, arrivals, 1860-1862 ... 5284, 5294, 5304, 5314, 5321, **5323**
British Crown Estates, Ireland, departures from, ca. 1850 1826
British Library documents on Palatines to England, 1709 9214
British Loyalists *see* Loyalists
British Queen, Scotland to Canada, 1790..........**1014**
Broad Bay, Me., Germans to, 1757 3341
Brooke, Robert, and family, to Md., 1650 ....**5997**
Brooklyn, Liverpool to Halifax, 1885 2529
Brother Jonathan, San Francisco to B.C., 1860 .....**5323**
Brothers, Belfast to Wilmington,
1789, 1790 .... 2044, 2046
Brown, Thos., and Georgia plantations, 18th c. **1245, 3430**
Brown family of New Jersey.....................0973
Brown County, Wis., naturalizations, 1841-1978 .. **3015.5**
Bruchhausen, Germans from, 1860-1866 5125
Brunner family to Maryland, 18th c. **3577**
Brunswick, Germans from, 1846-1871 2822
Brunswick troops
in American Revolution 0140, 1482, 7495
resettled after war 8560, 8562, 8670
Buchanan, Alexander, life of, Montreal **1001**
Buchanan, James, family, from Ireland, 19th c. **1001**
Buchannon, Ireland to New York, 1765 ....**6535**
Buckinghamshire, English from,
1663-1775 .... **1217.7**
17th, 18th c., to Pa. **2824**
Bucks County, Pa.,
arrivals recorded,
17th c. 7585
17th, 18th c. 9790
British to, 1687 and earlier 0418, 0428
inhabitants, to 1687 6463
Buedesheim, Germans from, to Texas, 1845 7405
Buffalo, N.Y.
arrivals, 1854-1864 .... **1133.18**
naturalizations, 1838-1842 .... **5867.1-.2**
Old Lutherans to, 1835-1854 ...... 3474, **7896,** 8655
Building tradesmen, from Netherlands and Scandinavia,
1631-1655 8134
Burgundy, French from, to Canada,
1653 through 1700s 1502
Burgundy,
Bremen to New Orleans, via England, 1848 5153
foundering of the, on British coast, 1848 5153
Burial records,
County Down, 19th, 20th c. **1194**
Irish in America, n.d. 6276, **9593**
Burial records *see also* Gravestone inscriptions
Burkholder, Hans, and Swiss Mennonites to Pennsylvania, 18th c. **1035.25**
Burlington,
Iowa, Swedes to, by 1855 ....**2090**
New Jersey, arrivals, 1677-1678 8070
Burwell, Lewis, Virginia, 1648 1297
Butte County, Calif., Great Register, 1878-1879 .... **1050.1-.7**

C

Caddo Parish, La., nat'zations, 1867-1925 .... **7129, 7130**
Cadillac, Mich., Swedes, citizenship,
1875-1882 ....**6717**
Cajun(s) *see* Acadians
Calaveras County, Calif., census, 1852 .... **1068.1-.3**
Calenberg, Germans from,
1753-1882 5080
1845, to Texas 5080
California,
arrivals,
1849-1875 at port of San Francisco...... 7875-91
1880's-1900s 5394
Augustan Library Irish files, 18th, 19th c. **1831**
Canadians to, 1880s-1900s 5394
census of Calaveras County, 1852 .... **1068.1-.3**
Germans to
by 1854 2932
1838-1859 .... 2053, 8656
Mexicans to, 1769-1835.......................**3365**
naturalizations,
1846-1850 (various counties) **6013.19**
1848-1872 (Santa Clara County) 1890
1856-1875 (San Francisco) 1888
1856-1887 (Los Angeles) **6410.20**
1860-1871 (Sacramento County) **7840.1-.51**
1866-1873 (San Diego County) **8361.1-.9**
1866-1877 (Kern County) **2763.54-.56**
1866-1878 (Siskiyou County) **8484.1-.38**
1871-1880 (Kern County) 0448-49
1872 (Tulare County) **2769.1-.10**
1875 (Sonoma County) **8865**
1878-1879 (Butte County) **1050.1-.7**
1879 (Siskiyou County) **3707.1-.19**
1880-1887 (San Diego County) **8361.30-.32**
1884 (Humboldt County) **4747**
1884 (Santa Clara County) **2763.20**
1884-1888 (Tulare County) 2765-68
1892 (Siskiyou County) **1820.1-.3**
1896-1898 (Fresno County) **2763.25-.33**
1898 and earlier (Mendocino County) 2764
1900 (Santa Clara County) **1981**
1903-1911 (Riverside County) 5394
1903-1925 (Riverside County) **5394.1-.7**
1936 (Yuba County) **6131**
19th, 20th c. (Contra Costa Co.) **2423**
Santa Clara County Grt. Register, 1900 ....**1981**
voting records, 1848-1875 .... 1888, 1890
Calumet County, Wis., nat'zations, 19th c. **3457.1**

Calvert, Leonard, colonial governor 7141
Cambria County, Pa.,
court records, n.d. **7138**
new citizens, 1835-1836 .... **1076.1-.4**
Cambridgeshire, English from, 1663-1775 .... **1217.7**
Campbell, John, and Scots to New Bruns., 1804... **0358.2**
Campbell, Lauchlin, Captain
and Highland emigration, 1736 6286
with Scots to Illinois, 1738-1740 6640
Canada,
Ansbach troopers to Nova Scotia, 1780s **6987**
arrivals,
Cape Breton Island, 19th c. **2919**
rescued from shipwreck, 19th c. **0358.17**
British Columbia, ships to, 1860-61 .... **5323**
British to
Atlantic ports, 1654-1685 0943
Pacific ports,
1860-1861 .... **5323**
1862 .... 5284, 5294, 5304, 5314, 5321
per English port books, 1618-1668 .... **1239**
Prince Edward Island, 1855 .... **4646**
Cape Breton Island census, 1818 .... **2919**
children to, from Fermanagh, 1846-1929 .... **1418**
colonists recruited for,
1653 .... 0172, 5374, 5751
1658 .... 1656, 2642
Compagnie du Nord-Ouest, 1797-1798 4762
Dutch to, 1789-1950 4880
English to,
from East Sussex, 1830s-1860s 1021, 1029
from Hertfordshire, 1836 .... **9628**
from Liverpool, 1841, 1864.......... **4906**, 6213
from London, 1862 5304
from Oxfordshire
1830s-1850s .... **2526.10, .40**
from Sussex
1832, 1836 .... **2043**, 2688, 8775
1830s-1862.................... 1021, 1029
from West Sussex, 1778-1874............. **4915**
indexed over three centuries **1862**
to Prince Edward Island
18th, 19th c. **1436, 1446.1-.3**
Foehr Islanders to, 1850-1875 .... **8596**
French from, to New England, 17th c. **7510.1-.2**
French to,
from Anjou, 1636 5811
from Burgundy, 1653- 1502
from LaRochelle,
17th, 18th c. 1462, 2632, 2642, 2662
from Lyons, 1632-1760 5583
from Normandy, 16th, 17th c. 9350
from Perche, 17th c 2612, **7510.1-.2**
from St. Malo, n.d. 3050-51
from several places, 1750-1752 .... **3745**
from Tourouvre, n.d. 5761
Montreal, 1653, 1659 .... 0172, 2662
on the *Saint-Jehan,* 1636 2682
Quebec, 1621-1700 6830
Germans to,
between 1750 and 1752 .... **3745**
from American Revolution,
1776-1783 .... 1482, 8640, 8643
1780s **6987, 7105**
from Baden, n.d. 0119
from Cottbus (Lower Lusatia), 1847-1883 ... 4467
from Dresden, 1850-1903 3914
from Hesse, 1753 5093
from Leipzig area, 1850-1855 3960
from Prussia, 19th c 8655
from Russia,
1849-1910 .... 1697, **1860, 2974.1, 4490**
from Thuringia, 1850 3948
via Rotterdam,
1751, 1752 .... **7076, 7079**
Hamburg ships to, 1850 .... 8656, **8657**
Huguenots to, 17th, 18th c. **7202, 7204**
"Indian Lands" for Scots, ca. 1817 0361
Irish Buchanan family to, 19th c. **1001**
Irish in Nova Scotia, 1820 .... **9554**
Irish in Ontario,
grave records, n.d. **9593**
Peterborough, 1825, 1975 1455
Irish to,
1815-1823 4986
1825 .... 2832, 1455
1830s **0358.21, 1500, 8867**
1839-1847 4575
1846-1929 .... **1418, 1433, 6213, 6413.20**
19th c. **7078**
from the North, n.d. **9254**
Loyalists,
to New Brunswick, n.d. **0358.41**
to Nova Scotia, 18th c. **7073**
Manitoba's Red River settlement,
1811-1816 .... 0998, 1000, 1014, 3600
1871 .... **7323**
Montreal census records, 1642-1667 5344-5346
New Brunswick,
British to, 1907 7630
English to, 1837 .... **0358.6, .13, .41**
Germans to, 1920s **2528**
Scots to, 1804-1840 ..... **0358.2, .13, .19, .26, .31**
unidentified arrivals, 1827, 1840s .... **0358.36, .46**
Northwest Company and settlers' contracts,
1797-1798 4762
Norwegians to, 1848 .... **5982**
Nova Scotia arrivals,
1749-1752 .... 0077, 0080, **7016, 7075**
1760, 1773 .... 1072, 3309, 5000
1774-1775 5675
1700s, unspecified 0860, **7073**
1818 .... **7005**
1829-1834 .... **3251**
1849-1910 .... **2974.1**
1800s **7078**
from Revolutionary War, 1784 .... **7105**
Ontario,
arrivals via New Brunswick, 1801 .... **5277**
English farm labor to, 1836 .... **9628**
government grants, early 19th c. 4502
in Ottawa public archives 0361, 1416
Irish in Peterborough, 1825-1975.......... 1455
Loyalists to Kingston, 1783 0398
naturalizations, 1828-1850 .... 5002, 5003
York settlement, 1799 2222

Canada, *cont'd*
Quebec,
Compton family, 1860s **1284**
ship lists, 1893 1697
see also Quebec as main entry
Rhode Islanders to Nova Scotia, 1760 3309
Russian Mennonites to, 1874-1880 ....**1865**
Russian refugees to, 1920s **2528**
Scandinavians to, 1619-1620 1898
Scots to
Hudson Bay, 1811, 1813 1000
Manitoba, 18th, 19th c. **1014**
Montreal, 18th c. **3370**
New Brunswick,
1804 .... **0358.2**
1815-1816 .... **0358.19** and **.31**
1837 .... **0358.13, .26**
Nova Scotia,
1771-1818 .... **4814,** 5000
1815-1816 5253
Ontario, 18th, 19th c. **1014,** 4918, **4968,** 4986
Prince Edward Island,
1772 ....**0924**
1848 ....**4649**
18th, 19th c. **1446.1-.3**
Quebec,
1774-1775 .... 1088, **3370**
1819-1832 ....**7199**
unspecified places, 1802 .... **5012.18**
ships to:
Brideship, 1862 5321
British Queen, 1790 ....**1014**
Clarendon, 1808 ....**1014**
Commerce, 1803 ....**1014**
Cyclone, 1862 5304
Dove of Aberdeen, 1801 ....**1014**
Dragonet, 1855 ....**4646**
Elizabeth & Ann, 1806 ....**1014**
Empress of Ireland, 1907 7630
Helen Thomson, 19th c. **0358.17**
Humphreys, 1806 ....**1014**
Isle of Skye, 1806 ....**1014**
Jane, 1790 ....**1014**
Lucy, 1790 ....**1014**
Montrose, 1924 2528
Mountain Wave, 1862 5314
Oughton, 1804 ....**1014**
Pacific, 1862 5294
Prince of Wales, 1813, 1815 ....**1014**
Saint Andre, 1659 2662
Saint Johan, 1636 2682
Sarah of Liverpool, 1801 ....**1014**
Sheffield, 1841 ....**4906**
Sierra Nevada, 1862 5284
Spencer, 1806 ....**1014**
Tynemouth, 1862 5321
see also under Nova Scotia, ships to
Swiss to, 1750-1752 .... **3745, 7076**
Ukrainians to, 1891-1900 3750
various nationalities to, 1757 4652
Welsh to, 17th-19th c. **1862, 7005**
see also specific place-names
Canada, Upper, *see* Ontario
Canadian
archives on Red River settlement, 19th c 5274
colonists recruited, 1653, 1659 .... 5364, 5374
militia, Montreal, members, 1663 5354
refugees to Lake Erie area, 1785 8660
Canadians
and land in New York state, 1775 .... 4930, 6147
in American Revolutionary War 1114, 8660
to California, 1880s-1900s...................5394
to New York, 1775 4930
see also Acadians
Canapus, Bremen to Galveston, 1848 ....**2518**
Canary Islands departures, 1778-1783..............9436
Canton, N.Y., naturalizations, n.d. **8525**
Cape Breton Island, Nova Scotia
census, 1818 ....**2919**
Loyalists to, 1784 4682
Scots to, 1829, 1843 .... 4970, 4980
Capellen tot den Pol,
Netherlands to Maryland, 1784 9902
ship with redemptioners who escaped, 1784.....9900
Captains, lists of,
on ships to Maryland, 18th c. **9897**
port of Philadelphia, 1727-1808 9041-9042
Cardiff, Wales, to New Orleans, the *Euphemia,*
1849 .... 2742, **3453**
Careers of Swiss immigrants, 16th-19th c. 4898
Caribbean area,
Acadian petition for Hispaniola, 1764 2394
Barbados families, n.d. **0773**
French from Santo Domingo, 18th, 19th c. 1712
see also specific place names
Caribbean Islands, British servants to, 1654-1685 0943
Carolina,
London to Virginia, 1773-1774 0225
to the Ashley River, S.C., 1669 1153
Carolina(s),
Acadian petition for Hispaniola, 1764 2394
Barbadians to, 1678 3280
Bermudans to, 17th, 18th c. **5400**
British to, a foot regiment, 1775-83 .... **8570.7**
early settlement of, 1584-1590 2875
English to, women prisoners, 1723-1724........0608
French to, from Normandy, 1564 0228
Germans to,
from Dossenheim, 18th c. 2917
from Hesse-Hanau, 1741-1767 8602
from Nassau-Dillenburg, n.d. 3233
from Palatinate,
1728-1749 3193
1732-1777 4280
1750-1771 .... 4357, 4364
indentured servants to, 1683-1684 6179
Scots deported to, 1684 ....**9842**
Swiss to, 1734-1752 .... 1946, 8945, 8955
Caroxbostel, Germans from, 1830-1848 5143
Carroll County, Ohio, naturalizations, 1833-1839....**7912**
Carroll Township, Cambria County, Pa., census
of 1900 ....**7137**
Cartier, Jacques, and Canadian explorers 3050-51
Cass County, Ind., nat'zations, 1870 ....**3246**
Catawba River area, N.C.,
Germans to, 1760s-1780s.....................**7755**

Catharine
Havana to New Orleans, 1820 .... **5034**
to New York and Philadelphia, 1742 0932
Cathay, N.D., Germans to,
from Rumania, 1899 .... **6404.6**
from Russia, late 19th c. 2529
Catherine, Volga Germans from, 1870s 1682
Catherine,
Amsterdam to New York, 1850 7355
Scotland to Nova Scotia, 1843 4970
see also the *Catharine*
Catholics
expelled from Georgia, 1756 6414
forcing Lutherans from Salzburg, 1739 9330
Polish, to Pennsylvania, 18th c. **2865**
Volga German,
to Canada, 1920s **2528**
to New York, 1875 2969
Catlenburg-Lindau, Germans from,
1831-1866 .... 5119, **5120**
Census records,
Acadians in Maryland, 1763 9880
Barbados, 1679-1680 .... **0776**
California (Calaveras Co.), 1852 .... **1068.1-.3**
Canada, 1663 9222
Cape Breton Island, 1818 .... **2919**
Georgia
1741 (Ebenezer) 9055
1850, 1860 1712
Islands of St. Pierre and Miquelon,
Acadian inhabitants, 1767 2354
Kansas (Kearny County), 1880 .... **3755**
Maryland (Acadians in), 1763 9880
Michigan (Clinton County), 1860 8017
Mississippi, 1816 .... **0926.49**
Missouri (2 counties), 1850 .... **3702**
Montreal, 1642-1667 5344-46
New York,
Germans in 1710 .... 5015, 5023, 6301, 6341
Italians, 1884-1930 .... **0692**
North Dakota landowners, 1918 .... **0090**
Pennsylvania,
1790 (statewide) **0926.4**
1900 (part of Cambria County) **7137**
Tennessee (Franklin County), 1850 2732
Virginia, colonial,
1607-1608 8745
1624/1625 3520
1625 (Isle of Wight County) 5907
Washington (Whitman County), 1889 .... **9473**
Central Europe,
arrivals in,
1712, 1737, 1787 .... **8606**
1750-1803 .... **8584**
departures from, 1850 .... 8656, **8657**
Central Europeans,
to California, 1848-1872 1890
to Kansas, 1876 2971
to Maryland, 1893 .... 9034, **9035**
to New York, 1893 .... 9034, **9035**
to Pennsylvania by 1900 .... **7137**
Ceres, Belfast to Philadelphia, 1817 3075
Certificates of removal, Quaker congregations,
from Ireland, 1682-1750 5917
various countries, 1682-1750 5924
Ceynosure, Liverpool to New York, 1855 1414
Chaleur Bay,
English to, 1837 .... **0358.13**
Irish to, 1837 .... **1500**
Scots to, 1837 .... **0358.13**
Champaign County, Ill.,
naturalizations, 1866-1892 .... **5012.40**
soldiers naturalized, 1866-1892 .... **5012.40**
Champneys family, Salem, N.J., 1675 1292
Charitas,
Sweden to Delaware, 1641 8002
Sweden to Pennsylvania, 1641 3766
Charles Crooker, Germany to N.Y., 1838-1868 .... **1133.23**
Charles Lottie, Gothenburg to N.Y., 1848 .... **6515**
"Charles Towne" (Charleston, S.C.), 1669 1288
Charleston, South Carolina,
English founding of, 1669 1288
French to, 1695, 1696 7192
Irish to,
1773 1594
1804-1806 3450
prisoners to, 1718 .... **4912**
Swiss to, 1695/1696 7192
"Charlestown" (Charleston, S.C.), 1773 .... 1288, 1594
Charlotte,
LeHavre to New York, 1833 .... **9037.1-.2, 9734**
out of Bremen, 1867 .... **1133.58**
Charlotte County, N.B., Scots to, 1804 .... **0358.2**
Charlotte Louise, Germany to N.Y., 1838-1868 .... **1133.23**
Charlottetown, P.E.I., British to,
on the *Clarendon,* 1808 .... **1446.3**
on the *Dragonet,* 1855 .... **4646**
on the *Valiant,* [19th c?] 8753
Charming Molly
Massachusetts to Nova Scotia, 1760 .... 1072, 9820
to Virginia, 1764-1765 .... **0614**
Chastain family, Virginia, 1700 0953
Chatelain family, from Switzerland, 1754 1148
Chavignaux family, to Canada, 1658 1656
Cherbourg, Acadians to, 1767 2344
Cherokee to Boston, Poles aboard, 1834 .... **4606**
Cheshire, English from,
bonded passengers, 1665-1775 .... **1217.8**
to Maryland, 1682 1587
to Pennsylvania, 1683 (Quakers) 5334
Chester County, S.C., naturalizations,
early 19th c 0069
Chicago, arrivals from Russia via New York,
1893 7941
Chicago Federal Archives and Records Center 1442
Children
apprenticed by Governor Hunter, New York,
1710-1714 5019
British poor, to Bermuda, 1850 9995
Dutch,
to New Amsterdam, 1655 1988
to New Netherland, 1755 8212
English, to Virginia, 1648-1685 .... **1257**
Irish, to U.S., Canada, 1846-1929 .... **1418**
orphans, sent from Netherlands, 1755 8212
Scottish, to Philadelphia, 1697-1698 .... **6185**

various origins, to Ohio, 1840s-1850s **3069**
Chile
Foehr Islanders to, 1850-1875 .... **8596**
Germans to,
1849-1855, from Bavaria 3879
1850 8657
1906-1912 8140
Chisago Lake, Minn., history of an
immigrant church, 1858-1983 .... **1832**
Cholera on ship from Hamburg, 1867 6447
Choptank River, Md., the *Submission* to, 1682 1587
Christenings of French in New France,
1621-1700 6830
Christians, German, flee State interference, 1830s ... **4058**
Christina, Del., the *Fama* from Stockholm, 1643 8000
Chronicle *see* Diary
Church emigration loans, Fressingfield,
Suffolk, 1836 7177
Church of England clergy to colonies,
1690-1811 .... 2120, 2144
Church of Jesus Christ of Latter-Day Saints
see Mormon(s)
Church of Scotland
family records, 19th c. **8893**
religious exiles, 1680s **9838, 9842, 9845**
Church of Seventh Day Adventists,
Bowdle, S.D., 1889 .... **1641**
Church of the Brethren,
Maryland, 1767-1772 6011
Pennsylvania, early 18th c 1732
Church of the pilgrims, New England, 17th c 5388
Church records,
Barbados, 1679-1680 .... **0776**
Germans from Russia in S.D. **0444**
Churchill Factory, Canada, Scots to, 1813 6765
Cimbria, Hamburg to New York, 1875 0439
Cincinnati, Germans to, 19th c 1578, 1582, **5747**
Citizenship *see* Naturalizations
City of Berlin, S.S., with Germans from Russia,
1875 1694
City of Chester, Russia to New York, 1874 9070
City of Richmond,
Liverpool/Queenstown to N.Y., 1888 .... **1133.44**
Russia to New York, 1874 9070
Civil liberties and new arrivals, 17th c. 3470
Clandestine immigration, young Germans, 1807 ..... **8646**
see also Desertions from mercenary troops
Clare, County, Irish from, 1850-1860 .... **6413.30**
Clarendon, Scotland to Canada, 1808 ...... **1014, 1446.3**
Clarion County, Pa., nat'zations, 1830-1900 .... **9155**
Clarissa, Norway to New York, 1842 .... **5985**
Clark County, Ind., nat'zations, 1888-1927 .... **1186**
Clark County, Ohio, nat'zations, 1890-1902 .... **6425**
Clarke, James, Liverpool departure, 1816 .... **1188**
Clearfield County, Pa., nat'zations, 1822-1862 ...... **0097**
Clergy,
British, to New England, 1690-1811 ..... 2120, 2144
Huguenot, in Virginia, 1750-1797 3630
Lutheran, from Austria, 1734-1739 9330
Maryland, colonial 9916
New England arrivals,
1630-1641 9170
1690-1811 .... 2120, 2144
Presbyterian, from Ulster, 1680-1820 5243
Clerks in the Northwest Company, 1797-1798 4762
Clindinnon, James, captain of *Brittania,* 1772 .... **5996**
Clinton, Illinois, naturalization records,
1850s-1870s 0024
Coblentz (Germany) official gazettes as research
source for 1824-1860 7524
Cochise County, Ariz., voter registrations,
1890 .... **1213.1-.3**
Cocke family, Virginia, 1700 0953
Colliers, Welsh to Maryland, ca. 1838 2920
Colonial arrivals,
clues to ancestry among **5820**
servants, British, 17th, 18th c. **1139.1, 1217.1-.9**
Colonial land grants, Va., 1690-1692 .... **6225**
Colonial law of naturalization, R. I. 7415
Colonial naturalizations,
German names **0926.52**
German/Swiss, 1729 .... **0926.18**
Germantown, Pa., 1691 .... **5650**
Palatines, 1740-1765 .... **0926.16**
Pennsylvania, 1709 .... **0926.26**
special, 1600s-1700s 3213-15
various .... **0926.16, .52, .63,** 2564
Virginia, 1652 .... **6251**
Colonial records
of Barbadoes, 1679-1680 .... **0776**
of British arrivals, 1621 .... **3279**
of Georgia, 18th c. 3388, **5996**
of Maryland, 1733-1773 1282-83
of North Carolina 9550
of Pennsylvania 6665-66
of Virginia,
1635 .... **1035.14**
1674-1702 .... **0620**
Colonies
of Germans, Texas, 1844 8150
of Mexicans, Calif., 1833 .... **3365**
Colonists
and debts owed in Eng., 1641-1736 .... **1235**
recruited for Montreal,
1653 .... 5374, 7690
1659 5364
Colorado
Germans from Russia to, 1889 .... **7242**
naturalizations,
Boulder County, n.d. **9678.1-.3**
statewide, 19th, 20th c. 6016-19
Columbia
Glasgow to N.Y., 1905 .... **1924**
to Baltimore, Germans aboard, 1856 .... **7200**
Commerce, maritime, 18th c. **9897**
Commerce,
Scotland to British N. Amer., 1803 .... **1014**
Scotland to New York, 1774-1775 .... 2202, 8425
Scotland to Nova Scotia, 1803 7088
Scotland to Quebec, 1821 4502
Compagnie du Nord-Ouest, Canada, 1797-1798 4762
Company of the Indies,
and French to Louisiana, 1718-1721 ..... 1542, 9190
recruits to Louisiana, 1719/1720 1542
Compton, William, and family, to Canada, 1860s ... **1284**

Concord,
England to Virginia, 1677 1252
to Pennsylvania,
Germans aboard, 1683 .... **9251, 9252**
Mennonites aboard, 1683 8490
Confederate passport records, 1855-1862 5223
Confidence, London to New England, 1638... **0232,** 8995
Congaree, South Carolina, Germans and Swiss to, 1732-1752 9480
Congregationalists in Minnesota, 1855-1867 6406
Connecticut,
colonial settlers, 1635 .... **3197**
English to, 1639 .... **9597**
Germans to, before 1700 .... 4822, 4830
Irish to, 19th c 2859
Loyalists from, to Canada 6407
naturalizations
1803-1844 (New Haven Co.) **8250**
New Haven arrivals on *Hector,* 1637-1638 1064
Scots to, 1685 2596
Society of *Mayflower* Descendants **6604**
Connewitz, Germans from, 1850-1855 3960
Conscription, military, as cause of emigration,
Northern Germany, 1838-1858 5135
Russia, 1874 .... 1677, 3872
Consolidated passenger and immigr. lists,
1600-1900 .... **2048.1-.2**
Consolidated ship list,
18th, 19th c., vessels arriving **0254, 5829**
Construction workers, Dutch and Scandinavian, New York, 1631-1655 8134
Contracts
between settlers and Northwest Company, Canada, 1797-1798 4762
for migration to Texas, 1830s 5011
for service, 1727-1731 2324
of indentured servants, from London,
1683-1686 9580
with French recruited for Canada,
1634-1715 .... 0172, 1462, 2642, 5374, 5751
Convicts *see* Prisoners
Cooper, William, of the *James* of London, 1635 1190
Copenhagen,
the *Catherine* from, to N.Y. and Philadelphia via London, 1742 0932
the *Guiding Star* to N.Y., 1869 0314
Scandinavians from, to New York, 1869 0314
Copernicus, Bremerhaven to New Orleans,
1838/1839 .... **2095**
Coppage family arrivals, 1648 1297
Coriolan, Bremen to New York, 1864 .... **1133.38**
Cork, Ireland,
the *City of Richmond* en route, 1888 .... **1133.44**
the *Paragon* from, to Newport, 1851 .... **6508.5**
the *Thetis* from, to New. Bruns., 1837 .... **1500**
Cornelia, Britain to New York, 1841 .... **4906**
Cornwall, English from, 1664-1775 .... **1217.5**
Cornwallis, Edward, Governor of Nova Scotia, 1749-1752 .... 0080, 7058
Cornwallis, and Acadian passengers, 18th c 5655
Correspondence *see* Letters about and by immigrants
Cost of board on the ship *Rensselaerswyck,* 1636-1637 9370
Costs *see* Passage payment; Subsistence account
Cottbus, Germans from, 19th c 4460, 4467
Court case: *Neptune* and its cargo, 1618/19 .... **1260**
Covenanters, Scotts, to New Jersey, 1685 2026
Covington, Ky., Germans in, 1830-1856 .... **9999.3**
Cowes, England, departures, 1743 0933
Craftsmen
from London guilds, ca. 1800 2135
from Netherlands and Scandinavia,
1631-1655 8134
Crawford County, Ind.
first papers, 1817-1824 .... **1385**
naturalizations, 1822-1896 .... **4598**
Crefeld (Krefeld), Germans from, 1683 .... **9251, 9252**
Crew *see* Seamen
Crimea, Bohemians from the 0008
Cromwell, and Scots deported, 1651-52 .... **1750**
Crown Estates, British, in Ireland, departures from, ca. 1850 1826
Crown Milligo, from London, 1677 0356
Cuba,
Catharine to New Orleans from, 1820 .... **5034**
English to, 1818-19 and 1853-58 .... **3028**
Irish to, 1818-19 and 1853-58 .... **3028**
Scots petition for naturalization, 1818-1858 3030
Spanish from, to New Orleans, 1840-1865 5030
Culloden, prisoners after battle of, 1746 .... **4913**
Cultivator, Liverpool to New York, 1867 .... **1133.26**
Cumberland County, N.C.,
land allotments to Scots, 1767 5009
Cumberland County, Pa., nat'zations, 1783-1801 .... **5630**
Cumberland, English from, 1665-1775 .... **1217.8**
Curke, John, seaman on the *Dove,* n.d. 6620
Customs lists
port of New Orleans, 1868-1870 .... **1536**
port of New York, 1846-1851 .... **1921.1-.4**
U.S.,
1819-1820 9258
1820-1834 .... **0253**
1850-1864 .... **1133.10**
Cyclone, London to British Columbia, 1862 5304
Czechoslovakia, Jauernig, archives of Freiwaldau, Silesia, from 1850 9985
Czechoslovakian newspaper lists, 1879 .... **8774**
Czechoslovakians
to Kansas (Decatur County), 1858-1901 8410
to Maryland, 1868 .... **8514**
to Nebraska, 1879 .... **8774**
to Pennsylvania, 18th c 0454
to Texas, 1858-1929 3830
via various ports, before 1880 .... **0205**
see also Bohemians

D

Dakota Territory, Germans from Russia,
1874, via Hamburg **9676**
1885 7931
1886, 1900 via Hamburg 7943

1888-1889, via Bremen **7951.3-.5**
1888, 1901, 1903 .... **1970**
Dakotas, arrivals from Russia,
1872-1899 ..... **0190, 2973.2,** 7171, 7921, 7941, **7948**
1900-1903 .... **2973.2, 3277, 6750**
Daleiden, Germans from, n.d. 5473
Dalhousie, N.S., Irish in 1820 ....**9554**
Dalmatia to California, Brac departures,
1891-1913 6785
Danes
from Island of Foehr, 1850-1875 ....**8596**
in New York, 17th, 18th c....................1898
naturalized in Boston, 1815-1840........... **6410.30**
to New York, 1869................... 0299, 0314
Danube, north of, Germans from, 1821-1823 ....**6572**
Danube-Swabian arrivals, ca. 1900 6740
Darby Township, Pennsylvania, 1687-1760 1018
Darmstadt, Germans from,
1834-1838, 1847 .... **0683,** 9780
19th c. **9072**
Darmstaedter Farm, German colony,
New Braunfels, Texas, 19th c...................9780
Davenport, John, to Connecticut, 1637-1638........1064
Davenport, Ia., naturalizations, 1842-1930 ....**2771**
David, Scotland to Quebec, 1821 4502
Dearborn County, Ind., nat'zations,
1838-1845 .... **1457.1-.3, 1459**
Death notices,
Germans from Russia, 1800s-1950s 6381
Irish, in *The Shamrock or Hiberian Chronicle,*
1811-1817 8099
Maryland, 18th c 0321, 0323, 0325
Debtors,
American, 17th, 18th c.........................**1235**
British, 1710-1712 4003
English in colonies, 17th, 18th c. **1235**
German, 1710-1713 1811
Irish, 1848-1860 .... **6413.20** and **.30**
Scottish, 1803 .... **0358.15**
Decatur County, Ind., nat'zations, 1867-1874 ....**3275**
Defections, military, *see* Desertions
DeKalb County, Illinois,
naturalizations:
1838-1908 .... **1498, 2421**
Scots to, 1738-1740 6640
Delaware
called New Sweden 7282
Dutch to, 17th c. **0464,** 1472
Finns to, 1640s 4870
Griffin
to Delaware River, 1689 ....**6099**
to Salem River, 1675 3580
Irish to,
1789, 1790 .... 2044, 2046, 7600
1831 .... **6508.3** and **.7**
naturalizations
1826-1858 (New Castle County) 6107-08
Scots to, 1831 .... **6508.7**
servants to, 1789..............................2044
ship and passenger arrivals, 1641-1825 ... 0717, 8370
South River Colony of New Netherland,
arrivals, 1661 1472
Swedes to, 17th c. 0040, **0464,** 7282, 8000, 8002
Welsh to
1701-1713 1798
1831 .... **6508.7**
see also New Sweden
Delaware Bay, ships to, 1681-1684 .... 0236, 0248
Delaware River,
Amelia of Belfast to, 1783....................9158
arrivals to Jersey shore, 1676 ...... 1681, 8370, 8390
Griffin to, 1689...........................**6099**
Irish to, 1789.............................7600
settlement, 1662, 1693 .... 0040, 6296, 7282
Delaware Valley
British to, 1675 .... 1292, 8450
Dutch to, 17th c. **0464**
Swedes to, 17th c. **0464, 8010**
Demerara, Scots from, on *Sophia,* 1871 .... **6508.6**
Den Norske Klippe, Norwegians to New York
on the, 1836, 1837 1056
Denization *see* Naturalizations
Denkershausen, Northeim, the Holzhausen family from,
to Baltimore 1831.............................3550
Denmark,
Catharine from, 1742.........................0932
departures from, for New York, 1869 0314
Guiding Star from, 1969 0314
Deportations,
Acadians to France, 18th c. 2384, 3050-51
British, 1760-1767 .... **8543, 8695**
English convicts to Md., 1722 ....**0340**
French, from Nova Scotia, 18th c. 2384, 3050-51
Scots,
from Battle of Culloden, 1746 ....**4913**
for political reasons, 1650-1775 ...... **1639, 1750,** 8170
for religious reasons, 1684-1687 ...... **9838, 9842, 9845**
Derbyshire, English from, 1671-1775 .... **1217.9**
Derry (N. Ireland) *see* Londonderry
Descendants
of first *Mayflower* passengers........... **6604, 8278**
of German arrivals:
18th c. **3771**
1833 ....**3300**
of Mennonites in Pa., 1710-1815 .... **3570.1-.5**
of Swiss arrivals, 16th-20th c...................4898
Desertions
from British troops in Amer. Revolution,
1775-1783 .... **8570.7, .10, .15**
from contracted service,
Maryland, 1745-1780................. **1357.1-.2**
from crew of *Amelia,* Philadelphia, 1783 9158
from crew of *Capellen tot den Pol,* Maryland,
1784 9900
from crew of *Stadacona,* Phila., 1864 9200
from mercenary troops in American
Revolution 8560,8562, 8570, 8640, 8643, 8665
from military,
American Revolution ......**8570.7, .10, .15,** 8905
Napoleonic Wars 7050
Des Moines County, Ia., naturalizations,
1849-1857 ....**1525**
Destination changed on high seas,
the *Eagle,* 1718 ....**4912**

Destitution as cause of deportation,
Dutch children, 1655, 1755 .... 1988, 8212
English children, 1830, 1850 .... 1794, 9995
Irish children, 1846-1929 .... **1418**
Destroismaisons family, Canada, 17th, 18th c 4846
Detmold, Germans from, 19th c. **7521, 9417**
Detroit, Mich., naturalizations, 1830-1900 .... **9097**
Dettingen, Germans from, 1751-1754 4445
Dettmar, Bremen to New York, 1849 .... **1133.36**
Deutsch-Dutch distinction 4822
Deutscher Pionier Verein *see* German Pioneer Society
Deutschland, Hamburg to New York, 1849 3967
Les Deux Amis and Acadians exiled to France 2384
Les Deux Freres, France to Louisiana, 1719 3418
Devon, English from, to New England
1650 and earlier **0977**
1664-1775 .... **1217.5, 8805**
Devonia, Glasgow to New York, 1893 9029
Devonshire *see* Devon
Diary
Norwegian American, 1839-1847 0209
of first Lutheran pastor, Wisc. **9074**
on Germans from Dill, 1850-1885 7730
Dick, John, and organized emigration, 1750 .... **7075**
"Dick Foreign Protestants,"
Nova Scotia, 1750-1752 .... **3745**
Dieburg, Germans from, 1834-1838 .... **0683,** 0685
Diepholz, Germans from, 1823-1860 .... 5045, 5051, 5055
Dieppe departures, for Carolina, 1565 0228
Dill area, Germans from, 1850-1885 7730
Dill River area, Germans from, ca. 1700 4493
Directory of Swedes in Boston, 1881 .... **6410.40**
District of Columbia, court records of
naturalizations in Eastern cities, 1817-1850 3530
Dobruja, Black Sea area, Germans from, 1885 2529
Dolphin
and Acadian passengers, 18th c 5655
Scotland to Canada, 1848 .... **4649**
Donau, with arrivals from Kolb, 1876 1702
Door County, Wis., naturalizations,
1870-1890 .... **2907.1-.2**
1904-1906 .... **2906**
Dorchester, Mass., founding, 1630 4477
Dorset, English from, 1664-1775 .... **1217.5**
Dossenheim, Germans from, 18th c 2917
Douglas, William, clergyman, Virginia, 18th c 3630
Dove, arrivals on the,
n.d. 3470, 6157
1634 .... 1036, 6070, 7141, 7976
to Maryland, 1634 .... 6070, 7976
to Nova Scotia, Scots, 1801 5007
see also *Pigeon*
Dove of Aberdeen, Scotland to Canada, 1801 .... **1014**
Down, County, Irish from, 19th, 20th c. **1194**
Dragonet to Prince Edward Island, 1855 .... **4646**
Drammen, Norwegians from, 1840, 1843 ..... 0209, 1208
Drebber, Germans from, 1839 2242
Dresden, Germans from,
1850-1903 .... 0628, 3914
to Australia, 1850-1903 3914
to New York via Hamburg, 1850-1903 3914
to Quebec via Hamburg, 1850-1903 3914
to San Francisco, 1850-1903 3914
to South America, 1850-1903 3914
Dresden, Mo., Germans to, 1838-1839 4803
Drought as cause of emigration, Russia, 1922 .... **2965**
Dublin, Irish from, to N.Y., 1849 .... **1133.24**
Dubuque County, Ia., naturalizations, 1832-56 ...... **3813**
Dubuque, Ia., naturalizations, 1868 .... **5228**
Le Duc de Noailles, France to Louisiana, 1719 3418
La Duchesse de Noailles, France to Louisiana,
1719 3418
Duderstadt, Germans from,
1822-1866 .... 3730, 5119, **5120**
Duesseldorf, state archives on 19th c 9560
Duke of Wirtemberg, with German immigrants,
1751-1752 4245
Dumfries, Scots from, to Nova Scotia, n.d. 6650
Dundas, Henry, Viscount Melville, 1803 9775
Dunkers,
from Maryland, naturalized in Pennsylvania,
1767-1772 6011
see also Church of the Brethren
Dupuy family, Virginia, 1700 0953
Durham, English from, 1665-1775 .... **1217.8**
Durlach, Germans from, 18th c. **8667**
Dutch
arrivals, 1820-1880 .... **9081, 9082, 9362**
children to New Netherland, 1755 8212
departures via Antwerp, 1855 .... **2885**
Mennonites to Ontario, 1800-25 .... **8363**
naturalizations, colonial N. Y. 0963, 0969
to Canada, 1789-1950 4880
to Delaware, 17th c. 1722, 1472
to Delaware Valley, 17th c. **0464**
to Iowa (Pella), 19th c 0675, 9385-87
to Maryland (Baltimore), 1847 0675
to Michigan, 1846, 1850 .... 6875, 6895, 7355
to New Jersey,
1630-1667 .... 4612, **7899**
1700s 0505
to New Netherland, 1620-1664 .... 3243-44, 8060
to New York,
17th, 18th c 0505, 1736, 1864, 4612, **7899**
19th c 4880
to Ontario, 1800-1825 .... **8363**
to Pennsylvania, 1683-1709 3313
to South Africa, 1835-1880 .... **9081**
to South America, 1835-1880 .... **9081**
to Southeast Asia, 1835-1880 .... **9081**
to U.S.A. *see* Dutch Arrivals
Dutch-Deutsch distinction 4822

E

Eagle, London to Charleston, S.C., 1718 .... **4912**
Earl of Buckinghamshire, Greenock, Scotland,
to Quebec, 1821 4502
East Indies, Germans to, from Cottbus, 19th c 4460
Eastern Europeans,
in Pennsylvania census, 1900 .... **7137**
to Maryland, 1893 9034
to New York, 1893 9034

Eaton, Theophilus, to Connecticut, 1637-1638 1064
Ebenezer, Georgia,
Austrians in, 1738-1739 .... **9332**
Austrians to, 1741 .... **3609**
inhabitants, 1741 9055
Ebensburg, Pa., county court records **7138**
Edenkoben, Germans from, 18th c 4252
Edinburgh, Germany to Philadelphia, 1748 0780
Edmund, Germans to New Orleans on the, 1849 5719
Edw. Downes, Belfast to New Orleans, 1821 .... **6121**
Edward, Belfast to New Orleans, 1821 .... **6121**
Egmont, Earl of, colonial founder **3605**
Egremont, Geo. Wyndham, Third Earl of,.... 4575, 4582
Egremont Papers, West Sussex, on emigration
ca. 1836 .... **2043**
Eider, S.S., to New York, 1889 1652
Eifel region, Germans from
n.d. (Pruem) 5428
1800s (Bittburg) 5422
1831-1911 (Adenau area) **5776**
1840-1845 (Ahr River towns) 3710
1843-1919 (Malmedy area) 3740
1845-1878 (Dueren area) 5550
Einbeck, Germans from, to Texas, 1845-1848 1636
Electoral Palatine *see* Palatine, Palatinate
Elisabeth,
Bremen to New York, 1832 0789
LeHavre to Carolina, 1564 0228
Eliza Warwick, Liverpool to Baltimore,
1841-1842 .... **6508.8**
Elizabeth,
Amsterdam to Philadelphia, 1819 6500
Germany to New York, 1838-1868 .... **1133.23**
London to Philadelphia, 1738 2554
London to Virginia, 1773-1774 0225
Elizabeth and Ann,
Britain to Canada (P.E.I.), 1806 .... **1446.3**
Scotland to Canada, 1806 .... **1014**
Elizabeth & Anne, Liverpool to Yorktown, 1716 .... **4727**
Elize to New York, Germans aboard, 1852 .... **8509.1**
Ellen, Scotland to Nova Scotia, 1848 5007
Ellida, Norway to New York, 1842 .... **5985**
Ellis County, Kan., German-Russians to,
1876-1878 .... **1677**
Elsaz, Dakota Territory, founded by Germans
from Russia, 1885 7931
Emelie, Norway and Sweden to N.Y., 1840 1208
Emeline, N. Ireland to Phila., 1825 .... **5033**
Emerald, LeHavre to New York, 1845 .... **1133.20**
Emilie, Norway to New York, 1842 .... **5985**
Emmons County, N.D., arrivals from Russia:
1885, 1888 .... 7931, 7934
Emperor to New York, Germans aboard, 1852 ...... **8499**
Empire State, Liverpool to New York, 1850 0305
Empire Union Loyalists *see* Loyalists
Empress of Ireland, England to New Brunswick,
1907 7630
Endeavour
and Acadian passengers, 18th c 5655
to Pennsylvania, 1683 .... 0418, 5334
Engel, Engell, Engels, Engle families, 1737-1773 1850
England,
Germans (Palatines) to, 1709 4772-73
Huguenots from, to Virginia, 1700 9230
port books, ship/passenger lists, 1618-1668 ..... **1239**
Quakers from, to Pennsylvania, 1677-1702 1137
Engle family arrivals, 1737-1773 1850
English
arrivals, 17th-19th c., indexed **1862**
departures, records of **9817**
from Cheshire, 1683 5334
from London to Va., 1648-1685 .... **1257**
from Oxfordshire,
1830s-1840s .... 1794, **2526.10** and **2526.40**
from Plymouth, 1630 4477
from Suffolk
1600-1649 3327
1836 7177
from Sussex, 1830s **0092, 4609**
from various counties, bonded,
17th, 18th c. **1217.1-.9**
from Yorkshire, to Canada, 1774, 1775 5675
Gautrey family arrivals, 1868 .... **2398**
in Dutch colony of New Netherland, 1639 1984
naturalized
in Indiana, 1833-1840 9625
in Texas, 1855-1907 0528
ports of departure for Irish, 18th c 6267
prisoners, bonded, 17th, 18th c. **1217.1-.9**
prisoners, women, 18th c 0608
Public Record Office, Kew, .. **3430, 8543, 9554, 9817**
purchasers of land in Pennsylvania,
1681-1682 .... 0032, 7570
Quakers to Pennsylvania, 1683 5334
records of departures for America .. **0092,** 8400, 8715
surname research **9078**
to American colonies,
1618-1668 .... **1239**
1624-1638, via Holland **2130.1-.4**
1718-1759 .... **3690.1**
to Barbados, 1654-1686 .... 1252, **3438.1-.6**
to Boston,
1620-1640 0263
1712 0154
to Canada
1830s-1850s .... **2526.10** and **.40**
from East Sussex, 1830s-1840s 1021
from Sussex, 1830s **2043,** 2688, 8775
from various ports, 1618-1668 .... **1239**
17th-19th c. **1862**
to Connecticut, 1635-1639 .... **3197, 9597**
to Cuba, 1818-19 and 1853-58 .... **3028**
to Georgia, 1774-1775 .... **1451.49**
to Indiana, 1850-1864 .... **1133.10**
to Louisiana,
1787 5213
1849 2742
to Maryland,
1650-1686 .... 1587, 3438, **5997**
1776 and earlier **0340,** 1372, **9832**
to Massachusetts, 1620-1640 ...... 0263, 0281, 4477
to New Brunswick, 1837 .... **0358.6, .13, .41**
to New England,
1572-1640 ... 0048, 0124, 0255, 0263, 0275, **0977,**
1660, **2130.1-.4,** 2713, 3327, 3540, **5820**
1631-1671 .... 1672, 4545, 4910, **5820**

English, *cont'd*
n.d. 1666, 1674
to New Jersey, 1675 1292
to New Orleans, 1849 . . . . . . **3453**
to New York,
1678 3438
1830 1794
1840-1841 . . . . . . **4905, 4906**
1850, 1855 . . . . . . 0305, 1414
1878 8330
to North Carolina, 1774-1775 . . . . . . 6167, 6169
to Nova Scotia,
1774, 1775 . . . . . . 4632, 5675
1864 6213
to Pennsylvania,
1680s 2979, 3438
17th, 18th c. **0926.21, 2824, 6441**
1852-1968 4950
to Plymouth Colony, 1620-1623 . . . . . . 0255, 2713
to South Carolina, 1669 . . . . . . 1153, 1288
to Tennessee, before 1850 2732
to Virginia
early 1600s 3273, **3820**, 5695
1634-1635 . . . . . . 0048, **1035.14**
1675-1677 . . . . . . 1252, 3438
to West Indies, 18th c 2324, 2328
see also British (may include Scots, Irish, and Welsh)
Enigheden, Norwegians to New York on the, 1836, 1837 1056
Enkenbach, Germans from, 1715-1928 0837
Ennistymon, County Clare, Irish from, 1850-1860 . . . . . . **6413.30**
Ensminger family arrivals, German, 18th c 0488
Enz, Germans from, 18th c 1815
Erbach, Germans from, 1830-1855 . . . . . . 3351, 3358
Erie County, N.Y., naturalizations, 1838-1842 . . . . . . **5867.1-.2**
Erie County, Pa., naturalizations, 1825-1906 . . . . . . **1869**
Erie, Lake, lands adjacent to, for refugees, 1785 8660
Erin, Dublin to New York, 1811 . . . . . . **6608**
Espiritu Santo Bay, English vessel wrecked, 1769 . . . . **4676**
Esquimalt, B.C., British to, on the *Tynemouth* (or *Brideship),* 1862 5321
Essenheim, Germans from, 18th c 4329
Essex County, Mass.,
British to, 1670, 1679 . . . . . . 9610, 9620
French inhabitants, after 1750s 1658
Essex County, Va., *Charming Molly* to, 1764-1765 . . . . . . **0614**
Essex, Eng., British from, 1572-1775 . . . . . . 0048, **1217.4**
Essex, Ont., Huguenots to, 17th, 18th c. **7204**
Ethnic societies,
Irish, Baltimore, 1831-1834 . . . . . . **9076**
German, Cincinatti, 19th c. **5747**
Swedish, Minneapolis, 19th c. **6410.35**
Etruria, Norway/Sweden to N.Y., 1892 . . . . . . **1133.46**
Eugenius to New Jersey, 1819 . . . . . . **3295**
Euphemia, Liverpool and Cardiff, to New Orleans, 1849 2742
Eureka, S.D. Germans from Russia to,
1889-1909 . . . . . . **4490, 4532, 7846**
Euroclydon, Liverpool to Halifax, 1864 6213
Europa, Liverpool to Halifax, 1864 6213
Euryal, Dublin to Philadelphia, 1746/1747 4732
Eutaw, Liverpool to U.S., 1841 . . . . . . **4903**
Evangelical Lutheran Church and German immigrants, 19th c. **3709**
Evangelicals, German search notices for emigrant, 1839-1865 4066
Evans, Nathaniel, and Welsh in Pennsylvania, 1701-1713 1894
Eveline,
Portsmouth to Montreal, 1832 2688
Portsmouth to Upper Canada, 1832 8775
Exiles,
Acadian *see* Acadians exiled
Polish, to U.S., 1831-1835 . . . . . . **4606**
Scottish, 1684-1687 . . . . . . 8170, **9838, 9842, 9845**
see also names of particular faith groups
Exon, England, prisoners from, 1722 . . . . . . **0340**
Expedition, Bristol to South Carolina, 1728 3510
Expedition against Canada, 1711 6321
Eyersheim, Germans from, n.d. 7314

F

Facsimiles of passenger lists
from five ships to La., 1720-1721 2100
from the *Manhattan,* 1820 6530
from the S.S. *Patria,* 1899 5183
Fah Kee, S.S., Cuba to New York, 1866 7790
Fairfield County, Oh., nat'zations, 1840-70 . . . . . . **1918**
Fairy Queen, New Brunswick to Maine, 1849 . . . . . . **5034**
Faja Maisan, formerly German colony of Huefel-Comuy, Chile 8140
Falmouth, England, to N.Y., the *Orient,* 1842 3796
Falmouth, Me., *Fairy Queen* to, 1849 . . . . . . **5034**
Falmouth, N.S., arrivals from Newport, R.I., 1760 2887
Fama, Sweden, to Delaware, 1643 8000
Families named *see* Individual surname
Family data on some early arrivals
British, 1600-1649 . . . . . . 0255, 3327
Dutch, 17th c. 1864, **7899**
English, 1635 and following **3197**
French, 1717-1731 . . . . . . **1290**
Germans, 1700-1784 . . . . . . **1290, 7105, 9981**
Huguenots, 17th, 18th c. **7204, 7899**
New Englanders, 1620-1692 1936
Scots in Canada, 18th c. **3370**
Swiss, 16th c. on 4898
Family histories
Barbadian families, n.d. **0773**
Dutch families
17th c. **1864**
1835-1880 . . . . . . **9081**
English families **9078**
German families, ... **0472, 9079**
Germans from Neckar Valley 3627
Germans in Maryland, 1700s 3577
Huguenot families, 17th, 18th c. **7204**
Irish families, 19th c. 0568
Liechtenstein families, 19th, 20th c. **3495**

Family histories, *cont'd*
- Santo Domingo families, 1870 . . . . . **1536**
- Scandinavian families, 18th c 6411-12, 1898
- Schwenkfelder families, 18th c. 0923
- Swedish families, 19th c. **0110.1, 2419.1-.3**
- Swedish, in Mich., 1875-1882 . . . . . **6717**
- Ukrainian-Canadian, 1891-1900 3750
- *see also* under specific family name

Famine as cause of emigration, Ireland, 1845-1846 . . . . . **1921.1-.4**
Fanny to Virginia, 1769-1770 0622
Farias Colony (Mexican) in Calif., 1833 . . . . . **3365**
Farmers,
- English, to Ontario, 1836 . . . . . **9628**
- German, from Reitzengeschwenda, n.d. 0548
- Prussian, to Wisconsin, 1853 . . . . . **1133.34**
- Scottish, to Vermont, 1774 . . . . . 3670, 9670
- Swiss, to Ohio, 1853 . . . . . **1133.34**
- various, North Dakota, 1918 . . . . . **0090**
- *see also* Planters

Faucon, Le Havre to Carolina, 1564 0228
Favourite, Scotland to Canada, 1815 . . . . . **0358.31**
Favrot, Captain, Louisiana, 1787 5213
Fayette County, Pa., nat'zations, 1802-15 . . . . . **1966.1-.8**
Feg family, from Palatinate, 1709-1710 9660
Fellbach, Germans from, 1735-1930 1291
Felons *see* Prisoners
Fenwick, John, and Delaware Valley settlers:
- moving to New Jersey, 1675 . . . . . 1292, 3580, 8450
- purchasing New Jersey land, 1664 1992

Fenwicke *see* Fenwick
Ferdinand,
- Bremen to Baltimore, 1834 3080
- Bremen to New York, 1864 . . . . . **1133.38**

Fermanagh, Irish from, 1846-1929 . . . . . **1418**
Fessenden, N.D., Germans from Russia to, 1902 2842
Financial aid, petition for, 18th c. **0926.42**
Finns
- to Delaware, 1640s 4870
- to Maryland, 1640s 4870
- to New Jersey, 1640s 4870
- to New Sweden, *see* Finns to Delaware
- to Pennsylvania, 1640s 4870

First settlers
- New England,
  - 1620, 1621 . . . . . **3077, 3279**
  - 1631-1671 . . . . . **1461**, 1672, **3197**
  - 17th c. 1666, 1672, 1674
- Virginia, 17th c. **3820, 9039**

Fisherman to American colonies, 1631-1635 5781
Fishmongers, British, in the colonies **1139.1**
Flemish Huguenots to Virginia, 1700 0953
Flenheim, Germans from, 1739-1920s 7552
Flint, Wales, bonded departures, 1665-1775 . . . . . **1217.8**
Florida
- arrivals, 1837-1868 4702-4703
- settlement attempted, 1562 0228
- Spanish to, 1538 8870-72
- West, in 1764 9600

Flying Hart, Britain to Virginia, 1621 . . . . . 2722, 2851
Foehr, Island of, departures, 1850-75 . . . . . **8596**
Fontaine family, Virginia, 1700 0953
Foot regiments
- 4th (King's Own) Regiment, 1783 8570
- 7th (Fusiliers) in Amer. Revolution **8570.7**
- 10th (N. Lincolnshire) in Amer. Rev. **8570.10**
- 15th (Yorkshire East Riding) in the Rev. **8570.15**
- 49th in Jamaica and N.Y., 1760-1763 8534
- 99th or Prince of Wales Tipperary, 1820 . . . . . **9554**

Fordnock, Scots from, to Canada, 1803 . . . . . **0358.15**
"Foreign Protestants" *see* names of faith groups
Fort Garry and route to Red River, 1871 . . . . . **7323**
Fort Wayne, Ind., naturalizations, n.d. **1451.6**
Fort William to Ft. Garry, Red R. route, 1871 . . . . . **7323**
Fortune
- from Britain to American colonies, 1621 . . . . . **3279**
- to Plymouth, 1621 . . . . . 0255, 2713, 3152, 3408, 4692, 9810

Forty-Five, Uprising of, *see* Jacobite Rebellion
Founders, miscellaneous,
- of Georgia Colony, 1730s **3605**
- of Guilford, Conn., 1639 . . . . . **9597**
- of Highland, Ill., 1831 . . . . . **9984**
- of Holland, Mich., 1847 6875
- of New England:
  - ancestry, 1620 ff. 1936, **5820**
  - 1631-1671 and n.d. 1660, 1666, 1672, 1674
  - research on, in British archives 1672, 1674
  - see also *Mayflower*
- of New Paltz, N.Y., 1678 2924
- of "New Sweden," 1637-1642 6351
- of Rhode Island colony, 1636 . . . . . 1926, 9110
- of Swedish settlements in Iowa, 1846 . . . . . **2090**
- of Swiss colony, Highland, Ill, 1831 . . . . . **9984**

Founding families, Huguenot and Dutch, 1630-1667 . . . . . **7899**
Franconia, Germans from,
- 1740s, to Pennsylvania 4525
- 1849-1855, to various countries 3879

Frankenthal, Germans from,
- n.d. 0180
- 18th c. 4175

Frankland to S.C., Germans aboard, 1766 . . . . . **0926.59**
Franklin County, Ind., nat'zations, 1830s **2180**
Franklin County, Tenn., labor camps, 1850 2732
Franklin County, Vt., nat'zations, 19th c. **5901**
Franklin, Hamburg to New York, 1849 . . . . . **1133.30**
Freckenfeld, Germans from, 18th c 4224, 4329
Fredericksburg, Tex., arrivals, 1845-1846 2534
Freiwaldau, Silesia, departures, 19th c 9985
French
- arrivals, 1613-1640 . . . . . **7510.1-.2**
- departures via Antwerp, 1855 . . . . . **2885**
- deported, Nova Scotia to St. Malo, n.d. 3050-51
- from Lyons to "New France," 1632-1760 5583
- from Moselle region, 19th c 5481
- in Mobile, Alabama, 1764 9600
- intending naturalization, S. Carolina, 1696 7192
- naturalized
  - in Carolina, ca. 1695 0228
  - in New York, 1790-1839 . . . . . 1140, 5942
- Protestants
  - in colonial records, 17th c 1158
  - in Nova Scotia, 1757 4652
  - *see also* Huguenots as main entry
- recruited for Canada, 1650s 0172, 2642, 2662
- to Boston, 1751 . . . . . 3333, 3335

French, *cont'd*
to Canada,
1636, 1659 .... 2636, 2682
17th, 18th c 2612, 2632, 1462, 2652
1765 2384
colonists recruited for Montreal, 1653 0172
from Alsace-Lorraine, 1727-1775 2883
from Burgundy, 1653 through 18th c 1502
from LaRochelle, 1634-1715 1462
from London, late 18th c 2222
from Lyons, 1632-1760 5583
from Normandy, 16th, 17th c 9350
from Picardy, 17th, 18th c 4846
from St. Malo, n.d. 3050-51
later exiled 2384
to Carolina, 1564, 1695 0228
to Florida, 1562 0228
to Georgia, 18th, 19th c 1712
to Iowa (Pella), mid 19th c 0675
to Louisiana
1717-1731 .... **1290,** 1542, 3418, 8420, 8422, 9190
1752-1800 .... 1548, 6695
to Massachusetts, 1750s 1658
to Montreal, settlers recruited,
1653, 1659 .... 5364, 5374, 5751
to "New France," 1621-1700 6830
to New Jersey, 1677-1710 4056
to New Orleans, 1850 9570
to New York,
1756, from Nova Scotia, ... 6414
1828-1848 .... **4900, 6515, 7640**
to Nova Scotia, 18th c. 0080, **3745**
to Ohio, 1833-1853 .... **1133.16, .18, .20, 9734**
to Pennsylvania
n.d. 8935
18th c. **7765**
to Rhode Island, 1686 6815
to South Carolina, 1679-1750s 1916, 5655
to Virginia,
1695-1732 .... 0953, 4622, 6223, 6710
1750-1797 .... 3630, 3640
French Canadians
and "Old France," 1763 2374
to Massachusetts (Boston) 1763 2374
French Guiana, Germans to, 18th c 0853
Fresno County, Calif., voters, 1896-98 .... **2763.25-.33**
Fressingfield, Suffolk, departures, 1836 7177
Freudenberg, Germans from, 1738 0212
Freudenstadt, Germans from, 1751-1752 4245
Friedelsheim, Germans from, 19th c 0813
Friedrich Lucas (or *Friedrich Jacob*), Bremerhaven to New Orleans, 1842-1843 7507
Friedrichstal, Germans from, to Pennsylvania, 1723-1739 9960
Friends *see* Quakers
Friends Adventure, to Pennsylvania, 1682 0418
Friendship, from Scotland,
to Canada, 1775 .... **1014**
to Maryland, 1716 .... 7385, 7983
to Philadelphia, 1774-1775 8425
Friesland, Antwerp to New York,
1893, 1900 .... **3844, 6750**
Frisian Islands
Foehr, departures, 1850-1875 .... **8596**
North, Germans from, 1850-1875 .... **8596**
West, Dutch from, 1661 1472
Frisians
to New York, 1855-1857 9664
to Vriesland, Mich., 1847 6895
Frohna, Mo., Germans to, 1838-1839 4803
Fuerstenberg area (Baden), departures,
1712, 1737, 1787 .... **8606**
1720-1806 8090
Fulda, Bremen to New York,
1886, 1889 .... 1765, **9225**
Fulton County, Pa., naturalizations, 19th c. **6013.7**

G

Gale,
Rotterdam to Halifax, 1751 .... **7076**
Stranraer, Scotland, to New York, 1774 2202
to Halifax, Germans aboard, 1752 .... **7016**
Galesburg, Illinois, Scots to, 1828-1909 7134
Galveston,
arrivals, 1845-1848 .... **2518,** 2534
arrivals from Russia, 1893-1910 .... **4485.1, .2,** 7941
Germans to,
1844-1847 2504
1850-1852 .... 2494, 2514, 3948
1897-1910 .... **4485.1, .2**
Galveston County, Tex., naturalizations, n.d. **1005**
Gardner, C.E., master of the *Margaret,* 1804 4672
Gautrey family arrivals from Sussex, 1868 .... **2398**
Gedern, Saxony, Germans from, 1748-1749 3848
Gemuenden, Hunsrueck, Germans from, 19th c 1612
Genealogical travel, Switzerland, 1900 .... **4480**
General Washington, Bremen to New Orleans, 1845 0544
Geneva, Swiss Huguenots to Virginia, 1700 0953
George Canning, Greenock Scotland, to Quebec, 1821 4502
George's Creek Coal and Iron Co. (Md.), naturalization records of 1839-1840 2920
Georgetown, P.E.I., Scots to, 1848 .... **4649**
Georgia,
Acadians from, to N.Y. state, 1756 6414
arrivals, 17th, 18th c. 1322, **5400**
Augusta, and Richmond County voting records, 1867 .... **1451.45**
Austrians to,
1730s-1740s **0926.36, 3609, 9332**
1734-1741 .... 1134, 7820, 9055
British to,
1730s-1740s 1312, 3388
1774-1775 .... **1245, 1451.49, 3430**
1775-1790 .... 1078, **8570.7**
1820-1868 9890
exiled Acadians from, to N.Y. state, 1756 6414
French to, 18th, 19th c 1712
German-speaking arrivals, 1733-1741 .... **3605**
Germans to,
17th, 18th c. **2855**
1720-1760 .... 0212, **0926.36,** 3610
headrights in Clarke County, 1803-1804 1198

Georgia, *cont'd*
Irish to,
1772 .... **5996**
1828-1841 9689
Moravians to, 1734-1775.......... 2262
naturalizations,
1790-1879 (Savannah) 6421
1793-1868 (Richmond County) .. **0056.1, 1451.45**
1820-1847 (Irwin County) **1307, 3371,** 9689
recipients of land grants, 1756-1909 4890
veterans and prisoners of war to, 1775-1783 .. **8570.7**
Georgia Packet, from Scotland, 1774-1775 ...... **1451.49**
Georgiana, German to N.Y., 1838-1868 .... **1133.23**
German
arrivals
1700 and earlier 4822, 4830
18th c. .... 1126, **3375, 4255,** and **4273**
1816-1817 .... **5745**
1830-1849 ..... **0683, 1133.22, .23, .30, .32,** 5163, 9248, 9640
1838-1900 .. **1133.22, .23, .28, .30, .32,** 9248, **9317**
18th, 19th c. **0926.10**
and log of Capt. J. Meyer, 1832-1849 9640
California records of 1830
during and after American Revolution,
heirs missing 9945
from the North,
1738 0212
1753-1882 5040-5163
18th c. **8655.20**
1838-1859 .... 2053, **8636**
see also Germans from [place-name]
Landers family, 17th-19th c. **4514**
Rumsfelds from Lower Saxony, 1860s **5633**
shipwrecked in Gulf of Mexico, 1769 ...... **4676**
via Baltimore, 1874 .... **5237**
via England, ca. 1709 9214
benefactors of Salzburg emigrants, 1730s **9332**
Catholic assoc. of German Canadians, 1924 .... **2528**
departures,
from Baden, 1830-1935 8120
from Bonfeld, 1710-1738 .... **3627**
from Bremen, 1849 .... **1136.36**
from Lippe, 1650s-1877 .... **9417**
from Lower Rhine Palatine villages,
1700s **8655.20**
via Antwerp, 1855 .... **2885**
Evangelicals in the U.S., 1839-1865 4066
Huguenots
naturalized, 1743-1746 6021
to Virginia, 1700 0953
Mennonites, to Ontario, 1800-1825 .... **8363**
mercenaries remaining after American
Revolution **8570.10,** 8643, 8650, 8670
Pioneer Society,
Cincinatti, 19th c. **5747**
Covington, Ky., 1830-1856 .... **9999.3**
membership list, 1877 .... **5747**
Newport, Ky., 1830-1856 .... **9999.3**
Toledo, Ohio 1770-1895 5603
Protestants and S. C. churches,
1788, 1794 .... **7119, 7121**
Russians, *see* Germans from Russia
ships,
of the Adelsverein, 1845 8302
with Balkan and Eastern Europeans aboard,
1845 6127
surname index, 18th c. **2884.1**
surname research **9079**
troops in American Revolution **1505,** 7495, 8560, 8562, 8620, 8905
Volga Republic (Russia), *see* Germans from Russia *and* Volga Germans
German Society of Maryland for Germans, 19th c ... 5113
German Society of Nobility (Deutsche Adelsvereinigung), and its Texas holdings, 1844 8150
German society of pioneers *see* German Pioneer Society
German-speaking settlers, 18th c. **1031.8, 3605**
Germania, Germans from, 1821-1823 .... **6572**
Germania, Antwerp to New York, 1863 .... **1133.4**
Germanic emigrants card file (Calif.) 1830
Germanna, Va., Germans to, 1714, 1717 ..... **3771,** 6102
Germans
from Aachen, n.d. 5436
from Adenau area, 1831-1911 .... **5776**
from Anhalt-Zerbst, 18th c. **1505**
from Appenhofen, 18th c 4259
from Asperg, 18th, 19th c 0638
from Auerbach (now Bensheim), 19th c. **9072**
from Baden, 1712, 1737, 1787 8606
from Baden-Durlach,
1738 4089
1749-1755 .... 4085, 4094, 4095 4322, 4417, 4435
from Bavaria,
various communities, 18th c 0558, 4329
via Hamburg, 1850-1851 3941
see also Bavaria as main entry
from Beihingen am Neckar,
1727-1934 8634
1895 and earlier 7537
from Beindersheim, 19th c 7967
from Bergzabern, Rhenish Palatinate, 18th c.... 4141
from Bernkastel, n.d. 5408
from Birkenfeld, 1697-1899 5728
from Bitburg, Eifel area, 19th c 5422
from Bonn area, 1814-1914 .... **9638**
from Breisgau, 18th, 19th c. 0121
from Bremen, *see* index entry Bremen
from Bruchhausen, 1860-1866 5125
from Calenberg, 1753-1882 5080
from Caroxbostel, 1830-1848 5143
from Catlenburg-Lindau, 1831-1866 ..... 5119, **5120**
from Cottbus, Lower Lusatia,
1847-1886 .... 4460, 4467
from Daleiden, n.d. 5473
from Detmold, Lippe
1851, 1861, 1863-1866 .... **7521**
from Dettingen, 1751-1754 4445
from Dieburg area, 1834-1838 0685
from Diepholz,
1823-1840 5045
1841-1860 .... 5051, 5055
from Dill area, 1850-1855 7730
from Dillheim area, ca. 1670-1719 4493
from Dresden, 1852-1857 0628

Germans, *cont'd*
from Duderstadt, Prussia,
1822-1866 .... 3730, 5119, **5120**
from Durlach, 18th c. **8667**
from East Frisia, 19th c.......................9664
from Edenkoben, 18th c 4252
from Eifel region,
1800s 5422, 5550
1843-1919 3740
from Enkenbach, 1715-1928...................0837
from Fellbach, 1735-1930 1291
from Foehr, 1850-1875 .... 0087, **8596**
from Frankenthal,
n.d.....................................0180
18th c 4175
from Freckenfeld, 18th c.....................4224
from Friedelsheim, 19th c....................0813
from Germania, 1821-1823 ....**6572**
from Germersheim, 18th c 4214, 4266
from Gieboldehausen, Prussia,
1839-1866 .... 5119, **5120**
from Harburg, 1830-1848 5143
from Heidelberg,
1726-1727 4450
1737-1754 .... 4119, 4196, 4422, 4440
from Heidenheim area, various communities,
1739-1920s, ...7552
from Herbolzheim, 18th, 19th c......... 0121, 4033
from Hesse,
1830-1840 3351
1846-1849 3004
1853-1855 3358
from Hesse-Cassel,
1832-1835 2828-29
1835-1839 ....**2829.1-.3**
from Hesse-Hanau,
1741-1767 .... 8600, 8602
1783 and later.........................8643
from Hildesheim, n.d. 5060
from Hoechstadt (Hochstadt)
18th c. 1032, **1033.4**
from Hohentruedingen, 18th c................0558
from Hungary, ca. 1900 6740
from Hunsrueck region, n.d. 4203
18th c.......................... 4154, 4161
19th c.................... 1612, 1616, 8652
from Jockgrimm, Rhenish Palatine, 19th c......**7140**
from Kaiserslautern, 18th, 19th c........ 0805, 0845
from Kell, n.d. 5463
from Kraichgau, 18th c. **1031.8**
from Lambsheim, in the Palatinate,
18th, 19th c 7312, 7314
from Landau, 18th c 4214
from Langenholtensen, 19th c.................**0472**
from Lauenstein, 1841-1866 5051
from Lein Valley, 1750-1883..................7810
from Leipzig area, 1850-1855 3960
from Lemfoerde, 1825-1840 5113
from Lettweiler, 18th c......................4168
from Lippe, 17th-19th c. 2602, **9417**
from Lippstadt, n.d. 4555
from Lower Alsace, 18th c....................**4255**
from Lower Saxony, 1830-1848 5143

Germans, *cont'd*
from Ludwigshafen am Rhein,
18th c......................... 0821, 0853, 0860
from Lueneburg,
1849-1853 .... 5040, 5071, 5109, 5111
from Malmedy, 1843-1919 3740
from Mecklenburg, 1850-1862 .... 2070, 3223
from military service to Nova Scotia, 1784 .....**7105**
from Minden, Westphalia, 1816-1900 ....**5860**
from Moessingen, 1829-1900 ....**2852**
from Mosbach, 1749-1750 .... 4119, 4422
from Mosel (Moselle),
1764 5685
19th c 5481
from Muenster, 19th c........................5851
from Nahe region, 18th c 4154, 4161, 4203
from Nassau-Dillenburg, 18th c. 2454, 2690
from Neckar Valley, 18th c. .. **2857, 3627,** 4404, 4422
from Neumagen, n.d.........................5408
from Neustadt area, Palatinate, 18th c ... 4371, 4385
from Niedersachsen (Lower Saxony), 1830-49...**8579**
from North Rhine-Westphalia,
1840s-1880s **8636,** 8653
from Obereichsfeld, 1832-1891................2692
from Odernheim am Glan, 1748 .... 0780, 4121
from Oldenburg, 1830-1849 ....**8595**
from Oppenheim area,
1742-1749 .... 4112, 4397
n.d.....................................4203
from Orenhofen, Prussian-Rhine province,
n.d.....................................5490
from Ostertal, n.d. **9982**
from Otterberg, 18th, 19th c........... 0891, 4301
from Palatinate,
1709-1787 .... **3375, 3624,** 3983, **8606**
18th c. **0856, 2857, 4255**
19th c. **9072**
n.d.........................**7127.2-.15, 9982**
via London, 1709 ... **0926.8,** 3983, 3990, 4772-73, 5013, 9214
from Pfeddersheim and Pfiffligheim,
1753-1766 1126
from Poland to Dakota(s), 1889 7921
from Prinzbach, 1839-1860...................**0635**
from Pruem, n.d. 5428
from Prussia, 1880s, 1890s **0123.1-.2**
from Ransweiler,
18th c 4168
1823-1842 ....**6194**
from Reitzengeschwenda, rural departures,
n.d.....................................0548
from Remmesweiler, 18th, 19th c 0468
from Rhenish Hesse, 18th c **4255,** 4308
from Rhineland,
colonial era **9968**
1700s-1860...................... **6104,** 7524
18th c. **2854, 2855.5, 4255, 4374, 4376**
1831-1911 .... 3935, **5776**
from Rhineland-Palatinate
1750-1803 ....**8584**
19th c. **7140**
n.d.....................................5408
from Rumania to N.D., 1899 ....**6406.6**

Germans from Russia,
arrivals:
1879-1923 .... **2974.5,** 7930
1880s, 1890s .... **0123.1, .2, 7124.1-.8**
1886-1911 .... **2004.5, .13, 2974.4**
19th c. (late) **9490**
1901, 1903, 1908 .... **2004.11, 2005**
n.d. **2978**
via Halifax, 1897-1899 .... **1860**
via Hamburg,
1876-1880 .... **5726.1-.2,** 6930
1892, 1900-1901 .... 6928, 6940
via London, 1877-1901 6921
death notices, late 1800s to 1950s 6381
Mennonites, 1870-1900 .... **1286,** 2973
to Argentina, 1877 6925
to Baltimore
1849-1910 .... 0438, 1882, 2969, **2974.1,** 6927, 7921
via Bremen,
1874-1876 .... 1882, 2966, 2972, 6950
1907 5263
to Boston
via Hamburg, 1877, 1898-1899 6927
to Brazil
1874-1886 ...... 6921, 6922, 6925, 6930, 6931
1892, 1900-1901 6928
to Canada,
1849-1910 ..... 2417, **2974.1,** 6929, 6951, 6954
19th c 0008, 1697, **1860,** 2529, **4490**
1920s **2528**
to Colorado, 1889 .... **7242**
to Dakota Territory via Bremen,
1888-1903 .... **1970, 7951.3-.5**
to Dakota Territy via Hamburg,
1874 .... **9676**
1876-1903 .... **1970, 2973.2,** 7942
to Dakota(s),
1872, 1873 7171
1878-1879 3203-3204
1885, 1889, 1893 .... 2529, 7931, **7948**
1895, 1898 .... **0190,** 7930
1900, 1901 .... 2417, **6750**
1903-1922 .... 2424, **2973.2, 3277**
n.d. 3372
to Frankfort on Oder, 1922 .... **2965**
to Halifax
1877-1901 .... **1860,** 6929
1902-1909 .... 6951, 6954
to Kansas
1874-1916 ...... **1677,** 1694, 4019, 4497, 8080
1876-1899, 1908, 1922 ..... 1694, 2971, **2973.2**
to Manitoba (Winnipeg), 1893 1697
to Nebraska,
1874-1880 .... 1694, **9676**
1893, 1905 .... 1697, **1924**
to Nevada, via Netherlands, 1874-1879 9510
to New York
1873-1876 .... 2969, **2974.3,** 6510
1876-1913 ... 0626, 1652, 1765, **2004.13,** 2320, **2974.2, .3, .4, .6,** 7930, 7931, 7934
to New York, via Bremen,
1874-1876 .... 1882, 2966, 2971, 2972
1884-1886 .... **8900, 9225**
1889, 1893, 1898 .... **7846, 7945, 7948**
1902, 1912 .... 2842, 3590, **4061**
to New York, via Glasgow, 1906 5263
to New York, via Hamburg:
1873-1878 ...... **0440,** 2960, 3872, 6920, 6921, 6922, 6923, 6924, 6925
1880-1898 .... 1882, 6926
1902-1903 6954
to New York, via Liverpool, 1876 2972
to North Dakota,
19th c., late **0626, 3844,** 7930, 7931
20th c., early **1924, 2338,** 2424, **4061**
to Nova Scotia, 1849-1910 .... **2974.1**
to Oklahoma, early 20th c. **0104**
to Pacific Northwest, 1874-1916 8080
to Paraguay, 1874-1880 .... 6925, 6930
to Saskatchewan, 1885 2529
to South Africa, via Hamburg, 1877-1901 ... 6929
to South America,
1800s 0008
1874-1880 .... **5726.1-2.,** 6921, 6922, 6925, 6930, 6931, **9674**
1881-1892 .... 6928, 6931
1900-1909 .... 6928, 6951
to South Dakota,
1877-1878 (prior to) **0971**
1878-1879 3203-04
1889 and earlier **1641, 7242, 7846**
1898, 1899 .... **2995, 4490, 4532, 7846**
19th c. (late) **0444**
1909 .... **4532**
to Texas, 1897-1910 .... **4485.1, .2**
to various places, 1879-1923 .... 2424, **2974.5**
to Washington state, 1876 .... **9473**
to Wisconsin, 1864-1922 1871
via England, 1872, 1873 7171
see also Volga Germans
Germans [resuming after Germans from Russia]
from Saar region, 1816-1908 .... 3786, 3788
from Saxony, various destinations,
19th c 8290, 8590, 8592
from Saxony-Weimar, 1854, 1859 .... 4040, 4046
from Schleswig Holstein, to Iowa, 1900 7252
from Sieg River area, 1857-1883 .... **8653**
from Simmern,
1750-1803 .... **8584**
19th c. 8652
from Speyer, 18th c. **2854,** 2856
from Sponheim, 18th c 4161
from Steinweiler, 17th-19th c 0849
from Steinwenden, 1684-1780 0885
from Thaleischweiler, 18th c 4231, 8470
from Thuringia, 1800s 2782, 3948, 8290
from Trier, 19th c 5540-45
from Ulm, 17th, 18th c. **2855**
from Urach, 1751-1754 4445
from Wachenheim, 18th c 4280
from Wangen, 1834-1880 3893
from Wegelnburg, 18th c 4147
from Wertheim County (Wuerttemberg-Baden area),
1750-1840 .... 4517, 4525
from Westphalia,

Germans, *cont'd*
1725 5877
1800s 5851, 5861
1900's (mid) 2602
from Wiesbaden-Biebrich, 18th c 0368
from Wolfersweiler, before 1750 . . . . 0478, **9881**
from Wuerttemberg, 18th c and early 19th c. . . . 4315, **4374, 8646**
from Wuerttemberg area, various locales
1770s-1920s and n.d. 4203, 7650
from Wuerttemberg-Baden,
18th, 19th c 0121, **2852**
from Yugoslavia, ca. 1900 6740
from Zweibruecken,
18th c 3193, 4133, 4141, 4145, 4147, 4214, 4266, **4268, 4349,** 4350, 4357, 4364, 8050
in Chile, 1906-1912 8140
in Illinois, 1842-1845 1976
in Mississippi, 1816 . . . . **0926.49**
in New Jersey, 1710 ff **1138**
in New York,
1710 . . . . **1138,** 5023, 6341
1777 0140
1886 1906
in Nova Scotia, 1757, 1780s 4652, **6987**
in Ohio,
early 19th c. 1582
1877 . . . . **5747**
in Pennsylvania,
1742-1779 . . . . 1911, 7207
1783 and later 8560
1806 . . . . **9950**
in South Carolina,
1788, 1794 . . . . **7119, 7121**
in Virginia, after American Revolution 8560
joining American forces, 1782-1783 8665
naturalized,
1740-1765 . . . . **0926.16,** 6021
18th c. . . . . **0926.52** and **.55**
1802 . . . . 6047, 6048
in Illinois:
1836-1855 0094
1886-1906 . . . . **5012.37**
in Indiana:
1833-1840 9625
1848-1852 . . . . **6327.1, .2, 7515.1, .2**
19th, 20th c. **0926.53**
in Kansas, 1907-1919 . . . . **6013.40**
in Maryland:
17th c. **1420**
18th c. **0926.51**
in New York,
1782-1785 . . . . 1906, 5841
1790-1828 1140
in Ohio:
1840-1884 . . . . **1918, 8404**
19th c. **0176.1-.12**
in Pennsylvania,
1798 . . . . 9031, 9032
18th c. . . . . **0926.18** and **.38**
1855-1856 . . . . **8864.1-.8**
19th c. **0515-0518, 6013.7**
in Texas, 1855-1907 . . . . 0528, 8350
in Virginia, 18th c. **0926.57**

Germans, *cont'd*
Northern, arrivals,
1753-1882 5040-5163
1831-1866 . . . . 3474, **5120**
Southern, arrivals,
1700s 0558, 4329, 4404
1727-1775 . . . . 2883, 4422
ca. 1776-1783 8905
1780s 8640
1846-1855 . . . . 0598, 3879, 3941
to Alabama (Mobile), 1832-1852 5203-04
to Argentina, 1878 . . . . **9674**
to Arkansas, 1833 . . . . **3300**
to Australia, 1850 . . . . **8657**
to Baltimore,
1820-1834 (many ships) **0253, 3704**
1834, on *Ferdinand* and *Johannes* 0285, 3080
1840, on *Helena* and *Neptune* 5613, 5623
1854, (numerous ships) 3705, **6912**
1854, from wreck of *Johanne* 2414
1874, 1875, out of Bremen 0438, 2966
1900 and earlier, from Lauscha 2782
port customs list **0253**
to Boston, 1751 . . . . 3333, 3335
to Brazil, 1827-1919 . . . . 1612, 3740, **8657**
to British colonies, 18th c 4378
to California, 1838-1859 . . . . 2053, 2932
to Canada:
1750-1752 . . . . **7012, 7016, 7076, 7079**
1780s 1482, **6987, 7105,** 8640, 8643
1850, 1893 . . . . 1697, **8657**
1920s **2528**
to Carolina(s),
n.d. 3233,
1709-1710 . . . . 7820, 8094
1728-1749 3193
1750-1771 . . . . 4357, 4364
18th c. 1739, 2917
to Chile, 1850 . . . . **8657**
to Connecticut before 1700 . . . . 4822, 4830
to Dakota(s), 1898 . . . . **0190**
to Eastern seabord, 18th c 1815
to England, 1709 . . . . 4772-4773, 9214
to Georgia,
1720-1760 . . . . 0212, 3610
17th, 18th c. **2855**
to Illinois,
1783-1850s 0689, 0797, 2940, 3710
1850-1883 . . . . **1133.38** and **.40, 7620, 7621**
to Indiana, 1820-1869 . . . . **1133.10,** 1692
to Iowa,
1838-1859 (Davenport) 2053
1840s to 1870s . . . . **1133.6, .8, .12,** 2946, 8580-81
1900, from Schleswig-Holstein 7252
to Kansas,
18th c. **8528**
1858-1901 (Decatur County) 8410
1873-1874 (Hillsboro) **9317**
to Kentucky,
1830-1856 . . . . **9999.3** and **.6**
1869 8700
to London from the Palatinate, 1709 5013
to Louisiana,
1717-1731 . . . . **1290,** 2100

Germans, *cont'd*
1842-1843 7505
to Maine, 1752-1764 .... 3341, **6104**
to Maryland,
17th c. colonial arrivals **1420**
18th c. **3577, 9897**
1840 .... 5613, 5623
1841 .... **8515, 9090**
1854-1855 .... 2414, 3705
1874 .... **5235**
see also Germans to Baltimore (above)
to Massachusetts,
1751 .... 3333, 3335, 4210
1777 0140
to Michigan,
1835-1854 (Detroit area) 8655
1840-1845 (from Eifel region) 3710
1846-1856 (S.W. part of state) 6890
1860 (Clinton County) 8017
19th c. (Washtenaw County) **3709**
to Minnesota,
1840-1845 3710
1859-1888 .... **1133.42, .44**
19th c. (late) 2802
to Missouri,
1833 0797
1838-1841 .... 2095, 4803
1850 and earlier **3702**
to New England, 18th c 1815
to New Jersey,
17th c. 4822, 4830
18th c. **0926.40,** 3610
1819 .... **3295**
1854 7830
to New Netherlands, 1620-1664 8060
to New Orleans,
1769 .... **4676**
1848 (via England) 5153
1850 .... 3967, 9570
1853 (via England) 3298
to New York,
1610-1674 .... 1898, 4830
1700 and earlier 4822
1708-1719 .... 4817, 5015, 5019, 9800
1709-1710 .... 0889, **0926.8, 3615,** 3620
1720-1760 .... 0932, 3610, 6860
18th c. **0926.40**
1820-1850 .... 1874, **7640**
1832 0789
1833 .... **9037.1-.2**
1837 .... **6346**
1838-1859 .... 2053, **7896**
1840-1841 .... 1976, **4900, 4905**
1843 1074-75
1849-1868 .... **6200, 8657**
1875, 1878 .... **0446.** 8330
1893 .... **9027, 9028,** 9031
to North America, 18th, 19th c. **7127.2-.15**
to North Carolina, 1760s-1780s **7755**
to Nova Scotia, 18th c. 0860, **3745,** 5093, **7012, 7016, 7075, 7076, 7079**
to Ohio,
1770-1895 (short history) 5603
1832-1833 .... 0789, **3704, 9037.1-.2,** 9734

Germans, *cont'd*
1838-1868 .... **1133.16, .18, .20, .22**
1869-1870 .... 1578, 8700
to Pennsylvania,
17th c. 4822, 4834, **9251, 9252**
17th, 18th c. **1873**
18th c. **1033.1,** 2544, 3610, 4294, 4357, 4364, 4409-4415, 4422, 4662, **6211, 7370**
18th, 19th c. **0926.10,** 3565-3570
n.d. **9966, 9968**
1710-1815 .... 3565-70, **3570.1-.5**
1720-1760 .... 2544, 3610, 4422
1727-1787 .... **0491, 0929,** 4294, 4409-4415
1750-1773 .... 4357, 4364, 4662, **9256**
Berks County, Pa., 18th c 0889, 1032, **1033.4**
Church of the Brethren, 1729-1735 1732
Coblentz archives, 1732-1785 4409-4415
Ensminger family, 18th c 0488
from Dossenheim, 18th c 2917
from Friedrichstal, 1723-1739 9960
from Hassloch and Boehl, 18th c. **1031.2**
from Ludwigshafen, 18th c 0860
from Mutterstadt, 18th c. **1031.5**
from Nassau (duchy) 1709 8094
from Neckar Valley, 1749-1750 4422
from Palatinate, n.d. 3233
1700s 0922, 3193, 6665-66, 8810
from Prussian province of Saxony,
1748-1749 3848
from Rhenish Hesse, 1743-1754 .... **1870**
from Ulm, 17th, 18th c. **2855**
from Wittgenstein, Westphalia, 1725 5877
from Wolfersweiler, 18th c 0478
from Wuerttemberg, 1738-1750 6860
Germantown, 1683-1709 3313
Hellertown, 1738 3686
Huguenots, n.d. 8935
via Rotterdam, 1700-1775 1632
see also Germans to Philadelphia
to Philadelphia
1683 8490
1727-1751 .... 0821, 0827, 0829, 0877, 0932, 1778, 2232, 4294, **4594**
1746-1787 .... **0925.21,** 1120, 4294, **4319,** 4594
from Pfeddersheim, n.d. 1129
via Denmark and London, 1742 0932
via Netherlands,
ca. 1758 9085
1804 4672
to Russian Poland, 1834-1838 .... **0683**
to South America, 19th c 5143, 8290
to South Carolina,
1732-1752 .... 8730, 9480
1765, 1766 .... **0926.42, .59**
17th, 18th c. **2855**
19th c. (mid) 8290
to Tennessee, before 1850 2732
to Texas
1835-1854 .... 0408-10, 1636, 2474-76, 2484, 2504, 5719, 8150, 8655, 8770
1849-1867 .... 0578, 2484, 2494, 2514, 8317, 8770
to Toledo, Ohio, 1770-1895 5603
to Utah, 1849-1868 .... **6200**
to various countries, 1750-1803 .... **8584**

Germans, *cont'd*
to Venezuela, 1842 4033
to Virginia,
1714-1717 .... **3771,** 6102, **7480**
18th c. .... **0926.44** and **.46**
to West Virginia
n.d. **0926.46**
1850s (Mason County) 4998
to Wisconsin,
1840s 3710, **5608,** 5821, **9074**
1852 .... **8499, 8505, 8509.1, .2**
1853-1856 .... **1133.48, 7200**
1861-1862 .... **1133.56** and **.62**
1864, 1867 .... **1133.52 .54, .58**
1907-1925 .... 1867, 1868
see also entries under the particular regions and faith groups; *and* Wends
Germantown, Pa.,
and William Penn, 1691-1692 6041
Dutch and Germans to, 1683-1709 3313
Germans to, from Krefeld, 1683 .... **9251, 9252**
Mennonites naturalized, 1691 .... **5650**
naturalizations, 1709 .... **0926.26**
Germantown, Va., Germans to, after 1714 6102
Germany,
Bremen emigration lists, 1832-1850 .... 3967, 9640
departures, various,
1709 8480
1743-1784 4189
1816-1900 .... **5860, 6572**
1830s, as religious protest, ... **4058**
Hamburg ship lists, 1850-1875 0087
see also under Hamburg as main entry, passenger lists.
Huguenots, a compilation 4916
letters from Rhineland, 18th c **9949**
Mennonites from Friedelsheim, 19th c 0813
North, departures from,
1753-1882 .... 2053, 5040-5163, **5120**
Palatines from *see main entries* Palatinate *and* Palatines
Saar departures, 1816-1908 .... 1834, 3786, 3788
South (Neckar Valley), 18th c. **2857, 3627,** 4404, 4422
Southwest, departures,
1739-1780 4126
1816-1817 .... **5745**
Swabians from, to Hungary and Yugoslavia, then overseas, by 1900 6740
Upper Rhine area, departures, 18th c. **2855.5**
see also particular regions and specific place names
Germersheim, Germans from, 18th c 4214, 4266
Gibson, John, Mayor of Philadelphia, 1772-1773 7222-23
Gieboldehausen, Germans from, 1839-1866 .... 5119, **5120**
Gil Blas, Bremen to N.Y., 1849 .... **1133.32**
Gildart, Liverpool to North Potomac, Md., 1747 1242
Gillespie County, Texas, arrivals, ca. 1845-1846 2534
Glanmuenchweiler Lutheran church register, Palatinate 4133
Glarus, Swiss from, to New Glarus, Wis., 1845 .... **4891**
Glasgow
Russian Mennonites via, 1874-1880 .... **1865**
Scots from,
to Baltimore, 1874 .... **5235**
to Carolina, 1684 .... **9842**
to New Brunswick, 1815 .... **0358.31**
the *Columbia* from, 1905 .... **1924**
the *Lulan* from, 1848 .... **1446.3**
Mt. Stewart Elphinstone from, 1849 .... **1133.14**
Glassworkers, Belgian, in Pa., 1889-1904 .... **7664**
Glengarry "Indian Lands," Ontario, ca. 1817 0361
Gloucestershire, English from, 1663-1775 .... **1217.6**
Gluecksthaler Gebiet, Odessa, Germans from, 1876 1882
Goeshe, Bremen to New York, 1868 .... 7620, **7621**
Goethe, from Bremen
to Baltimore, 1854 3705
to New York, 1868 .... **1133.44**
Goetschy (Goetschius) family, 1735 .... 3000, 4487
Goetzendanner family to Md., 18th c. **3577**
Goisern, Austrians from, 1850-1882 2172
Golden Eagle, Amsterdam to Delaware R., 1661 1722
Golreppen (Hallingdal) Norway, depart's, 1853 .... **4030**
Good Speed, Scotland to Maryland, 1716 .... 7395, 7990
Goodman family, from Germany 9460, 9461
Goschenhoppen burial register, Pa., 1752-1772 .... **9256**
Gothenburg, Swedes from, 1848 .... **6515**
Gotland, Swedes from, 1819-1890 .... **6410.15**
Government-aided emigration:
Germany, 1765 .... **0926.42**
Ireland, ca. 1850 1826
New Brunswick, 1841-1842 .... **0358.36**
Government supported *see* Grant recipients *and* Subsistence accounts
Graafschap, Michigan, Dutch to, 1846-1847 6895
Grant County, S.D., Scandinavians in 1880 .... **7667**
Grant recipients
Georgia, land, 1756-1909 4890
Ireland, ca. 1850 1826
Nova Scotia, 1761, 1783 .... 2887, 6650
Upper Canada, 19th c 4502
Virginia, land, 17th, 18th c 6219-23, 6264, 9025
Gravesend, British from, to Barbados, 1677 9450
Gravestone inscriptions, Ireland, 19th, 20th c. **1194**
Gray family to Philadelphia, 1800-1906 .... **2763.10**
Great Britain *see* England; Ireland; Scotland; Wales
Great Register poll lists, Arizona, Cochise County, 1890 .... **1231.1-.3**
Great Register poll lists, California,
Butte County, 1878-79 .... **1050.1-.7**
Contra Costa County, 19th, 20th c. **2423**
Fresno County, 1896-98 .... **2763.25-.33**
Humboldt County, 1884 .... **4747**
Kern County, 1866-77 .... **2763.54-.56**
Mendocino County, 1891-98 2764
Sacramento County, 1860-71 .... **7840.1-.51**
San Diego
1866-1873 .... **8361.1-.9**
1880-1887 .... **8361.30-.32**
Santa Clara County,
1848-1872 1890
1884 .... **2763.20**
1900 .... **1981**
Siskiyou County,
1866-1878 .... **8484.1-.38**
1879 .... **3707.1-.19**
1892 .... **1820.1-.3**

Great Register, *cont'd*
Tulare County,
1872 .... **2769.1-.10**
1884-1888 2765-68
Great Register poll lists, Oregon, Klamath County, 1869 .... **3840.1-.3**
Great Registers, history of 1890
Great Yarmouth to New England, British, 1637-1639 3540
Greene, John, master of the *John and Sarah,* 1652 ... 8171
Greene County, Ia., naturalizations, n.d. **2770**
Greenock, Scots from,
to Halifax, on the *Polly,* 1799 7080
to N.B. on the *Rosina,* 1803 .... **0358.15**
to N.Y. on the *William,* 1817 5741
to Pictou, Nova Scotia, on the *Hector,* 1773 5000
Grey *see* Gray
Griffin, the
to Delaware River, 1689 .... **6099**
to Delaware Valley, 1675 1292
to New Jersey:
1675, 1689 .... 6097, 8450, 3580
ca. 1721 8760
Griffith see *Griffin*
Gronau, I.C., pastor, leader of Salzburg group to Georgia, 1730s **9332**
"Gruber's Group," German Lutherans, 1839-1841 ... **2095**
Guadeloupe, W.I., some departures after 1671 0228
Guerriera, Trieste to N.Y., Poles, 1831 .... **4606**
Guessing area (Austria), departures 1884-1939 2762
Guiana, French and Germans to, 18th c 0853
Guichart family, to Canada, 1658 1656
Guiding Star, Copenhagen to New York, 1869 .... 0299, 0314
Guilds, English, emigrant members, ca. 1800 2135
Guilford, Conn., English founders, 1639 .... **9597**
Guillory family arrivals, New Orleans, 1870 .... **1536**
Gulden Arent, Amsterdam to Delaware River area, 1661 1722
Gulf of Mexico, shipwreck of Germans and Acadians, 1769 .... **4676**
Guntersblum, Germans from, 18th c 4308
Gunzenhausen, Bavaria, Germans from, 18th c 0558
Gutman(n) family arrivals, Germans 9460-61

H

H.H. Meier, Bremen to New York, 1893 .... **7945**
Hague, N.D., Germans from Russia to, 1893 .... **3844**
Haiti to New Orleans, Guillorys and others, 1870 .... **1536**
Halifax,
arrivals, various, 1750-1752 .... **7016**
English to,
1750 4742
1774-1781 4632
1864 6213
Germans from Russia to,
1849-1910 .... **1860,** 2529, **2974.1,** 6929
1902-1909 .... 6951, 6954
Germans to,
1750, 1784 .... **7012, 7105**

Halifax, *cont'd*
Irish to,
1799 7080
1805-1806 and earlier 7050, 7065
1830 and earlier 7058
1864 6213
Loyalist refugees to, for provisions
n.d. 6407
1778 7072
New Englanders to
n.d. 6407
1750 4742
Scots to, 1784, 1799 .... 6650, 7080
Swiss to, 1750 .... **7012**
Welsh to, 1818 .... **7005**
Hallingdal, Norway, departures, 1853 .... **4030**
Hamburg,
Czechs from, for Nebraska, 1879 .... **8774**
departures,
for Brazil, 1850 8656
for Chile, 1849-1855 .... 3879, 8656
for Quebec, 1850 3948
for Sou. Amer. ports unnamed, 1850 3948
see also Hamburg passenger lists *and* ship lists
Foehr Islanders sailing from, 1850-1875 0087
Germans from Rumania via, 1899 .... **6404.6**
Germans from Russia via,
1873-1903 ... 0439, **0440,** 1697, 2960, 2970, 2972, 3872, 6920-6931, 6951, 6954, **9033**
1905-1907 .... **2974.6**
Germans from, to California, 1845-54 2932
Old Lutherans from, 1835-1854 .... 3474, **7896**
passenger lists
for 1850-1855 .... 3960, 8656, **8657**
for 1876-1878 .... **5726.1-.2**
ship lists,
Bavarian departures, 1849-1855 ...... 3879, 3941
Central German departures, 19th, 20th c 3948
Deutschland, the, 1849 3967
Foehr Islanders, 1850-1875 0087
Franklin, the, 1849 .... **1133.30**
Germans from Russia, 1874 3872
indexing project 3935
John Bertram to N.Y., 1864 .... **1133.18**
Kopler, the, 1853 .... **1133.48**
Leipzig departures via, 1850-1855 3960
microfilm of, in Salt Lake City 6920-31
Thuringian departures, 1850 3948
via England, early 1860s 3956
to Chile, Germans, 1849-1855 .... 3879, 8656
to Galveston, Germans, 1850 8656
to New Orleans, Balkan and Eastern Europeans, 1845 6127
to New York,
1847-1865 .... **1133.6, .12,** 2960, 3879, 3921, 3948, 8656
1873-1878 2960
to Quebec,
from Thuringia, 1850 3948
Liebig, 1868 2802
numerous ships, 1849-1855 .... 3879, 8656
to San Francisco, Germans,
1850, 1854 .... 2932, 8656
to Texas, Germans, 19th c ... 2494, 2504, 3879, 8656

Hamilton, James, Mayor of Philadelphia, 1745 .... 6054-56, 8357-58
Hamilton County, Illinois, Germans to, 1841-1845 1976
Hammer, Thomas Christian, Nova Scotia, 1753 5093
Hammonia, Hamburg to New York, 1876 .... **0440**
Hampshire County, Mass., French inhabitants, Acadians, after 1750 1658
Hampshire, English from, 1664-1775 .... **1217.5**
Hancock Co., Miss., nat'zations, 1856-1923 .... **6656**
Hannah and Elizabeth to Boston, 1679 .... 6560, 9610
Hannibal, Germany to N.Y., 1838-1868 .... **1133.23**
Hanover, Germans from, 1846-1871 3249
Hansa, Bremen to New York, 1852 .... **8506**
Happy Return, Plymouth, England, to Boston, 1670 9620
Harburg, Germans from, 1830-1848 5143
Harrietsfeld, N.S., Germans to, 1784 .... **7105**
Harris County, Tex., naturalizations,
  1886-1894 .... **0678.1-.3, 1006.1-.5**
  1896-1903 .... **6013.55, 6254, 6659**
  1903-1906 .... **2910**
Harrison County, Ind., nat'zations, 1841-44 .... **6758**
Harvard College graduates up to 1662 1936
Harvey, Col. Alexander, Vermont, 1774 .... 3670, 9670
Harvey, N.D., Germans from Russia to, 1902 2842
Hassloch, Palatines from, 18th c. **1031.12,** 1034
Hastings, Major L. H., with British to Brazil 5705
Haurida, Swedes from, 1851 .... **6412.50**
Haustadt, Germans from, 1816-1908 3786
Havana, Cuba,
  English and Irish to, 1818-19, 1853-58 .... **3028**
  Spanish from, 1840-1865 5030
  the *Catharine* from, to New Orleans, 1820 .... **5034**
Haverhill, Mass., Acadian French in exile 1658
Havre, France,
  departures for New York,
    1828-1842 .... **7640**
    1848-1882 .... **6428.1-.16**
  French from, 1841 .... **4900**
  Germans to N.Y. via, 1841 .... **4900**
  mixture of nationals from,
    1845 .... **1133.18** and **.20**
    1849-1853 .... **1133.16**
  ships from:
    Emerald, 1845 .... **1133.20**
    Havre, 1845 .... **1133.18**
    Langen, 1853 .... **1133.16** and **.34**
    Oneida, 1845, 1849 .... **1133.16** and **.18**
    St. Nicholas, 1849 .... **1133.16**
    Tremont, 1848 .... **6515**
    various, 1562-1671 0228
Havre de Grace *see* Havre (Le Havre)
Headlands, New Jersey, records of, 1664-1703 6097
Headrights claimed,
  Georgia
    1756-1909 4890
    1785-1790 1078
    1803-1804 1198
  Virginia,
    1677-1679 .... **1659**
    1734-1870 .... **0614,** 2302, **2915**
Headrights *see also* Land grants
Heathfield, Sussex, English from, 1830-1831 1023
Hebe, Trieste to N.Y., Polish exiles, 1831 .... **4606**
Hector
  Norway to New York, 1842 .... **5985**
  Scotland to British N. America, 1773 .... **1014**
  Scotland to Nova Scotia
    1773 and n.d. 5000, 5007, 6650
  to Boston, 1637-1638 1064
Hedge family, Salem, New Jersey, 1675 1292
Hefte family from Norway, 1853 .... **4030**
Heidelberg, Germany, departures
  n.d. 4203
  1726-1727 4450
  1737-1754 .... 4119, 4196, 4422, 4440
Heidelberg, Pa., Moravians to, 1752 3179
Heidenheim area, Germans from, 1739-1920s 7552
Heilbron area, Germans from, 1750-1883 7810
Helen Thomson, shipwreck, Gulf of St. Lawrence, 19th c. **0358.17**
Helena, Prussian brig, to Baltimore, 1840 5623
Helena Sloman, Hamburg to New York, 1850 3921
Helene, Bremen to New York, 1849 0689
Heller family arrivals, Pennsylvania, 1738 3686
Henrico County, Virginia, French to, 1714 6710
Henry and Francis,
  from Newcastle, England, 1685 0973
  Scots to New Jersey on the, 1685 .... 2026, 2596, 9738
Henry and Sarah to Jamaica, 1675 .... **7852**
Herald, Liverpool to Baltimore, 1834 .... **5034**
Herbolzheim, Germans from,
  18th, 19th c and n.d. 0121, 4033
Hercules of Sandwich,
  British on the, n.d. 0732, 0744
  to Jamaica, with slaves, 1675 .... **7852**
  to New England, 1634-1637 .... 0378, 6600, 7111
Herefordshire, English from, 1663-1775 .... **1217.6**
Herman, S.S., Bremen to Baltimore, 1889 7921
Hermine to New York, Germans aboard, 1852 .... **8499**
Hertfordshire, English from,
  1646-1775 .... 1098, **1217.4**
  1836 .... **9628**
Herzog, Volga Germans from, 1870s 1682
Hesse, Germans from,
  to Baltimore, 1854, 1855 2414
  to Nova Scotia, 1753 5093
  to Pennsylvania:
    1743-1754 .... **1870**
    1777 and earlier 8630
  to various destinations, 1835-1839 .... **2829.1-.3**
Hesse-Cassel, Germans from, 1835-1839 .... **2829.1-.3**
Hesse-Darmstadt, 1834-1838 .... **0683**
Hesse-Hanau,
  Germans from,
    1741-1767 .... 8600, 8602
    1783 and after 8643
    to Canada after 1783 8643
  soldiers from, in Canada, 1783, 1784 .... 1482, **7105**
Hessian arrivals,
  1832-1835 2828-29
  1846-1849 3004
Higgins, capt., master of the *Ocean,* 1841 .... **9090**
"High Germans" to Virginia, 1717 .... **3771**

Highland Scots *see* Scottish Highlanders
Hijar-Padres Colony, California, 1769-1835 .... **3365**
Hilbringen, Germans from, 1816-1908 3786
Hildesheim, Germans from, n.d. 5060
Hill, William, ship's master, 1727 1632
Hillsboro, Kans., Germans to, 1873-1874 .... **9317**
Hinman, Edward, descendants of, Connecticut **3197**
Hippenstiel family, late 18th c. **3208**
Hobson, John, master of the *Nightengale,* 1669 0354
Hoechst (Hochst), Germans from,
1834-1838 .... 1683, **0685**
Hoechstadt (Hochstadt), Palatines from,
18th c. 1032, **1033.4**
Hohentruedingen, Germans from, 18th c. 0558
Hohenzollern, S.S.,
Bremen to Baltimore, 1886 .... **3260**
Bremen to New York, 1895 7930
Holland, Michigan,
founded, 1846 6875
colonized, 1846-1856 6890
Holstein, East, Germans from, 1838-1859 2053
Holzhausen family to Maryland, 1831 3550
Holzminden, Germans from, to Texas, 1849 5719
Home Counties, English from the, 1655-1775 ..... **1217.4**
Hope, Alexander, ship's master, 1738 1788
Hope, Scotland to Nova Scotia, 1848 5007
Host Church, Berks Co., Pa., 18th c. 1032, **1033.4**
Houlton, Me., Swedes naturalized 1837-1900 ..... **6410.5**
Hudson Bay, Scots to, 1811 1000
Huefel-Comuy, German colony in Chile,
1906-1912 8140
Hueffelsheim, Lutheran church register, 18th c. 4161
Huguenot
arrivals, 16th, 17th c. 0228, 2564
expeditions, 1562-1565 0228
land patents, Virginia, 1695-1732 6223
Huguenots
exiled, 17th, 18th c. **7204,** 9230
French, 16th, 17th c. 0228
1700 .... 0953, 3633, 3640, 7850
18th c. **7765**
French, Swiss, Genevese, German, and Flemish,
1700 .... 0953, 9230
Germans, 18th c. 6021, **7765**
in Germany, n.d. 4916
London to Virginia, refugees, 1700 9230
naturalized, colonial era **0926.63,** 6021
Swiss,
to Phila. via Rotterdam, 1735 3000
to Virginia, 1700 0953
to Canada, 17th, 18th c. **7202, 7204**
to Carolinas, 17th, 18th c. **7204**
to England, ca. 1735 3000
to French West Indies, then continental North
America, 1671 0228
to Massachusetts, 1681 0228
to New England, 17th, 18th c. **7204**
to New Jersey:
1630-1667 .... **7899**
1677-1710 4056
to New York:
1630-1667 ("New Amsterdam") **7899**
1678-1820 (New Paltz) 4592
1681 (N.Y.C.) 0228
1687-1776 (New Rochelle) 8280
17th, 18th c. **7204**
to Pennsylvania, 17th, 18th c. **7204, 7765,** 8935
to Rhode Island, 17th, 18th c. **7204**
to South Carolina,
1679 1916
16th, 17th c. 0228
to Virginia,
17th, 18th c. 6223, **7204**
1700 .... 0953, 3633, 7850
1750-1797 3630
Hull, England, to Nova Scotia, Yorkshire settlers,
1774 9975
Humboldt County, Calif., voters in 1884 .... **4747**
Humphreys, Scotland to Canada, 1806 .... **1014**
Hungarian centennial, S. Bend, Ind., 1982 .... **0611**
Hungarians
in Boston, 1882 .... **0611**
in Pennsylvania, 1900 census **7137**
to Indiana, 1882-1982 .... **0611**
to N. Dakota before 1918 .... **0090**
Hungary, Germans to,
1700s 0853, 6740
1738-1750 2282
Hunsrueck, Germans from,
n.d. 4203
18th c. 4154, 4161, **8584**
19th c. 1612, 1616, 8652
Hunter, Robert,
colonial governor 1811
New York, 1710-1714 .... 5019, 6311
Huntingdon County, Pa., naturalizations,
1798-1802 .... **3330.1-.4**
Huntingdonshire, English from, 1663-1775 .... **1217.7**
Huntington Bay to Kingston, Loyalists, 1783 0398
Hutchinson County, S.D., Germans from Russia to,
1878-1879 3202-04

I

Illingen, Germans from, 1833-1836 1834
Illinois,
arrivals, 1850-1883 .... 7620, **7621, 1133.38**
Germans to:
1783-1850s 0689, 1976, 2940
1850-1883 .... **1133.38** and **.40**
19th c., Palatines 0797, 8430
naturalizations,
Champaign County,
1866-1896 .... **5012.37** and **.40**
1903-1906 .... **5012.37**
DeKalb County,
1838-1845 .... **1498**
1853-1908 .... **2421**
DeWitt County, 1850s-1870s 0024
Iroquois County,
1867-1889 1452
1891-1929 .... **3455.1-.5**
Madison County, 1816-1900 .... **8368**

Illinois, *cont'd*
Morgan County, 1835-1894 3368
Oquawka, 1836-1855 0094
Richland County, n.d. **1638**
Rock Island County, 1855-64 . . . . **6410.25**
Rockford, 1859-1870 . . . . **6410.10**
St. Clair County, 1816-1905 1003
Schuyler County, 1828-1886 7318
Southern District, 1856-1864 1442
Vermilion County, 1880-1900 . . . . **2341.1-.2**
Norwegians to, 1835-1850s 2574, 2580
Scots to,
1738-1740 6640
1828-1909 7134
Swiss to, 19th c. **6154, 9984**
Imperial Circle of Vohenstrauss (Bavaria),
Austrians from, 1843-1877 4596
Importation
as proof of headrights, Va., 1734-1870 2302
oaths concerning, Va., 1739-1741 4627
Importations [Virginia],
1734-1870 2302
1739-1740 5831
1746 and earlier **2915,** 4627
Indentured servants,
British, arrivals
1637-1886 . . . . **1139.1,** 2162, 2524, 3090, 3438, 6179, 9580
1686-1716 . . . . 2212, 2524, **4727**
1718-1775 . . . . **1451.49,** 2554, 3510, 3690, **3690.1,** 4642, **4727**
British to Barbados, 1654-1686 . . . . **3438.1-.6**
English,
1774 . . . . **9832**
17th, 18th c **1217.1-.9**
escaped from *Capellen tot den Pol,* 1784 9900
headrights claimed, Va., 1677-79 . . . . **1659**
Irish,
1749-1750 4790
1769-1770 0622
1787, 1789 . . . . 2044, **4049**
missing, *see* Missing persons
to Georgia, 1774-1775 . . . . **3430**
to Maryland, 1774 . . . . **9832**
to New Jersey,
1664-1703 6097
1787 . . . . **4049**
to Philadelphia,
1745-1746 . . . . 6054-56, 8357-58
1771-1773 . . . . 7207, 7222-7223
1775 4642
to Virginia, 1674-1702 . . . . **0620**
to West Indies, 1682-1686 . . . . **1139.1**
see also Servants
"Indian Lands," Glengarry, Ont., Scottish settlers of,
ca. 1817 0361
Indian Queen, Liverpool to Halifax, 1864 6213
Indiana,
arrivals, 1840-1870s **3246, 1133.10**
foreign-born in Scot County, 1817-1894 . . . . **0633**
Germans to, 1820-1869 1692
Hungarians in, 1882-1982 . . . . **0611**
Mennonites to, from Russia, 1870-1885 3100
naturalizations

Indiana, *cont'd*
Allen County, n.d. **1451.6**
Cass County, 1870s **3246**
Clark County, 1888-1927 . . . . **1186**
Crawford County, 1817-1896 . . . . **1385, 4598**
Dearborn County:
1800-1830s 4990
1838-1840s **1457.1-.3, 1459**
Decatur County, 1867-1874 . . . . **3275**
Dubois County, 1852-1869 1692
Franklin County, 1826-1839 . . . . **2180,** 2182
Harrison County, 1841-1844 . . . . **6758**
Jennings County, 1865-1900 . . . . **3509**
Knox County, 1852-1945 . . . . **3018**
Lawrence County, 1852 . . . . **4537**
local courts up to 1907 . . . . **3434**
Marion County, 1843-1853 . . . . **1450.1**
Monroe County, 1854-1859 . . . . **5755**
Montgomery County, 1850-1930 . . . . . 6003, **9754**
Ohio County, 1848-1852 . . . . **6372.1-.2**
Orange County, 1840-1905 . . . . **4599**
Pike County, 1857-1906 5815
Ripley County:
1818-1843 . . . . **2525.15**
1850s **7515.1-.2**
Rush Country, 1857-1868 7825
Switzerland County, 1825-1829 . . . . **2525.40**
Tippecanoe County, 1834-1850 3010
Vanderburgh County:
1820-1854 . . . . 9115-9116, **9117**
various counties, 19th, 20th c. **0926.53**
Wayne County, 1833-1840 9625
Wells County, n.d. **5817**
Indianola, Tex., Germans to, 1852 2494
Indostan, Germans on the, 1804 8610
Industrial trades, New York, 1631-1655 8134
Interpreters in the Northwest Company,
1797-1798 4762
Inverness County, Scot., Macmillans, 1802 . . . . . . **5012.17**
Inverness Township, Que., early settlers, 1819 . . . . **7199**
Iowa
arrivals,
from Germany on *Kopler,* 1853 . . . . **1133.8**
from Netherlands, 1847-1860 9385-9387
via German ports, 1848-1865 . . . . . **1133.6 and .12**
Dutch to Iowa, 19th c 0675
French to Iowa, 19th c 0675
Germans to
1838-1859 (Davenport) 2053
1840s-1870s 2946, 8580-81
1848-1865 . . . . **113.6, .8, .12**
from Friedelsheim, 19th c. 0813
from Schleswig-Holstein, 1900 7252
naturalizations,
Des Moines County, 1849-1857 . . . . **1525**
Dubuque County:
1832-1856, 1868 . . . . **3813,** 5228
Greene County, n.d. **2770**
Jefferson County, 1846-1905 . . . . **9094**
Plymouth County, 1872-1886 9596
Polk County, 1848-1889 . . . . **6778**
Scott County, 1842-1930 . . . . **2771**
statewide, 1838-1853 . . . . **8773**
Swedes to, by 1855 . . . . **2090**

Irad Ferry, with Swiss to N.Y., 1843 . . . . **3810**
Ireland,
  Aide-de-Camp from, to Halifax, 19th c **7078**
  crop failure and mass emigration,
   1846-1851 . . . . **1921.1-.4**
  departures from,
    for American colonies, 1660-1775 4790
    from Crown Estates, ca. 1850 1826
    from various places, 18th, 19th c. **1831**
  Friends of, polit. assoc., 1831-34 . . . . **9076**
  Lord Dunluce from, 1773 1594
  Northern, departures
    for American colonies up to 1717 4790
    for Delaware, 1789, 1790 . . . . 2044, 2046
    for New England, 1718 0648
    for Pennsylvania, 1836 1384
    for South Carolina, 1773 1594
    for various ports, 1804-1806 3450
    from Belfast,
      1789, 1790 . . . . 2044, 2046
      1817 3075
      1833-1835, 1836 . . . . 1384, 2080
    from Fermanagh, 1846-1929 . . . . **1418**
    from Larne, 1773 1594
    from Londonderry:
      1620-1822 8790
      1831, 1838 . . . . **0358.21, 6508.3**
    from Newry,
      1765 . . . . **6535**
      1803-1831 . . . . **5033,** 9198
    Quakers from, to Pa., 1677-1702 1137
    Sarah Sheaffe from, to Phila., 1836 1384
    ships from:
      1681-1775 4790
      1810-1812 . . . . **3806**
    State-aided emigration, ca. 1850 1826
Irish
  arrivals,
    1620-1822 . . . . 2151, 3040, 6575, 6588, 8790, 9198
    1830-1860s . . . 2080, 3040, **6413.20, .30, 8867,** 9198
    1864-1871 9200
  children to U.S. and Canada, 1846-1929 . . . . **1418**
  convict servants to Md., 1745-1780 . . . . **1357.1-.2**
  deserters, Napoleonic Wars, 1805-1806 7050
  families, histories of some 0568, **9254**
  family searches, through notices in *Boston Pilot,*
   19th c 6417
  from Dublin to N.Y. on *Russia,* 1849 . . . . **1133.24**
  from Ennistymon workhouse, 1850-1860 . . . . **6413.30**
  from Limerick workhouse, 1848-1860 . . . . **6413.20**
  from Liverpool to N.Y. on *New World,* 1853 . . . 2016
  from Royal Constabulary, emigrating,
   1834-1845 . . . . **9576**
  from various Irish ports, 1660-1775 4790
  genealogy, handbook on 3040
  gravestone transcriptions, n.d. **9593**
  in Nova Scotia, 18th, 19th c 7095-98, **9554**
  in West Indies, 17th c 2851
  mentioned in the *Boston Pilot,* 1846 7035
  naturalized
    in Georgia, 1820-1847 . . . . **1307,** 3371
    in Indiana, 1838-1867 . . . . . . **4537, 6372.1-.2,** 7825
    in Iowa, 1868 . . . . **5228**
    in Maryland, 19th c 6454
    in New York,
      1800-1855 (various counties) 0016
      1802-1814 (N.Y.C.?) 9870
      1807-1828 (Allegany County) 5972
      1816-1870 (Courtland County) 1568
      1830s (Wayne County) 5978
      1830-1839 (Onondaga County) 5942
      19th c. (Saratoga County) 5934, **5935**
    in Pennsylvania:
      1783-1801 (Cumberland County) **5630**
      1795-1888 (Washington Co.) 8276-8277
      1798-1802 (Huntingdon, York
       counties) **3330.1-.4, 9972.3-.4**
      1802-1815 (Fayette, York
       counties) **1966.1-.8, 9972.7-.8**
      1822-1862 (Clearfield, Somerset
       counties) **0097,** 6047-48
      1835-1836 (Cambria County) **1076.1-.4**
      19th c. (Berks County) . . **0515-0518, 4504.1-.3**
    in South Carolina, 1800-1825 . . . . **2428,** 8354
    in Texas:
      1880-1905 (Cooke County) 8350
      19th c. (Dallas County) **1447.1-.4**
    in Vermont, 19th c. (Franklin Co.) **5901**
    in Virginia, 1828-1854 9830
  Northern Presbyterians, departures,
   1680-1820 5243
  opposed to British Act of Union, 1801 7065
  purchasers of land in Pennsylvania,
   1681-1682 0032
  Quakers in Pennsylvania, 1682-1750 5917
  railroad builders 2732
  surname interests **9254**
  to Alabama (Mobile), 1832-1852 5203-5204
  to America, 19th, 20th c. **1194**
  to Australia,
    1834-1845 . . . . **9576**
    1848-1860 . . . . **6413.20**
  to Canada,
    1830s **1500,** 2080, **8867**
    1839-1860 . . . . **1433,** 4575, **4906, 6413.20, .30**
  to Cuba, 1818-19, 1853-58 . . . . **3028**
  to Delaware:
    1789 . . . . 2044, 7600
    1831 . . . . **6508.3** and **.7**
  to Georgia:
    1772 . . . . **5996**
    1828-1841 . . . . **1307,** 9689
  to Kansas, 18th c. **8528**
  to Louisiana, 1813-1837, 1849 . . . . 2742, **6121**
  to Maryland,
    1776 and earlier 1372
    1820-1834 . . . . **0253, 9076**
    1841-1842 . . . . **6508.8**
    19th c (early) 1742, 2859, 6468, 8795-97
    out of English ports, 18th c 6267
  to Massachusetts,
    1620-1775 1642
    18th, 19th c 7095-98
  to New Brunswick, 1838 . . . . **0358.21**
  to New Castle, 1803-1806 1762
  to New England, 1716-1769 6270

Irish, *cont'd*
to New Hampshire, 1718 0648
to New Jersey, 1687-1741 .... **4049,** 8380
to New London, 19th c. 2859
to New Orleans, 1849 .... **3453**
to New York
early 19th c 2859
1803-1855 ..... 1742, 1762, 1826, **1921.1-.4** 3040, **3806, 6608,** 8795-97
1827-1868 .... **1133.22,** 2792, **4906**
1845-1907 ...... 0305, 0568, **1133.24,** 1414, 2016, 5791, 8330
to North America, 18th, 19th c. **1194, 1831**
to Nova Scotia
1770 (approx.)-1799 .... **7073,** 7080
1800-1806 .... 7050, 7065
1830 and earlier 7058
1864 6213
19th c. **7078**
to Ohio, 1838-1868 .... **1133.22**
to Ontario (Lanark County), 1815-1823 4986
to Pennsylvania
1682-1750 .... 2979, 5917
1746/1747 4732
1785-1788 6800
early 19th c 1742, 1762, 2859, 3075, 8796
1845 .... **6508.6**
19th c. **0097**
to Quebec, 1830s 8867
to Rhode Island, 1851 .... **6508.5**
to South Carolina, 1773 1594
to Tennessee before 1850 2732
to Texas, 1829 .... 7365, 7740, 7745
to Virginia
1600s 2851, 6258, 6276
1700s 0622, 6276
to Wisconsin, 1852 .... **8505**
Ironworkers, Scots in Mass., 1651-52 .... **1750**
Iroquois County, Ill., naturalizations, 1891-1929 .... **3455.1-.5**
Irwin County, Ga., naturalizations, 1820-1847 .... **1307, 3371**
Isaac Allerton, Liverpool to N.Y., 1841 .... **4906**
Isabella,
Bremen to New Orleans, 1832-1839 8890
Bremen to New York, 1832-1839 8890
Isabella G. Briggs, Liverpool to Baltimore, 1841-1842 .... **6508.8**
Isle of Skye, Scot., to Canada, 1806 .... **1014, 1446.3**
Isle of Wight, departures for Virginia, 1620-1621 3273
Isle of Wight County, Va., records of 1618-1623 and 1625 5907
Italia, with Central and Eastern Europeans,
to Baltimore, 1893 .... 9034, **9035**
to New York, 1893 .... 9034, **9035**
Italians
in N.Y. census records, 1884-1930 .... **0692**
in U.S. forces in W.W.I. **0692**
to New York, 1884-1930 .... **0692**
Italy, departures
from Messina, 1870 0289
via Antwerp, 1855 .... **2885**
Itzstein and Welcker, Bremen to New Orleans, 1850 3967
Ivernia, S.S., Liverpool to Boston, 1903 2424

J

Jabel, Mecklenburg, Germans from, 1850-1857 2070
Jackson County, Tex., naturalizations, 1890-1920 (approx.) **6660**
Jacobidrebber, Germany, departures from, 1839 2242
Jacobite Rebellion, Scotland, and prisoners, 1745, 1746 .... 1242, **4913,** 4920, 6904-05
Jacobites, transported to colonies, 1716 .... 2989, 8690
Jamaica,
Barbadians to, 1679 .... **8408**
British to,
1675 .... **7852**
1760-1763 8534
indentured servants to, 1683-1684 6179
prisoners to, Jacobites, ca. 1745 4920
Scots to,
1685 .... **9845**
1716 8690
1774-1775 1088
James, Captain of the *Oxford,* 1776 3110
James,
Hampton, England, to New England, 1635 1190
to Bermuda, with London children, 1850 9995
James Eduard, Germany to Maryland, 1833 .... **3704**
James Goodwill, Rotterdam to Philadelphia, 1727 .... **4594**
Jamestown, Va.,
arrivals, 1606-1624 .... 7860, 8745, 9238
inhabitants, 1624 9238
legislators, 1629, and dates of arrival 6064
Jane,
Britain to Canada (P.E.I.) [18th c.?] **1446.1**
Scotland to Canada, 1790 .... **1014**
Jason, to Baltimore, 1833 .... **3704**
Jauernig, Czechoslovakia, Freiwaldau Archives at 9985
Jeannette, Pa., and Belgians naturalized, 1889-1904 .... **7664**
Jeannette, Haiti to New Orleans, 1870 .... **1536**
Jefferis, James, captain of the *Brothers,* 1789 2044
Jefferson, Oh., naturalizations, 1875-1906 .... **0160**
Jefferson County, Ia., naturalizations, 1846-1905 .... **9094**
Jennings County, Ind., naturalizations, 1865-1900 .... **3509**
Jenny, Hull, Eng., to Ft. Cumberland, N.S., 1775 5675
Jersey, West, British to, 1664 1992
Jews in the American colonies, 1600-1700 .... 0061, 3253, 3283, 3303
naturalized,
Maryland, colonial era 3253
New York, colonial era 3253, 3303
Pennsylvania, colonia era 3253
South Carolina, colonial era 3253
Jobson, John, captain of the *Confidence,* 1638 .... **0232**
Jockgrimm, Germans from, 19th c. **7140**
Johan Georg, Bremerhaven to New Orleans, 1838/1839 .... **2095**
Johanna, Drammen, Norway, to N.Y., 1843 0209
Johanne, foundering of the, Frisian Islands, 1854 2414

Johannes,
Bremen to Baltimore, 1834 0258
Emden, Germany, to Charleston, 1857 9664
John, England to Barbados, 1677 1252
John Bertram, Hamburg to N.Y., 1864 .. **1133.18, .38, .54**
John and Dorothy, England to New England, 1637-1639 3540
John and Sarah, England to New England, 1651-1652 .... 0269, 8170, 8171
John Barry, Irish to Canada on the, 1825 2832
John Hancock, Liverpool to New York, 1853 .... **9668**
"Johnsburg" and McHenry County, Ill., Germans, 1840-1845 3710
Johnson, Robert, Gov. of S. Carolina, 1732 8730
Johnson County, Kans., citiz. applica., 1870-90 .... **0770**
Johnson, Liverpool to Port Oxford, Md., 1747 .... 1242, 8005
Jones, William, ship captain, 1678 2075
Joseph and Thomas from Bristol, England, with passengers for Virginia, 1707 0666
Juchereau family, France to Canada, n.d. 5761
Jugoslavs *see* Yugoslavs
Juniata County, Pa., nat'zations, 1789-1848 .... **0926.12**
Jupiter, Bremen to New York, 1864 .... **1133.52**

K

Kaiser Wilhelm der Grosse, Bremen to New York, 1888-1903 .... **1970, 2995, 4061**
Kaiserslautern, Germans from,
18th, 19th c 0805, 0845, **0856**
to Ontario, n.d. **7202**
Kalmar Nyckel, Sweden to New Sweden, 1641 3766
Kansas,
arrivals, 1858-1901 8410
census of Kearny County, 1880 .... **3755**
Germans to, from Central Europe, 1876 2971
Germans to, from Russia
1874-1876 .... 0008, **1677,** 1682, 1694, 4019, 7720
1876-1922 .... 0008, **1677, 2973.2,** 7720
German-Irish family to, 18th c. **8528**
Germans to Newton and Burton, 1878 .... **9556**
Kearny County census, 1880 .... **3755**
naturalizations:
1866-1892 (Riley County) **7470**
1870-1890 (Johnson County) ... 1512, 1513, **0770**
1907-1919 (Montgomery Co.) **6013.40**
1907-1921 (Lawrence) **1828**
1909-1937 (Kearny County) **3755**
Russians to, 1870s **3394**
Volhynian Mennonites to, 1874 9070
WPA listing of Germans, 1873-1874 9317
Karlsruhe, Germany,
Heidelberg emigration records,
1726-1727 4450
1737-1754 4196
state archives 4287, 4440
Kasserin Maria Theresa, Bremen to N.Y., 1900 3596
Katharinenburg, Germans from, 18th c 4133
Katharinental, Russia, Germans from, 1891 .... **0626**
Katzka, Russia; possibly Kratzka **3394**
Kearny County, Kans., nat'zations, 1909-1937 .... **3755**
Kedar, Liverpool to Halifax, 1864 6213
Kell, Germans from, n.d. 5463
Kendall County, Ill., Norwegians to, 1835-1837 2574
Kent, British from,
1634-1637, to New England 0378
1655-1775, bonded passengers **1217.4**
1721-1773, to Virginia **8435**
n.d. 0732, 0744
Kent, Ont., Huguenots to, 17th, 18th c. **7204**
Kent, to New Jersey,
1677, 1721 (approx.) 8070, 8760
with English Quakers, 17th c. 8070
Kentucky,
Germans to,
1830-1856, 1869 .... 8700, **9999.3** and **.6**
naturalizations, 1828-67 (Todd County) **2158**
Swiss to Laurel County, 1881 f. 8054
Kern County, Calif., voters, 1866-1877 .... **2763.54-.56**
Kesh County, Irish from, 1846-1929 .... **1418**
Kew, Eng., passenger lists records **3430, 8543, 9817**
Key of Kalmar, Sweden to Delaware, 1641 8002
Key West, arrivals, 1837-1868 4702-03
Kidnappings
1648-1685, for the colonies **1257**
1697-1698, of Scots for Pennsylvania **6185**
King family, Virginia and N. Carolina, 1694 .... **9824**
King of Prussia to Philadelphia, with Palatines and servants, 1764 .... **0926.21,** 6441
King William Village, Henrico County, Va., French Protestants to, 1714 6710
Kings County, N.Y., Dutch to, 17th c. 0505
Kirchschaffenei Archiv, Zweibruecken, ... 4357, 4364
Kirkwall, Scots from, 1774-1775 .... **1451.49**
Kittery, Maine, Scots to, 1651-1652 0269
Klamath County, Ore., voters in 1869 .... **3840.1-.3**
Kleeburg, Germans from, 18th c 4133
Klein family arrivals, 1732-1774 3428
Klein Schifferstadt, Germans from, to Maryland, 18th c. **3577**
Kleinliebental to New York on S.S. *Kasserin Maria Theresa,* 1900 3596
Klungler family arrivals, German 9460-9461
Knickerbocker families, 17th c 1864
Knight family arrivals, n.d. **1439**
Knox County, Ill., Scots to, 1828-1909 7134
Knox County, Ind., nat'zations, 1852-1945 .... **3018**
Koblentz *see* Coblentz
Kocherthal, Joshua, clergyman, 18th c.
Palatine paster 4817, 5990
with Germans to N.Y. 6137, 6316, 9800
Koeckelwick, Germans from, 1846 5851
Koepfli family, Illinois, 1831 .... **9984**
Kolb, departures for America, 1876 1702
Kopler, Germans to New York on, 1853 .. **1133.8** and **.48**
Kowal-Kowalski-Kowalczik variations, ... **7138**
Kraichgau, Germans from, 18th c. **1031.8**
Kratzka, Russia, departures for Kansas, 1870s **3394**
Krause, L.F.E., Lutheran pastor, 19th c. **9074**
Krefeld, Germans from, to Pennsylvania,
1683 .... **9251, 9252**
n.d. 6199

Kreuznach, Germans from, 18th c.................4161
Kreis Adenau *see* Adenau, Germans from
Kronoberg County, Swedes from, to Minnesota, 1855-1867 6406
Kroonland, Antwerp to New York, 1906 ....**4810**
Kulm, Bessarabia, Russia, to South Dakota, Germans, 1878-1879 3203-04
Kulm, N.D., Germans from Russia to, 1902 ....**4061**
Kunigrude, Bremen to New York, 1852 ....**8508**
Kutschurgan area, South Russia, to North Dakota,
  Germans from, 1895 7930
  other departures, 1888.......................7934

L

Laborers,
  British, to New Brunswick, 1837 .... **0358.13**
  Dutch and Scandinavian in N.Y., 1631-1635 8134
  English, to Canada, 1836 ....**9628**
  German, in Lancaster, Pa., 1777 8630
  Irish, in Tennessee by 1850 2732
  Scottish, to New Brunswick, 1837 .... **0358.26**
Lady Emily Peel to Philadelphia, Irish aboard, 1864 9200
Lady Gray, Scotland to Nova Scotia, 1841 5007
Lady Mary to N.Y. via Newfoundland, 1842........9770
Lahave, N.S., 18th c. arrivals **3745**
Lahn, S.S., Bremen to N.Y., 1893 .... 7937, **7945**
Lambsheim, Germans from, in the Palatinate,
  1709-1764 7314
  18th, 19th c 7312
Lanark County, Ontario,
  British to, 1821 4502
  Scots to, 1815-1823 4986
Lancashire, English from, to Maryland, 1665-1775 .... **1217.8,** 1587
Lancaster, Pa.,
  German laborers to, 1777 8630
  Swiss Mennonites to, 18th c. **1035.25**
Lancaster County, Pa.,
  French to, 18th c...........................**7765**
  German/Swiss in, 1729 .... **0926.18**
  Huguenots to, 18th c. **7765**
  Mennonites from, to Canada, 1800s 8363
  naturalizations,
    18th c. .... **0926.18** and **.38**
    19th c. **4504.1-.3**
  Swiss to, 17th, 18th c. **0926.18, 4483**
Lancaster [Eng.] *see* Lancashire
Land,
  alien-owned,
    New Jersey, 1664 1992
    New York, 1790-1825 8222
    North Dakota, 1918......................**0090**
    Pennsylvania, 1681-1682 .... 0032, 7570
    South Dakota, 1901 ....**7667**
    Texas, 19th, 20th c......................0538
  allotments of, South Carolina, 1761 7343
  called "Welsh Tracts," Pennsylvania, 1681......0983
  claims on, in Virginia, 1746-1750.............**2915**
  entitlement of Canadians to, New York, 18th c 4930
  entitlement proceedings, Virginia, 1739-1740....3816
  for Canadian and Nova Scotia refugees, N.Y., n.d. and 1785 .... 6147, 8660
  for English arrivals, New Brunswick, 1837.... **0358.6**
  for immigrants transported to New Jersey, 1664-1703 6097
  for immigrants transported, Virginia, 1677-1679 ....**1659**
  for Irish arrivals, 18th c......................6276
  for Scots, 1767 5009
  grants,
    Georgia,
      1730s-1909.................... 3388, 4890
    Louisiana, 1719 3418
    New York, 1785, 1798, n.d. 1114, 6147, 8660
    North Carolina, 1753-1767 .... 2272, 5009
    Nova Scotia, 1716, 1784 .... 2887, **7105**
    Ohio, 1798..............................1114
    Quebec, 1650-1655.......................6830
    South Carolina, 1761.....................7343
    Texas, 1830s 5011
    Virginia, 1623-1878 ...... **0614, 1659,** 6219, 6276
    West Virginia, 18th c. **0926.46**
  grants and land patents, Virginia
    1623-1666 .... 9025, 6220
    1666-1695 .... 6221, **6225**
    1695-1732 6223
    17th-19th c.............................6264
  grants and sales, Pennsylvania,
    1681-1682 .... 0032, 2979, 7570
  holding of, permits to resident aliens, N.Y.,
    1790-1848 .... 8222, 8258
  owners,
    Canada, 1663 9222
    New York, 1777-1901 2956
    North Dakota, 20th c.....................**0090**
    South Dakota, 1901......................**7667**
    Virginia, 18th c. **0926.46**
  patents *see* grants and patents under Land
  sales,
    Pennsylvania, 1681-1682....... 0032, 2979, 7570
    West Jersey, 1664.......................1992
Land Office Acts, Georgia, repeal of, 1909 4890
Land Office records, Annapolis, Md. 4507-11, 6157
Landau, Germans from, 18th c 4214
Landers family arrivals, 17th-19th c................**4514**
Lane, Sir Ralph, colonial governor, 1530?-1603 2875
Langen, LeHavre to New York, 1853 .... **1133.16** and **.34**
Langenholtensen, Germans from, 19th c............**0472**
Larne, Ireland, departures for Carolina, 1773 1594
La Rochelle, French from,
  to Canada, 17th, 18th c 1462, 2632, 2652
  to Massachusetts, 1681 0228
  to New York, 1681.........................0228
Larson, Daniel, and Swedish immig., 1851 ...... **6412.50**
LaSalle County, Ill, Norwegians to,
  1835-1850s....................... 2574, 2580
Lau, Bishop Daniel Friedrich......................3928
Laudenheim, Germans from 1709-1710 ....**3615**
Lauenstein, Germans from, 1841-1866 5051
Laura, from England with prisoners, 1748..........1232

Laurens County, S.C., nat'zations, 1800-1825 .... **2428**
Lauscha (Thuringia), Germans from, to 1900 2782
Lauthier family from France, 17th c. **7510.1-.2**
Law, federal, on naturalization, 1798 9931-9932
Lawrence, Kan., naturalizations, 1907-1921 .... **1828**
Lawrence County, Ark., naturalizations, 1855-1887 .... **3688**
Lawrence County, Ind., naturalizations, 1852 .... **4537**
Laws in N.Y., 1886, excerpts on naturalization 1906
Laws on naturalization records, summary 1442
Leander, Londonderry to Wilmington, 1831 ...... **6508.3**
Lebanon County, Pa., Moravians, 1752 3171
Lee family, Virginia and N. Carolina, 1694 .... **9824**
Leeward Islands, W.I., Scottish rebels to, 1716 8690
Legislative permits for ownership of land, New York, 1790-1825 8222
LeHavre *see* Havre
Lehigh County Pa.,
  and Swiss arrivals, 18th c. **7607**
  gravestones of Irish **9593**
  naturalization records, 1798 9931-32
Lehman, Hans, Bishop and German Mennonite, 1727 .... **4594**
Leicestershire, English from, 1671-1775 .... **1217.9**
Lein Valley, Germans from, 1750-1883 7810
Leipzig area, Germans from, 1850-1855 3960
Leith, Scotland, the *Henry and Francis* from,
  to Perth Amboy, N.J., 1685 2596
  to Port Hawkesbury, Nova Scotia, 1829 4980
Lemfoerde, Germans from, 1825-1840 5113
Lemfoerde *see also* Diepholz
Letters about and by immigrants:
  from Austrians in Georgia, 1739 .... **9332**
  from Canadian archivist on arrivals of 1860s.... **1284**
  from Germans in midwest, 1840-1845 3710
  from Germans of Herbolzheim, 1840s 4033
  from Germans of Nassau-Dillenburg, 1709 2690
  from Germans of Palatinate, 18th c 4168
  from Germany to Pennsylvania, 18th c. **9949**
  from Lord Selkirk on Canada, 1889 1000
  from Pennsylvania to Germany, 1806 .... **9950**
  from Robt. Taylor, Phila., 1836 1384
  from Secretary of State...with list, 1819, 1820 ... 9258
  from Swedish settler on Delaware, 1693 0040
  of Duc de Nivernois, 1763 9880
Lettwiler, Germans from, 18th c 4168
Lewis, Fielding, 18th c 0622
Leyden
  city records, n.d. 5897
  to Plymouth Colony, arrivals, 17th c 3152
Liberty, with Loyalists to Quebec, 1784 7328
Lichtenberg, Germans from, 1834-1838 0685
Liebental and Kleinliebental departures 3596, 7921
Liebenthal,
  departures via Bremen, 1889 7921
  Volga Germans from, 1870s 1682
Liebig, Hamburg to Quebec, 1868 2802
Liechtenstein, arrivals from, 19th, 20th c. **3495**
Limerick, Irish from, 1848-1860 .... **6413.20**
Licenses *see* Permits
Lichtenberg, Germans from, 1834-1838 .... **0683**
Limping Messenger, Swiss to Carolina, 18th c. 9630
Lincolnshire, English from, 1671-1775 .... **1217.9**
Lipinski-Lupinski-Lapinski variations **7138**
Lippe, Germans from, 19th c., ... 2602, **7521, 9417**
Lippstadt, Germans from, n.d. 4555
Lipsia to New York, Polish exiles aboard, 1834 ..... **4606**
List, [Georg] Friedrich, 1789-1846, and German emigration **5745**
Little James, to Plymouth, 1623 .. 0255, 2713, 3152, 4692
Little Strength, Rotterdam to Philadelphia, 1743 0933
Lively, Britain to Prince Edward Island, 1775 ..... **1446.3**
Liverpool,
  as port of call from the Continent, 1848-82 .... **6428.1-.16**
  British from,
    1669, 1686 .... 0354, 2162
    1816, 1841 .... 1188, 4903
    1849, 1850 .... 0305, 0544, 2742
    1874, 1882 .... **5233, 5235**
  departures,
    Aurania, 1888 .... **1133.44**
    City of Richmond, 1888 .... **1133.44**
    Cultivator, 1867 .... **1133.26**
    Eliza Warwick, 1841-1842 .... **6508.8**
    Empress of Ireland to Canada, 1907 7630
    Endeavour to Delaware River, 1683 5334
    Euphemia to New Orleans, 1849 ..... 2742, **3453**
    Eutaw, 1841 .... **4903**
    Isabella Briggs, 1841-1842 .... **6508.8**
    John Hancock to N.Y., 1853 .... **9668**
    Louisa to Baltimore, 1834 0294
    Marmion to N.Y., 1849 .... **1133.60**
    Mexico, 1830 4860
    numerous ships to Savanah, 1820-68 9890
    Pleiades to Delaware, 1831 .... **6508.7**
    Stephen Baldwin, 1845 .... **6508.6**
    Texas to Baltimore, 1882 5233
    Wm. D. Sewall to New Orleans, 1849 0544
  English from, 1849, 1850 .... 0305, 0544, 2742
  Indentured servants from, 1697-1707 2212
  Irish from,
    1838-1868 ..... 0305, 0544, **1133.22,** 2742, **6508.8**
  Russian Mennonites via, 1874-1880 .... **1865**
Liverymen, from London, ca. 1800 2135
Lochaber, Scotland, and MacMillan family, 1802 .... **5012.17**
Lock, Robert, Master of the *Speedwell,* 1656 4910
Loewenstein-Wertheim-Rosenberg and Freudenberg, Princely Archives (Germany) 4517, 4525
Logan, Le Havre to New York, 1833 0797
Logansport, Ind., alien residents, 1840-1876 .... **3246**
London,
  British from,
    to New England, 1687 6570
    to Pennsylvania, ca. 1682 2979
  children from,
    to Bermuda, 1850 9995
    to Virginia, 1648-1685 .... **1257**
  court depositions and debts of Americans, 1641-1736 .... **1235**
  departures,
    bonded emigrants, 1656-1775 .... **1217.3**
    1800 (approx.) 2135
    Cyclone to Victoria, B.C., 1862 5304
    guild members/liverymen, 1800 2135

Medora to New York, 1712 .... **3836**
ships to Boston, 1712 0154
ships to Virginia, 1773-1774 0225
Huguenots from, to Virginia, 1700 0953
Palatines to, 1709 4772-73
Palatines to N.Y. via, 1710 .... **0926.8**
prisoners transported from,
1617-1775 .... 1222, 1223
public record office **3430,** 8530, **8543, 9817**
London, the, Scotland to Nova Scotia, 1848 5007
Londonderry, Irish from,
1620-1822 8790
1831, on *Leander* **6508.3**
1838, to Canada **0358.21**
Londonderry, N.H., arrivals from N. Ireland,
1718 0648
Long Island,
arrivals, 1620-1675 1936
documents on the 1600s 1984, 1988
Lord Broughton, S.S., Hamburg to N.Y., 1867 6447
Lord Dunluce, Northern Ireland to South Carolina,
1772, 1773 .... 1594, 8980
Lord Melville,
Portsmouth to Montreal, 1832 2688
Portsmouth to Upper Canada, 1832 8775
Lost naturalization records, Palatines, 18th c **0926.55**
"Lost" relatives sought *see* Missing persons
Louisa, Liverpool to Baltimore, 1834 0294
Louisiana,
Acadians to, 1769 .... **4676**
arrivals,
1717-1731 .... **1290,** 1542
1843 .... **5231**
as French colony, 1752-1758 1548
Attakapas area, non-Acadians, 1795-1823 9424
Canary Islanders to, 1778-1783 9436
Czechs to, before 1880 .... **0205**
English to, 1700s 0608, 5213
French to,
1717-1731 .... **1290,** 3418, 8420-22, 9190
1796-1800 6695
1843, 1850 .... **5231,** 9570
Germans to,
1717-1769 .... **1290, 4676**
1842-1850 .... 7507, 9570
naturalizations,
1800s (Avoyelles Parish) 6209
1820-1850 (Natchitoches Parish) 5665
1839-1898 (New Orleans) 2110
1850-1877 (Natchitoches Parish) 5667
1867-1925 (Caddo Parish) **7129, 7130**
New Orleans customs record, 1813-1821 3480
prisoners to, 18th c 0608
Pyramid to, 1850 9570
Spanish to, 1538-1559 8870-8872
Yugoslavs to, 1813-1870 9520
Louisiana State Museum Library, customs lists,
19th c 7460-7461
Lovely Nelly
1774, 1775, Scotland to Canada **1014**
1775, [1806?], to Prince Edward Island **1446.1-.2**
"Low German" family information, 19th c. **0472**
Lower Alsace, Germans from, 18th c. **4255**
Lower Rhine Palatine village, Germans from,
18th c. **8655.20**
Lower Saxony
archives, Hanover, Germany 5085
Germans from, 1830-1849 .... 5143, **8595**
Loyal Judith
to Georgia, 1741 .... **3609**
to Pennsylvania, 1740 0877
Loyalists,
from Connecticut to New Brunswick, n.d. 6407
from Long Island to Kingston, Ont., 1783 0398
to Cape Breton Island, 1784 4682
to New Brunswick, n.d. **0358.41,** 6407
to Nova Scotia, 18th c. 7072, **7073**
to Ontario, 1776-1834 .... 0398, **7202**
to Quebec, 1784 7328
Lucas County, Ohio, Germans to, 1770-1895 5603
Lucerne, Swiss from, to Illinois, 1831 .... **9984**
Lucilla, Bremen to Baltimore, 1840 .... **5911**
Lucy
Britain to Prince Edw. Isl., 18th c. **1014**
Scotland to Canada, 1790 .... **1446.1**
Ludwigsburg,
emigration records, 1700s 4210, 4245, 4315
Germans from, 1770s-1920s 6860, 7650
Ludwigshafen am Rhein, Germans from,
18th c 0853, 0860, 0829
to French Guiana, 18th c 0853
to Philadelphia, 1730 .... 0821, 0827, 0829
Lueneburg, Germans from,
1849-1853 .... 5040, 5071, 5109, 5111
Lulan, from Scotland,
to Nova Scotia, 1848 5007
to Prince Edward Island, 1848 .... **1446.3**
Luneburg *see* Lueneburg
Lunenberg, N.S., French, German, and Swiss
Protestants to, 1757 4652
Lunenburg, Va., land claims, 1746-1750 .... **2915**
Lusatia, Lower, Germans from Cottbus,
19th c 4460, 4467
Lusatian Wends *see* Wends
Lutheran and Reformed Church, German 0893, 1739
Lutheran Church, Buffalo Synod, 19th c 3474, 8655
Lutherans,
from Austria to Georgia, 1734-1739 9330
from Pfeddersheim & Pfiffligheim, 1753-1766 ... 1126
in S. Carolina, 1788, 1794 .... **7119, 7121**
petition to settle in N.Y., 18th c 6137
to Georgia, 1734 .... 9055, 9330
to Michigan, 19th c **3709**
to Missouri, 1839-1841 .... **2095**
to North Carolina, 18th c 1739
to South Carolina, 1732-1752 9480
to Virginia, 1714-1717 .... **7480**
to Wisconsin, from 1840's **9074**
Lutherans, Old, *see* Old Lutherans
Luxembourg,
arrivals from, 1848-1882 .... **6428.1-.16**
arrivals naturalized, Iowa, 1868 .... **5228**
Luxembourg Society, Wisconsin **6428.1-.16**
Lydia, Rhode Island to Nova Scotia, 1760 .... 2887, 3309
Lynn, Maine, Scots to, 1651-1652 0269
Lynn, Mass., Scottish ironworkers, 1651-1652 ...... **1750**

Lyon, Bristol to Boston, 1631 9110
Lyons, French from, 1632-1760 5583

M

McCorkell, William & Co., Londonderry, 1864-1871 9200
McIntosh County, N.D., arrivals from Russia, 1885, 1888 .... 7931, 7934
MacKinnon, C., and some 1860s arrivals **1284**
MacMillan, Archibald, and family, to Canada, 1802 .... **5012.17**
McNab Township, Ontario, Scots to, 1825 .... **4968**
McNaughton, Alexander, on Scots to Illinois, 1738-1740 6640
Madison County, Ill.,
- naturalizations, 1816-1900 8368
- Swiss to, 19th c. **6154**

Magdeburg, Germans from, 1850-1852 3886
Magnet, Bremen to Galveston, 1851 .... 2514, 8317
Maine,
- arrivals before 1630 8880
- Gaelic arrivals via Canada, 1849 .... **5034**
- Germans to, 1752-1764 .... 3341, **6104**
- naturalizations,
  - 1780-1830 (Kennebec County) 8202
  - 1873-1900 (Aroostook County) **6410.5**
- Scots to, 1651-1652 0269

Mainz, Bremen to New York, 1900 .... **2307**
Malmedy, departures, 1843-1919 3740
Malouins, colonists of Canada from St. Malo, n.d. 3050-3051
Manakin Town, Va., Huguenots to, 1700-1797 .... 0957, 3630
Mandan, N.D., Germans from Russia to, 1900 .... **2338**
Manhattan, British in Dutch colony of, 1639 1984
Manhattan, Kan., naturalizations, 1866-1892 .... **7470**
Manhattan, Liverpool to New York, 1820 6530
Manitoba,
- Germans from Russia to, 1893 1697
- Red River settlement, 1811-1826 .... 0998, 1000, 3600, 5274, 6765

Manitoban, corrected to S.S. *Brooklyn* 2529
Mankin, Michael, commander of the *Friendship,* 1716 7983
"Mannachin Town," Virginia, Huguenots to, 1700-1797 .... 0957, 3630
Mannhaven, N.D., arrivals, misc., by 1918 .... **0090**
Manufacturing trades, workers for, 1631-1655 8134
Marburg, Germany, state archival records of former principality of Hesse-Hanau 8600, 8602
Le Marechal d'Estrees, France to Louisiana, 1719 3418
Marey Anne, Great Yarmouth to New England, 1637-1639 3540
Margaret,
- German passengers on the, 1804 4672
- Mobile, Ala., to Para, Brazil, British, 1866 5705

Marianne, Bremen to Baltimore, 1855 .... **7200**
Mariendrebber, Germany, departures from, 1839 2242
Marienthal, Argentina, German founding of, 1878 .... **9674**
Marion County, Ind., nat'zations, 1843-1853 .... **1450.1**
Marion County, Ore., naturalized voters, 1900 .... **1451.15-.16**
Maritimes, Canada, Huguenots to, 17th, 18th c. **7204**
Markgroeningen, Germans from, 1770s-1920s 7650
Marksville, Louisiana, Avoyelles Parish, court records, 19th c 6209
Marmion, Liverpool to New York, 1849 .... **1133.60**
Marriage records,
- Dutch in New Netherland, ca. 1755 8212
- English departing for Virginia, 1620-1621 3273
- German-American, New York, 1708-1719 4817
- Irish in America, 17th-19th c. 6276
- Irish in Nova Scotia, (Halifax) 18th, 19th c 7095-98
- Maryland in, 18th c 0321, 0323, 0325, 0327
- Moravians in Pennsylvania, 18th c 0454

Martha,
- from England, 1677 8070
- to New Jersey, 1721 8760

Martin, William, clergyman, head of migrant group, 1772 8980
Mary, to Philadelphia, 1743 5645
Mary and Ann to Virginia, with Huguenots, 1700 9230
Mary and James, Belfast to South Carolina, 1772 8980
Mary and John,
- England to Massachusetts, 1630 .... 0281, 3323, 4477
- of the Winthrop Fleet, 1630 .... **8877**
- to New England, 1634 6600

Marye family, Virginia, 1700 0953
Maryland,
- Acadians from, to Louisiana, 1767 .... **1139.6**
- Acadians in, ca. 1763 9880
- arrivals,
  - 1714 6077
  - 1820-1834 .... **0253**
- birth records *see* Maryland, marriage, birth, death announcements
- British to, from these places:
  - Bridewell, 1700s 0608
  - Bristol, 1654-1685 .... 0943, 3438
  - Gravesend, 1677 9540
  - Hertfordshire, 1646-1775 1098
  - Hull, 1669 0354
  - Liverpool, 1682, 1686, 1882 .... 1587, 2162, **5233**
  - London, 1718, 1774 .... **4912, 9832**
  - Newgate, 1740 9725
  - Plymouth, 1704 .... **8805**
- Brooke family to, 1650 .... **5997**
- colonial era 6077
- Czechs to, 1868, 1879 .... **0205, 8514**
- death records *see* Maryland, marriage, birth, death announcements
- Dutch to, 1847 .... 0675, 9385
- English to,
  - 1650, a family and their servants, ... **5997**
  - 1682, on the *Submission* 1587
  - 1774 on the *Nancy* 9832
  - 1776 and earlier, recruited 1372
- Finns to, 1640s 4870
- French inhabitants, 1524-1800 9880

Maryland, *cont'd*
Germans from Russia to
1873-1876 .... 0438, 2966, 2969, 4019, 6950
1875-1907 .... 1882, 4497, 5263, 6927
Germans to,
17th c. **1420**
18th c. **0926.51, 3577, 9897**
1840, 1841 .... 5613, 5623, **5911, 8515, 9090**
1854-1856 .... 2414, 3705, **7200**
1874, 1895 .... 0438, **9207**
history of............ 6077, 7976, 7983, 7990, 7997
Holzhausen family to Baltimore, 1831 3550
indentured servants to,
1654-1686 .... 3438, 6179
1686-1707 .... 2162, 2212
Irish to,
18th c 1372, 6267
19th c 2859, 6468
Jews naturalized in, colonial era 3253
land records,
1634-1655 4507-4511
1678 2075
marriage, birth, and death announcements,
18th c 0321, 0323, 0325, 0327
military recruits of 1776 1372
naturalizations, by acts of legislature,
1660-1750 7997
naturalizations, colonial
1600s-1700s 3213-3215
1660-1775 .... 0993, 6725, 7997, 9916
1733-1773 .... 1282-1283, 6011
naturalizations, federal
1785-1799 (Frederick County) 1180-1181
1797-1853 (Baltimore) 3432
1798 (Washington County)................1422
1700s (German immigrants) **0926.51**
1799-1850 (Frederick County) 1182
1830-1839 (Harford County) 6454
1839-1840 (Allegany County).............2920
1857-1864 (Harford County) 6454
newspapers,
arrivals listed in,
1727-1785 .... 0321, 0323
1786-1795 .... 0325, 0327
Pennsylvania-German, items on Maryland,
18th c 9900, 9902
Poles to,
Baltimore pioneers, n.d. **1163**
on the *Stuttgart*, 1895 ....**9207**
prisoners to,
from England
1646-1775 .... 1098, 9725
1718 (diverted to S.C.) **4912**
18th c. 0608, 9725
from Scotland
1716 .... 7385, 7395, 7983, 7990
1747 .... 1242, 8005
Protestants to, colonial era...................2564
runaway servants, 1745-1780 .... **1357.1-.2**
Scots to,
1716 .... 7983, 7990, 8690
1747 .... 1242, 8005
servants
deserting, 1745-1780 .... **1357.1-.2**

Maryland, *cont'd*
in Northampton Forge, 1772-74 1362
see also indentured servants under Maryland
settlement of, 1634 7141
ships to
American Merchant, 1714 6077
Ark, n.d. 6157
1634 .... 6070, 7141, 7375, 7976
Capellen tot den Pol, 1784 9902
Dove, n.d. 6157
1634 .... 6070, 7141, 7375, 7976
Ferdinand, 1834 3080
Friendship, 1716.................. 7385, 7983
Gildart, 1747 1242
Goethe, 1854..............................3705
Good Speed, 1716 .... *7395, 7990*
Helena, 1840 5623
Hohenzollern, 1886 ....**3260**
Johanne, 1854-1855 2414
Johannes, 1834 0285
Johnson, 1747.................... 1242, 8005
Lucilla, 1840 ....**5911**
Mechanic, 1804 6468
Neptune, 1840............................5613
North America, 1784 9902
Ohio, 1873-1876 .... 2969, 4019
Oldenburg, 1903...........................2424
Submission, 1682 1587
Texas, 1882 ....**5233**
Tiberias, 1838 2920
various, unnamed, 1874 ....**5235**
York, 1740 9725
Welsh to,
1682 1587
1838 2920
Marylanders naturalized in Pennsylvania,
1767-1772 6011
Marysville, Calif., naturalizations, 1936 ....**6131**
Mason, John, and New Hampshire arrivals,
ca. 1630 2056
Mason County, W. Va., Germans to, 1850s.........4998
Massachusetts,
Acadians to, 1750s, 1764.............. 1658, 2394
arrivals,
1629-1662 .... 1936, 4782
1715-1769 9750
1798-1800 3130
Bay Colony arrivals, 1620-1675 .... 0263, 1936
British to,
1630 3323
1712 0154
correction of data...........................8825
English to,
1620-1640 .... 0263, 2713
1630-1639 .... 1432, 4477
Essex County court records, 1670 9620
freemen admitted to colony, 1630-1662 1936
French Canadians to, 1736 2374
French to, 1681, 1751 .... 0228, 3333, 3335
Germans to, 1751, 1777...... 0140, 3333, 3335, 4210
Huguenots to, from LaRochelle, 1681 0228
Irish to, 1700s-1800s 1642, 3450, 7095-98
naturalizations, 1815-1840 (Boston) **6410.30**
Plymouth Colony established, 1620-23 ... 0162, 2713

Massachusetts, *cont'd*
Quakers to Boston, 1656 1352
Scandinavians in Boston, 1815-1840 .... **6410.30**
Scots to, 1652 .... 0269, 8170, 8171
ship(s) from: *Charming Molly*
to Nova Scotia, 1760 1072
ships to:
Arbella, 1630 7660
Hannah & Elizabeth, 1769 .... 6560, 9610
Mary & John, 1630 4477
Mayflower, see that entry
Nathaniel, 1679 9610
Matty, Scotland to New York, 1774 .... 3670, 9670
Maury family, Virginia, 1700 0953
Mayflower,
arrivals on, 1620
ancestries 0255
and their fate **1461,** 3140, **5390**
classified by occupation 3219
descendants **6604, 8278**
from a 19th-c. history 2713
from *Hist. of Plymouth Plantation* 4692
from *Nat'l Genealogical Soc'y Quarterly* 0162
from *New England Hist. & Gen. Register*
in 1847 8440
history and genealogy 3152
in a British source **3077**
in modern literature 2404, 9810
list of Gov. Wm. Bradford 0756, 0768, 4692
places of origin of **5390**
Society of Mayflower Descendants' list 4722
arrivals on, 1629 .... 3152, 9810
Mayflower, Cork to New Jersey, 1787 .... **4049**
Mayflower Compact, signers of 6540
Mechanic, Dublin to Baltimore, 1804 6468
Mecklenburg, Germans from, to U.S., 1850-1862 3223
Mecklenburgh County, N.C., land allotments to Scots,
1767 5009
Medora, London to New York, 1836 .... **3836**
Megantic County, Quebec, pioneers, 1800-1978 ..... **7199**
Melville, Henry Dundas, Viscount, papers of 9775
Mendocino County, Calif., voters, 1898 2764
Menno, S.D., Germans from Russia to, 1899 .... **4490**
Mennonite descendants, located, 1977-1980 3565-70
Mennonite Historical Library, Goshen College,
Indiana 6478
Mennonite migrant group leaders, 1874-1880 .... **1865**
Mennonites,
French, arrival of, 1831-1840 6431
from Maryland naturalized in Pennsylvania,
1767-1772 6011
from the Palatinate, 18th c 4343
from Russia,
C. Mueller and others, 1870s **1286**
to Indiana, 1870-1885 3100
to Quebec, 1874-1880 .... **1865**
via Bremen-New York, 1878 6478
German, arrival of,
18th c **3570.1-.5,** 4343
1800-1815 .... 0813, **3570.1-.5**
1831-1840 .... 0789, 6431
1852 0805
1875-1876 2970
Germans from Russia,
living in Kansas, 1873-1874 .... **9317**
naturalized in Pa., 1709 .... **0926.26**
to Nevada, 1874-1879 9510
to New York, 1874 3872
Swiss
named in cantonal archives, 18th c. **3545**
to Louisiana, 1830 6431
to Pennsylvania,
17th c. **4483**
18th c. **1035.25, 8042**
Volhynians, arrival of, 1874 9070
to Middle West, 1878 6478
to Ontario, 1800-1825 .... **8363**
to Pennsylvania,
n.d. **8363**
1683-1754 .... **3545,** 8490
1710-1815 .... 3565-70, **3570.1-.5, 4594**
Volga German, to N.Y., 1875-76 2970
Mercenary troops of Amer. Rev. **1505,** 8560, 8562
Anhalt-Zerbst soldiers **1505**
Ansbach-Bayreuth troops 8640, 8905
background study, with names 8620
Brunswick soldiers 0140, 7495, 8562
Hesse-Hanau rangers 1482, 8643
muster rolls and POW lists 8630, 8650
resettling *see* Desertions
Mercer County, N.D., landowners, 1918 .... **0090**
Merchants, Germans from Hamburg to California,
1845-1854 2932
Mercury,
Netherlands to Philadelphia, Swiss aboard,
1735 .... 4487, 3161
Rotterdam to Philadelphia, 1735 3000
Merrimeche River area, Acadians to, 1763 2374
Merseburg, Germans from, 1850-1852 3886
Merzig, Germans from, 1816-1908 .... 3786, 3788
Messina, Italians from, to New York, 1870 0289
Meta, Bremen to New Orleans or New York, 1842 ... 8890
Methodist immigrants, Minn., 1855-1867 .... **1832**
Mexicans to California, 1769-1835 .... **3365**
Mexico, Scandinavians to, 16th, 17th c. 1898
Mexico from Liverpool, British aboard, 1830 4860
Meyer, Captain Juergen, head of migrant groups
from Bremen, 1832-1849 9640
Miami Valley, Ohio, Quakers to, 18th c. **1634**
Michigan
arrivals from French, Belgian, German ports,
1845-1864 .... **1133.18**
Dutch to,
1846-1856 .... 6875, 6890, 6895, **9362**
via New York, 1846-1850 .... 7355, **9362**
Germans to, 19th c. **3709,** 6890, 8017
naturalizations,
1810-1900 (Eastern District) **1443, 9097**
1875-1882 (Wexford County) **6717**
Middle West arrivals,
Germans from Friedelsheim, 19th c. 0813
Mennonites from Russia, 1878 6478
via Bremen-New York, 1852 .... **8506**
see also specific place names
Middlesex, English from, 1617-1775 .... **1217.2,** 1222
Middlesex, to New York, Germans aboard, 1852 .. **8509.1**

Middlesex County, Ontario, Scots to, 19th c........4918
Middlesex County, Va., arrivals, 1674-1702.........**0620**
Military
bounty lands in New York state, n.d. 6147
conscription and emigration, 1838-1874 .. 3872, 5135
deserters *see* Desertions
discharges,
British, 1775-1783 .... 8570, **8570.7** and **.10,** 8650
British in Nova Scotia, 1820...............**9554**
Irish in Nova Scotia, 1820 ....**9554**
naturalizations (Ill.), 1866-1892 .... **5012.40**
recruits to Maryland before 1776.............1372
registration for War of 1812, British in N.Y. 5952
Militia of 1663, Montreal 5354
Militia rolls, Barbados, 1679-1680................**0776**
Millet family, to Canada, 1658....................1656
Milwaukee,
arrivals, 1852, 1867 .... **1133.58, 8508**
Germans to:
1840s-1860s .... **1133.54, .56, 8499, 9074**
Norwegians to, 1845 ....**9667**
Minden, Westphalia, Germans from, 1816-1900 .....**5860**
Mineral Ridge, Ia., Swedes to, 1846-1855 ....**2090**
Miners
to Maryland from Wales, 1838 2920
to Virginia from Germany, 1714 4894
Ministers *see* Clergy
Minneapolis, Swedes in, 1876-1888 .... **6410.35**
Minnehaha to Philadelphia, Irish aboard, 1864 9200
Minnesota
arrivals, various:
1859-1892 ....**1133.4, .44, .46,** 2802
19th c. 4602-4604
via Hamburg-Quebec, 1868 2802
British to, 1888 .... **1133.44**
Germans to: 1868, 1878............... 2802, **9556**
Irish to, 1888.......................... **1133.44**
Methodists to Chisago Lake, 1858-1983........**1832**
Norwegians to, 1892 .... **1133.46**
Swedes in, 1858-1983............... **1832, 6410.35**
Swedes to:
1855-1867 6406
1880-1904 .... **1133.46, 5038**
Swedish Congregationalists to, 1855-1867 6406
Minors naturalized
in Illinois: 1858-1906 .... **5012.37, 6410.25**
in Ohio: 1859-1860.........................**3069**
Miquelon, Acadians to, 1767 .... 2344, 2354
Missing persons, newspaper notices for
crew of
the *Amelia,* Philadelphia, 1783 9158
the *Capellon tot den Pol,* Pa., 1784.........9900
the *Stadacona,* Philadelphia, 1864..........9200
Germans
from Wuerttemberg, 1807.................**8646**
in Pennsylvania:
1742-1779 1911
1825 9945
Irish
in Boston, 1846..........................7035
in Philadelphia, 1783.....................9158
relatives traced, 1811-1817 8099
runaway servants, apprentices, soldiers,
1775-1783 8242-8245
Swiss, Pennsylvania, 1742-1779 1911
Mississippi
German residents, 1816 .... **0926.49**
Irish gravestone records, n.d. **9593**
naturalizations,
1798-1906 (statewide) 6401
1856-1923 (Hancock County)........ 5193, **6656**
Misssissippi River settlement, Missouri, 1839-1841 ..**2095**
Missouri,
arrivals, via LeHavre, 1833...................0797
French to, 1843 ....**5231**
Germans to,
from Thuringia, 1838-1839 4803
from Westphalia, 19th c...................**3702**
Lutherans, 1839-1841 ....**2095**
naturalizations intended, 1838-1849 1492-93
Scandinavians to, from the *Emelie,* 1840 1208
Mobile, Ala.,
arrivals,
1821-1822 5715
1832-1852 5203-04
to 1857............................ 1386-98
French inhabitants, 1764.....................9600
Mobile County, Ala., nat'zations, 1833-1871 ... **1398-1401**
Moerbe family, Texas, 1854 1067
Moersfeld, Germans from, 18th c 4329
Moessingen, Germans from, 1829-1900 ....**2852**
Mohawk Valley, N.Y., Germans to,
1709-1710 .... **0926.8** and **.40**
Mohongo to Philadelphia, Irish aboard, 1864.......9200
Monarchists *see* Loyalists (British); Royalists (French)
Monin family from Switzerland, 1754 1148
Monmouthshire, English from, 1663-1775 .... **1217.6**
Monroe County, Indiana,
naturalizations, 1854-1859 ....**5755**
some inhabitants, 1860-1862..................**5755**
Monroe County, Ohio, Germans and Swiss to,
1819 ....**3295**
Montgomery County, Ind., nat'zations, 1850-1930 ...**9754**
Montgomery County, Kans., nat'zations,
1907-1919 .... **6013.40**
Montreal,
arrivals, various,
1642-1667 ....5344-5346, 5374, 7690
English from East Sussex, 1840-1862 1029
French recruited as settlers, 1653... 0172, 5374, 5751
Germans from Russia to, 1899................**4490**
Scots to, 18th c. and later **3370**
the *Helen Thomson* passengers, 19th c. **0358.17**
the *Saint Andre* to, 1659 2662
Montreal, the, Sweden to Boston, 1851 .... **6412.50**
Montrose, Hamburg to St. John, N.B., 1924........**2528**
Moravian register of members, 1727-1754 7267
Moravians
to New York, 1734-1767 3654
to New York and Pennsylvania,
1700s 0454, 0932, 0933, 3660-61
to North Carolina, mid 18th c 2272, 3660-61
to Pennsylvania,
1734-1767 ....3650, 3652, 3654, 3660-3661
1752 .... 3179, 3171, 3183
to Saxony, 1772 6087

Index

Morehouse, La., French to, 1797 6695
Morgan County, Ohio, naturalizations:
1819-1832 .... **9892**
n.d. **5819**
Mormon
index of Palatine arrivals, 18th c 2883
records of Swiss arrivals, 1650-1800 4916
Mormons, German, arrivals via Liverpool, 1853 3928
Morris, John, to Pennsylvania, 1697, 1698 1302
Mosbach, Germans from, 1749-1750 .... 4119, 4422
Mosel, Germans from,
1764 5685
1800s 5481
Mosel, S.S.,
Bremen to New York, 1876 2971
with Germans from Russia aboard
1876-1878 .... **0971, 9473**
Moselle departures,
18th c 5685
19th c 5481
Mt. Stewart Elphinstone, the, Glasgow to N.Y.,
1849 .... **1133.14**
Mountain Lake, Minn., Germans to, 1878 .... **9556**
Mountain Wave to Victoria, B.C., 1862 5314
Muehlhausen, Thuringia (now East Germany),
19th c. emigration files 2692
Mueller, Christian, Mennonite from Russia, 1870s ... **1286**
Muenster,
German state archives 5861
Germans from, 19th c 5851, 5861, **8636**
Mull, Isle of, Scots from, to North Carolina, 1767 ... 5009
Munjor, Volga Germans from, 1870s 1682
Munroe, J. B., Boston, 1851 5328
Murdoch to Halifax, Germans aboard, 1751 .... **7076**
Mutterstadt, Germans from, to Pennsylvania,
18th c. **1031.5**

N

Nacogdoches, Texas, 1824-1834 1752
Nahe [River], Germans from region of,
18th c 4154, 4161, 4203
Nancy, London to Maryland, 1774 .... **9832**
Napoleonic Wars, Irish settlers' desertions from,
1805-1806 7050
Narragansett County, R.I., French to, 1686 6815
Nashville and Chattanooga Railroad, foreign laborers,
1850 2732
Nassau, Germany, departures, 1806-1866 9061
Nassau-Dillenburg,
Germans from, 18th c 2454, 2690
Germans from, to Pennsylvania, n.d. 3233
Nassau-Siegen, Germans from, to Virginia,
1713-1714 6102
Nathaniel to New England, 1679 9610
Nattheim, Germans from, 1739-1920s 7552
Naturalization,
Canada, 1828-1850 5002-5003
colonial,
special, 17th, 18th c. 3213-3215
various .... **0926.16, .63,** 2564
correction of records **0926.63**
following colonial era 9530
of Acadians, 1778 9880
of British subjects, 1811-1816 6031
of German Huguenots, 1743-1746 6021
of German Protestants, 18th c. **0926.52**
of Huguenots, colonial era **0926.63,** 2564, 6021
of Jews, under Act of 1740 .... 3253, 3303
of Mennonites, 1709 .... **0926.26**
of Palatines, 18th c. 0498, **0926.55**
of Quakers, colonial era **0926.26,** 6680
Naturalization law, colonial
New Jersey, 1702-1776 6117
New York, 1740 9860
Rhode Island, n.d. 7415
Naturalization law, federal, of 1798 9931-9932
Naturalization oaths, ca. 1778 .... **9530**
Naturalization records,
found, Palatines, 18th c. **0926.55**
guide to 6421
sources compared, 18th c. **0926.4**
Naturalizations
Alabama,
1764 (Mobile) 9600
1800s (Selma) 5218
1833-1871 (Mobile) 1386-98, **1398.1-1401**
1880-1930 (Southern district) 4565
Arkansas, 1855-1887 (Lawrence County) **3688**
Atlantic coast ports, 1817-1850 3530-34
California
1846-1850 (various counties) **6013.19**
1848-1872 (Santa Clara County) 1890
1856-1875 (San Francisco) 1888
1856-1887 (Los Angeles County) **6410.20**
1860-1871 (Sacramento County) **7840.1-.51**
1866-1877 (Kern County) **2763.54-.56**
1866-1878 (Siskiyou County) **8494.1-.38**
1871-1880 (Kern County) 0448-0449
1872 (Tulare County) **2769.1-.10**
1875 (Sonoma County) **8865**
1879 (Siskiyou County) **3707.1-.19**
1884 (Humboldt County) **4747**
1888 and earlier (Tulare County) 2765-2768
1892 (Siskiyou County) **1820.1-.3**
1896-1898 (Fresno County) **2763.25-.33**
1898 and earlier (Mendocino County) 2764
19th, 20th c. (Contra Costa County) **2423**
1903-1925 (Riverside County) 5394, **5394.1-.7**
1936 (Yuba County) **6131**
Colorado,
n.d. (Boulder County) **9678.1-.3**
19th, 20th c 6016-6019
Connecticut, 1803-1844 (New Haven County) ... **8250**
Delaware, 1826-1858 (New Castle County) .. 6107-08
Georgia,
1790-1879 (Savannah) 6421
1793-1868 (Richmond County) .. **0056.1, 1451.45**
1820-1847 (Irwin County) **1307, 3371,** 9689
Illinois,
1816-1900 (Madison County) **8368**
1816-1905 (St. Clair County) 1003
1828-1886 (Schuyler County) 7318

Naturalizations, *cont'd*
1835-1894 (Morgan County) 3368
1836-1855 (Henderson County) 0094
1838-1845 (DeKalb County)...............**1498**
1850s-1870s (DeWitt County) 0024
1853-1908 (DeKalb County)...............**2421**
1855-1864 (Rock Island County) **6410.25**
1856-1864 (Southern District) 1442
1859-1870 (Rockford) **6410.10**
1866-1892 (Champaign County) **5012.40**
1867-1868 (Iroquois County) 1452
1880-1900 (Vermilion County) **2341.1-.2**
1886-1896 (Champaign County) **5012.37**
1888-1929 (Iroquois County) 1452, **3455.1-.5**
1903-1906 (Champaign County) **5012.37**
n.d. (Richland County) **1638**
Indiana,
1800s-1845 (Dearborn County) **1457.1-.3, 1459,** 4990
1817-1896 (Crawford County) **1385, 4598**
1818-1843 (Ripley County) **2525.15**
1820-1854 (Vanderburgh Co.) .. 9115, 9116, **9117**
1825-1829 (Switzerland County) **2525.40**
1826-1839 (Franklin County) **2180,** 2182
1832-1842 (Marion County) 1450
1833-1840 (Wayne County) 9625
1834-1850 (Tippecanoe County) 3010
1840-1905 (Orange County) **4599**
1841-1844 (Harrison County)..............**6758**
1843-1853 (Marion County) **1450.1**
1848-1852 (Ohio County) **6372.1-.2**
1850s (Ripley County)...............**7515.1-.2**
1850-1930 (Montgomery County) **9754**
1852 (Lawrence County)..................**4537**
1852-1869 (Dubois County) 1692
1852-1945 (Knox County).................**3018**
1854-1859 (Monroe County) **5755**
1857-1868 (Rush County) 7825
1857-1906 (Pike County)..................5815
1865-1900 (Jennings County) **3509**
1867-1874 (Decatur County) **3275**
1870s (Cass County) **3246**
1888-1927 (Clark County).................**1186**
1907 and earlier (local courts) **3434**
19th, 20th c. (sev'l counties) **0926.53**
n.d. (Allen County) **1451.6**
n.d. (Wells County) **5817**
Iowa,
1832-1856 (Dubuque County) **3813**
1838-1853 (general) **8773**
1842-1930 (Scott County) **2771**
1846-1905 (Jefferson County).............**9094**
1848-1889 (Polk County) **6778**
1849-1857 (Des Moines County) **1525**
1868 (Dubuque) **5228**
1872-1886 (Plymouth County) 9596
n.d. (Greene County).....................**2770**
Kansas,
1866-1892 (Riley County) **7470**
1870-1890 (Johnson County) **0770**
1886 (Finney County) 1512, 1513
1907-1919 (Montgomery Co.) **6013.40**
1907-1921 (Lawrence) **1828**
1909-1937 (Kearny County) **3755**

Naturalizations, *cont'd*
Kentucky, 1828-1867 (Todd County) **2158**
Louisiana,
1839-1898 (New Orleans) 2110
1867-1925 (Caddo Parish)........... **7129, 7130**
Maine,
1780-1830 (Kennebec County) 8202
1873-1900 (Aroostook County) **6410.5**
Maryland,
17th c. (Germans)........................**1420**
[ca. 1660-1750] (colonial) 0993, 7997
1666-1775 (colonial)....1282-83, 6011, 6725, 9916
1785-1850 (Frederick County) .. 1180, 1181, 1182
1797-1853 (Baltimore) 3432
1798 (Washington County).................1422
18th c. (Germans)................... **0926.51**
1830-1864 (Harford County) 6454
1839-1840 (Allegany County) 2920
Maryland, by acts of legislature, 1666-1750 7997
Massachusetts, 1815-1840 (Boston) **6410.30**
Michigan,
1810-1900 (Eastern district) **1443, 9097**
1875-1882 (Wexford County) **6717**
Mississippi,
1798-1906 (statewide) 6401
1856-1905 (Hancock County)........ 5193, **6656**
Missouri, 1838-1849 (St. Louis) 1492-93
New Hampshire, 1792-1849 (Rockingham County) 8232
New Jersey,
1702-1776 (colonial)................ 6117, 9010
1838-1844 (several counties) **8209**
New York
n.d. (colonial) 3303, 8270
1664 (colonial) 0963, 0969
1687 (colonial) 6236, 7680
1715-1773 (colonial)................ 0498, 9860
1782-1784 (statewide) 1906
1782, 1785 (legislative acts)...............5841
1789 (statewide) **6686**
1790-1828 (N.Y. District) 1140
1792-1840 (general) **8197**
18th c. (Mohawk Valley)............... **0926.40**
1800-1855 (several counties) 0016
1802-1814 (N.Y.C.?)......................9870
1807-1828 (Allegany County) 5972
1816-1848 (Cortland County)...............1568
1820-1839 (Steuben County) **5970**
1830s (Onondaga, Wayne counties)... 5942, 5978
1830s-1840s (Cayuga County) 5962
1838-1842 (Erie County) **5867.1-.2**
19th c. (Saratoga County)........... 5934, **5935**
n.d. (St. Lawrence County) **8525**
New York, by legislative act,
1714-1772 .... **0926.40, 1138,** 6248
1782, 1785 (statewide) 5841
North Carolina, 1763-1767 (Rowan County) **7755**
Ohio
1807-1830 (Cincinnati) 1582
1814-1858 (Shelby County)..... 0050, **8365.6-.11, .25-.27, .40-.45, .52-.57**
1819-1832 (Morgan County) **9892**
1833-1839 (Carroll County) **7912**
1840-1870 (Fairfield County) **1918**

Naturalizations, *cont'd*
1852-1884 (Mercer County) **8404**
1856-1873 (Darke County) 1448
1859-1880s (Sandusky County) **3068, 3069**
1875-1896 (Richland County) 9224
1875-1906 (Ashtabula County) **0160**
1890-1902 (Clark County) **6425**
19th c. (Auglaize County) **0176.1-.12**
n.d. (Morgan County) **5819**
Oklahoma,
1907-1935 (Washita County) **0104**
n.d. (Washita County) **0101**
Oregon,
1850-1853 (Territory) **7228**
1853-1926 (Washington County) **0251**
1869 (Klamath County) **3840.1-.3**
1900 and before (Marion Co.) **1451.15-.16**
Pennsylvania
1691-1692 (Germantown) **5650,** 6041
1709 (Germantown) **0926.26**
1727-1775 (colonial) 1804, 6011, 6680
1729 (Lancaster County) **0926.18**
1777-1789 (general) 9680
1783-1801 (Cumberland County) **5630**
1789-1848 (Juniata County) **0926.12,** 5593
1794-1880 (Philadelphia) 9290-9314
1795-1888 (Washington County) 8276-8277
1798 (Lehigh County) 9931-9932
1798-1799 (Western district) **5825**
1798-1799 (York County) **9972.3-.4**
1798-1802 (Huntingdon County) **3330.1-.4**
1798-1869 (Allegheny County) 9695-9697
18th c. (Lancaster County) **0926.38**
1802 (York County) **9972.7-.8**
1802-1815 (Fayette County) **1966.1-.8**
1802-1852 (Westmoreland County) **9155**
1835-1836 (Cambria County) **1076.1-.4**
1849-1854 (Beaver County) **6002**
1853 (Westmoreland County) **9717.1-.4**
1855-1856 (Somerset County) **8864.1-.8**
1880-1906 (Allegheny County) **9700, 9702**
1889-1904 (Westmoreland County) **7664**
19th c. (Bedford County) **6013.7**
19th c. (Berks County) **0515-0518**
19th c. (Fulton County) **6013.7**
19th c. (Lancaster County) **4504.1-.3**
n.d. (Bedford County) **0470.1-.2**
n.d. (Cambria County) **7138**
Rhode Island, 1701-1766 (colonial) 7415
South Carolina,
1695, 1696, 1732 (colonial) 7192, 8730
1790-1860 (Charleston) 3020, 8965
1800-1825 (Laurens County) **2428**
1800-1830s (Chester County) 0069, 8354
1840-1903 (Charles County) 8777-78
1846-1871 (Pickens District) 3249
South Dakota,
1877-1878 (Hutchinson County) **0971**
1910-1914 (Tripp County) **2984**
Texas
1800s (Calhoun County) 4933
1824-1835 (Nacogdoches) 1752, 4079
1846-1847 (three counties) 6231-6232
1847-1932 (Waller County) 0538

Naturalizations, *cont'd*
1850-1906 (McLennan County) 5771-72
1851-1923 (Bastrop County) 6238
1855-1907 (Grayson County) 0528
1857-1880 (Washington County) **0540,** 8770
1858-1929 (Ellis County) 3830
1880-1905 (Cooke County) 8350
1881-1886 (Menard County) 3507
1886-1906 (Harris County) . . **0678.1-.3, 1006.1-.5, 2910, 6013.55, 6254, 6659**
1890-1920 (Jackson County) **6660**
19th c. (Dallas County) **1447.1-.4**
n.d. (Galveston County) **1005**
Vermont, 19th c. (Franklin County) **5901**
Virginia
1652 (Northumberland) **6251**
1777 (Powhatan County) **1211**
1783-1794 (Henrico County) 1782
1784-1794 (statewide) 1772
18th c. (Augusta County) **0926.57**
1811-1816 (general) 6031
1828-1854 (Norfolk County) 9830
Washington,
1853-1883 (Thurston County) **3436**
1888-1973 (Douglas County) **1654.1-.2**
1916-1920 (Pierce County) **1728.4-.5**
Wisconsin,
1870-1890 (Door County) **2907.1-.2**
19th c. (Calumet County) **3457.1**
1904-1906 (Door County) **2906**
1907-1925 (statewide) **1867-1868**
Nebraska,
Czechoslovakians to, 1879 . . . . **8774**
Germans from Russia to,
1874-1905 . . . . 1694, 1697, **1924, 9676**
Germans to, 1878 . . . . **9556**
Neckar River Valley, Germans from,
1710-1766 . . . . **3627,** 4404, 4422
18th c. **2857**
Neptune,
to Maryland, Germans aboard, 1840 5613
to Virginia, 1618-1619 . . . . **1260**
Nether-Hesse, Germans from, 1835-1839 . . . . **2829.1-.3**
Netherlanders *see* Dutch
Netherlands,
and ships from Leyden to Plymouth Colony,
ca. 1620 3152
and ships to Maryland, 1784 9902
British call on way to New England
1624-1638 . . . . **2130.1-.4**
children from, to New Amsterdam, 1655 1988
departures for
Delaware (New Amstel), 1661 1722
New Jersey and New York,
17th, 18th c. 0505, **7899**
departures from,
Dutch,
to Delaware River, 1661 1722
to Iowa, 1847 0675
to New York, 1848-1882 . . . . **6428.1-.16**
French to Iowa, 1847 0675
Germans to Philadelphia, 1700s 9085
Moravians to Pennsylvania, 1743 0933
Palatines to England and America, 18th c . . . 3990

Netherlands, *cont'd*
Swiss to Philadelphia, 1735 4487
departures indexed:
1820-1880 .... **9081, 9082**
19th c. **9362**
Leyden city records 5897
Neumagen, Germans from, n.d. 5408
Neustadt area, Germans from, 18th c ... 0860, 4371, 4385
Nevada, Germans from Russia to, 1874-1879 9510
New Amstel, Delaware
Dutch to, from Netherlands, 1661 1722
in 17th-century Dutch archives 1722
New Amsterdam *see* New York
New Bedford, Northern Irish, to, 1804-1806 3450
New Bergholz settlement, New York 1843 1074-1075
New Braunfels, Germans to, 1840s 0408-0410
New Brunswick,
arrivals,
1801, for Upper Canada, ... **5277**
1837, English requesting land **0358.6**
Empress of Ireland to, 1907 7630
Fairy Queen from, to Maine, 1849 .... **5034**
Germans to, from Russia, 1924 .... **2528**
Helen Thomson shipwrecked, 19th c. **0358.17**
Irish to: 1838, 1847 .... **0358.21, 1433**
Loyalists to, 18th c. **0358.41**
provincial support of newcomers,
1841-1842 .... **0358.36**
Scots to:
1804 .... **0358.2**
1815, 1816 and before .... **0358.19, .31**
1837 .... **0358.26**
New Castle, Del., Irish to, 1803-1806 1762
New citizens in the new republic, 1778 .... **9530**
New Ebenezer, Ga., Austrians to, from Salzburg,
1734-1739 9330
New England,
arrivals,
n.d. 6630, 8855
corrected data 8825
from Great Yarmouth, 1637-1639 3540
from London, 1638 8995
in the Winthrop Fleet, 1630 0388
passengers and ships, 1620-1640 .... **6111.1-.13**
see also *Mayflower*
British to,
early voyages, 1620-1638 .... 1660, **2130.1-.4,** 2713
from Essex, 1687 6570
from Kent, 1634-1637 0378
from Norfolk, 1633-1639 1432
from Southampton, 1638 .... **0232,** 6606
from Suffolk, 1600-1649 3327
from Waymouth, 1635 6545
on the *Hercules,* 1635-1637 7111
prisoners, 17th, 18th c 0269, 1046
servants, 1654-1686 .... 0943, 3440
see also New England, English to
clergymen to, 1630-1641 9170
English to,
n.d. 1666, 1674
1572-1640 ..... 0048, 0124, 0263, 1660, **2130.1-.4,** 5781, 8780
1620-1692 .... 0275, **0977,** 1672, 1936
1650 and earlier **0977**
1654-1685 .... 0943, 9610, 9620
1700-1775 0658
1843-1849 7906-07
French to, 1613-1640 and later **7510.1-.2**
Germans to, 18th c 1815
Huguenots to, 17th, 18th c. **7204**
indentured servants to, 1697-1707 2212
Irish to, 1716-1769 6270
James of London to, 1635 1190
prisoners to, British, 1600s, 1700s 0269, 1046
Scots to, 1651-1652 .... 0269, **1750**
servants from Bristol, 1657-1686 3440
ships to
Arabella, 1671 6550
Bevis, 1638 6606
Confidence, 1638 .... **0232**
Hannah and Elizabeth, 1679 .... 6560, 9610
Hercules, 1634-1637 .... 6600, 7111
James, 1635 1190
Mary and John, 1634 6600
Mayflower see that main entry
Susan and Ellen, 1635 9163
Winthrop Fleet, 1630 0388
New Era shipwrecked, New Jersey, 1854 7830
"New France," French to,
1600s-1700s 1462, 2632, 6830
see also Canada *and* Quebec
New Glarus, Wis., Swiss colony, 1845 .... **4891**
New Hampshire,
arrivals, 1631 0053
Irish to, from North, 1718 0648
naturalizations, 1792-1849 (Rockingham Co.) ... 8232
New Hampshire, Antwerp to N.Y., 1847 .... **1133.20**
New Haven Co., Conn., nat'zations, 1803-1844 .... **8250**
New Jersey
archives, colonial 6097
arrivals in the Delaware River,
1676-1681 .... 8070, 8390
1689 .... **6099**
British to,
1664, 1675 .... 1292, 1992
called West Jersey (colony), 1664 1992
Dutch to,
1636-1642 4612
1700s 0505
English Quakers to, 1677 8070
Finns to, 1640s 4870
French Huguenots to, 1677-1710 4056
Germans to,
1700 and earlier 4822, 4830
on *New Era,* 1854 7830
Palatines, 1720-1760 3610
indentured servants to, 1683-1684 6179
Irish gravestone records, n.d. **9593**
Irish to, 1687-1741, 1787 .... **4049,** 8380
naturalizations,
1702-1776 (colonial) 6117, 9010
1838-1844 (sev'l counties) **8209**
prisoners to, Scots, deported, 1685 9840
Scots to, 1685 .... 2026, 2590, 2596, 9738, 9840
ships to,
1676-1681 8390
1721 and earlier 8760

New Netherland,
arrivals
n.d. 0508-0509
1620-1664 .... 0220, 3490, 5635, 6291, 8060
for Delaware River colony, 1661, 1662 .... 1472, 6296
on the *Rensselaerswyck,* 1637 9370
Dutch colony of, 1639 1984
Germans to, 17th c 4822, 4830
see also New York
New Orleans,
Acadians to,
1767 .... **1139.6**
1769, on English ship **4676**
1785, expelled from France 7445
Ajax to, 1820 .... **5034**
arrivals,
1813-1840 .... 3480, 5028, **6121,** 7460-61
1840-1865 .... 0544, 5030, 9570
Balkan and Eastern Europeans to, 1845 6127
British to, from Liverpool, 1849 .... 0544, 2742, **3453, 5034**
Catharine to, 1820 .... **5034**
Cubans to, 1840-1865 5030
Czechs to, 1880 and before **0205**
French to,
1820-1843 .... 5028, **5231**
Germans to:
1769 .... **4676**
1820-1843 .... 1976, **2095, 3300,** 5028, 7507
1848-1853 .... 0544, 3928, 3967, 5153
1849, en route to Texas 5719
Guillory family arrivals, 1870 .... **1536**
Irish to, 1849 .... **3453**
Mormons to, Germans, 1853 3928
naturalizations indexed, 1839-1898 2110
Spanish to, some military, 1820-1865 .... 5028, 5030
Yugoslavs to , 1813-1870 9520
New Packet, New York to Texas, 1829 .... 7740, 7745
New Paltz, N.Y.
Huguenot founders, 1678 2924
Palatines to, 1678-1820 4592
New Plymouth, English to, 1620-1623 2713
New Sweden,
Finns to, 1640-1655 4870
founding of, 1637-1642 6351
inhabitants of, 1693 .... 0040, 1999
Swedes to, 1638-1693 .... 1999, 3560, 3760, 3766
see also Delaware; Pennsylvania
New Sweden, Maine, Swedes naturalized, 1873-1900 .... **6410.5**
New World, Irish to New York on the, 1853 2016
New York
arrivals
for midwestern states, 1852 .... **8506**
for Rensselaerswyck,
1630-1658 .... 8360, 9365, 9370
from German ports, 1853-1865 .... **1133.6, .8, .12**
from Russia,
1875-1893 .... 0439, 7934, 7937
from various countries: 1828-1870 .... 0289, **1133.10, .16, .18, .20, .22, 7640**
Illinois bound, 1850-1883 .... **1133.38, .40**
unspecified, 1657-1664 .... 6291, 6520
via several ports, 1893 9031
Wisconsin bound, 1845 9666
Barbadians to, 1679 .... **8408**
Belgians to, 1906 .... **4810**
British to,
1631-1685 .... 0943, 1984, 3438, 5781
1760-1763 8534
1820-1834 .... 1794, 6450, 6530
1840-1868 .... 0305, 1414, 3378, 3796, **4905, 6200**
called New Amsterdam (N.Y.C.) and New Netherland 4822, 4830
Canadians to, 1775 4930
Central Europeans to, 1893 .... 9034, **9035**
Clinton County refugee tracts, 1798 1114
colonial manuscripts 0969, 8198
Czechs to, 1879 .... **0205, 8774**
Danes to, on *Guiding Star,* 1869 0299
Dutch children to,
1655 1988
1755 8212
Dutch to,
1600s 0505, 1736, 1864, 4612, 8134
1846-1856 .... 4880, 6890
Eastern Europeans to, 1893 .... 9034, **9035**
English to, 1836 .... **3836**
French to,
1712 and earlier 7820
1841, on the *Rhone,* **4900**
German arrivals, for Midwest:
Illinois, 1841, 1849 .... 0689, 1976
Michigan, 1846-1856 6890
Wisconsin, 1852 .... **8499,** 8500, 8503, **8505**
German Protestants to, early 18th c 6137, 9800
Germans to,
1700 and earlier 1898, 4822, 4830
1712 and earlier **3615,** 7820
1840-1841 .... **4902, 4905**
1849-1868 .... **6200**
from Alsace-Lorraine, 1820-1850 1874
from Bavaria, 1849-1855 3879
from Bremen,
1832, 1834 0789
1840-1841 .... 3080, **4902**
1875, 1882 .... **0446,** 6206
from Dresden, 1850-1903 3914
from Eastern Holstein, 1838-1859 2053
from French port, 1841 .... **4900**
from Frisian Islands, 1855-1857 9664
from Hamburg,
1847-1855 .... 3879, 3921, 3948, 5821, 8656
1867-1899 .... 2960, 5183, 6447
from Palatinate,
1709-1710 .... 0889, **3615,** 3620, 5015, 6301, 9660
from Pomerania, 1843 1074-75
from Prussia, 1869 0299
from Rhineland, 1820-1850 1874
from Rumania, 1899 .... **6406.6**
from Russia
1849-1876 .... **0440,** 2966, 2969, **2974.1, .3,** 4019, **9676**
1876-1899 .... **0626,** 1652, 1765, 1882, 1970,

New York, *cont'd*
2004.13, 2320, **2944.4, 2973.2**
1900-1922 ... **0626, 1970, 2004.13, 2320,** 2338, 2842, **2944.4, 2973.2, 2974.1, .2 2974.3, .6,** 3590, 3844, **7951.3-.5,** 8900, **9225**
from Wuerttemberg, 1738-1750 6860
Ochling family, 1837 ....**6346**
on the *Samuel M. Fox,* 1852 0805
New Bergholz settlement, 1843 1074-75
on *Charlotte* and *Sully,* 1833 ....**9734**
via England, early 1860s 3956
West Camp, 1708-1719 4817
Huguenots to,
colonial era 0228, 2564
New Paltz, late 17th c 2924
New Rochelle, 1687-1776 8280
indentured servants to, 1683-1684 6179
inhabitants, 17th, 18th c 6303, 8198
Irish to:
early 1800s ... 1742, 1762, 2859, 3450, **3806, 6608**
1827-1849 .. 0568, **1133.24,** 1826, **1921.1-.4,** 2792, 3040, 5791
1850-1907 .....0305, 1414, 1826, **1921.1-.4,** 2016, 2792, 5791, 8505
Italians to, 1884-1930 ....**0692**
Jews naturalized, colonial era 3253
Kleinliebental arrivals on the *Kasserin Maria Theresa,* 1900 3596
laws, 1886, excerpts on naturalizations.........1906
Long Island, colonial documents, 1620-1675 1936
Manhattan arrivals, early,
1620-1675 .... 1936, 1984
naturalizations,
n.d. (colonial) 3303, 8270
1664 (colonial) 0963, 0969
1687 (colonial) 6326, 7680
1710-1773 (colonial).........0498, **0926.40,** 9860
1782, 1785 (general) 1906, 5841
1789 (statewide) **6686**
1790-1828 (N.Y.C.) 1140
1800-1855 (various counties) 0016, **8197**
1802-1814 (general) 9870
1807-1828 (Allegany County).............5972
1816-1870 (Cortland County).............1568
1820-1839 (Steuben County) **5970**
1830-1839 (Onondaga, Wayne Cos.) .. 5942, 5978
1830-1849 (Cayuga County) 5962
1838-1842 (Erie County) **5867.1-.2**
19th c. (Saratoga County)........... 5934, **5935**
n.d. (St. Lawrence County) **8525**
by act of legislature,
1714-1772 .... **1138,** 6248
1782, 1785 5841
newspapers, Irish named in,
1810-1812 (port arrivals)..................**3806**
1845-1907 (New York City) 5791
Norwegians to,
1825-1845 ....0209, 0588, 1056, 1208, **5985,** 7700, **9667**
Palatine families, 1709-1750 ....**3624**
Palatines
to Mohawk Valley, 1710 .... **0926.8**
to Newburgh, 1708.......................5990

New York, *cont'd*
Protestants to, colonial era 2564
regimental recruits, British, 1760-1763 8534
Rensselaerswyck manufacturing and industry, 1631-1655 8134
resident aliens and land holdings, 1790-1825 8222
Rumanians to, via Germany, 1900 ....**2307**
Scandinavians to,
17th, 18th c 1898, 8134
1869, 1892 ....0299, 0314, **1133.46**
see also N.Y., Danes to; Norwegians to; Swedes to;
Scots to
1685 2596
1774-1775 .... 1088, 2202, 8425, 9670
1893 9029
from Aberdeen, 1834 .... 6450, 8520
from Glasgow, 1849.................. **1133.14**
from Greenock, 1803, 1817.......... 5741, 9775
from Highlands, 1736 on 6286
from Perthshire, 1803 9775
ships from, to San Francisco, 1850-1853 .. 7156-7162
ships to:
Albert, 1858 .... **1133.28**
Anchoria, 1892....................... **1133.46**
Atlantic, 1834 .... 6450, 8520
Belgique, 1857 .... **1133.18, .38**
Commerce, 1774-75 8425
Coriolan, 1864 .... **1133.38**
Cornelia, 1841 ....**4906**
Cultivator, 1867 .... **1133.26**
Dettmar, 1849......................... **1133.36**
Deutschland, 1849 3967
Devonia, 1893...........................9029
Emerald, 1845......................... **1133.20**
Etruria, 1892......................... **1133.46**
Ferdinand, 1864 .... **1133.38**
Franklin, 1849 .... **1133.30**
Germania, 1863 .... **1133.4**
Gil Blas, 1849 .... **1133.32**
Goeshe, 1868............................7620
Havre, 1845.......................... **1133.18**
Helene, 1849 0689
Irad Ferry, 1843 ....**3810**
Isaac Allerton, 1841 ....**4906**
John Bertram, 1864 .... **1133.18, .38**
Jupiter, 1864 .... **1133.52**
Kasserin Maria Theresa, 1900 3596
Kopler, 1853 .... **1133.48**
Langen, 1853 .... **1133.16, .34**
Lord Broughton, 1867 6447
Matty, 1774.............................9670
Mt. Stewart Elphinstone, 1849.......... **1133.14**
New Hampshire, 1847 .... **1133.20**
Oder, 1875.............................**0446**
Olympia, 1857 .... **1133.38**
Oneida, 1845, 1849.............. **1133.16, .18**
Orient, 1842 3796
Patria, 1899............................5183
Restoration, 1825........................7700
Russia, 1849 .... **1133.24**
St. Nicholas, 1849 .... **1133.16**
Salier, 1882 .... 6202, 8130
Samuel M. Fox, 1852 0805
Southerner, 1846 4880

New York, *cont'd*
Spaarndam, 1891 .... **0626**
Union, 1868 .... **1133.20**
Wallace, 1834 3080
West Point, 1849 3378
Wyoming, 1892 .... **1133.46**
state lands for Canadian refugees, 18th c 4930
Swedes to, 1820-1850... 0299, 1208, 6411, 6412, **6515**
Swiss to, 1842 .... **3810**
New York *see also* New Netherland
"New York Group," German Lutherans, 1839-1841 .... **2095**
New Zealand, Germans to, from Calenberg, 1753-1882 5080
Newburgh, N.Y., Palatines to, 1708 3997
Newburyport, the *Medora* out of, 1836 .... **3836**
Newcastle, England,
British from,
1685 0973
1806 .... **1446.3**
the *Henry and Francis* from, 1685 0973
the *St. Lawrence* from, 1800s 4980
Newfoundland and foundering ships,
the *Britannia* 1842 9770
the *Helena Sloman* 1850 3921
Newgate, English prisoners from,
1656-1716 1223
1723-24, 1740 .... 0608, 9725
Newhaven, with Scots to Jamaica, 1685 .... **9845**
Newport, Ky., Germans to, 1830-1858 .... **9999.6**
Newport, Rhode Island,
departures for Nova Scotia, 1760 3309
Irish arrivals, 1851 .... **6508.5**
Newport News, Va., Irish to, 1621, 1623 2851
Newry, Northern Ireland departures,
1765 .... **6535**
1803-1831 .... **5033,** 9198
Niagara, Ont., Huguenots to, 17th, 18th c. **7204**
Nicholson, Francis, Governor of Virginia, 1700 .... 0953, 7850, 9230
Niederheimbach, Germans from, 1847-1900 8030
Niederhochstadt, Germans from, 1732-1751 1032
Niederkirchen, Germans from, 18th c 4329
Nightengale, England to Maryland, 1669 0354
Nivernois, Duc de, correspondence of, 1763 9880
Norden, Norwegians to New York on the, 1836, 1837 1056
Norfolk, English from,
1633-1639 1432
1663-1775 .... **1217.7**
Norka, Volga Germans from, 1875 1694
Normandy,
French from,
to Canada, 16th, 17th c 9350
to Carolina(s), 1564 0228
to Florida, 1562 0228
to New York, 17th c. 0228
Norske Klippe, Norwegians to New York on the, 1836, 1837 1056
North America, Netherlands to Maryland, 1784 9902
North Carolina,
arrivals, 1674-1702 .... 2334, 9550
colonial records, 1674-1701 9550
English to, 1774-1775 .... 6167, 6169
Germans to:
1700s 1739
1709, 1710 7820
1760s-1780s **7755**
Huguenots to, 17th, 18th c. 7204
King family to, 1694 .... **9824**
Lee family to, 1694 .... **9824**
Moravians to, mid 1700s 2272, 3660-3661
naturalizations, 1763-1767 (Rowan County) **7755**
Protestants to, colonial era 2564
records, land and tax, 1674-1701 .... 9550, 7204
Scots to,
1767 5009
1771-1818 .... **4814,** 6167, 6169
see also Carolina(s)
North Dakota,
arrivals
from Russia, 1903 2003
miscellaneous, by 1918 .... **0090**
Germans from Russia to,
n.d. 3372
late 1800s 2529
1885, 1887 .... 0008, 7931
1890s **0190,** 3844, **6406.6,** 7930
1900-1910 .... **1924,** 2417, 2424, 2842, **4061**
Germans to, late 19th c 2802
see also Dakota Territory *and* Dakota(s)
North Dakota Herold records, 1917 .... **0626**
North Dakota landowners, foreign born, 1918 .... **0090**
North Rhine-Westphalia, Germans from,
1840-1845 3710
1857-1889 .... **8653,** 9560
19th c. 2602, **7521**
North Rhineland, Germans from Siegen area, 1738 0212
Northampton Forge, Md., servants to, 1772-1774 1362
Northamtonshire, English from, 1671-1775 .... **1217.9**
Northfield Township, Washtenaw County, Mich., Germans to, 19th c. **3709**
Northumberland, English from, 1665-1775 .... **1217.8**
Northumberland, Va., oaths of allegiance, 1652 .... **6251**
Northwest Company and Canadian settlers, 1797-1798 4762
Norway, departures from,
1840, 1843 .... 0209, 1208
1853, Hefte family **4030**
Norwegian arrivals, 19th c. **4908.1-.3**
"Norwegian Mayflower," the *Restoration,* 1825 7700
Norwegians
to Canada, 1848 .... **5982**
to Illinois,
1835-1850s 2574, 2580
to Minnesota, 1859-1892 .... **1133.42, .46**
to New York,
17th, 18th c 1898
1821-1840 .... 0115, 0117, 0588, 1056, 7700
1840-1869 .... 0209, 0314, 1208, **5985**
to South Dakota, 1877-1920 .... **7667**
to Texas, 1840s, 1850s 4026
to Wisconsin, 1845 .... **9667**
Nottinghamshire, English from, 1671-1775 .... **1217.9**
Nova Caesaria *see* New Jersey

Nova Scotia,
Acadians
banished, 1755-1768 .... 3503, 7430
to Louisiana from, 1767 .... **1139.6**
to Massachusetts from, 1750s 1658
Ansbach troopers settle in, 1780s 6987
arrivals,
1750, on the *Ann* 7075
1760, from Boston 9820
1774-1775, several ships 5675
1799, on the *Polly* 7080
1815-1838, for settlement in Pictou 5253
British to,
1750, some from New England 4742
1774, 1775, from Yorkshire 4632, 5675, 9975
Cape Breton Island census, 1818 2919
departures, 1815-1838 5253
see also Acadians
French deported to St. Malo, n.d. 3050-51
French Protestants in, 1775 4652
French to, 1750-1752 .... **3745**
Germans from Russia to, 1849-1910 .... **2974.1**
Germans to:
1700s 0860
1750s 3745, 4652, 5093, 7016, 7079
1780s 6987, 7185
Irish to,
1770 (approx.) **7073**
1830 and earlier 7050, 7058, 7065
19th c. **7078**
land grants, 1761 2887
Loyalists to, 1770 (approx.), 1778 .... 7072, **7073**
newspapers, vital statistics in, 1829-1834 .... **3251**
New Englanders to, 1750 4742
Pictou County history 5253, 6650
refugees from, to New York, 1775, 1785 .. 4930, 8660
see also Acadians
Rhode Islanders to, 1760 .... 2887, 3309
Scots to,
1771-1818 .... **4814,** 5000, 5007, 5253, 7088, 9775
1801-1849 .... 4970, 5007
Mabou, Cape Breton, 1843 4970
Pictou from Glasgow, 1803 9775
ships to:
Aide de Camp, 19th c. **7078**
Albion, 1774 .... **5675**
Ann, 1750 7075
Catherine, 1843 4970
Charming Molly, 1760 1072
Commerce, 1803 7088
Hector, 1773 5000
Jenny, 1775 5675
Lydia, 1760 .... 2887, 3309
Polly, 1799 7080
Providence, 1775 5675
Sally, 1760 .... 2887, 3309
Squirrel, 1774 5675
Two Friends, 1774 5675
Swiss to, 18th c. **3745,** 4652, 8945, 8955
Nova Scotians
entitled to land in New York state, n.d. 6147
in American Revolutionary War 1114
to Lake Erie area, refugees, 1785 8660
Nueces River, Texas, Irish and others to, 1829 7740

O

Oath, objections to swearing of, 1709 .... **0926.26**
Oath of abjuration or allegiance *see* Naturalizations
Oban, Scots from,
to North Carolina, 1767 5009
to Prince Edward Island, 1808 .... **1446.3**
Obereichsfeld, Germans from, 19th c 2692
Oberfranken and Oberfalz, Bavaria, Germans from, 1849-1855 3879
Oberhochstadt, Germans from, 1732-1751 1032
Obermoschel, Germans from, 18th c 4329
Obituaries *see* Burial records; Death notices
Ocean, Bremen to Baltimore, Germans aboard, 1841 .... **9090**
Ochling family from Germany, 1837 .... **6346**
Odenwald area, Germans from, 1830-1855 .... 3351, 3358
Oder, Bremen to New York, 1875 .... **0446**
Odernheim am Glan, Germans from, 1748 .... 0780, 4121
Odessa to Baltimore, Germans from Russia, 1876 ... 1882
Oggenhausen, Germans from, 1739-1920s 7552
Ohio
arrivals via New York:
1838-1868 .... **1133.16, .18, .20, .22, .23,** 6426
Cincinnati, association of immigrants, 1877 ..... **5747**
Darke County arrivals, 1831-1868 1448
German-speaking arrivals, 1819 .... **3295**
Germans to:
1800s 0813, **1133.16**
1832, 1833 .... 0789, **3704, 9037.1, .2, 9734**
1840, 1869 .... 5613, 8700
1877 and earlier **5747**
Licking County, refugee tracts, 1798 1114
naturalizations,
1807-1830 (Cincinnati) 1582
1814-1858 (Shelby County) .... 0050, **8365.6-.11, .25-.27, .40-.45, .52-.59**
1819-1832 (Morgan County) **9892**
1833-1839 (Carroll County) **7912**
1840-1870 (Fairfield County) **1918**
1852-1884 (Mercer County) **8404**
1856-1873 (Darke County) 1448
1859-1880s (Sandusky County) **3068, 3069**
1875-1896 (Richland County) 9224
1875-1906 (Ashtabula County) **0160**
1890-1902 (Clark County) **6425**
n.d. (Morgan County) **5819**
Quakers to Miami Valley, 18th c. **1634**
Swiss to:
1819 .... **3295**
1833 .... **9037.1-.2, 9734**
1849 .... **1133.16**
1853 .... **1133.16, .34**
Volga Germans to Sandusky, 1875 1694
Ohio, the
German Catholics to New York on, 1875 2969
Germans from Russia to New York on, 1875 ... 2969

1875 2969
Oklahoma
naturalizations:
1907-1935 (Washita County) **0104**
n.d. (Washita County) **0101**
Olav Kyre, Bergen to Quebec, 1848 .... **5982**
Olbers, Bremen to New Orleans, 1833-1839 ... **2095, 3300**
Old Lutherans,
and formation of Buffalo Synod 3474
and Heinrich von Rohr, 1839 .... **7896**
from Brandenburg, 1835-1854 3474
from Dresden area, 1838-1839 4803
from Hamburg, 1835-1854 3474
from Pomerania, 1835-1854 .... 1074-1075, 3474
from Prussia, 1835-1854 .... 3474, 8655
from Silesia, 1835-1854 .... 3474, 7422
to Canada, 1835-1854 .... 3474, 8655
to Michigan, 1835-1854 8655
to Missouri, 1838-1839 4803
to New York, 1835-1854 .... **7896,** 8655
to Texas, 1835-1854 8655
to Wisconsin, 1835-1854 8655
Old Wuerttemberg, Germans from, 18th c. 4245
Oldenburg, Germans from, 1830-1949 .... **8595**
Oldenburg, S.S., Bremen to Baltimore, 1903 2424
Olympia, Bremen to New York, 1857 .... **1133.38**
Oneida County, N.Y., Irish to, 1827-1867 2792
Oneida, LeHavre to New York, 1845-49 ..... **1133.16, .18**
Ontario,
American colonists to, 1776-1834 .... **7202**
arrivals, 1801, 1802 .... **5277, 7202**
English to,
from Hertfordshire, 1836 .... **9628**
from Sussex, 1832 3801
Huguenots to, 17th, 18th c. **7204**
Irish gravestone records, n.d. **9593**
Irish to, 1815-1825 .... 1455, 4986
Loyalists to Kingston, 1783 0398
Ops township arrivals by 1829 1416
Peterborough arrivals, 1825 1455
Scots to,
1825 .... **4968**
19th c 0361, 4918, 4986
Oppenheim, Germans from
n.d. 4203
1742-1749 .... 4112, 4397
Opposition to emigration, Northern Germany,
1727-1761 5113
Ops Township, Ontario, in 1829 1416
Orange County, Ind., naturalizations, 1840-1905 .... **4599**
Orange County, Va., land entitlement proceedings,
1739-1740 3816
Oregon,
naturalizations,
1850-1853 (Territory) **7228**
1853-1926 (Washington County) **0251**
1869 (Klamath County) **3840.1-.3**
1900 and earlier (Marion County) **1451.15-.16**
Oregon, the,
to British Columbia, 1861 .... **5323**
to New Orleans, French aboard, 1843 .... **5231**
Orenhofen, Germans from, n.d. 5490
Orient, Falmouth, England, to New York, 1842 3796
Orkney Islands, Scots from,
on *Marlborough,* 1774-1775 .... **1245**
to Georgia, 1774-1775 .... **1451.49**
Ormsheim, Germans from, n.d. 7314
Ornen out of Antwerp, 1843 .... **5608**
Orphans,
Dutch to New York, 1755 8212
Germans to New York, 1710-1714 6311
Orpheus, Bremen to New York, 1861 .... **1133.56**
Osage County, Mo., French to, 1843 .... **5231**
Osgood to Philadelphia, 1819 .... **3208**
Ostergotland, Swedes from, 1850s **9161**
Ostertal, Germans from, n.d. **9982**
Otterberg, Germans from,
18th c 4301
mid-18th to mid-20th c 0891
Ottersheim Reformed Church records, 18th c 4287
Ouachita, Louisiana, French to, 1797 6695
Oughton, Scotland to Canada, 1804 .... **1014**
Overseers, English, of Sussex emigrants, 1832 .... **0092**
Owen, Thomas, of the *William Galley,* ca. 1697 1302
Oxford, Scots to Virginia on the, 1776 3110
Oxford Circuit, English from, 1663-1775 .... **1217.6**
Oxfordshire paupers to New York, 1830 1794
Oyer family arrivals from Switzerland, 1830 6431

P

Pacific, steamer from San Francisco, to British Columbia,
1862 5294
Pacific Northwest, German-Russia arrivals,
1874-1916 8080
Paitzdorf (Mo.), Germans to, 1838-1839 4803
Palatinate,
Church of the Brethren members from, early
18th c. 1732
Germans from:
18th c **0856, 2884.1,** 3610, 4010, 4122, 4133, 4182, **4255,** 4343, **4376,** 4428, **8606, 8655.20**
19th c 1382, **6194, 9072**
Huguenots from, to New York, 1678 2924
Mennonites from:
1710-1815 .... **3570.1-.5**
18th c. 4343
Northern departures, 18th c. **8655.20**
Reformed Church members before 1750 .... **9981**
Southern departures, 18th c. 0893, 0895
to North America via Rotterdam and London,
1709-1710 .... **0926.8,** 3990
see also Palatines *and* Rhineland Palatinate
Palatine
connection with Huguenots, 18th c. **7765**
names in Waterloo Township, Ont., n.d. **7202**
population,
of New York, 1710 .... **1138,** 5015, 6301
of "West Camp," N.Y., 1710 .... 5023, 6341
registry, Simmendinger's, 1709 .... 4010, 8480
state archives, Speyer, Germany ... 4385, 4392, 4428
Palatine, Illinois, arrivals, 19th c. 8430

Palatines
  called "Seventeen-niners" **3375**
  child apprentices, New York, 1710-1714 .. 5019, 6311
  departures
    via LeHavre, 1833 0797
    via Netherlands and England, early
      18th c **0926.8,** 3990
  from Adenau area, 1831-1911 .... **5776**
  from Jockgrimm, 19th c **7140**
  from lower Neckar region, 18th c **2857**
  from Nassau-Dillenburg, n.d 3233
  from Ostertal, n.d **9982**
  from Wolfersweiler before 1750 .... **9981**
  identification of 2883
  in London, 1709-1710 .... **0926.8,** 3983
  in Mississippi, 1816 .... **0926.49**
  in New York,
    1709-1710 .... **1138, 3624,** 5015, 5023, 6301
  indexed by surname, 18th c 2883, **2884.1**
  naturalized:
    1709 (in Pennsylvania) **0926.26**
    1714-1773 (New York) 0498, **0926.16, 1138**
    18th c. (Maryland & elsewhere) ..... **0926.51, .55**
    19th, 20th c. (in Indiana) **0926.53**
  on the *King of Prussia,* 1764 .... **0926.21**
  to Brazil, n.d 1129
  to British colonies, 18th c 4378
  to Carolina(s)
    n.d 3233
    1728-1777 .... 3193, 4280, 9480
  to England, 1709 .... **0926.8,** 3983, 3990, 4772-4773, 5013, 9214
  to Georgia, 1730s-1740s **0926.36**
  to Kansas, 18th c **8528**
  to New York:
    1678-1820 .... 3997, 4592, 5015, 5990
    18th c. **0926.40, 3615,** 6137
  to North America, 18th, 19th c **7127.2-.15**
  to Nova Scotia, 1750-1752 .... **7075, 7079**
  to Pennsylvania:
    1709-1749 ... 0780, 0869, 1034, 1632, 4112, 4280, 4287, 8810
    1710-1815 .... 1032, 3193, 3565-3570, 3610, 4122, 4280, 4294, 4428, 6441, 7820
    18th c. .... **0856,** 0915, 0922, **0926.10, 0929, 1031.5, .12, 1033.4,** 4280, 4371, 4385, 4392
    19th c. **0926.10**
  to South Carolina, 1732-1752 9480
  to Virginia, 18th c **0926.44**
  see also Germans from specific locales
Para, Brazil, British to, via Mobile, 1866 5705
Paragon, Ireland to Rhode Island, 1851 .... **6508.5**
Parana, Argentina, Germans to, 1878 .... **9674**
Parish aid to immigrants, St. Andrews, N.B.,
  1827 .... **0358.46**
  1841-1842 .... **0358.36**
Parish-organized departures from East Sussex,
  1823-1832 1026
Parish registers *see* Church records
Parthia, with passengers Minnesota-bound,
  19th c. **1133.42**
Passage payment:
  England to Canada, 1855 .... **4646**
  Germany to Georgia, 1730s-1740s **0926.36**
  Germany to Pennsylvania, 1732, 1733 2544
  Germany to South Carolina, 1765 .... **0926.42**
  Oxfordshire sponsors' expenses,
    1834-1860 .... **2526.10** and **.40**
Passenger arrivals, State Dept. lists,
  1819-1820 9258
  1821-1823 9268
Passenger lists,
  consolidated, 1600-1900 .... **2048.1-.2**
  discussion of **0253**
  reconstructed, Hamburg, 1850 8656
  San Francisco, ca. 1850 7156-62
  see also Ship(s)
Passenger ships, consolidated lists,
  18th, 19th c. **0254, 5829**
Passenger steamship arrivals, 1890-1930 .... **5829**
Passport records, confederate and federal, ... 5223
Pastorius, Francis Daniel, and others, freemen,
  Pennsylvania, 1691-1692 6041
Patria, Hamburg to New York, 1899 5183
Patricia, to New York, Germans aboard, 1852 .... **8509.1**
Patterson, W., master of brig *Ceres,* 1817 3075
Patuxent River, Md., British to, 1704 .... **8805**
Pauline,
  Bremen to New Orleans, 1839-1842 8890
  Bremen to New York, 1839-1842 .... 2242, 8890
Paupers
  Dutch from almshouses 1988, 8212
  English to Australia, 1830s-1850s ...... **2526.10, .40**
  English to Canada:
    1825, 1827 .... **0358.46,** 1455
    1830s-1850s .... **0358.36, 2526.10, .40**
  English to New York:
    1830, from London 1794, 9995
    1832, from Aldingbourne **0092**
  Irish to
    New York, 1846-1851 .... **1921.1-.4**
    Upper Canada, 1825 1455
  see also Destitution
Paxson family to Pennsylvania, 17th, 18th c. **2824**
Pearl, to Halifax, Germans aboard, 1751, 52 .. **7076, 7079**
Pelican, to Louisiana, 1704 0608
Pella, Iowa, Dutch, French to, 19th c 0675, 9385-87
Penn, William,
  and Dutch Quakers to Pennsylvania, 1683 3313
  and Francis Daniel Pastorius, 1691-1692 6041
  and land in Pennsylvania,
    1681-1682 .... 0032, 2979, 7570, 0983
  and land in "West Jersey," 1664 1992
  and the *Welcome,* 1682 .... 0132, 1342, 4752
  and "Welsh Tract" lands, 1681 0983
  ships of, to Delaware Bay, 1681-1682 .... 0248, 4752
Pennsylvania
  arrivals
    1641-1819 9120
    1682-1687 .... 0236, 2313, 4752, 6460
    17th c. **8010,** 9623
    1727-1776 .... 5645, 7820
    1786-1808 1804
    Berks County, 1740 .... 0867, 0889
    Brand family from Germany, 1749 .... **4319**

Pennsylvania, *cont'd*
Bucks County: 17th, 18th c.......... 6463, 9790
census records, Cambria County, 1900...... **7137**
Chester County, 1687-1760................ 1018
Delaware River area,
17th c. **8010**
1789 7600
from Russia, via New York, 1893 7941
Germantown, 1683-1709 3313
Tulpehocken, 1720s, 1730s 0867, 0889
British to, from Bristol, 1654-1686 ...... 0943, 3438
English to, 1852-1968 4950
Finns to, 1640s 4870
French to, 18th c. **7765**
German influence in 1632, 4822
Germans to:
17th c. **1873,** 3313, 4822, 4834, **9251-9252, 9966, 9968**
1709 and earlier 3313
1709-1786 .... 4357, 4364, 4409-4415, 9960, 9964
1710-1815 .... **0491, 0929, 3570.1-.5,** 9041-42
1773-1825 .... 4462, 9945
18th c. .... **0926.4, .10, 1873, 4255, 6211, 7370, 9256, 9966, 9968**
19th c. **0926.10**
Berks County, 1740 .... 0867, 0889
from Baden-Durlach, 1710-1815 .... 3565-70, 4287, 4322
from Bavaria, 1846-1852................. 0598
from Boehl, Rhineland-Palatinate,
1726-1764 1034
from Dossenheim, 18th c 2917
from Hassloch, 1726-1764................ 1034
from Hesse, 1777 8630
from Hesse-Hanau, 1741-1767 8602
from Hochstadt (Palatinate) 18th c. .... 1032, and **1033.4**
from Krefeld, Lower Rhine,
1683 .... **9251, 9252**
n.d. 6199
from Ludwigshafen, 1730 .... 0827, 0860
from Nassau-Dillenburg 3233
from Oppenheim, 1742-1749 4112
from Otterberg, 18th to mid-20th 0891
from Palatinate,
see under Palatines, to Pennsylvania
from Pfeddersheim, 1738 3686
from Rhenish Hesse, 1743-1754 2192
from Rhineland, 1732, 1733 2544
from Saarland, 1709 ff **1033.11**
from Speyer, 18th c. **2854**
from Staudernheim, 1739-1741 2292
from Ulm, 17th, 18th c. **2855**
from Vogelsberg-Spessart area, 1738-1751 ... 2232
from Wernigerode, 1748-1749 3848
from Wertheim, Franconia, 1740s 4525
from Westphalia, 1725 5877
from Woerrstadt, 1743-1754.............. **1870**
from Wolfersweiler, before 1750 0478
from Wuerttemberg, 1738-1750 6860
from Zweibruecken, 1728-1749 3193
Germantown, 1683-1709 3313
Tulpehocken, 1720s, 1730s 0867, 0889
Huguenots to,

Pennsylvania, *cont'd*
n.d. 8935
18th c. **7765**
indentured servants to,
1683-1684 6179
1697-1707 2212
Irish gravestone records, n.d. **9593**
Irish to,
1682-1750 5917
1817, 1825 .... 3075, **5033**
Jews naturalized, colonial era 3253
Kowalski family name, with variations, n.d. **7138**
land sales, 17th c 7570
letter from, to Germany, 1806 .... **9950**
Lipinski family name, with variations, n.d. **7138**
Mennonites from, to Ontario, 1800-1825 .... **8363**
Mennonites to:
1694-1754 .... **3545**
17th c. **4483**
1710-1815 .... **3570.1-.5, 4594**
18th c. **1035.25**
Moravians to, 18th c. 0454, 3171, 3179, 3183, 3650, 3652, 3654, 3660-61
naturalizations,
1691-1692 (colonial)............... **5650,** 6041
1709 (colonial) **0926.26**
1727-1775 (colonial)........... 1804, 6011, 6680
1729 (Lancaster County) **0926.18**
1777-1789 (statewide) 9680
1783-1801 (Cumberland County) **5630**
1789-1848 (Juniata County) **0926.12,** 5593
1794-1888 (Washington & others) ...... 8276-77, and 9290-9314
1798-1799 (Western district)............. **5825**
1798-1799, 1802 (York County) .. **9972.3, .4, .7, .8**
1798 (Lehigh County) 9931-32
1798-1802 (Huntingdon County) **3330.1-.4**
1798-1869 (Allegheny County) 9695-97
18th, 19th c. (Lancaster County) .... **0926.38, and 4504.1-.3**
1802-1815 (Fayette County) **1966.1-.8**
1802-1853 (Westmoreland County) 3460, **9717.1-.4**
1802-1856 (Somerset County) 3458, 6047-48, **8864.1-.8**
1820-1840 (Western district).............. 2847
1822-1862 (Clearfield County) **0097**
1825-1906 (Erie County) **1869**
1830-1900 (Clarion County) **9155**
1835-1836 (Cambria County) **1076.1-.4**
1849-1854 (Beaver County)............... **6002**
1880-1906 (Allegheny County) **9700-9702**
1889-1904 (Westmoreland County) **7664**
19th c. (Bedford County) **0470.1-.2, 6013.7**
19th c. (Berks County) **0515-0518**
19th c. (Fulton County) **6013.7**
n.d. (Cambria & Berks Cos.) **0470.1-.2, 7138**
Paxson family to, 17th, 18th c. **2824**
Poles to, 18th c. **2865**
Protestants to, colonial era.................. 2564
Provincial Council records, 1717-1745 6665-6666
Schwenkfelders to, 1731-1737 .... **0923**
Scots to, 1685 .... 2590, 2596
Silesians to, 1731-1737 .... **0923**

Pennsylvania, *cont'd*
Swedes to,
17th c. 0040, 0041, 3263, **8010**
1734-1744 1946
Swiss to:
17th c. **4483**
1694-1754 ....**3545**
17th, 18th c. **1873**
1709-1787 .... **0929,** 1946, 3161, 8945, 8955, 9964
18th c, ... **1035.25, 7607, 8042**
tax records, Berks County, 1727-1757..........3258
Welsh to:
1681 0983
1701-1713 1894
William Penn's ships to, 1681-1682 0248
see also New Sweden
"Pennsylvania Dutch" (really Palatines)
18th c. 0915, 0922, 4822
Pennsylvania Germans, list of hundreds, 18th c. ... **1031.8**
Pensioners, Arkansas, 19th c.......................**3688**
Perceval, Sir John, 1st Earl of Egmont, 1683-1748 ...**3605**
Perche, French from,
17th c. to Canada.................2612, **7510.1-.2**
17th c. to New England.................. **7510.1-.2**
n.d...5761
Perkiomen, Pa., Germans in, 1752-1772............**9256**
Permits to emigrate,
England, 1624-1638 ....**2130.1-.4**
Germany, Northern, 19th c............. 5055, 5125
Malmedy, 1843-1919 3740
Muenster in Westphalia, 19th c 5851
North Rhine-Westphalia, 1857-1889 9560
Oberreichsfeld, Germany, 19th c 2692
Palatinate, 18th c 4133
Permits to reside,
Cuba, 19th c, ...**3028**
New York, 17th, 18th c. 8270
Perreau, Daniel, Commander of the *Peter and Anthony,* 1700 4622
Perrie, Nicholas, crewman on the *Dove,* n.d.........6620
Persecution, religious, as cause of emigration,
Austria, 18th c.............................9330
Germany, 19th c. **4058**
Perth Amboy, Scots to, 1685 .... 2026, 2590, 2596
Perthshire, Scots from, to Nova Scotia, 1803 9775
Peru, Spanish to, 1560-1594.......................5801
Peter, with Germans for Wisconsin aboard, 1852 .... **8509.2**
Peter and Anthony, to Virginia, 1700 .... 0953, 4622
Peterborough, Ontario, families, 1825, 1975 1455
Petit Guerard Colony, 17th c 1158
Petworth Emigration Committee, 1830s-1840s 9979
Petworth House Archives, England 4575
Pfaelzer *see* Palatines *and* Germans
Pfalz *see* Palatinate *and* Germany
Pfeddersheim, Germany, departures for Philadelphia,
before 1787 1120
n.d...1129
Pfeifer, Volga Germans from, to Kansas, 1870s 1682
Philadelphia,
apprentices and servants, 1745 8357-58
arrivals
1682-1687 6460
1693 and earlier 9623
1697-1698, minors **6185**
17th c., corrected 7585
1743, on the *Mary* 5645
1785-1788, from Irish ports 6800
1791-1792 3776
1819, from Amsterdam 6500
Bishop Hans Lehman to, 1727 ....**4594**
Brand family to, from Germany, 1749 ....**4319**
British servants to:
18th c. 2554, 4642, 6441, **7855**
children kidnapped for, 1697-1698 ....**6185**
German Mennonites to, 1683 8490
German redemptioners, 1771-1773 7207
Germans and others to, 1738 1788
Germans to,
1727-1808 .... 1788, 9041-42
1730 .... 0821, 0827, 0829
1740, 1764 .... 0877, 6441
1771-1773 7207
1787 and earlier 1120
via Amsterdam, 1804.......................4672
Gray family, 1800-1906 .... **2763.10**
Hippenstiel family, 1819 ....**3208**
indentured servants, 1771-1773 7207
Irish, Northern to, 1804-1806 3450
Irish to,
1682-1750 .... 4732, 5917, 5924
early 1800s 1762, 2859, 3450
1811-1817 .... 1742, 3075, 8796
1825, 1845 .... **5033, 6508.6**
Mennonites to, 1683 8490
Moravians to, 1734-1767......................3654
Palatines and servants to, 1764 .... **0926.21**
Quakers to, 1682-1750................. 5917, 5924
Sarah Sheaffe from Belfast to, 1836 1384
Scots to,
1697-1698 ....**6185**
1774-1775 .... 1088, 8425
ships to,
1681-1684 .... 0236, 0248
1727-1776 7280
Swedes to, 17th c. **8010**
Swiss to, via Netherlands, 1735 .... 3161, 4487
Picardy, French from, to Canada, 17th, 18th c 4846
Pictou, Nova Scotia,
inhabitants, n.d. 6650
Scots to,
1773, 1784 .... 5000, 6650
1803, 1816 .... 5253, 7088
Pigeon (or *Dove),* Scotland to Nova Scotia, 1801....5007
"Pilgrim Fathers," 17th c...........................**3077**
"Pilgrim ships" 3408
Pine Barrens of New Jersey, gravestone records **9593**
Pioneers' Home, Sitka, Alaska, 1920 ....**0158**
Pirate raid on the *Eagle,* 1718 ....**4912**
Place names, colonial Maryland 9916
Plague,
on German ships to Louisiana, 1720-1721 2100
on S.S. *Lord Broughton* to N.Y., 1867 6447
Plantation labor, Virginia, 1620....................**3820**
Planters,
British,
1628-1640 7237

1704 .... **8805**
on the *Mayflower* 3219
to Maryland, 1704 .... **8805**
to Massachusetts, 1620-1640 0263
to Virginia, 1606-1616 .... 7860, 8745, 9025
Plittershagen, Germans from, 1738 0212
Plymouth, England, departures
for Maryland, 1703 .... **8805**
for Massachusetts, 1630 4477
Plymouth Colony,
arrivals, 1620s 0162, 1674, 2713
the *Anne*, the *Fortune*, and the *Little James* to, 1621-1623 2713
the *Mayflower* to, 1620 .... 0162, 2713
Poland,
departures from, 18th-20th c. **5723**
exiles from, 1831-1835 .... **4606**
Germans to, 1834-1838 0685
Germans to, from Calenberg, 1753-1882 5080
Old Lutherans from, 1835-1854 3474
Old Lutherans to Australia, 1835-1854 3474
Poles
to Baltimore:
1895 .... **9207**
n.d. **1163**
to Boston, 1834 .... **4606**
to New York:
1831-1835 .... **4606**
1895 .... **9207**
to Pennsylvania, 18th c. **2865**
to Texas, 1854 1067
Political conditions, Germany, 18th c 2454
Political uprisings, Scotland
1685 1110
1715-1716 7983
1745 .... 1242, 4920, 6904-6905
Polk County, Ia., first papers, 1848-1889 .... **6778**
Polly,
Ireland or Scotland to Canada (Halifax), 1799 7080
Scotland to Canada (Prince Edward Island), 1803 8345
with Loyalists to Quebec, 1784 7328
Polynesia, Germany to New York, 1888-1903 .... **1970**
Pomerania, Old Lutherans from, 1835-1854 .... 1074-75, 3474, 8655
Port arrivals (U.S.), various, 1890-1930 .... **5829**
Port Royall, men aboard the, 1669-1676 1153
Portland, and wreck of the *Helen Thompson*, 19th c. **0358.17**
Portland, Me., the *Fairy Queen* to, from Canada, 1849 .... **5034**
Portsmouth, Eng., Sussex emigrants to Montreal, 1832 2688
Portsmouth, N.H., arrivals, 1631 0053
Posen *see* Poznan
Poverty
among Irish emigrants, 1848-1860 .... **6413.20, .30**
among N. German emigrants, 1838-1858 5135
in Massachusetts among arrivals, 1847-1851 5328
see also Destitution *and* Paupers
Powell, David, to Pennsylvania, 1697, 1698 1302
Powhatan County, Va., naturalizations, 1777 .... **1211**
Poznan, Old Lutherans from, to Australia, 1835-1854 3474
Presbyterians, clergy and laity from N. Ireland, 1680-1820 5243
Prince Edward Island,
British to:
1855, on the *Dragonet* **4646**
n.d., from Hull 8753
English to:
1817 on the *Valiant* **1436**
18th, 19th c. **1446.1-.3**
Scots to,
1770-1775 .... **0924**, 1088, 9412
18th, 19th c. **1446.1-.3**
1803 8345
1848 .... **4649**
Prince of Wales,
Scotland to Canada, 1813, 1815 .... **1014**, 6765
to Hudson Bay, 1813 1000
Prince William County, Va., Germans to, 1714 4894
Princess Royal, London to British Columbia, 1861 .... **5323**
Printz, Lt. Colonel Johan, leader of Swedes to Delaware, 1643 8000
Prinzbach, departures from, 1839-1860 .... **0635**
Priscilla to Boston, 1751 .... 3333, 3335, 3341
Prisoners,
as plantation labor, New Jersey, 1685 9840
as servants, Maryland, 1772-1774 1362
British,
claiming headrights, Va., 1677-1679 .... **1659**
on the *Laura* out of Kent, 1748 1232
out of West Sussex, 1778-1853 .... **4915**
to American colonies,
1600s 1046
1646-1775 .... 1098, 1223
1700s, unspecified 0608, 1046
1716-1775 .... 1222, 1232, 3700, 9725
1760-1767 .... 8530, 8534, 8541, **8543, 8695**
to Australia, 1778-1853 .... **4915**
to Barbados and Jamaica, 1646-1775 .... 1098, and 1235
to Canada, 1778-1853 .... **4915**
to Maryland, 1646-1775 .... **0340**, 1098, 9725
to South Carolina, 1718, 1728 .... 3510, **4912**
to Virginia:
1646-1775 .... 1098, **1659, 4727, 8435**
English, to colonial America,
17th, 18th c. **1217.1-.9**
French, to South Carolina, 1755-1756 5655
German, in American Revolution 8670
Irish, arriving 1735-1754 4790
of war:
British in North America,
1775-1783 .... **8570.7, .10, .15**
1783 and after 8570
Germans in American Revolution 8630, 8650
Scots from Battle of Dunbar, 1651-1652 0269
pardoned, Arkansas, 19th c. **3688**
Scottish, to American colonies:
to Carolina, 1684 .... **9842**
to Maryland,
1716 .... 7385, 7395, 7983, 7990

1747 . . . . . 1242, 8005
to Massachusetts, 1652 . . . . . 8170, 8171
to New England,
1651-52 0269
1685 1110
to New Jersey, 1685 . . . . . 2590, 9840
to Pennsylvania, 1685 2590
to various colonies, unnamed:
1650-1775 . . . . . **1639**
1716 . . . . . 2989, 8690
1746 . . . . . **4913**
to Virginia, 1776 3110
to West Indies,
1685 . . . . . **9845**
1745 (approx.) 4920
late 1740s 6904, 6905
Probate records of Irish in America, 18th c 6276
Probstei region, East Holstein, Germans from, 1838-1859 2053
Probus, the, to New York,
Germans aboard, 1852 . . . . . **8499**
Norwegians aboard, 1845 . . . . . **9667**
"Proof of Importations," Virginia, 18th c 2891-2893
Protest, colonial, New Netherland, 1650 . . . . . 3490, 6331
Protestant Church records, 18th c., Zweibruecken, Germany 4350
Protestants,
arrivals, 18th c, ... **0926.4**
Austrian, to Georgia, 1734-1739 . . . . . 9055, 9330
English, to American colonies, n.d. 2564
French,
arrivals, 17th c 1158
naturalized in colonial era 2564
to South Carolina, 17th c 7192
to Virginia,
1695-1732 6223
1700s 3640, 6710
German,
in South Carolina, 1788, 1794 . . . . . **7119, 7121**
naturalized, colonial era . . . . . **0926.16, .52,** 2564, 6680
petition to settle, New York, 18th c 6137
to New York,
18th c 6137, 6316, 9800
19th c 2970
to Pennsylvania, 1731-1737 . . . . . **0923**
to Virginia, 1714-1717 . . . . . **7480**
naturalized in Pa., 1740-1773 6680
Silesian, to Pennsylvania, 1731-1737 . . . . . **0923**
Swiss, to South Carolina, 17th c 7192
to Nova Scotia, French, German, Swiss
1750-1752 . . . . . **3745, 7012, 7016, 7076**
1757 4652
to South Carolina,
1679 and ca. 1732 . . . . . 1916, 8730
1763-1773 . . . . . 1158, 7343
to various colonies 2564
to West Indies, 18th c. **0926.4**
see also Huguenots *and* names of specific denominations
Providence, the
Amsterdam to Baltimore, 1833 . . . . . **3704**
Britain to Virginia, 1623 2722
to Nova Scotia (Halifax), 1775 5675
to Virginia, Irish servants aboard, 1623 2851
Prudence, N. Ireland to Canada, 1838 . . . . . **0358.21**
Pruem, Germans from, n.d. 5428
Prussian
arrivals,
Australia, Canada, U.S., 19th c 8655
on the *Guiding Star,* 1869 0299
on the *Helena,* 1840 5623
on the *Indostan,* 1804 8610
on the *Russia,* 1893 . . . . . **9027**
on the *Sorrento,* 1893 . . . . . **9028**
departures from
Cottbus, 1847-1886 . . . . . 4460, 4467
Diepholz, 1823-1840 5045
Duderstadt, 1839-1866 5119
East Prussia, 1880s, 1890s . . . . . **0123.1** and **.2**
Gieboldhausen, 1839-1866 5119
Hildesheim, n.d. 5060
Lueneburg, 1849-1851 . . . . . 5040, 5109, 5111
Magdeburg, 1850-1852 3886
Malmedy, 1843-1919 3740
Merseburg, 1850-1852 3886
Russia, 1880s, 1890s . . . . . **0123.1** and **.2**
Saxony, 1838-1900 9248
Prussian-Rhine departures,
Aachen, n.d. 5436
Bitburg, 19th c 5422
Neumagen, n.d. 5408
Orenhofen, n.d. 5490
Pruem, n.d. 5428
Trier, 19th c 5441-45, 5463, 5473, 5490, 5540
Prussians
in Pennsylvania, 1900 . . . . . **7137**
to New York, 1848-1882 . . . . . **6428.1-.16**
to various countries, 19th c. 8652
to Virginia (Prince William County), 1714 4894
to Wisconsin, 1853 . . . . . **1133.34**
see also Germans from specific locales
Publications on the 1709ers **3375**
Puerto Rico, arrivals in, 19th c 1168
Puisaye, Count Joseph de, French royalist, Upper Canada, 1799 2222
Purmerender Kerck (or *Purmerlander Kerck*) (ship), 1661 . . . . . 1472, 1722
"Purrysburgh," S.C., 1732 8730
Pyramid to New Orleans, French and Germans aboard, 1850 9570

Q

Quakers,
English to New Jersey, 1677 8070
Irish, to Pennsylvania, 1682-1750 5917
living in Barbados, n.d. **0773**
naturalized in Pennsylvania,
1709 . . . . . **0926.26**
1740-1773 6680
to Boston, 1656 1352

to Ohio, 18th c. **1634**
to Pennsylvania,
1677-1702 1137
1682-1750 (Philadelphia).......... 5917, 5924
1683-1709 (Germantown) 3313
1683 (Delaware River).......... 5334
Quebec
Buchanan family to, 19th c. **1001**
Compton family to, 1865-1869.......... **1284**
English to, from East Sussex, 1840-1862 1029
French to,
from LaRochelle, 17th, 18th c.......... 2652
from Lyons, 1632-1760 5583
from Perche, 17th c. .... **7510.1, .2**
on *Le Taureau,* 1658 2642
Germans to,
from Bavaria, 1849-1855.......... 3879
from Dresden, 1850-1903 3914
from Russia, 1899 .... **4490**
from Thuringia, 1850.......... 3948
Irish to,
1848-1849 .... 1826, **8867**
19th c., unspecified **1001**
Montreal arrivals, 1647-1667 .... 5344-5346, 5374
Norwegians to, 1848 .... **5982**
Russian Mennonites to, 1874-1880 .... **1865**
Saint-Jehan to, 1636 2672
Scots to:
18th c. 1088, **3370**
1819-1832 .... **7199**
Queen Elizabeth to Philadelphia, 1738 1788
Queenstown (now Cobh), Irish from, to Minnesota, 1888 .... **1133.44**
Questions and answers,
German imigration, 18th, 19th c.......... **7127.2-.15**
on Germans from Russia, 1880s **7124.1-.8**
Quinte, Bay of, Ont., Huguenots to, 17th, 18th c.......... **7204**
Quitopehille, Moravian settlement, 1752 3171

R

Raalte, Albertus Christiaan van, founder of Holland, Mich., 1846.......... 6875
Rainbow, to New York, 1843.......... 1074-1075
Rambler, Britain to Prince Edward Island, 1806... **1446.2**
Ransweiler, Germans from,
18th c 4168
1823-1842 .... **6194**
Readers' queries on German immigration, 18th, 19th c **7127.2-.15**
Readers' queries on Germans from Russia **7124.1-.8**
Real estate *see* Land
Rebecca Francis to Baltimore, 1833 .... **3704**
Rebels transported to Colonies,
1685, English **1217.5**
1716, English and Scottish **4727,** 8690
1745-1746, Scots.......... 4920, 6904-05
see also Jacobite Rebellion; Jacobites; *and* Prisoners
Recklinghausen area, Germans from, 1840s-1850s ... **8636**
Recruitment,
of colonists for Montreal, 1653, 1659 .... 5364, 5374, and 5751
of French military for Louisiana, 1719-1720 1542
Red River, Manitoba,
Scots to, 1811-1816 .... 0998, 1000, **1014,** 3600, 5274, 6765
Swiss to, 1821 1000
Red River Route and British settlers, 1871 .... **7323**
Redemptioners *see* Indentured servants
Reform, Bremen to Galveston, 1851 .... 2514, 8317
Reformation, Exon, England, to Baltimore, 1722.... **0340**
Reformed Church, German,
departures before 1750 .... **9981**
destination, North Carolina, 18th c.......... 1739
registers, 18th c. 4141, 4182, 4287
Reformed Church, Odessa, S. Dakota, 19th c. **0444**
Reformed Church, Swiss, members of, to South Carolina, 1732-1752 9480
Refugee tracts granted, New York, Ohio, 1798 1114
Refugees,
Austrian Protestants to Georgia, 1734 9330
Canadians from English Crown, 1775, 1785 ... 4930, and 8660
Germans from Russia,
1922, from Minsk.......... **2965**
1924, to Canada **2528**
Regulations and measures against emigration, Northern Germany, 1727-1761.......... 5113
Reitzengeschwenda, German farmers from, n.d. 0548
Religious affiliations of Palatines, 18th c. **2884.1**
Religious emigration/immigration *see* names of specific faith groups
Religious intolerance and migration
of Austrians, 1734-1739.......... 9330
of French: *see* Huguenots
of Germans, 17th, 18th c. **1873**
of Scots, 17th c. **9838, 9842, 9845**
of Swiss, 17th, 18th c. **1873**
Remmesweiler, Germans from, 18th, 19th c.......... 0468
"Remonstrance," New Netherland, 1650 .... 3490, 6331, 9400
Renfrew County, British to, 1821 4502
Rensselaer, Kiliaen Van, in New York, 1636-1642 ... 4612
Rensselaerswyck, N.Y.,
arrivals, 1630-1658 .... 6306, 8360, 9365, 9370
Dutch to, 1631-1655 8134
Scandinavians to, 1631-1655 8134
Rennselaerswyck (ship), costs of passage owed, 1636-1637 9370
Renunciation of foreign allegiance *see* Naturalizations
Repealers, Irish, at Halifax, Nova Scotia, 1843...... 7065
Republic, out of Bremen:
to New Orleans, 1838-1839 .... **2095**
to New York, 1856, 1868.......... **1133.44,** 1842
Rescue at sea,
Acadian families in Gulf of Mexico, 1769 ...... **4676**
Eagle to South Carolina, 1718 .... **4912**
Germans on way to New Orleans **4676**
Helen Thomson in Gulf of St. Lawrence, 19th c. **0358.17**
Resettlement of Germans from Russia, 19th c....... 0008
Resolution, Irish to Canada on the, 1825.......... 2832

Restaurationen see *Restoration*
Restoration, the
Norway to New York, 1825 .... 0588, 7700
Norwegians for Illinois on, 1835-1837..........2574
Reudnitz, Germans from, 1850-1855...............3960
Revolution of 1848, Germany 2602
Revolutionary War, American,
Ansbach troops from, 1780s..................**6987**
British troops in **8570.10-.15**
German troops in British forces during .. 0140, 1482, **1505,** 7495, 8560, 8562, 8620, 8905
Hessians from, to Nova Scotia, 1784 ....**7105**
Loyalists from, to Nova Scotia, 18th c. **7073**
Rheinhessen *see* Rhenish Hesse
Rhennish emigration *see* Rhineland, Germans from
Rhenish Hesse, Germans from,
18th c.............................. **4255,** 4308
to Philadelphia, 1743-1754 2192
to Texas, 1845 7405
Rhine, right bank, departures from, 18th c....... **2855.5; 2857, 6572**
Rhine area emigration, research on, (Forschungen zur Rheinischen Auswanderung) 5728
Rhine-Main region, Germans from, 1751...........4210
Rhine valley departures for Maryland, 18th c. **3577**
Rhineland,
arrivals from
Adenau, 1840-1860 8017
Enkenbach, 1715-1928...................0837
Speyer, 18th, 19th c. **2854,** 7524
via Hamburg, 1850-1851..................3935
Wuerttemberg, 18th c......................**4374**
Zweibruecken, 18th c. **4268, 4349, 4594**
see also Zweibruecken as main entry
departures for
Maine, 1752-1764.........................**6104**
New York, 1820-1850 1874
North America, colonial era..............**9968**
Pennsylvania,
1732-1733 2544
1743-1754 ....**1870**
1806 ....**9950**
n.d.......................... **9966, 9968**
Rhineland, Lower, departures from Krefeld, n.d. 6190
Rhineland Palatinate, Germans from,
1750-1803 ....**8584**
18th c. **4376**
1823-1911 .... **5776, 6194**
19th c **7140,** 7967, 8652
n.d................................ 4203, 5473
see also Palatinate *and* place-names in that region
Rhode Island
arrivals,
1631 9110
1636 1926
departures for Nova Scotia, 1760 2887
French to, 1686 6815
Huguenots to, 17th, 18th c. **7204**
Irish to, 1851.............................**6508.5**
naturalizations, 1701-1766 7415
Rhodt, Germans from, 1749......................**4319**
Rhone, LeHavre to New York, 1841...............**4900**
Rhum, Island of, Scots from, 19th c. 4980
Richland County, Ill., naturalizations, n.d. **1638**
Richmond, Huguenots to Carolina on the, 1679 1916
Richmond County, Ga.,
naturalizations,
1793-1868 ....**0056.1**
1867 ....**1451.45**
records and sources 1712
Ried, Andrew, Esq., and British prisoners, 1740 9725
Ringuette family from France to North America, 17th c. **7510.1-.2**
Rio de Janeiro, departures from, for N.Y., 1870 0289
Ripley County, Ind., naturalizations, 1818-1843, 1850s **2525.15, 7515.1-.2**
Risch family, from the Palatinate, 1709-1710 9660
Rissavouin family to Canada, 1658................1656
Riverside County, Calif., naturalizations, 1903-1925 ....**5394.1-.7**
Robert Watt, Scotland to Canada, 1837......... **0358.26**
Robertson, Major Sterling C., and Texas colony, 1830s 5011
Robinson, Peter, and organized emigration to Canada, 1825 1455
Rock Island County, Ill., Swedes, 1858-1862..... **6410.25**
Rockbridge County, Virginia, arrivals, 1739-1740 ...5831
Rockett, John, ship captain, 1828-1842 ....**7640**
Rockford, Ill., Swedish residents, 1860s **6410.10**
Rohr, Heinrich von, and Old Lutherans, 1839 ......**7896**
Roon, Bremen to New York, 1912 3590
Rose, Great Yarmouth to N. England, 1637-1639....3540
Rosina, Scotland to Canada, 1803 .... **0358.15**
Rothenburg, Wends from, to Texas, 1854 0578
Rotterdam,
Dutch from,
to Iowa, 1847-1860................. 9385-9387
to New York, 1846-1847 ....**9362**
Germans from,
to Halifax, 1750 ....**7012**
to Wisconsin via New York, 1847-1848 5821
Moravians from, to Phila. via England, 1743 ...0933
Swiss from, to Halifax, 1750 ....**7012**
Rowan County, N.C., Salisbury arrivals, 1763-1767 ....**7755**
Roy Guillaume d'Henrico parish, Virginia, French to, 1750-1797 3640
Royalists,
British, to Barbados, 1656 ....**1235**
French, to Upper Canada, 18th c 2222
Royer family, Lancaster, Pa., 18th c. **7765**
Ruhr, Germans from, 1840s-1850s **8636**
Rum Isle, Scotland, to Gut of Canso, Nova Scotia, Scots, 1829 4980
Rumania, Germans from, to N. Dakota, 1899..... **6406.6**
Rumanians,
in California, 19th c. 1890
to Baltimore, via Bremen, 1907 5263
to New York,
via Germany, 1900 ....**2307**
via Glasgow, 1906 5263
to North Dakota before 1918..................**0090**
Rumsfeld (or Rumsfield) family from Saxony, 1860s, 1870s **1012, 5633**
Runaways *see* Desertions *and* Missing persons
Ruperti, George, German clergyman, 18th c .. 4772-4773,

and 9214
Rush County, Kan., Germans-Russians to, 1876-78 .... **1677**
Russell County, Kansas, arrivals, 1870s **3394,** 7720
Russia
colonies of Germans, 19th c. **7945**
departures:
for Colorado, 1889 .... **7242**
for Dakota Territory, 1888-1903 .... **1970**
for Kansas, 1874-1878 .... **1677,** 7720
for Maryland, 1874 .... **5237**
for N.Y., 1886-1894 .... **2004.13,** 2320, 7937, **7948**
for North America (unspecified)
1893-1903 .... **2004.5, .11, 2005**
ships, comprehensive list 2978
for N. Dakota,
1888, 1900, 1903 .... 2003, **2338,** 7934
for South Dakota, 1889 .... **7242**
Germans from *see* Germans from Russia
Mennonites from,
C. Mueller and others, 1870s **1286**
to Indiana via Hamburg, 1870-1885 3100
to New York, 1874 9070
via Bremen, 1874-1893 .... **5237,** 7937, **7948**
via Hamburg, 1892-1893 .... 0439, **9027, 9033**
Volga area, Mennonites from, to N.Y. 9070
Russia, the,
Dublin to New York, 1849 .... **1133.24**
Hamburg and LeHavre to New York, 1893 ..... **9027**
Russian-born in Kearny Co., Kans., 19th, 20th c. **3755**
Russian Germans *see* Germans from Russia *and* Volga Germans
Russian Mennonites to Quebec, 1874-1880 .... **1865**
Russian Poland, Germans to, 1834-1838 ..... **0683,** 0685
Russians [and Germans from Russia] in Pa., 1900 ... **7137**
Rutland county, English from, 1671-1775 .... **1217.9**

S

Saale, S.S., Bremen to New York, 1893 7941
Saar, Germans from,
1709 ff. **1033.11**
1816-1908 .... 1834, 3786, 3788
Saarland *see* Saar
Sachsen *see* Saxony
Sacramento County, Calif., voter registrations, 1860-1871 .... **7840.1-.51**
Sailors *see* Seamen
St. Albans, Vt., naturalizations, 19th c. **5901**
Saint Andre, French to Canada on the, 1659 2662
St. Andrews, N.B.,
aid to immigrants, 1827-1842 .... **0358.36, .46**
English to, 1837 .... **0358.6**
Scots to, 1804, 1837 .... **0358.2, .26**
St. Charles County, Mo., Germans to, by 1850 ...... **3702**
St. Christopher, West Indies,
arrivals, 1634-1635 8835
departures from, 1870 0289
Huguenots to, 1671 0228
Scots to, 1716 8690
St. Clements Island, Md., *Ark* and *Dove* to, 1634 .... 6070, 7375, 7976
St. Goar County, Germans from, 1847-1900 8030
Saint Jehan to Canada, French aboard, 1636 .... 2672, 2682, 5811
St. John, N.B.,
Fairy Queen from, to Maine, 1849 .... **5034**
from Liverpool, the *Empress of Ireland,* 1907 ... 7630
from Londonderry to, the *Prudence,* 1838 ... **0358.21**
Helen Thomson rescued, 19th c. **0358.17**
Irish to, 1838, 1847 .... **0358.21, 1433**
Scots to, 1815, 1816 .... **0358.19, .31**
St. John Island, Scots to, 1774-1775 1088
see also Prince Edward Island
St. John River, N.B., and return of Loyalists, [18th c.] **0358.41**
St. Kitts, W.I., departures from, 1870 0289
St. Lawrence, Gulf of,
Acadian destination, 1763 2374
shipwreck in, 19th c. **0358.17**
Saint Lawrence, Scotland to Nova Scotia, 1829 4980
St. Lawrence County, N.Y., naturalizations, n.d. **8525**
St. Malo, French from, to Canada, n.d. 3050-3051
St. Marc, Haiti, to New Orleans, Guillory family, 1870 .... **1536**
St. Martinville, La., church records, 1795-1823 .... 9424, 9880
St. Marys, Pa., Germans to, 1846-1852 0598
St. Nicholas, LeHavre to New York, 1849 .... **1133.16**
St. Pancras, London, children from, 1850 9995
St. Paul, Minn., arrivals from Antwerp, 1863 ..... **1133.4**
St. Peter, Loyalists to Quebec on the, 1784 7328
St. Pierre, Acadians to, 1767 .... 2344, 2354
St. Vincents, Pa., Germans to, 1846-1852 0598
Salehurst, East Sussex, departures, 1838-1862 1029
Salem, Mass., arrivals, 1798-1800 3130
Salem, N.C., Scots to, 1774-1775 1088
Salem, N.J., English to, 1674-1681 3580
Salem River, the *Griffin* to, 1675 1292
Salier, Germany to New York, 1882 .... 6206, 8130
Salisbury, N.C., naturalizations, 1763-1767 .... **7755**
Salliman, Ralph, captain of the *Robert Watt,* 1837 .... **0358.26**
Sally, Rhode Island to Nova Scotia, 1760 .... 2887, 3309
Salzburg, Austrians from, to Georgia,
1730s-1740s **0926.36,** 1134, 3609, 7820, 9055, 9330, **9332**
Salzkammergut region, Austrians from, 1850-1882 .. 2172
Samos, Norway to New York, 1842 .... **5985**
Samuel M. Fox, the, Germany to New York, 1852 .... 0805, 0807
San Bruno, Calif., naturalization records (state) 1846-1850 .... **6013.19**
San Diego County, Calif., registered voters,
1866-1873 .... **8361.1-.9**
1880-1887 .... **8361.30-.32**
San Francisco,
arrivals, 1849-1875 7875-91
Germans to,
from Dresden, 1850-1903 3914
from Thuringia, 1850 3948
the *Pacific* to British Columbia, 1862 5294
the *Sierra Nevada* to British Columbia, 1862 5284

voting records, 1856-1875 1888
Yugoslavs to, 1870-1875 9100
San Patricio colony, Texas, 1829 7365
Sandusky, Ohio, minors naturalized, 1859-1860 .... **3069**
Sandusky County, Ohio, applications for citizenship, 1860s-1880s **3068**
Sandwich, Kent,
British from, 1634-1637 .... 0378, 0732, 0744
history of 0732
prisoners from, 1721-1773 .... **8435**
Santa Clara County, Calif., voter lists, 1848-1900 .... 1890, **1981, 2763.20**
Santee River, S.C., settlers on the, 1695, 1696 7192
Santiago, Cuba, to New York, the steamer *Fah Kee,* 1866 7790
Santo Domingo,
Acadians in, 1767 .... **1139.6**
French from, to Georgia, 18th, 19th c. 1712
Guillory family from, to New Orleans, 1870 .... **1536**
Sarah, Scotland to Nova Scotia, 1801 5007
Sarah of Liverpool, Scotland to Canada, 1801 .... **1014**
Sarah Sheaffe, Belfast to Philadelphia, 1836 1384
Saratoga, N.Y., and American-German genealogical research 0140
Saratoga County, N.Y., naturalizations, 19th c. **5935**
Saratov, Russia, and Kansas arrivals, 1870s **3394**
Savannah, Georgia,
arrivals on the *Ann,* 1733 6494
numerous ships, 1820-1868 9890
Scots to, 1774-1775 1088
Saxe-Gotha, Germans from, to S. C., 1732-1752 9480
Saxe-Weimar-Eisenach, Grand Duchy of, *see* Saxony
Saxony,
Bohemians and Moravians to, 1772 6087
Dresden departures, mid 19th c 0628, 3914
emigration records, 1859 4046
Germans from,
19th c 3474, 3848, 4040, 4046, 5085, 5143, 8290, 8590, 8592, 9248
to Texas, 1854 0578
Old Lutherans from, 1835-1854 3474
permits to emigrate from, 1852-1857 0628
Rumsfeld family from, 1860s **5633**
Schwenkfelders from, to Pa., 1731-1737 .... **0923**
Scandinavia,
Danes to New York, 1869 .... 0299, 0314
Norwegians to New York, 1825 .... 0115, 0117
Swedish arrivals, 1820-1850 .... 6411, 6412
see also Denmark; Norway; Sweden
Scandinavians
and founding of New Sweden, 1637-1642 6351
in California, 1856-1887 .... **6410.20**
in Canada, 1619-1620 1898
in Massachusetts, 1815-1840 .... **6410.30**
to Mexico, 1532-1740 1898
to Minnesota, 1859-1892 .... **1133.42, .46**
to New York, 17th-19th c. 1208, 1898, 8134
to South Dakota, 19th c. **7667**
to Wisconsin
1870-1890 .... **2907.1-.2**
1904-1925 .... 1867-68, **2906**
see also Danes; Norwegians; Swedes
Scarborough, England, to Nova Scotia, Yorkshire settlers, 1774 9975
Schaefferstown, Pa., Germans and Swiss to, 1727-1787 .... **0929**
Schaffhausen, Swiss from, 1709-1786 .... 8945, 8955, 9964
Schatte family immigration, 1854 1067
Schleswig-Holstein, departures for Iowa, 1900 7252
Schoenchen, Volga Germans from, 1870s 1682
Schoolteachers, English, to colonies, 1690-1811 2144
Schutterwald (Baden), Germans from, 1830-1935 8120
Schuylkill Valley, Pa., Swiss and Germans to, 17th, 18th c. **1873**
Schwenkfelders, Silesia to Pa., 1731-1737 .... **0923**
Schwenkfeldians *see* Schwenkfelders
Scotchfort, P.E.I., Scots to, 1772 .... **0924**
Scotland,
departures for American colonies,
1651-1652 .... **1750**
1716-1774 .... **1014, 1255, 1639,** 9412
departures for New York,
the *Atlantic,* 1834 .... 6450, 8520
the *Matty,* 1774 3670
Scotland, S.D., Germans from Russia to, 1889 .... **7242**
Scots,
arrivals:
1625-1685 .... **1640.1-.2**
1855 and earlier **1640.1-.2, 8893,** 9760
departures,
see Scots to specific places
deported:
1650-1652 .... 0269, **1639**
1684-1687 .... 1110, **9838, 9842, 9845**
1775 and earlier 0269, **1639, 4913**
naturalized:
in Cuba, 1818-1858 3030
in Pennsylvania, 1802 .... **9972.7-.8**
to Canada:
Hudson Bay, 1811 1000
MacMillans of Inverness, 1802 .... **5012.17-.18**
Manitoba, 1811-1816 .... 0998, 1000, **1014**
New Brunswick, 1803-1837 .... **0358.2, .15, .19, 0358.26, .31**
Nova Scotia:
1771-1800 .... **4814,** 5000, 5007, 7080
1801-1848 .... **4814,** 4970, 4980, 5007, 5253, 7088, 9775
Ontario, 1800s 0361, 4918, **4968,** 4986
Prince Edward Island:
1770-1774 .... **0924,** 9412
1803, 1848 .... **4649,** 8345
18th, 19th c. **1446.1-.3**
unspecified places, 17th, 18th c. **3370, 5012.18**
Upper Canada, 1821 4502
to Georgia, 1774-1775 .... **1245, 1451.49**
to Illinois, 1828-1909 7134
to Maryland:
1871, 1874 .... **5235, 6508.6**
on the *Friendship,* 1716 .... 7385, 7983
on the *Good Speed,* 1716 .... 7395, 7990
on the *Johnson,* 1747 8005
on the *Sophia,* 1871 .... **6508.6**
to Massachusetts, 1652 .... 0269, 8170, 8171
to New Jersey, 1685 .... 2026, 2590, 9738, 9840
to New York:

Scots, *cont'd*
1736 and later 6286
1774-1775 .... 2202, 8425, 9670
1803-1849 .... **1133.14,** 5741, 8520, 9775
1893 9029
to North Carolina, 1767-1818 ...... **4814,** 5009, 6167, and 6169
to Pennsylvania:
17th c. 2590, 2979, **6185**
1774-1775 8425
to Philadelphia, on the *Friendship,* 1774-1775 ... 8425
to Red River, Manitoba, 1811, 1813 ..... **1014,** 6765
to Texas, 1880s **9777**
to various colonies:
1650-1775 .... **1255, 1639, 1750**
1700s **1014,** 1088, 2989
to various ports, 1821-1822 6580
to Vermont (Barnet), 1774 .... 3670, 9670
to Virginia, 1776 3110
to West Indies:
1685, Jamaica **9845**
1774-1775, Antigua and Jamaica 1088
with Capt. Lauchlin Campbell, 1738-1740 6640
Scott County, Ind., foreign-born residents, 1817-1894 .... **0633**
Scott County, Ia., naturalizations, 1842-1930 .... **2771**
Scottish
arrivals, religious exiles, 1684, 1685, 1687 ..... **9838, 9842, 9845**
children to Philadelphia, 1697-1698 .... **6185**
Covenanters to New Jersey, 1685 2026
Highlanders,
arrivals:
1783 and earlier 5009
18th, 19th c. **1014**
to Halifax, 1784 6650
to Middlesex County, Ont., 1800s 4918
to New York, from 1736 6286
to North Carolina, 1767-1818 .... **4814,** 5009
to Nova Scotia, 1771-1818 .... **4814,** 6650
to Ontario, 19th c. 4918
parochial registers, early 19th c. **8893**
purchasers of land in Pa., 1681-1682 0032
rebels,
to Maryland,
1716 .... 7385, 7395, 8690
1747 1242
to South Carolina, 1716 8690
to various colonies, 1715-1746 .. **1639,** 2989, **4913**
to Virginia, 1716 8690
to West Indies, 1716 8690
Sloane family, 19th c. 8520
uprising *see* Jacobite Rebellion
Scythia, British to New York on, 1878 8330
"Sea Congregations," Moravian, 1742, 1743 .. 0932, 0933
Sea Venture shipwrecked, Bermuda, ca. 1610 9227
Seaboard, Eastern,
from Barbados to, 1678 3280
Germans to, 18th c 1815
naturalizations, mixed, 1817-1850 3530-3534
Seamen,
crew of the *Stadacona* jump ship, Phila., 1864 9200
crew on the *Ark,* n.d. 6620
crew on the *Dove,* n.d. 6620
crew on the *Joseph and Thomas,* 1707 0666
crews on seven Acadian transports, 1785 7445
Scandinavian, naturalized in Boston, 1815-1840 .... **6410.30**
Swedes, jump ship, 1841-1858 .... **6412.40**
Seattle, arrivals, 17th c 1748
Seelitz, Mo., Germans to, 1838-1839 4803
Sehlin, J.B., Captain of the *Helena,* 1840 5623
Selkirk, Thomas Douglas, 5th Earl of, colonizer, 1811-1821 .... 0998, 1000, 3600, 6765
Selkirk Scots to Prince Edward Island, 1803 8345
Selkirk settlers of Red River, 1811-1814 ...... 5274, 6765
Seneca Falls, N.Y., Italians to, 1884-1930 .... **0692**
Serbin, Texas, Wendish settlement, 1854 1067
Servants,
British,
defecting, Maryland, 1745-1780 .... **1357.1-.2**
from Bristol, 1654-1686 3438
from London records, 1682-1692 2524
indentured, London, 18th c. **3690.1**
to Georgia, 1774-1775 .... 1245, 3430
to Newport News, Va., 1621 2722
to Philadelphia, 18th c. 6441, **7855**
West Indies, 17th, 18th c. 0943, **1139.1,** 2328
to Yorktown, 1716 .... **4727**
Dutch, to New Netherland, 1629-1663 3243-44
English,
arriving with Palatines, 1764 ...... **0926.21,** 6441
settling in Maryland, 1774 .... **9832**
German military, in American Revolution 8670
Irish,
to Philadelphia, women, 1746/1767 4732
to Virginia, 1621, 1623 .... 2722, 2851
missing *see* under Missing persons
on the *Mayflower* 3219
to Delaware, from Belfast, 1789 2044
to Maryland (Northampton Forge), 1772-1774 1362
to New Hampshire, ca. 1630, 1631 ...... 0053, 2056
to New Jersey, 1664-1703 6097
to New Sweden, 1638-1656 3560
with Brooke family, to Maryland, 1650 .... **5997**
see also Indentured servants
Servitude of convicts, Maryland, 1745-1780 .... **1357.1-.2**
"Seventeen-niners," Palatine arrivals, 1709-1710 .... **0926.8, 3375, 3615**
Seventh Day Adventists, Bowdle, S.D., 1889 .... **1641**
Seville, Spain, Archives of the Indies 5801
Shallop and the pilgrim fathers, 1622 9810
Shamrock newspaper, N.Y., passenger lists, 19th c. **3806**
Sheboygan, Wis., Germans from Russia to, 1864-1922 1871
Sheffield, Liverpool to U.S. and Canada, 1841 ...... **4906**
Shelburne, Nova Scotia, Welsh to, 1818 .... **7005**
Shelby County, Ohio,
arrivals, early 19th c. 0050-0052
citizenship records, 1814-1858 ... **8365.6-.11, .25-.27, 8365.40-.45, .52-.57**
Shenandoah Valley, Va., naturalizations, 18th c. **0926.57**
Shepherd family (various spellings), New Jersey arrivals,

1687 8380
Sherman, John, and family, n.d. **8395**
Shield,
English on the, 1684 4940
to New Jersey, 1678, 1721 .... 8070, 8760
Ships
and ship masters,
English, 17th c. **1239,** 3438, 3440
Maryland, 18th c. **9897**
consolidated lists:
comprehensive, of Germans from Russia **2978**
general, 17th-19th c. **0254, 5829, 8370**
Dept. of State list for 1821-1823 9268
from Antwerp, 1855 .... **2855**
from Bremen, 19th c. **1970, 5237**
from British ports, 17th c. **1239**
from Hamburg, 1850, 1883-1903 .... 8656, **1970**
from Irish ports, 1681-1775 4790
German Adelsverein, 1845 8302
to Alabama, 1832-1852 .... 5203-5204, 5715
to Barbados, Bermuda, Amer. colonies,
17th c. 3283
to California via N.Y., mid-19th c. 7156-7162
to four N. American ports, 1890-1930 .... **5829**
to Maryland:
18th c. **0926.51**
1820-1834 .... **0253**
1874 .... **5235, 5237**
n.d. **1163**
to New England, 17th c. 3197, **6111.1-.13**
to New York from Bremen, Hamburg, and Rotterdam,
1847-1848 5821
see also New York, ships to
to Nova Scotia, 1767-1849 .... **3251,** 4632, 5007
to Pennsylvania, Moravian immigration,
1734-1767 .... 3650, 3652
to Quebec, with Mennonites, 1874-1880 .... **1865**
to Texas, 1840s 0408-0410
to Virginia:
17th c. **0614, 0620,** 4782
18th c. **0926.44**
with English from Oxfordshire,
1830s-1850s .... **2526.10, .40**
with Germans from Russia (comprehensive) **2978**
with Mennonites:
to Canada, 1874-1880 .... **1865**
to Pennsylvania, 1691 .... **5650**
with Moravians to Pa., 1734-1767 3650-3652
with Poles:
covering 200 years **5723**
to Baltimore, n.d. **1163**
Shipping statistics, 18th c. 6276
Shipwrecks,
Amalia, ca. 1839, 1840(?) **2095**
Britannia, near Newfoundland, 1842 9770
Burgundy, on British coast, 1848 5153
English vessel in Gulf of Mexico, 1769 .... **4676**
Helen Thomson, Gulf of St. Lawrence,
19th c. **0358.17**
Johanne, off Frisian Islands, 1854 2414
New Era, New Jersey coast, 1854 7830
Sea Venture, off Burmuda, ca. 1610 9227
Shipwrights to American colonies, 1631-1635 5781
Shreveport, La., nat'zations, 1867-1925 ...... **7129, 7130**
Shropshire, English from, 1663-1775 .... **1217.6**
Sicily, departures for New York, 1870 0289
Sieg River area, Germans from, 1857-1883 .... **8653**
Siegburg, Germans from, 1875-1889 9560
Siegen, Germans from, 1714, 1738 .... 0212, 4894
Sierra Leone, departures from, for N.Y., 1870 0289
Sierra Nevada, San Francisco to Victoria, B.C.,
1862 5284
Silesia, Lower, departures from, 1835-1854 ... 3474, 8655
Silesians,
arrivals, 1839-1843 7422
departures from Freiwaldau, 19th c 9985
to Pennsylvania, 1731-1737 .... **0923**
"Simmendinger Register" (German arrivals),
early 18th c 4010, 8480
Simmern, Germans from,
18th c 4161, **8584**
19th c 1616, 8652
Sir Robert Peel, Hamburg to New York, 1862 ... **1133.62**
Siskiyou County, Calif., voter lists, 1866-1879,
1892 .... **1820.1-.3, 3707.1-.19, 8484.1-.38**
Sitka, Alaska, arrivals, 19th, 20th c. **0158**
Skye, Scots from, to N. America, 1771-1818 .... **4814**
Slaves transported to Jamaica, 1675 .... **7852**
Slavs,
Old Lutherans, from homelands, mid-19th c 3474
Ukrainians, to Manitoba, 1891-1900 3750
Yugoslavs, to New Orleans, 1821-1870 9520
see also Central Europeans; Wends; *and* specific
place names: Bohemia(ns), Czechoslovakia(ns);
Poland, Poles; Silesia(ns); Yugosalvia(ns)
Sloane family, New York, 19th c. 8520
Smelters to Virginia from Germany, 1714 4894
Smeltzer family, Kansas, 18th c. **8528**
Smidt, with passengers Minnesota-bound,
19th c. **1133.42**
Smith, Matthew, clergyman, Prince Edward Island,
1898 .... **1436,** 8753
Smith, Robert, Captain of the *Thetis,* 1837 ...... **0358.13**
Society of Swedes, Minneapolis, 1876-1888 ...... **6410.35**
Soldiers,
defecting *see* Desertions; Missing persons
French, to Louisiana, 1719 3418
German, in American Revolution .. 0140, 1482, 8905
Loyalist,
to Nova Scotia, 1780s 7073
to Quebec, 1784 7328
naturalizations of, Ill., 1866-1892 .... **5012.40**
Swedes, to New Sweden, 1638-1656 3560
Somers Islands, planters to, 1615 9227
Somerset, English from, 1664-1775 .... **1217.5**
Sonoma, Calif., naturalizations, 1875 .... **8865**
Sophia, Scotland to Baltimore, 1871 .... **6508.6**
Sophie, Hamburg to Texas ports, 1852 2494
Sorel, Quebec, inhabitants, 1668-1681 6830
Sorrento to New York, Austrians and Prussians aboard,
1893 .... **9028**
Sources of information compared, 18th c. **0926.4**
South Africa,
Dutch to, 1835-1880 .... **9081**
Germans to, 19th c. 4460

South America,
  Dutch to, 1835-1880 .... **9081**
  Germans to,
    19th c 1612, 1616, 5085, 8290
    from Dresden, 1850-1903 3914
    from Northern areas, 1838-58 5135
    from Rhineland, 1715-1928 .... 0837, 3935
    from Russia, 19th c 0008, **5726.1-.2**
    from Thuringia, 1850 3948
  Scandinavians to, 1532-1640 1898
  ships from, to N.Y., 1870 0289
South Bend, Ind., Hungarians in, 1882-1982 .... **0611**
South Carolina,
  Acadians to, 1755-1756 5655
  arrivals before 1676 1153
  British to, 1718, 1728 .... **0624**, 3510, **4912**
  English to, 1669 1288
  French to,
    1671 0228
    1695-1696 7192
    1755-1756 5655
  Germans in, 18th, 19th c. **0971, 7119, 7121**
  Germans to:
    1732-1766 .... **0926.42-.59**, 9480
    17th-19th c. **0971, 2855**
  Huguenots to, 17th, 18th c. **7204**
  Irish to, 1773 1594
  Jews naturalized, colonial era 3253
  naturalizations,
    1695, 1696, 1732 (colonial) 7192, 8730
    1790-1860 (Charleston) 3020, 8965
    1800-1825 (Laurens County) **2428**
    1800-1830s (Chester County) 0069, 8354
    1840-1903 (Charles County) 8777-8778
    1846-1871 (Pickens District) 3249
    1877-1878 (Germans from Russia) **0971**
  Protestants to, colonial era 2564, 7343
  Scotch-Irish arrivals, 1772 8980
  Scots to,
    1716 8690
    1772-1775 .... 1088, 8980
  Swiss to,
    1695, 1696 7192
    1732-1752 9480
  Witherspoon family to, 1734 and later **0624**
  see also Carolina(s)
South Dakota,
  Germans from Russia to,
    n.d. 3372
    1878-1879 3203-3204
    1889-1899 .... **0190, 1641, 2995, 4490, 4532, 7846**
    19th c. **0444**
    1901-1909 .... 2417, 2842, **4532**
  naturalizations:
    1877-1878 (Hutchinson County) **0971**
    1910-1914 (Tripp County) **2984**
  Scandinavians to, 1877-1920 .... **7667**
  Volhynian Mennonites to, 1874 9070
South River Colony, New Netherland, 1661 1472
Southampton to New England,
  the *Bevis*, 1638 6606
  the *Confidence*, 1638 .... **0232**
Southeast Asia, Dutch to, 1835-1880 .... **9081**
Southerner, Rotterdam to New York,
  1846 .... 4880, 6875, 6895
Spaarndam to New York, 1891 .... **0626**
Spain,
  departures from, 1492-1592 7800-7801
  General Archives of the [West] Indies,
    Madrid 7800-7801
    Seville 5801
Spanish,
  to Florida, 1509-1559 8870-8872
  to Louisiana,
    1538-1559 8870-8872
    1820-1865 .... 5028, 5030
  to Peru, 1560-1594 5801
  to Spanish America, 1509-1559 8870-8872
  to West Indies, 1509-1559 8870-8872
Speedwell, the
  to Boston, Quakers aboard, 1656 .... 1352, 4910
  to Halifax, Germans aboard, 1751 .... **7076**
Speier, Russia, Germans from, to N.D., 1900 .... **2338**
Spencer, the
  Britain to Prince Edw. Isl., 1806 .... **1446.3**
  Scotland to Canada, 1806 .... **1014**
Spessart area, Germans from, to Phila., 1738-1751 2232
Speyer, emigration records, 18th c. **4376**
Speyer, Germans from, 18th c. **2854**, 2856, **4376**
Sponheim, Germans from, 18th c 4161
Sponsored emigration, refugees, 1924 .... **2528**
Spotswood, Alexander, Governor of Virginia,
  18th c. **7480**
Spotsylvania County, Va., arrivals, 1769-1770 0622
Squirrel, Poole, England, to Halifax, 1774 5675
Stadacona, Irish to Philadelphia on the, 1864 9200
Stade, Germany, regulation of emigration,
  1727-1761 5113
Staffordshire, English from, 1663-1775 .... **1217.6**
State aid *see* Government-aided emigration
Staudernheim on the Nahe, Germans from,
  1738-1750 .... 2282, 2292
Steerage passengers, *Hohenzollern*, from Bremen,
  1886 .... **3260**
Steinhoft, Germans to N.Y., via France, 1893 9031
Steinweiler, Germans from, 18th, 19th, 20th c 0849
Steinwenden departures, 1684-1780 0885
Stephen Baldwin, Liverpool to Phila., 1845 .... **6508.6**
"Stephen Emigration," Thuringia to Missouri,
  1838-1839 4803
Steuben County, N.Y., nat'zations, 1820-1839 .... **5970**
Stilwell, John, captain of another *Mayflower*,
  1787 4049
Stolberg-Gedern, Germans from, 1748-1749 3848
Stonemasons, Scottish, to Texas, 1880s **9777**
Stranraer, Scots from, to New York, 1774-1775 2202
Strassburg, S.S.
  Bremen to New York, 1878 6478
  with Germans for Midwest destina., 1878 .... **9556**
Sturm family to Maryland, 18th c. **3577**
Stuttgart, S.S., Bremen,
  to Baltimore, 1895 .... **9207**
  to New York, 1893, 1895 .... 9031, **9207**
Stuttgart area, Germans from Fellbach, 1735-1930 1291
Stuyvesant, Peter, in New Amsterdam, 1655 1988
Submission, Liverpool to Maryland, 1682 1587

Subsistence account,
aboard the *Rennslaerswyck,* 1636-1637 9370
for English from Sussex, 1832 ....**0092**
of Acadians in Cherbourg, 1767 2344
of British debtors, New York and Hudson River settlements, 1710-1712.......................4003
of Palatines in New York, 1710-1713 1811
of poor in New Brunswick, 1841-1842 .. **0358.36, .46**
Suffolk, English from, 17th c. **1217.7,** 3327
Suffolk Court, Mass., and Scottish prisoners, 1651-1652 ....**1750**
Sully to New York, French, Germans, Swiss aboard, 1833 ....**9037.1-.2, 9734**
Superior, Le Havre to New Orleans, 1830 6431
Surname index of German arrivals, 18th c. .. 2883, **2884.1**
Surname Index Project (Seattle) 1748
Surname research:
English.................................**9078**
German **9079**
Irish **9254**
Surnames cited *see* individual surnames
Surrey, English from,
1639, to Conn. **9597**
1655-1775, bonded **1217.4**
Susan and Ellen, to New England, 1635 9163
Susanna, London to Virginia, 1773-1774 0225
Susquehanna Valley, Pa., Germans and Swiss to, 17th, 18th c. **1873**
Sussex, British from,
1639, to Conn. **9597**
1655-1775 .... **1217.4**
1830s-1840s 1021, **2043,** 2688, 3801, 8775, 9979
1838-1862 1029
Gautrey family from, 1868 ....**2398**
Sussex, West,
British from, 1830s.........................**4609**
prisoners from, 1778-1853...................**4915**
Sussex Archives for 1839-1847.....................4575
Sutherland Scots, from Orkney to Churchill Factory, Canada, 1813 6765
Sutley, S.D., and Reformed Church family register, 19th c. **0444**
Sutton, Neb., Germans to, 1878..................**9556**
Svanen, Sweden to Delaware, 1643 8000
Swabian arrivals via Hungary and Yugoslavia, ca. 1900 6740
Swatara Valley, Pa., Moravians to, 1752 3183
Swede Bend, Ia., Swedes to, 1846-1855 ....**2090**
Swede Point, Ia., Swedes to, 1846-1855 ....**2090**
Sweden,
the *Emelie* from, 1840 1208
the *Fama* from, 1643 8000
the *Svanen* from, 1643.......................8000
Swedes
in Illinois, 1859-1870 .... **6410.10**
in Massachusetts, 1881 .... **6410.40**
in Michigan, 1875-1882......................**6717**
in Minnesota; 1855-1888 .... 6406, **6410.35**
in Pennsylvania, 1693 .... 0040, 0041, 1999
naturalized:
in California, 1856-1887 .... **6410.20**
in Illinois, 1855-1864 .... **6410.25**
to Delaware, 17th c..... 3760, 3766, 7282, 8000, 8002
to Delaware Valley, 17th c...................**0464**
to Iowa, 1846-1855...........................**2090**
to Maine, 19th c. **6410.5**
to Massachusetts, 1851 .... **6412.50**
to Minnesota, 1859-1904......... **1133.42, .46, 5038**
to New Sweden, 17th c............ 0040, 1999, 3560, 3760, 3766
to New York,
17th, 18th c 1898
19th c. 0299, 0314, 1208, 6411-12, **6515**
to Pennsylvania, 17th c. 3263, 3760, 3766, **8010**
to South Dakota, 1877-1920.................**7667**
Swedish
arrivals,
crews jumping ship, 1841-1858.......... **6412.40**
documented, corrected lists, 1820-1850..... 6411, and 6412
with family details, 19th c. **0110.1, 2419.1-.3**
departures
from Gotland, 1819-1890 .... **6410.15**
from Ostergotland, 1850s **9161**
directory for Boston, 1881 .... **6410.40**
mutual aid society, 19th c. **6410.35**
places linked to Minn. Congregationalists, 19th c 6406
Sweet, Wm. H., master of *Ceynosure,* 1855 1414
Swiss,
arrivals,
16th-20th c 4898
1650-1800 4916
1709-1710 ....**4480**
1727-1775 .... 2883, 3000, 4487
1830 6431
see also Swiss to [specific places]
cantonal archives 4916
departures:
from Basel, 1709-1795 .... 1960, 8040
from Bern, 1709-1795 .... 1148, 1960, 8040
from Geneva, 1700..........................0953
from Russia, 1874 9070
from Tramelan (canton of Bern), 1754 1148
from Zurich, 18th c............ 1946, 1952, 8040
via Antwerp, 1855 ....**2885**
via Germany, 1684-1780 0885
Goetschy family and 200 others to Pa., 1735 4487
Huguenots
to Philadelphia, 1700.......................3000
to Virginia, 1700...........................0953
see also under Huguenots as main entry
in Carolina, ca. 1695 0228
in Pennsylvania, search for, 1742-1779 1911
intending nat'zations, S. Carolina, 1696 7192
listed with Palatines, 18th c...................2883
Mennonites to Ontario, 1800-1825 ....**8363**
naturalized, 1695, 1729, 1798 ..... 0228, **0926.18, .38**
to Canada, 18th, 19th c. **3745, 7012, 7076, 8363**
to Carolinas, 1734-1752...... 1946, 1952, 8945, 8955
to European places of settlement, 1694-1754 ....**3545**
to Illinois, 19th c.................... **6154, 9984**
to Kentucky, from 1881 8054
to Louisiana, 1720-1721 2100
to Manitoba, 1821-1826 1000
to Minnesota, via Manitoba, 1826..............1000

to New Jersey, 1819 .... **3295**
to New York, 1828-1853 .... **7640, 9037.1-.2, 9668**
to Nova Scotia (Halifax):
1734-1752 .... **3745, 7012, 7076,** 8945, 8955
1757 4652
to Ohio:
1833 .... **9037.1-.2, 9734**
1849-1853 .... **1133.16, .34**
to Pennsylvania,
17th c. (late) **1873, 3545, 4483**
1727-1787 .... **0929, 1873,** 1946, 1952, 3000, 3161, 4487, 8945, 8955
18th c. (unspec. date) **1035.25, 1873, 3545, 7607, 8042**
to South Carolina, 1732-1752 .... 8730, 9480
to western states, 1843 .... **3810**
to Wisconsin, 1843-1853 .... **3810, 4891, 9668**
Switzerland, departures traced:
1709-1710 .... **4480**
1843 .... **3810**
Switzerland County, Ind. nat'zations 1825-29 .... **2525.40**

T

Tables of ships, ships masters, bondmasters .. 3438, 3440
Tanner, Thomas, of Company of Fishmongers, 17th c. **1139.1**
Le Taureau, French to Canada on, 1658 2642
Taylor, Robert, letter from Philadelphia, 1836 1384
Teachers, British, to colonies, 1690-1811 2144
Tecklenburg, Germans from, to Missouri, 19th c. **3702**
Tennessee, Irish to, before 1850 2732
Tennyson, S.S., Buenos Aires to New York, 1907 ... 2424
Tensas River Valley, La., English to, 1787 5213
Texas,
arrivals,
Fredericksburg and Gillespie County, mid-19th c 2534
Galveston from Bremen, 1848 .... **2518**
Menard County, 1868-1884 3507
New Braunfels, 1840s 0408-0410
Nueces River area, 1829 7740
under contract, 1830s 5011
Czechs to, before 1872 .... **0205**
Germans, or Wends, to, 1854 ...... 0578, 1067, 1858
Germans to,
1844-1847 .... 2474-2476, 2504
1847-1861 .... 2484, 2514, 3879, 8317
from Calenberg, 1753-1882 5080
from Duchy of Nassau, 1806-1866 9061
from Einbeck, 1845-1848 1636
from Holzminden, 1849 5719
from Prussia, 1849-1867 8770
from Rhenish Hesse, 1845 7405
from Russia, 1897-1910 .... **4485.1-.2**
from Thuringia, 1850 3948
Karlshafen, port of, 1844 8150
New Braunfels area, 1840s 8150, 9780
Irish to, 1829 .... 7365, 7740, 7745
naturalizations:
Bastrop County, 1851-1923 6238
Calhoun County, 19th c. 4933
Cooke County, 1880-1905 8350
Dallas County, 19th c. **1447.1-.4**
East Texas, 1824-1835 .... 1752, 4079
Ellis County, 1858-1929 3830
Galveston County, n.d. **1005**
Grayson County, 1855-1907 0528
Harris County, 1886-1903 ... **0678.1-.3, 1006.1-.5, 2910, 6013.55, 6254, 6659**
Jackson County, 1890-1920 .... **6660**
McLennan County, 1850-1906 5771-5772
Menard County, 1881-1886 3507
three counties, 1846-1847 6231-6232
Waller County, 1847-1932 0538
Washington County, 1857-1880 ...... **0540,** 8770
Norwegians to, 1840s, 1850s 4026
Nueces River area arrivals, 1829 7740
Poles to, 1854 1067
Robertson's Colony, 1830s 5011
Scots to, 1880s **9777**
Wends from Germany to Serbin, 1854 ... 0578, 1067, and 1858
Texas, Liverpool to Baltimore, 1882 .... **5233**
Texel, Netherlands, Dutch from, 1661 1472
Thaleischweiler, Germans from, 18th c .... 4231, 4329, and 8470
Thames River, Ont., survey, names from, 1793 ...... **7202**
Thetis, from Ireland and Scotland, to New Brunswick, 1837 .... **0358.13, 1500**
Thirsby, Plymouth to Maryland, 1704 .... **8805**
Thistle of Glasgow to Philadelphia, 1730 .... 0821, 0827, 0829, 0869
Thomas family to Maryland, 18th c. **3577**
Thomas and Benjamin to New Jersey, 1684 6097
Thuringia, Germans from,
1838-1839, Dresden area 4803
1900 and earlier 2782, 3948, 4803, 8290
Thurston County, Wash., nat'zations, 1853-1883 .... **3436**
Thusneleta, Bremen to New York, 1861 .... **1133.56**
Tiberias, Newport, Wales, to Baltimore, 1838 2920
Tischer, Rev. Jacob, and Swiss families, 1819 .... **3295**
Tobermory, Scotland, ships from:
Catherine, to Nova Scotia, 1843 4970
Rambler, to Prince Edw. Island, 1806 .... **1446.2**
Todd County, Ky., naturalizations, 1828-1867 ...... **2158**
Toledo, Ohio, Germans to, 1770-1895 5603
Tombigbee River Valley, La., English to, 1787 5213
Torrance, Calif., Augustan Library emigrant files **1831, 1862**
Tourouvre, French from, to Canada, n.d. 5761
Trabue family, Virginia, 1700 0953
Traders, British, 1628-1640 7237
Trades, Dutch and Scandinavians in building and manufacturing, 1631-1655 8134
Trafford, Edward, captain of the *Elizabeth & Anne,* 1716 .... **4727**
Tramelan, Swiss from, 1754 1148
Transportation bonds **1217.1,** 1222, 1223
see also Prisoners
Trave, Bremen to New York via England, 1893 9031
Travel diaries, refugees, 18th c 9330

Treatment of prisoners transported, 1740s 6904-6905
Tremont, Le Havre to New York, 1848 .... **6515**
Treves *see* Trier
Tribekko, John, German clergyman, 18th c...... 4772-73
Trier, Germans from, 19th c............ 5441-5445, 5540
Tripp, S.D., Germans from Russia to, 1902.........2842
Tripp County, S.D., naturalizations, 1910-1914 .....**2984**
Tristram and Jane, London to Virginia, 1636-1637 ..3090
Triton, Norway to New York, 1842................**5985**
Trois-Rivieres, Quebec, inhabitants, 1668-1681......6830
Troon, Scotland, the *Thetis* from, to Ireland and Canada, 1837 ....**1500**
True Friendship, from Barbados, 1678 3280
Trustee's charge *see* Passage payment
Tudway Papers, Somerset Record Office, England ..2328
Tuisko, the
  with passengers Minnesota-bound, 19th c.... **1133.42**
  with passengers Ohio-bound, 1838-1868..... **1133.23**
Tulare County, Calif., voter list, 1872.........**2769.1-.10**
Tulpehocken, Pa., Germans to, 1720s... 0867, 0889, **7370**
Tuscarawas County, Ohio,
  Germans to, 1833......................**9037.1-.2**
  Swiss to, 1833.........................**9037.1-.2**
Tuslina, Norway to New York, 1842...............**5985**
Two Brothers, Carmarthen to Halifax, 1818 ....**7005**
Two Friends, Yorkshire to Nova Scotia, 1774 .... 5675, 9975
Tynemouth, England to Esquimalt, B.C., via San Francisco, 1862 5321

U

Uekermark region of Pomerania, Old Lutherans from, to western New York, 1843................ 1074-1075
Uhland, Bremen to New Orleans or N.Y., 1849......8890
Ukrainians to Manitoba, 1891-1900 3750
Ulm, Germans from, 17th, 18th c..................**2855**
"Ulster Scots" to Canada, 1827-1830 ....**7199**
Ulster *see* Ireland, Northern; *and* individual ports
Ulysses to Baltimore, 1833 ....**3704**
Umstadt, Germans from, 1834-1838 .... **0683,** 0685
Union, Bremen to N.Y., 1868................. **1133.20**
United Empire Loyalists *see* Loyalists
U.S. citizens and citizenship *see* Naturalizations
U.S. Department of State, record of arrivals, 1819-1834 .... **0253,** 9258, 9268
U.S. oaths of allegiance ca. 1778 ....**9530**
Upper Canada *see* Ontario
Upper Franconia (or Oberfranken), Bavaria, Germans from, 1849-1855......................3879
Urach, Germans from, 1751-1754 4445
Uster, Swiss from, to Carolina and Pennsylvania, 1734-1744 1946
Utah arrivals, 1849-1868 ....**6200**
Utah, Salt Lake City, Palatine Index **2883**

V

Valiant, the
  England to Canada, 1817 ....**1436**
  Hull, Eng., to Charlottetown, P.E.I., n.d. 8753
Van Raalte, Albertus C., founder of Holland, Mich., 1846 6875
Van Rensselaer, Kiliaen, in N.Y. State, 1636-1642 ...4612
Van Tienhoven, Cornelius (or Cornelis), 1650...... 3490, 6331, 9400
Vanderburgh County, Ind., nat'zations, 1820-1850...**9117**
Vaughan Charitable Charter School, Fermanagh **1418**
Vaughan Township, York County, Ont., arrivals from Pa., 1802 ....**7202**
Venezuela, Germans to,
  from Baden, 1842..........................4033
  from Calenberg, 1753-1882...................5080
  from Duchy of Nassau, 1806-1866.............9061
Vermilion County, Ill., nat'zations, 19th c. **2341.1-.2**
Vermont,
  naturalizations, Franklin County, 19th c........**5901**
  Scots to, 1774 9670
Vesta, Rotterdam to New York, 1847 6895
Victoria, B.C.,
  arrivals, 1862,
    on the *Sierra Nevada,* 5284
    on the S.S. *Pacific* 5294
    on the *Cyclone* 5304
    on the *Mountain Wave* 5314
  newspaper lists of docking ships, 1860-61.......**5323**
Victoria, Kans., Germans from Russia to, 1875, 1876 4019
Victoria County, Ontario, arrivals, 1829 1416
Village Belle to Philadelphia, Irish aboard, 1864.....9200
Ville-Marie *see* Montreal
Virginia,
  Alexandria County arrivals, 1801-1832.........1768
  Amelia County, headrights, 1737-1745 0618
  arrivals:
    1606-1624 .... **1260,** 1272, 5907, 7860, 9238
    1623-1635 .... 2772, 3520, 4782, 8845, 8862
    1635-1800 .... 1297, 8925, 9824
    1734-1870 .... **0614,** 2302
    17th c. **9039**
    17th, 18th c. **5400**
    18th c. **0926.44,** 2891-93, 3816, 5831
  Barbadians to, 1678, 1679.............. **3280, 8408**
  Bermudians to, 17th, 18th c...................**5400**
  British to:
    1621-1635 .... 0048, 2722
    1654-1702 .... **0620,** 0943, 1252, **1659**
    from Bristol, 1675-1677.....................3438
    from Gravesend, 1677 9540
    from Liverpool, 1686........................2162
    from London, 1648-1685.....................**1257**
  children to, 1648-1685 ....**1257**
  colony, 1620 arrivals **3820**
  Coppage family arrivals, 1648 1297
  county records, colonial and state 6264
  English to:

Virginia, *cont'd*
1623 and earlier 3273, 5695, **3820**
1631-1635 ....0048, 5781, **1035.14**
French to:
early 1700s 3633, 4622, 6710
1750-1797 .... 3630, 3640
Germanna Colony, 1717 ....**3771**
Germans to, 1714-1717 ...... **3771,** 4894, 6102, **7480**
headrights claimed, 1677-1679 ....**1659**
Huguenots to, 18th c. 3630, 3633, 7850
see also Virginia, Protestants to
importation oaths, 1739-1741.................4627
indentured servants to, 1683-1707 .... 2212, 6179
Irish to,
17th c....................... 2851, 6258, 6276
18th c........................... 0622, 6267
King family to, 1694 ....**9824**
land grants and land patents, 1623-1878....... 6219, 6220, 6221, **6223, 6225,** 6264
Lee family to, 1694 ....**9824**
legislators of, and their arrival dates, before 1629 6064
naturalizations,
Augusta County, 18th c................ **0926.57**
Henrico County, 1783-1794 1782
Norfolk County, 1828-1854 9830
Northumberland County, 1652 ....**6251**
Powhatan County, 1777 ....**1211**
statewide, 1784-1794 .... 1772, 6031
Neptune to, with very early arrivals, 1618-1619 ....**1260**
new citizens, 1784-1794, per British Public Record Office...................................1772
planters to, 1607-1616 .... 8745, 9025
prisoners arriving, diverted to S.C., 1718 ....**4912**
Protestants to, colonial era...................2564
see also Virginia, Huguenots to
Scots to, 1716 8690
settlement attempted, 1584-1590 2875
ships from London to, 1773-1774 0225
State Land Office records, Richmond.... 2772, 6258
Virginia,
Bremen to Baltimore, 1841 ....**8515**
London to Virginia, 1773-1774 0225
Virginia Company, sponsor of the *Sea Venture,* 1609-1610 9227
Vogelsberg area, Germans from, to Philadelphia, 1738-1751 2232
Vohenstrauss, Imperial Circle of, Austrians from, 1843-1877 4596
Volga Germans,
Catholic,
to New York, 1875......................2969
to South America, 1878 ....**9674**
Protestant, arrivals, 1875-1900.......... 2970, 2973
refugees from Minsk, 1922 ....**2965**
to Baltimore, then Kansas, 1875 4019
to Kansas, 1876f..................... 1682, 4019
to Wisconsin, 1864-1922 1871
see also Germans from Russia
Voter registrations:
Arizona, Cochise County, 1890 .... **1213.1-.3**
Irish to, 17th c 2851
California:
Contra Costa County, 19th, 20th c..........**2423**
Fresno County, 1896-1898 .... **2763.25-.33**
Kern County, 1866-1877 .... **2763.54-.56**
San Francisco, 1865-1875 1888
Santa Clara County, 1848-1900 .... 1890, **1981, 2763.20**
Siskiyou County, 1879, 1892 .... **1820.1-.3, 3707.1-.19**
Tulare County, 1872-1888.... 2765-68, **2769.1-.10**
Washington, Pierce County, 1916-1920 ...... **1728.4**
Voyage, difficulties of, France to Montreal, 1653 5374

W

WPA *see* Work Projects Administration *and* Works Progress Administration
Wachenheim, Germans from, 1732-1777 4280
Wages,
Book of Monthly, New York, 17th c...........8360
paid to colonists imported, Montreal, 1653 .... 5374, 7690
Wales,
departures from,
for New Orleans, 1849.............. 2742, **3453**
for Pennsylvania, 1681 0983
Euphemia from, to Louisiana, 1849 2742
Paragon from, to Rhode Island, 1851 .... **6508.5**
see also Welsh
Wallace, Bremen to New York, 1834 3080
Wangen, Germans from, 1834-1880 3893
Wanger family arrivals, 1717-1868 2006
War of 1812, British in the United States during.....8195
Wariscoyack, Va., inhabitants, 1625 5907
Warren County, Mo., Germans to, by 1850.........**3702**
Warwickshire, English from, 1671-1775 .... **1217.9**
Washington,
Germans from Russia to, 1876-1889 ....**9473**
naturalizations:
Douglas County, 1885-1973 ....**1654.1-.2**
Pierce County, 1916-1920 ....**1728.4-.5**
Thurston County, 1853-1883 ....**3436**
Waterville County, 1888-1973 .... **1654.1-.2**
Seattle arrivals, 17th c 1748
Washington, Norway to New York, 1842...........**5985**
Washington County, Ore., new citizens, 1853-1926 ..**0251**
Washington County, Tex., nat'zations, 1872-1880 ...**0540**
Washita County, Okla., first papers
1907-1935 ....**0104**
n.d...**0101**
Waterloo Township, Ont., and Kaiserslautern, Germany, a matching of surnames **7202**
Waterville, Wash., nat'zations, 1888-1973 ...... **1654.1-.2**
Waymouth, England, to New England, British, 1635 6545
Wayne County, N.Y., Germans from Rhineland to, 1820-1850 1874
Wegelnburg, Germans from, 18th c.......... 4147, 4392
Weimar, S.S., with Central and Eastern Europeans
to Baltimore, 1893 .... 9034, **9035**
to New York, 1893.................... 9034, **9035**
Weisenheim am Sand, Germans from, n.d. 7314

Weiser, Johann Conrad, from Germany, 1709-1710 9660
Welcome, the
and William Penn 0132, 1342
passengers on, 1682 .... 0242, 1342, 4960-63, 6610, 4752
Welcome Society of Pennsylvania, accepted list of *Welcome* passengers 6610
Wells County, Ind., naturalizations, n.d. **5817**
Welsh
arrivals, 17th-19th c. **1217.8, 1862**
to Canada, 17th-19th c.... **1862, 7005**
to Delaware, 1701-1713....1798
to Louisiana (New Orleans), 1849 2742
to Maryland,
1682 1587
1838 2920
to Nova Scotia, 1818 ....**7005**
to Pennsylvania,
1681-1698 .... 0983, 1302
1701-1713 .... 1798, 1894
Wends,
to Australia, 19th c 1858
to Texas,
1844-1847 2504
1854 .... 0578, 1067, 1858, 2504
see also Germans
Wengen, departures from, 1717-1868 2006
Wenger, Christian, family of, 1718 2006
Wernigerode, Germans from, 1748-1749 3848
Wertheim, Germans from, to Pennsylvania, 1709-1786 9964
Wertheim County, Germans from, 1740s-1840.... 4517, 4525
Wesenberg im Mecklenburg, Northern Germans, to U.S., 1850-1862 3223
West Camp, N.Y., Germans to,
1708-1719 .... 4817, 5023, 6341
"West Florida" arrivals, 1764 9600
West Indian archives, Spain
Madrid 7800-7801
Seville 5801
West Indies,
arrivals from Island of Foehr, 1850-1875 ....**8596**
British to,
1631-1635 5781
1646-1775 1098
1654-1685 0943
1682-1686 .... **1139.1**
1697-1707 2212
1727-1731 2324
1752-1756 2328
departures from,
1671 and after....0228
for American colonies, 17th, 18th c. **0773**
for New York, 1870 0289
French from,
1671 and after....0228
in 1870....0289
Huguenots to, 17th c 0228
indentured servants to,
1682-1707 .... **1139.1,** 2212, 6179
Protestants from England to, colonial era 2564
Scots to, 18th c. 1088, 4920, 8690
Scottish prisoners to, ca. 1745 4920
Spanish to, 1492-1592 .... 7800-01, 8870-72
West Jersey *see* New Jersey
West Point, Liverpool to New York, 1849 3378
West Sussex records of departures, 1830s **4609**
West Virginia,
German landowners in 18th c. **0926.46**
Germans to, after 1850 4998
Western Company, sponsor of French departures for Louisiana, 1718-1721....9190
Western states, Swiss to, 1843 ....**3810**
Westmoreland County, Pa., and Belgian glassworkers, 1889-1904 ....**7664**
Westmorland, English from, 1665-1775 .... **1217.8**
Westphalia, Germans from,
1714, 1725 .... 4894, 5877
1816-1900 .... **3702, 5860, 8653**
19th c. 2602, 5851, 5861
Weymouth, England, departures, 1635....6545
Wexford County, Mich., Swedish residents, 1875-1882 ....**6717**
Whavon, the *Lovely Nelly* from, to Canada, 1775 .... **1446.1**
Whitby, Yorkshire, servants to Georgia, 1774-1775 ....**1245**
Whitfield, Rev. Henry, and founding of Guilford, Conn., 1639 ....**9597**
Whitman County, Wash., Germans from Russia in, 1889 ....**9473**
Wiegand, C., captain of the *Salier,* 1882....6206
Wiesbaden archives for Nassau-Dillenburg 3233
Wiesbaden-Biebrich, Germans from, 18th c. 0368
Wight, Isle of, departures for Virginia, 1620-1621....3273
William, Scotland to New York, 1817 5741
William and Sarah, Rotterdam to Philadelphia, 1727 1632
William D. Sewall, Liverpool to New Orleans, 1849 0544
William Galley to Pennsylvania, 1697, 1698 1302
William Henry to New Brunswick, 1827.... **0358.46**
Williams, Roger, clergyman, founder of colony of Rhode Island 9110
Williamsburg County, S.C., arrivals, 18th c. **0624**
Willing Mind, to New Jersey, ca. 1721 8760
Wilmington, Del.,
British to, on the *Pleiades,* 1831.... **6508.7**
Brothers, from Belfast to, 1789, 1790 .... 2044, 2046
Dutch to, 17th c. **0464**
Irish to, on *Leander,* 1831.... **6508.3**
Swedes to, 17th c. **0464**
Wilmington, N.C., Scots to, 1774-1775....1088
Wiltshire, English from, 1664-1775 .... **1217.5**
Winger family arrivals, 1717-1868 2006
Winnipeg, Manitoba, Germans from Russia to, 1893 1697
Winston County, Miss., and Irish gravestones **9593**
Winthrop Fleet, 1630.... 0281, 0388
Wisconsin,
arrivals:
1852 ....**8507**
via Antwerp, 1843 ....**5608**

Wisconsin, *cont'd*
via Bremen, 1867 .... **1133.58**
via Hamburg, 1862 .... **1133.62**
via Liverpool, 1849 .... **1133.60**
via New York, 1845-1864 ..... **1133.48, .52,** 5821, 8500-03, **8508, 9666**
Belgians to, 1843 .... **5608**
British to, 1849 .... **1133.60**
Germans to:
1840s **5608,** 5821, **9074**
1850s .... **1133.48,** 1842, **7200, 8499,** 8500-03, **8509.1, .2, 8636**
1860s .... **1133.54, .56, .58, .62**
Irish to, 1852 .... **8505**
Lutherans and Pastor L. Krause, 19th c. **9074**
naturalizations:
Brown County, 1841-1978 .... 3015, **3015.5**
Calumet County, 19th c. **3457.1**
Door County, 1870-1906 .... 2906, **2907.1-.2**
statewide, 1907-1925 1867-1868
Norwegians to, 1845 .... **9667**
Prussians to, 1853 .... **1133.34**
Swiss to, 1845, 1853 .... **4891, 9668**
Witherspoon, Robert, and family history, 1780 ...... **0624**
Wittenberg, Mo., Germans to, 1838-1839 4803
Wittgenstein, Germans from, 1725 5877
Woerrstadt, Germans from, to Philadelphia, 1743-1754 .... **1870,** 2192
Wolfenbuettel, Germany,
files on Germans in British military forces in America during Revolutionary War 8560
state archives 7495, 8560
Wolfersweiler, Germans from, before 1750 .... 0478, **1033.11, 9981**
Women prisoners to colonial America, 18th c. 0608
Women servants to Philadelphia,
British, 18th c. **7855**
Irish, 1746, 1747 4732
Worcestershire, English from, 1663-1775 .... **1217.6**
Work Projects Administration
Louisiana port list, New Orleans, 1868-1870 .... **1536**
see also Works Progress Administration
Workers *see* Laborers; *and* Trades
Workhouses, Irish from
Ennistymon, 1850-1860 .... **6413.30**
Limerick, 1848-1860 .... **6413.20**
see also Almshouse
Works Progress Administration,
naturalization records ... **3434,** 5815, 6401, 9290-9314
records of Hillsboro, Kan., 1873-1874 .... **9317**
Wuerttemberg,
Germans from,
1770s-1920s 7650
18th c. 2434, 2444, 2464, 4315, **4374**
18th, 19th c. 0121, 2883, 4245, **8667**
19th c. **3709, 5745, 8646**
n.d. 4203
to Michigan, 19th c. **3709**
to Pennsylvania, 1709-1786 .... 6860, 9964
Urach and Dettingen, 1751-1754 4445
Wye River Merchant, Devon to Maryland, 1703-1704 .... **8805**
Wyndham, George, Third Earl of Egremont, and Sussex emigration to Canada 4575, 4582
Wyoming, Norway and Sweden to N.Y., 1892 ... **1133.46**

Y

York, Upper Canada, French to, 1799 2222
York County, Ont., arrivals from U.S.A., 1802 ...... **7202**
York County, Pa., naturalizations,
1798-1799 .... **9972.3-.4**
1802 .... **9972.7-.8**
Yorkshire, English from,
1665-1775, bonded passengers **1217.8**
1774-1775, to Georgia **1245**
1774-1781, to Nova Scotia 4632, 5675, 9975
Yorktown, Va., British to, 1716 .... **4727**
Yuba County, Calif., naturalizations, 1936 .... **6131**
Yugoslavs,
arrivals, 1900s 6740
to California, 1870-1913 .... 6785, 9100
to New Orleans, 1821-1870 9520

Z

Zeeland, N.D., Germans from Russia to, 1893 ...... **3844**
Zurich, Swiss from,
cantonal and parish records, 1650-1800 4916
to Carolina(s), 18th c. 1946, 9630
to Pennsylvania,
17th c. **4483**
1734-1744 .... 1946, 3161
"Zurich Lists," 18th c, additions/corrections to 8040
Zweibruecken, Germans from, 18th c
per local departure records:
Bavarian archives: 3193
church registers:
Lutheran 4133
Protestant church of Zweibruecken 4350
Reformed Church 4141, **4349**
various 4214, 4357, 4364
miscellaneous official archives 4214, 4266
Speyer state archives 4133, 4141, 4145, 4147, **4349**
to American colonies ... 3193, 4141, 4145, 4147, 4214, 4266, **4268, 4349,** 4350, 4357, 4364, 4394, **4594,** 8050